lessons of a century

A Nation's Schools Come of Age

By the staff of Education Week

To order copies of this book or other publications
from Editorial Projects in Education, call (800) 346-1834.

Visit us on the Web at edweek.org.

Front cover photos: top, courtesy of Burton Historical Collection,
Detroit Public Library; left, by Corbis-Bettmann; right, by Benjamin Tice Smith.
Back cover photos: top left, by Corbis-Bettman; top right,
courtesy of Archdiocese of Chicago; bottom, Corbis-Bettmann.

ISBN 0-9674795-0-9
$24.95

Though many people contributed in many ways to *Lessons of a Century*, the writers and editors at *Education Week* would especially like to thank the following people and institutions for their assistance:

David Ment and Bette Weneck in the Special Collections department of the Milbank Library at Teachers College, Columbia University. The library houses uncounted textbooks, journal articles, curriculum guides, and photos that have been collected from school districts across the country and meticulously catalogued and preserved since the 19th century.

Historians David L. Angus, Daniel J. Boorstin, Carl F. Kaestle, Marvin Lazerson, Jeffrey E. Mirel, Diane Ravitch, and David B. Tyack.

Olga Montgomery of the Finney County Historical Museum in Kansas; former high school teacher Bernadine Sitts of Garden City, Kan.; former Garden City school board member and local historian Pat Fishback; Donald Stull, a professor at the University of Kansas; Mark Grey, a professor at the University of Northern Iowa; Ben Barrett, the director of legislative research for the state of Kansas; Garden City School District 457; and the faculty of Garfield School.

Sharon A. Britton, the director of communications for Phillips Academy at Andover, Mass.; Bruce Cooper, a professor of education at Fordham University; Ruth Quattlebaum, the archivist at the Phillips Academy; Scott Somerville, an attorney for the Home School Legal Defense Association; Patricia M. Lines, a senior fellow at the Discovery Institute in Seattle; Patrick Farenga, the president of Holt Associates; Charles L. Glenn Jr., the author of *The Myth of the Common School*; and Charles J. O'Malley, the former executive director of the National Council for Private School Accreditation.

Raquel Irrizarry of Corbis and Mike LeTourneau of AP/Wide World for their invaluable assistance in locating photographs. Artist Brett Helquist for the illustrations that appear in the Perspective section of each chapter.

Steve McShane of the Calument Regional Archives at Indiana University Northwest in Gary.

Copy editor Diane Barry, proofreader Ihsan K. Taylor, and researcher Sharita Jacobs.

In addition, we would like to thank the numerous people featured in the pages that follow for sharing their memories and thoughts with the writers at *Education Week*.

Acknowledgments

This book involved the work of many people. And while each cannot be acknowledged by name, suffice it to say that all who contributed to this project deserve special recognition.

Lessons of a Century represents one of the most significant and ambitious projects *Education Week* has ever undertaken. Beginning in January 1999, the newspaper published a yearlong series of articles that reflected on the issues, forces, changes, and personalities that shaped American education during the 20th century.

The project was the epitome of a collaboration. Every member of *Education Week*'s staff contributed directly or indirectly to the project—from the research assistants who gathered historical source materials and proofread pages to the editors who conceived the project and shepherded each installment through its final production.

Several *Education Week* editors deserve special recognition for their hard work in planning the series. At the top of that list is the newspaper's managing editor, Gregory Chronister. In the six months before the series was launched, he received substantial help from several insightful colleagues, most especially Senior Editors Lynn Olson and M. Sandra Reeves and Deputy Managing Editor Steven Drummond. Assistant Managing Editor Karen Diegmueller also played a significant role in shaping major portions of the series.

Virtually every staff writer had at least one assignment for the series. The staff writers, whose bylines appear in the following pages, were the front-line workers who spent weeks reporting and writing their articles even as they continued to turn out stories in their regular beats. Working side by side with them was a small, dedicated team of researchers, led by Librarian Kathryn Dorko and Assistant Librarian Barbara Hiron.

Laura Baker, the newspaper's design director, deserves plaudits for both designing and directing the production of the 10 installments of the series and for designing and producing this book. Her art department colleagues, too, went well above and beyond the call of duty in turning out the beautiful pages that grace the series and book. Photo Editor Benjamin Tice Smith warrants a special mention for coordinating the photography that illustrated both the series and the book, as well as shooting several of the assignments himself.

Behind the scenes, the business staff—marketing, promotion, circulation, and advertising—attended to all the details so crucial to the success of a project like this. In particular, Circulation Director Peter LeMaster played a pivotal role in the completion of this project.

Were it not for the deft editing hand and superb organizational skills of Senior Editor Sandra Graziano, the completion of this book would not have been possible. She oversaw the myriad tasks that it took to transform a newspaper series, which by definition tends to be somewhat ephemeral, into this book, which we hope makes a useful contribution for years to come.

Several hundred people were interviewed and consulted during the course of this project. We are deeply grateful to all of those thoughtful, articulate, and committed people whose insights and wisdom inform our pages—not only in *Lessons of a Century*, but throughout the year in the columns of *Education Week*.

We want to express special gratitude to the Ford Foundation and the Carnegie Corporation of New York for providing grants to underwrite the editorial and production costs of producing the series in *Education Week*. In particular, we're grateful to Janice Petrovich, the director of Ford's education, knowledge, and religion program, and to Vivien Stewart, the chair of Carnegie's education program, and her colleague Michael Levine, the deputy chair.

Finally, the trustees of Editorial Projects in Education, the nonprofit organization that publishes *Education Week*, must be acknowledged for their enthusiastic support of this project. They were generous and constructive with their encouragement, time, and ideas.

Virginia B. Edwards
Editor and Publisher
January 2000

CONTENTS

A Nation and Its Schools Come of Age

Lawrence A. Cremin, the late dean of American education historians, once warned school reformers that they should not expect any lasting fame from their efforts, whatever the results. "For reform movements," he wrote, "are notoriously ahistorical in outlook. They look forward, rather than back; and when they do need a history, they frequently prefer the fashioning of ideal ancestors to the acknowledgment of mortals."

The same could be said of America's view of its schools. Nothing of the moment is ever quite enough to match expectations.

And when we need a history—some ideal marker on which to calibrate progress—we prefer the fashioning of golden ages to the acknowledgment of mortal cycles of reform.

By any measure, the educational achievements of the past 100 years are heroic in scale: universal public schooling; broad-based access to college; the democratization of a melting-pot culture; and provision of the skills and wherewithal to power an economic miracle, win two world wars, land on the moon, and defeat Communism.

But the story of 20th-century education is not a simple, linear progression to greatness. It is a tale of cycles of reform. A fitful journey of stops and starts through the social, political, and philosophical conundrums of a defining age.

Its triumphs are fueled more often by the frustration of necessity than by grand design. And its contradictions and crosscurrents run as deep as those of democracy itself.

What can this 20th-century journey teach us about ourselves, our past, and our future?

This book, produced by the staff of *Education Week* with contributions from leading scholars, explores that question. *Lessons of a Century* examines aspects of the educational landscape of 20th-century America—the people, trends, historical milestones, enduring controversies, political conflicts, world events, and socioeconomic forces that have made this period a time of unparalleled growth and influence for the field.

If the lessons of history reveal themselves in recurring patterns, education in the 20th century provides a veritable textbook of *déjà vu*.

The century opened with John Dewey's call for a "science of education." It closes with new promise from the cognitive sciences. At the end of the 19th century, the industrial-age needs of an expanding U.S. economy led to a push for greater curricular rigor, new forms of schooling, and systematized ways of measuring school results.

As the 20th century ends, the information-age needs of a global economy are spurring a drive for rigorous educational standards, national testing, and, again, new forms of schooling.

Even the *fin de siècle* social dynamics that complicated schooling 100 years ago are eerily re-emerging.

Today, as then, educators must deal with historic levels of immigration. And now, as then, the dislocations and social fissures caused by population shifts and cultural change are producing a search for political cohesiveness.

At the end of the 19th century, migration from the farms to the factories built up teeming cities, with the urban blight, machine politics, and ethnic strife that came with them.

Today's echo of that tumult is in suburban sprawl, the rise of hate groups and divisive politics, and the decline in community life.

What happened between these periods is, quite simply, the coming of age of a nation, with its education system providing the stimulus. These 100 years represent a span of accomplishment so transforming that by its end, the link between education and national progress was firmly established in the public mind.

But the ascendancy of education was a double-edged sword.

Library of Congress

It set up an all-things-to-all-people contradiction at the heart of the emerging national consensus on education's purposes.

And this, in turn, has led to enduring tensions that define the role, scope, and nature of movements to change the schools.

Nothing, in fact, so characterizes this educational age as its prevailing metaphor: the swing of the pendulum back and forth between extremes.

Wide, cyclical shifts in public mood and professional thinking have left unsettled to this day such fundamental questions about the enterprise of learning as what makes a good curriculum, how teachers should be trained, who best decides the policies and practices of a school, and where the proper balance lies between public needs and private destinies.

Though such questions may persist, in the end, writes Jerome S. Bruner, "Each generation must define afresh the nature, direction, and aims of education to assure such freedom and rationality as can be attained for a future generation."

The generations of the 20th century leave a legacy of optimism, activism, and faith in education's capacity to be, as Dewey said, "the fundamental method of social progress."

If the 20th century is, as commentators have proclaimed it, "the American century," then those qualities surely helped make it so.

—*Sandra Reeves*

opening the doors

Americans in the 20th century have gone to tremendous lengths to create, in the words of Noah Webster, "a system of education that should embrace every part of the community." This chapter explores how the United States in this century built on the foundations envisioned by Webster and others soon after the American Revolution and laid down during the 1800s. Though most Americans already were receiving some formal schooling before 1900, policy decisions and social and economic forces since then have brought millions more students into the public schools, for longer periods of time and for more varied purposes.

But while access to education has been assured, questions remain about the quality of schooling and, ultimately, the value of a diploma.

Students board a New York City school bus in 1930. The 20th century has seen enormous growth in access to public schooling: More doors opened for more and more Americans, and a high school diploma became a given for the vast majority of young people.

Photo by Corbis-Bettmann

Corbis-Bettmann

The Common Good

Providing a free public education to all has been a success for the United States, but ensuring equal quality in what is offered continues to challenge the nation.

By Lynn Olson

I f one word could summarize American education in the 20th century, that word would be "more." Today there are more students attending school for more of the year and for a longer period of their lives than at any time in our history.

It's a stunning achievement—yet one that is often overlooked, given Americans' rising educational aspirations.

"Education is opening the paths for people, and that's what our system of public education has done," says Daniel J. Boorstin, a distinguished historian and a former librarian of Congress.

At the beginning of the century, a majority of Americans ages 7 to 13 attended school. But only one in 10 remained in school beyond age 14, and fewer than 7 percent of 17-year-olds graduated from high school.

Now, at the century's close, high school enrollment is virtually universal. More than eight in 10 young adults have a high school diploma. And more than six in 10 enroll in college immediately after graduation. President Clinton wants to make universal access to two years of college the next frontier.

"By most standards, the history of the United States in terms of access is a success story," says Larry Cuban, an education professor at Stanford University.

But while access to schools is no longer an issue, access to quality is. Despite enormous progress, the opportunities students have to learn, and how well they are expected to do so, vary significantly based on where they live, what their parents earn, and the color of their skin. It's as if, having invited everyone to the banquet, some are served an appetizer and others a five-course meal.

"I think the issue now," says John I. Goodlad, an education professor at the University of Washington, "is to make our schools commonly good."

NEW ROLE FOR HIGH SCHOOLS

Early in the 20th century, "access" primarily meant securing enrollment in a public high school. By the late 1800s, reformers had largely won the battle for publicly financed elementary schools. But public high schools were still a rarity. They remained primarily an urban and middle-class phenomenon into the 1870s, with selective admissions based on entrance exams and modest enrollments.

Where high schools existed outside the big cities, they were typically small and varied greatly in curriculum and organization, notes Marvin Lazerson, an education historian at the University of Pennsylvania. Most students left school by age 13 to get a job. And a high school diploma was not required for college or the workplace.

But from the late 1800s until 1940, high schools underwent a remarkable transformation. On average, Stanford education historian David B. Tyack points out, Americans built one new high school a day from 1890 to 1918. High school enrollment swelled from about half a million in 1900 to 2.4 million in 1920 and to more than 6.5 million in 1940. By that year, more than three-fourths of Americans ages 14 to 17 were in secondary school. And, for the first time, more than half of 17-year-olds had earned a diploma.

David F. Labaree, an assistant professor of education at Michigan State University, captures the early years of that explosive growth in his history of Central High School in Philadelphia. When the school opened its doors in 1838, it was the only public high school in the city. Two-thirds of its students came from middle-class homes. By 1885, in response to a public clamor for secondary education, the school board had added Central Manual Training School a few blocks away, which served a higher proportion of students whose parents were among the "employed" middle class rather than proprietors or professionals. Five years later, it built Northeast Manual Training School, and the enrollment at Central High itself had doubled. By 1915, Philadelphia had 13 secondary schools, including two normal schools (for training teachers), a vocational school, and 10 regional comprehensive high schools, of which Central was one.

Historians point to a web of economic and social factors to explain the boom in secondary education. From 1890 to 1920, 18 million immigrants poured into the country, and many more Americans abandoned the farms for the nation's increasingly crowded and industrialized cities. Those population shifts provided the concentrated pool of young people needed to sustain large high schools. At the same time, new technologies replaced jobs once held by children, shrinking the labor market for minors. Laws restricting or banning child labor also pushed youngsters out of the workplace, while compulsory-attendance laws pulled them into the schools. Massachusetts enacted the first compulsory-attendance law in 1852. By the turn of the century, 33 states and the District of Columbia had followed, with laws aimed primarily at 8- to 14-year-olds.

'AMERICANIZATION'

Often, the targets of compulsory-attendance laws were the poor, immigrant children arriving daily on American shores. Many educators saw a desperate need to instill "civilized" values in these alien newcomers. Often, the concern was less to prepare an educated workforce than to preserve American democracy and morals.

In 1922, as part of a strategy to "Americanize" the Oregon schools, the Ku Klux Klan and the Scottish Rite Masons organized a voter referendum requiring all children between 8 and 16 to attend public schools. Parents or guardians who refused to comply were subject to a maximum punishment of a $100 fine and a 30-day jail term.

"The assimilation and education of our foreign-born citizens in the principles of our government, the hopes and inspiration of our people, are best secured by and through attendance of all children in our public schools," stated a resolution in favor of the ballot measure. "We must now halt those coming to our country from forming groups, establishing schools, and thereby bringing up their children in an environment often antagonistic to the principles of our government."

The measure was opposed—unsuccessfully—by members of the Evangelical Lutheran Synod, Seventh Day Adventists, private school principals, members of the Presbyterian Church, and the Catholic Civil Rights Association. But in 1925, the U.S. Supreme Court declared the law unconstitutional, saying it forced children to "accept instruction from public teachers only."

"Americanization," however, was never the only goal of public education. As the elementary schools filled up, parents also came to view the high schools as offering their children a distinct economic and social advantage.

As Robert S. and Helen Merrell Lynd observed in *Middletown*, their classic 1929 study of Muncie, Ind.: "This thing, education, appears to be desired frequently not for its specific content but as a symbol—by the working class as an open sesame that will mysteriously admit their children to a world closed to them, and by the business class as a heavily sanctioned aid in getting on further economically or socially in the world."

It was the Great Depression, however, that gave children a final shove out of the workforce and cemented the idea of high school as a virtual necessity in the minds of Americans. The value of children in the job market plummeted. And they competed with unemployed adults for those jobs for which they remained eligible. In response, many states raised the age of compulsory school attendance from 14 to 16.

"From my own experience at that time, all of a sudden, the enrollments above the elementary school began to increase enormously," Goodlad recalls.

CURRICULUM WARS

The question of what kind of education would suit this much larger and more diverse population of high school students had perplexed educators since the late

A high school mathematics class in 1900. At the time, high school was largely the province of urban youths from white, middle-class families. Many schools had selective admissions and taught a rigid academic curriculum.

Corbis-Bettmann

19th century. But the issue would become increasingly pressing as the ranks of students swelled.

On one side of the argument was the 1893 report from the Committee of Ten, chaired by President Charles W. Eliot of Harvard University. The group, composed largely of college presidents, argued that all students should master an equally rigorous curriculum: "Every subject which is taught at all in secondary school should be taught in the same way and to the same extent to every pupil so long as he pursues it, no matter what the probable destination of the pupil may be, or at what point his education is to cease."

The committee recommended at least four years of English, four years of a foreign language, and three years each of mathematics, science, and history.

Eliot was hardly a populist, however. At the time the committee wrote its report, only a small fraction of young Americans graduated from high school. And the committee itself described secondary schools as being for a small—but important—proportion of children who could profit from a prolonged education and whose parents could afford it.

Opposing the committee were men who favored a much more utilitarian curriculum for students who were not bound for college. In 1906, a report by the Massachusetts Commission on Industrial and Technical Education argued that the schools were "too exclusively literary" for the great body of youths. What most youngsters needed, the commission concluded, was "training of a practical character" that would prepare them for jobs in industry.

In 1918, the National Education Association published the "Cardinal Principles of Secondary Education," which endorsed different curricula for different students, with separate courses of study in such fields as industrial and fine arts. It suggested that secondary education be oriented around seven broad objectives: health, command of fundamental processes (literacy, numeracy), worthy home membership, vocation, citizenship, worthy use of leisure, and ethical character. The academic disciplines were barely mentioned.

Reformers of the day wanted to stem the tide of young people dropping out of high school, a problem they attributed to the dominance of bookish, academic coursework. By providing students with more options that would "best fit our boys and girls for life," the reformers saw themselves as increasing access to education. True, those pathways would have different standards and different academic content, but at least everybody would come away with a diploma.

TRACKING TAKES HOLD

Over time, such arguments proved persuasive. High schools responded to the polyglot mix of youths by stratifying and diversifying the curriculum.

"At the moment that the expansion really booms, you find high schools like Central and a lot of the others that were already in existence shifting to a tracking system," Labaree observes.

By 1919, the Philadelphia school had four courses of study: academic, commercial, mechanical, and industrial. Those would continue into the late 1930s, when Central High became once again a selective-admissions school.

To Labaree, tracking served an invidious purpose. It enabled public high schools to nominally meet their democratic agenda (serving all youths), while preserving the value of the high school credential for the few young people who made it into the academic track.

Tracking was reinforced—and made easier—by the new generation of intelligence tests, which purported to be able to assign children to different programs based on their abilities. In 1917, a Harvard psychologist, Robert Yerkes, devised the first multiple-choice intelligence test, called the Army Alpha, to help screen and place military recruits during World War I.

The use of multiple-choice tests that could be administered on a mass scale quickly spread to the schools. By 1932, three-fourths of large U.S. cities reported using such written, standardized intelligence tests to assign pupils. Typically, working-class, minority, and immigrant children scored worst on such exams and ended up in the lowest tracks.

ON THE 'GENERAL' TRACK

Detroit was a national leader in the adoption of a differentiated curriculum. In their new book, *The Failed Promise of the American High School, 1890-1995*, historians David L. Angus and Jeffrey E. Mirel detail how the Motor City shifted from a predominantly academic curriculum in the high schools to a watered-down mixture of course offerings.

By the 1920s, they note, Detroit's system reflected that in many other big cities, with four tracks: college preparatory, commercial (or business), vocational (industrial arts and home economics), and general. Still, three-quarters of student course-taking remained in the academic categories.

Soon, though, the Depression brought thousands of working-class children into the schools. Between 1929 and 1934, enrollment in Detroit's comprehensive high schools jumped by more than 43 percent. And the general track, designed to serve students without specific college or career plans, boomed.

"By the middle of the 1930s, educators have pretty much given up on vocational education because none of these kids were getting jobs," says Mirel, a professor of education at Emory University. "So the gen-

Corbis-Bettmann

Corbis-Bettmann

eral track becomes a place where you can keep them in school, not demand a tremendous amount, and at least give them a diploma."

By 1934, only about 62 percent of student course-taking in Detroit was in the academic category. And school officials lowered standards and weakened the content of the remaining academic courses. Science laboratory courses gave way to large lecture classes in biology, chemistry, and physics. In social studies, required courses in civics and economics were replaced by classes that dealt with such topics as juvenile delinquency, finding a job, and traffic safety.

By the late 1940s, the general track was serving the largest percentage of Detroit students of any of the four tracks—a pattern that would do a long-term disservice to the African-Americans who were migrating from the South and filling the city's schools.

DECLINE IN ACADEMICS

The same pattern occurred nationally. In 1928, Mirel and Angus say, more than 67 percent of the courses taken by American students were academic. Six years later,

the proportion of academic course-taking had fallen to 62 percent. Over the next two decades, the proportion continued to drop, to 57 percent in 1961.

Winifred Weislogel, who was a teenager in Elizabeth, N.J., in 1943, remembers having to choose a high school track. "In 9th grade, you had to choose between a general course, a commercial course, or an academic course," says the 71-year-old Arlington, Va., resident. "The general course included things like basic shop and basic math and arithmetic," she recalls. The commercial course offered typing, shorthand, and bookkeeping, "and then there was the academic course, which was where you were expected to take at least one foreign language, mathematics, science, English, history."

"I took the commercial course and then switched" to the academic track, she adds. "In those days, not quite so many people thought they would go on to college, and a lot of us who did were the first in our families to do so."

Weislogel graduated from Barnard College in New York City in 1949 and eventually went into the Foreign Service. She retired from the U.S. State Department in 1983.

Above: A classroom scene from the early 1900s. In the early decades of the 20th century, compulsory-attendance and child-labor laws broadened public school enrollment.

Left: Students at a Missouri school for African-American children during the Depression.

CALLS FOR REALIGNMENT

With the passage of the GI Bill during World War II, a college education suddenly became affordable for millions of Americans, and questions of access largely shifted to higher education. Those changes had two notable effects on the high schools.

First, increased access to college devalued the high school diploma in the job market. Second, it temporarily resurrected concerns about the quality of the college preparation that many young Americans were receiving. A prominent historian, Arthur Bestor, led the attack against the "anti-intellectual" nature of high schools in his 1953 book, *Educational Wastelands: The Retreat From Learning in Our Public Schools.*

Bestor was particularly alarmed by the "life adjustment" movement of the 1940s, which involved lessons in "the problem of improving one's personal appearance," the "problem of developing and maintaining wholesome boy-girl relationships," and other practical-sounding studies. Such programs were primarily aimed at the "60 percent" of American youths whom educators assumed were not fit for either college or technical careers.

Bestor lambasted educators for de-emphasizing mathematics, science, history, and foreign languages in favor of such topics. The onset of the Cold War also created demands for reinvigorating the high school curriculum, particularly in math, science, and foreign languages. But as much emphasis was placed on accelerating education for the best students as on changing the content of what most young people learned.

The Big Yellow Bus

By Kerry A. White

In 1937, Frank W. Cyr, a young professor of rural education at Teachers College, Columbia University, conducted a first-of-its-kind survey to find out how students across the nation were getting from their homes to school.

What he discovered was, any which way they could.

Most, of course, walked. But some students rode to school in horse-drawn carts borrowed from local farmers; others commuted in a hodgepodge of trucks and automobiles. And while most children who didn't walk, Cyr learned, caught rides in motorized school buses of some sort, there were virtually no standards in place for such vehicles. The first school buses, purchased mainly in the 1920s, came in all shapes and forms and in every color of the rainbow.

A few Wyoming districts had merely added engines to covered wagons. In one New York district, students rode in small purple buses; in another, in the name of patriotism, buses wore red, white, and blue stripes.

While manufacturers at the time were complaining that a lack of standards prevented them from turning out school buses more cheaply on an assembly line, school administrators complained of the high cost of buses—at a time when consolidation of widely scattered schools had increased the need for transportation. And even though the earliest school buses barely surpassed speeds of 20 mph, safety was a mounting concern.

NEW STANDARDS

The need for safety and manufacturing standards was obvious to Cyr, and in 1939, he gathered together state officials, school leaders, and bus engineers to hammer out the first national benchmarks for school transportation.

Participants in that seven-day conference in New York City adopted 44 new standards on bus size, engine specifications, and, most notably, color. A shade of yellow that soon came to be called National School Bus Chrome was selected for its visibility from dawn to dusk and through fog and rain.

While most of the standards have changed, and many more state and federal rules have been added, the familiar hue endures and is on file with the National Bureau of Standards.

Today, most students—about 60 percent—ride one of the 450,000 yellow school buses that traverse American roadways to and from school, extracurricular activities, and field

GROSS INEQUALITIES

Even without tracking, access to education would hardly have been equal. For much of the century, large segments of the population were excluded from a high-quality public education.

Differences in educational opportunity based on race, class, ethnicity, geography, and gender would come to dominate the nation's consciousness from midcentury onward.

"It's hard for us to remember how fatally unequal schools were, say, about 1930 or 1940," Tyack of Stanford University says. "If you think, not of the big cities, but of the rural areas, there were whole big swaths of the country and whole groups of people—especially black people—who had no access to high schools."

Before World War II, he notes, many rural areas in the South, the Dust Bowl, and other impoverished regions had no public high schools. In 1899, the Supreme Court had ruled in *Cumming* v. *Richmond County Board of Education* that the doctrine of "separate but equal" did not mean that black students automatically had the right to a high school because white students had one.

In 1913, a survey of Atlanta's black schools found that enrollment exceeded seating capacity by 2,111 children and that students without seats were forced to stand or sit on the floor. Because of the use of double sessions, 5,000 children received only three hours of instruction a day, in classrooms filled with 60 children per session. Despite repeated petitions from the city's black residents, the At-lanta school board made no provision for black high schools until 1920, when the district had 7,100 black students and 21,300 whites.

In his book on education during the Depression, *Public Schools in Hard Times*, Tyack and his colleagues Robert Lowe and Elisabeth Hansot describe the conditions of black children in a Southern school, where they experienced an "educational inequality so gross that one questions whether the term 'education' is appropriate." Four grades of youngsters squeezed into an unheated shack, where they crowded onto broken benches. While the youngest children were learning to write their names and draw pictures of dogs and cats, the older ones memorized lines from an antiquated grammar lesson and multiplied

trips. And because of the strict regulations, they're considered the safest way to get to school, beating walking, bicycles, and Mom and Dad's car.

"School buses are the safest mode of transportation on the road," says Karen Finkle, the executive director of the National School Transportation Association.

WORRIES REMAIN

Still, that status doesn't make her job worry-free. On average, 25 students are killed in school-bus-related accidents each year: About one-third are struck by their own buses in the loading and unloading zone, one-third are hit by motorists passing stopped school buses, and one-third are killed as they walk to or from bus stops. Very few are killed as passengers inside their school buses. By comparison, roughly 5,500 children die each year in accidents involving other types of vehicles.

And while the current figures on school bus fatalities are a vast improvement from years past, much remains to be done, Finkle says. "We'll work on improving the training of the drivers and educating the students," she vows, "until that number is down to zero." Seat belts are the biggest unresolved safety issue.

Though school bus seats are already designed to cushion children in most crashes, some safety groups say adding

Corbis-Bettmann

seat belts would help safeguard students in the event of rollover accidents or side-impact collisions. But opponents of using seat belts, including many bus drivers, say the cost and associated difficulties would hardly be worth it since most school-bus-related deaths occur outside the vehicles themselves. And drivers say they would have a hard time ensuring that each child was properly buckled in.

Carolyn Thornton has driven a school bus for the Princeton City schools outside of Cincinnati for 25 years. "I think it's coming," she says of a seat belt rule, "but it's going to be tough for drivers to enforce, especially for the little kids." ∎

In 1939, state officials, school leaders, and bus engineers met and adopted standards for the nation's school buses, including the shade of yellow that was soon known as National School Bus Chrome.

and checked their sums by counting on their fingers.

Even into the 1960s, conditions in black schools, particularly in the South, remained grossly unequal. James D. Anderson, the head of the department of educational policy studies at the University of Illinois at Urbana-Champaign, recalls his years as a student at Carver High School in Utah, Ala., in a county that was about 80 percent African-American.

"The white high school had a gymnasium, science labs, football fields with lights—most of the things you would expect in an American high school," says Anderson, who was the valedictorian of the Class of 1962. Carver, which served grades 1-12, was an amalgam of brick and wood-frame buildings dating to the 1920s.

It lacked janitorial services, so Anderson and the other boys scrubbed and waxed the floors themselves and raised and lowered the high windows with long sticks. In the winter, they carried buckets of coal from a pile out back to keep the school warm. "We had only one science teacher, and he taught biology, physics, and chemistry. We didn't even have a gymnasium until my senior year," Anderson recalls.

"One of the things people don't realize," he says, "is how recent access has been for some populations in this country. My mother's generation didn't even have a high school. They only went to 9th grade. And so it was really my generation, in the 1960s, that was the first generation of African-Americans to have universal public high school education."

Students at Central High School in Manchester, N.H. By the second half of the 20th century, access to a high school education was a given for most Americans.

"It's hard for us to remember how fatally unequal schools were about 1930 or 1940."

David B. Tyack
Education Historian,
Stanford University

PUSH FOR QUALITY

The civil rights movement that began in the 1950s and the federal "war on poverty" in the 1960s, combined with aggressive intervention by the federal courts, finally caused Americans to confront such inequities. Slowly, then with gathering speed, the schoolhouse door opened for large numbers of previously excluded youths: African-Americans, handicapped children, and those who spoke little or no English.

Through court battles and helped by federal legislation, poor children, migrant children, girls, disabled youngsters, and those wanting bilingual education clamored for—and got—special programs to serve their needs.

But, argues education historian Diane Ravitch, while many Americans gained greater access to schools, too little attention was paid to the content of what they learned once they got there. In *The Troubled Crusade: American Education, 1945-1980*, she writes: "Sometimes those who led the battles seemed to forget why it was important to keep students in school longer; to forget that the fight for higher enrollments was part of a crusade against ignorance, and that institutions would be judged by what their students had learned as well as by how many were enrolled."

Indeed, the social turmoil of the 1960s temporarily overwhelmed the schools, which tried to respond with a host of changes to make education more "relevant," more engaging, and less structured than it had been before. Often, though, such innovations came at the expense of a strong, core curriculum and an emphasis on high achievement. It wasn't until the 1970s, and the back-to-basics movement, that states began to impose minimum-competency tests to ensure that high school graduates could at least read, write, and compute at an 8th grade level.

The proportion of 17-year-olds with a high school diploma peaked in 1968-69, at 77.1 percent, in part as a result of the civil rights movement and federal anti-poverty efforts and in part as young people stayed in school to avoid the draft during the Vietnam War.

Although that figure had fallen to 69.7 percent in 1996-97, such figures do not include the many young people who obtain alternative credentials, such as a General Educational Development diploma. The United States, notes Cuban of Stanford University, is remarkable as a "second chance" system. The eventual graduation rates, including GED holders, are now "higher than they've ever been," says Tom Snyder, the director of annual reports for the National Center for Education Statis-

tics. In 1996, 87.3 percent of Americans ages 25 to 29 had a high school diploma.

By the 1980s, most states were rushing to raise the standards for a high school education by mandating new tests, lengthening the school year, raising salaries and entrance requirements for beginning teachers, and tightening their graduation standards. There is evidence that this burst of activity, coming after the earlier gains from the civil rights battles and the war on poverty, has begun to pay off.

Test scores have risen gradually since the early 1970s. Academic course-taking among high school students is up. More than half of all high school graduates now take four years of English and three years each of math, science, and social studies.

Some of the biggest gains have been posted by poor and minority students. From 1971 to 1984, black students ages 9 to 13 showed significant gains in scores on the National Assessment of Educational Progress, a federal program that tests a sampling of students in core academic subjects.

The enormous performance gap between students in high-poverty and low-poverty schools—more than two grade levels in math—also has begun to close. And young African-Americans now graduate from high school at about the same rate as their white counterparts, although the rate for Hispanics remains significantly lower.

DISSATISFACTION CONTINUES

Despite these advances, Americans remain dissatisfied with their public schools. And their aspirations, both for themselves and for what schools should accomplish, continue to rise.

In part, that's because schools continue to reflect the inequalities in the larger society. "On the one hand, kids have gotten access to education, and that includes all kids," observes Kati Haycock, the executive director of the Education Trust, a nonprofit advocacy group for poor and minority students. "That said, if you ask the question, 'Do they have access to schools of equal quality?' the answer is decidedly not, and the results show that."

In particular, she argues, the rigor of the academic courses taken by many poor and minority students in urban areas does not match that offered in schools in more affluent suburbs. Equally troubling, the neediest and least skilled students typically end up with the least experienced, least qualified teachers.

Meanwhile, the whole notion of "access" is shifting. An overwhelming majority of Americans now believe that a college edu-

cation, not just a high school diploma, is necessary to get and keep a good job.

"Now, to get a good job, you need to go to college," Labaree of Michigan State says. "And now that college is filling up, you've got to go to graduate school. The race continues." President Clinton, for one, has declared: "Our goal must be nothing less than to make the 13th and 14th years of education as universal to all Americans as the first 12 are today."

Whether the goal of universal access to higher education is justified is hotly debated by academicians and economists. "It's nice to be worried about universal access to higher education," Mirel of Emory University says. "But there's only one way that's going to happen, and that's if we really begin to make a concerted effort to make our middle schools and our high schools institutions that offer outstanding college-preparatory education."

At the same time, the most highly educated group of parents in history has brought a demanding, consumer-oriented attitude to their relationship with the public schools. Increasingly, parents are clamoring not for access to a common school, but for access to the school of their choice—whether it's a private school, a charter school, or a magnet school in a neighboring district.

Labaree cautions that, as such attitudes deepen, there is a danger that public education may increasingly be viewed as "a public subsidy for private ambition."

If such views prevail, he and others caution, it could serve to widen the educational gap between the haves and have-nots in American society, rather than supporting the schools' traditional democratic purpose.

FOCUS ON STANDARDS

That's one reason Mirel and others contend the movement by states to adopt academic standards for what students should know and be able to do is so important.

By focusing on the substance of what young people are learning in their courses—and how well they are learning it—the standards movement has the potential to ensure that all students have access to a top-quality curriculum.

Standards, "wisely developed and applied, can greatly benefit American education," Mirel and Angus write. "Such measures could constitute major steps toward equalizing educational quality and ensuring that all American students, particularly poor and minority students, have access to the same challenging programs and courses that students in the nation's best schools now receive."

But others are skeptical that the movement will live up to its promise. By 2004, for example, all students in Virginia will be expected to pass new tests based on detailed academic standards to graduate from high school. Test results also will help determine whether students are promoted to the next grade, and whether schools maintain their accreditation.

"I think all kids can learn," says R. Wayne Ellis, a high school math teacher in Richmond, Va., "but I don't think they can all learn at the level we're setting right now, as far as everybody is going to learn algebra when they're in 9th grade, and everybody can learn geometry in 10th grade, and so on."

"I think we need to take a serious look at the rate of student learning," adds Ellis, who teaches at the city's Huguenot High School. "And I think the standards are not age-appropriate."

The declaration that "all children can learn" may be even more difficult to fulfill given the changing demographics of the United States. In 1997, the country's population of children roughly equaled the record set when the baby boomers were coming of age—69.5 million in 1997, compared with 69.9 million in 1966.

An increasing proportion of U.S. children are poor and minority, groups that historically have been the least well-served by the public schools.

"The unfinished agenda will continually be the low-income minorities, basically poor people," Cuban of Stanford says. "And that inequity, which reflects the larger inequalities in this society, will remain what I would call a persistent kind of illness in the American educational system and the body politic." ∎

Century Snapshots

1900

U.S. population:
76.1 million

Children in public schools:
15.5 million

Number of new immigrants:
3.7 million (1891-1900)

High school graduates:
62,000, or 6.4 percent of 17-year-olds

■ *By the turn of the century, 33 states and the District of Columbia have enacted compulsory-education laws.*

Corbis-Bettmann

1910

U.S. population:
92.4 million

Children in public schools:
17.8 million

Number of new immigrants:
8.8 million (1901-10)

High school graduates:
111,000, or 8.8 percent of 17-year-olds

■ *Between 1900 and 1910, nine additional states enact compulsory-education laws.*

■ *The foreign-born make up 14.7 percent of the population–the highest level reached at any time in U.S. history. Fifty-seven percent of foreign-born residents live in one of six states: Illinois, Massachusetts, New Jersey, New York, Ohio, and Pennsylvania.*

Corbis-Bettmann

1920

U.S. population:
106.5 million

Children in public schools:
21.6 million

Number of new immigrants:
5.7 million (1911-20)

High school graduates:
231,000, or 16.8 percent of 17-year-olds

■ *Between 1910 and 1920, the six remaining states–Louisiana, Alabama, Florida, South Carolina, Georgia, and Mississippi–enact compulsory-education laws. The Great Depression begins in 1929 and lasts through much of the 1930s.*

1930

U.S. population:
123.1 million

Children in public schools:
25.7 million

Number of new immigrants:
4.1 million (1921-30)

High school graduates:
592,000, or 29.0 percent of 17-year-olds

1940

U.S. population:
132.1 million

Children in public schools:
25.4 million

Number of new immigrants:
528,000 (1931-40)

Corbis-Bettmann

High school graduates:
1.1 million, or 50.8 percent of 17-year-olds

■ *The post-World War II population surge known as the baby boom begins in 1946 and lasts until 1964.*

Corbis-Bettmann

1950

U.S. population:
152.3 million

Children in public schools:
25.1 million

Number of new immigrants:
1.0 million (1941-50)

High school graduates:
1.1 million, or 59.0 percent of 17-year-olds

1960

U.S. population:
180.7 million

Children in public schools:
36.1 million

Number of new immigrants:
2.5 million (1951-60)

High school graduates:
1.6 million, or 69.5 percent of 17-year-olds

1970

U.S. population:
205.1 million

Children in public schools:
45.6 million

Number of new immigrants:
3.3 million (1961-70)

High school graduates:
2.6 million, or 76.9 percent of 17-year-olds

■ *The children of the early baby boomers begin to flood the schools. In 1971, a then-record 51.3 million children enroll in the nation's public and private K-12 schools.*

■ *After declining since 1910, the percentage of the nation's population that is foreign-born hits 4.8 percent.*

1980

U.S. population:
227.7 million

Children in public schools:
41.7 million

Number of new immigrants:
4.5 million (1971-80)

High school graduates:
2.7 million, or 71.4 percent of 17-year-olds

■ *Seventy-five percent of all immigrants coming to the United States in the 1980s settle in California, Florida, Illinois, New Jersey, New York, and Texas.*

1990

U.S. population:
249.4 million

Children in public schools:
40.5 million

Number of new immigrants:
7.3 million (1981-90)

High school graduates:
2.3 million, or 72.4 percent of 17-year-olds

■ *In 1996, the number of children in U.S. public and private schools hits 51.7 million, an all-time high fueled by soaring immigration and a second surge in population known as the baby boom echo.*

2000

U.S. population:
267.6 million (as of 1997)

Children in public schools:
45.9 million

Jefferey M. Boan

NOTES: Immigration data are compiled by decades beginning with 1891-1900 through 1981-1990 and do not include illegal immigration. Hawaii and Alaska had compulsory-education laws on their books before becoming states in 1959.

SOURCES: U.S. Census Bureau; U.S. Department of Education's National Center for Education Statistics; U.S. Immigration and Naturalization Service; and *State Legislation on School Attendance*, Urban Institute.

Public Foundation

By
Lynn
Olson

In the 20th century, the United States opened wide the schoolhouse doors to the vast majority of its young people. But those advances built on a solid foundation that had been established long before, when the nation embraced the principle of free, universal public education.

"It goes back to the New England tradition of literacy," says historian Daniel J. Boorstin, "and the belief that all young people should be inducted into the ideas that govern the nation and the community."

In Colonial times, many towns had schools, but attendance was voluntary, and parents usually paid a fee, notes Carl F. Kaestle, a professor and historian at Brown University. School subjects generally were confined to reading, writing, and arithmetic. And students in rural areas might attend for only a few months each year.

"Nowhere was schooling entirely tax-supported and compulsory," Kaestle writes in *Pillars of the Republic: Common Schools and American Society: 1780-1860.* That gradually began to change in the 19th century, as states in the new republic moved toward greater financial support for public schooling, at least in the elementary grades.

In 1795, Connecticut sold its land in the Western territories for $1.2 million and used the proceeds to establish a permanent school fund, which by 1810 was providing annual assistance to schools. New York state created such a fund in 1805. By the 1820s and '30s, several more states had followed suit, although the money covered only a fraction of the costs of education.

In 1852, Horace Mann, the secretary of the Massachusetts board of education, helped pass the first compulsory-attendance law in the nation, for children of elementary school age.

Mann and other advocates of universal schooling had an almost boundless faith in the ability of public education to advance both national and individual progress. "Never will wisdom preside in the halls of legislation," Mann wrote, "and its profound utterances be recorded on the pages of the statute book, until Common Schools ... shall create a more farseeing intelligence and a purer morality than has ever existed among communities of men."

WIDER ACCESS

By the Civil War, Kaestle notes, state governments in the North generally had created common school systems, by enacting laws for tax-supported elementary schools and appointing state school officers. Support for public schooling came later to the South. And while 16 states had compulsory-attendance laws by 1885, most of those laws were sporadically enforced.

Enrollment grew throughout the 19th century, spurred by the establishment of district schools, population increases, and the growing acceptance of education for

Library of Congress

Educator Horace Mann helped pass the nation's first compulsory-attendance law in Massachusetts in 1852.

girls. By 1900, girls outnumbered boys, six to four, at the high school level.

Concerns about maintaining social order and preventing crime and delinquency also prompted philanthropic efforts to reach out to poor and immigrant children. Although these institutions took many forms—ranging from church-operated charity schools to programs for infants and toddlers—some eventually became incorporated into the burgeoning public school systems.

By 1830, most white Americans in the North had access to schooling, though the quality was uneven. And by midcentury, about half of all children under age 20 went to school, though they attended on average only about 78 days a year.

By 1860, writes David B. Tyack, an education historian at Stanford University, most large cities divided schoolchildren into grades, and by 1870, the concept had spread almost everywhere there were enough students to classify. That year, about 61 percent of Americans ages 5 to 18 were enrolled in some school, Tyack points out. By 1898, that figure was 71 percent, and the typical young American could expect to receive five years of schooling.

Indeed, so many young people wanted to go to school that educators often had nowhere to put them. In 1878, the Detroit school system turned away almost 800 children for lack of seats. And it educated others in rented basements. In 1881, New York City refused admission to 9,189 students for lack of room.

The situation was much worse for black Americans. In 1870, fewer than 10 percent of African-Americans ages 5 to 19 were in school for even part of the year.

WHO WILL PAY?

As Kaestle observes, though Americans supported the idea of public education, many took issue with the concept of state control and state financing. Attempts to gather all groups into a common school system with a common curriculum met with resistance.

On one side of the debate were reformers like Mann, who supported a standardized curriculum, better-prepared teachers, graded schools, a longer school year, and greater state supervision and regulation. On the other side was a loosely knit opposition made up of advocates of local control, tax resisters, defenders of religious freedom who worried about the dominant Protestant ideology of the schools, and supporters of private education.

Those groups, however, were "not upset about the same things about public education," Kaestle says. "So there's considerable opposition, but it's fragmented." ∎

The GI Bill

Most Americans today think of higher education as an inalienable right. With more than 4,000 colleges and universities to choose from, virtually every high school graduate who is so inclined can win admission somewhere.

Paving the way for this wide-open access was the GI Bill, part of the Servicemen's Readjustment Act of 1944.

Before that historic legislation, higher education was almost entirely the province of the well-to-do. Soon after the law was passed, college came to be seen as a reachable and even necessary goal.

In 1940, less than 5 percent of the U.S. population age 25 or older had completed four years of college. About 24 percent of Americans in that age group hold bachelor's degrees today.

"The bill made going to college normal rather than exceptional for American young people," says Charles Moskos, a sociology professor at Northwestern University.

By Julie Blair

Some 7.8 million World War II veterans took advantage of the GI Bill during the seven years benefits were offered, nearly doubling the college population.

But the law's greatest legacy was that it provided the same opportunities to every veteran, regardless of the person's background. "For the first time," education historian Diane Ravitch writes in *The Troubled Crusade: American Education, 1945 to 1980*, "the link between income and educational opportunity was broken."

Efforts to improve access for women and members of minority groups have challenged additional barriers.

In 1940, women made up 40 percent of U.S. college students. That share dropped to 29 percent in 1947 as a result of the GI Bill, which mostly benefited men. It wasn't until the mid-1970s, in the era of the women's liberation movement and the 1972 federal anti-discrimination law known as Title IX, that the number of women in higher education equaled the number of men. Today, women make up a slight majority of college students.

Black students benefited greatly from the civil rights movement of the 1960s and the widespread adoption of affirmative action policies in admissions by the early 1970s. Black enrollment in higher education tripled during the 1960s, from 174,000 to 522,000, then nearly doubled to 1 million by 1976.

By 1997, 13 percent of blacks 25 or older

Corbis-Bettmann

had at least four years of higher education, compared with just 1 percent of all minorities in 1940. Among Hispanics, 10 percent had four years of higher education in 1997, compared with 5 percent in 1974.

New Forms of Aid

Federal leaders have followed up the GI Bill with new forms of student financial aid over the past 40 years.

In 1958, at a time when Cold War competition had been heightened by the Soviet Union's launch of the first space satellite, Congress authorized college aid for students whose skills were deemed necessary to defend the nation.

That action was followed by the Higher Education Act of 1965, which created what are now called Pell Grants to help the neediest students attend college. President Lyndon B. Johnson's administration also instituted work-study programs, which enabled students to help pay their school debts by performing services for their colleges, and started the federal TRIO program, which offered scholarships to first-generation college students from low-income families.

Financial aid changed under President Ronald Reagan in the 1980s. The emphasis shifted from need-based grants, which don't have to be repaid, to student loans.

And in a reminder of the political appeal of student aid, President Clinton pushed through legislation in 1997 that provides higher education tax credits for middle-class families. From 1998 to 2002, the credits are expected to total about $40 billion.

The increase in the number of Americans attending college remains nothing short of remarkable.

No longer is higher education only for a fortunate few. ■

World War II veterans line up to buy textbooks and other supplies for college in January 1945. The GI Bill "made going to college normal rather than exceptional."

THE GI BILL

The GI Bill of Rights was passed in 1944 as part of the Servicemen's Readjustment Act. Designed to prevent unemployment among returning veterans of World War II, it subsidized the cost of tuition, books, and fees at any postsecondary institution a veteran chose to attend. In the seven years benefits were offered, about 7.8 million veterans, 98 percent of them men, took part.

Below are excerpts from the law.

Any such eligible person shall be entitled to education or training at an approved educational or training institution for a period of one year plus the time such person was in the active service on or after September 16, 1940, and before the termination of the war. ... The Administrator shall pay to the educational or training institution ... the customary cost of tuition, and such laboratory, library, health, infirmary, and other similar fees as are customarily charged, and may pay for books, supplies, equipment, and other necessary expenses ... as are generally required for the successful pursuit and completion of the course by other students in the institution.

SOURCE: *American Education in the Twentieth Century: A Documentary History.*

CHINESE • GERMAN • CZECHO-SLOVAKIAN • BRAZIL • SPANISH • JEWISH • SCOTCH • ROUMANIAN • ENGLISH • AUSTRIAN • SLAVIC •

Corbis-Bettmann

Immigrants Adapt

By Lynn Schnaiberg

Chicago

The 20-room annex at William G. Hibbard Elementary School shows just how much immigration has changed the 1,200-student school.

Before the annex opened in fall 1998, some class sizes hovered in the 40s. Students, mostly immigrants and the children of immigrants, attended classes in stairwell landings and hallways.

The Northwest Chicago neighborhood where the pre-K-6 school sits has long been a port of entry for new immigrants. Assistant Principal Ron Lyons, who has worked at Hibbard for more than two decades, recalls an influx of Greek immigrants early in his tenure. These days, the students' names printed on paper snowmen hanging outside Nancy Samra's 1st grade classroom represent a range of nations: Carlos, Ruqia, Cuong, Vannak, and Walid.

Almost half of Hibbard's students lack proficiency in English. The school's English-as-a-second-language program enrolls children who speak 17 languages. Hibbard offers bilingual programs that teach students partly in their native languages: Spanish, Bosnian/Serbo-Croatian, Arabic, Vietnamese, and Khmer—for now.

"We're always in a state of flux here," Lyons says.

Beginning with the huge influxes of immigrants to the United States in the early part of the 20th century, public schools have had to adapt to immigrant students—however reluctantly—and, in turn, help those students adapt to America. And the politics of the day have always shaped the schools' response to the newcomers.

Sheer numbers of immigrants aside, 1910 remains the high point for the percentage of the U.S. population made up of those born elsewhere. That year, 14.7 percent of Americans were foreign-born; in 1998, the figure was 9.8 percent.

In the century's first decade, 9 million immigrants arrived in the United States, most from Southern, Central, and Eastern Europe. At the close of the century, immigrants were most likely to come from Latin America and Asia.

The trends are no fluke.

Laws passed in the 1920s to restrict immigration set a downward curve that didn't reverse itself until the 1970s. A 1965 law undid the national-origin quotas set in the early part of the century that barred virtually all Asian immigrants and favored those from Northern and Western Europe.

In 1990, compared with 1910, proportionately more foreign-born residents had been in the United States 10 years or less. Such new arrivals are less likely to be fluent in English. And Jeffrey S. Passel, an immigration expert at the Urban Institute in Washington, points out that the issue of illegal immigration is relatively new. Immigrants here illegally, he says, are more likely to fear contact with institutions such as school.

Immigration is still largely an urban phenomenon—about half of all immigrants arriving in the 1980s lived in just eight metropolitan areas—but far from exclusively so. Immigration has touched suburban and rural schools and communities as well as urban areas.

How schools accommodate their immigrant pupils is inextricably linked to broader societal attitudes about immigration. And schools throughout the century have found themselves in a recurring pendulum swing between assimilation and pluralism.

BECOMING AMERICANS

It's easy to point to schools' explicit adaptations to immigrant and non-English-speaking students: bilingual and ESL classes, most obviously. But some aspects of school now considered "mainstream" emerged in the century's early years at least partly in response to the flow of immigrants.

"Immigration really has the impact of introducing and enlarging a new set of things we now commonly take for granted in school," says Marvin Lazerson, an education historian at the University of Pennsylvania. "It broadened the definition of what schools ought to be about."

In the early 20th century, urban schools, to a large degree, were about helping immigrant children become better and healthier citizens.

Immigrants served as a partial trigger—or at least a crucial clientele—for a range of social services in school: from hygiene lessons and vaccinations, to extended-day and summer programs, to

POLISH ▪ RUSSIAN ▪ TURK ▪ GREEK ▪ IRISH ▪ LITHUNIAN ▪ PORTUG

Students representing 19 nations pose for a group photo at a New York City public school in 1926.

school meals and playgrounds.

The schools were seen as one of the best places to reach and assimilate newly arrived immigrant students and their families.

Education historians say such newcomers also gave added impetus to the expansion of kindergarten, vocational education, and civics.

Compulsory-attendance laws were crafted in part to reach immigrant children, who figured disproportionately in big cities' truancy rosters. Immigrants were not the exclusive motivator for attendance laws, "but a very powerful one," says David B. Tyack, an education historian at Stanford University. "The notion was: How can they become Ameri—

Gary, Indiana? ➚

classes the New York City schools held to give new arrivals a crash course in English. Newcomer programs today often offer intensive language help and an orientation to the American school system and the cities where their students live.

While policymakers continue to grapple with difficult issues of ensuring such students' equal access to a good education, the question of school access at the beginning of the 20th century was often a starkly literal one: Many immigrant students were turned away because there was simply no room.

Schools across the country varied widely in how much they were affected by immigration and, in turn, how they responded to it. But the perception of the immigrant as a distinct "other"—early in the century when Southern and Eastern

European ethnic groups were considered "races"—helped shape the ways schools adapted.

Historians point to a movement among educators in the first quarter of the century—supported by the U.S. Bureau of Education and such civic and community groups as the YMCA—to foster the "Americanization" of immigrant students. Schools were seen as places where polyglot populations went to be homogenized into the larger society.

⇐ good info

...ics and sewing to teach gi... maintain an American home. Schools reached out to Americanize immigrant parents, too, by offering naturalization classes and free lectures.

Some historians view Americanization as coercive, nativist, and denigrating. Others see it as having provided immigrants needed structure and direction in a difficult new environment.

But most agree that the movement took on a harsher bent as anti-foreign tensions heated up at the time of the First World War. Many states passed laws banning German in classrooms, on the street, and in church. In the wake of the war, many states legislated English as the basic language of instruction or forbade foreign-language study in the elementary grades.

But as the flow of new immigrants waned in the 1930s, so too did society's fears. A new movement took hold in what some describe as a gentler approach to assimilation. Without waves of newcomers to manage, the leaders of the "interculturalism" movement of the 1930s and 1940s focused on "the second-generation problem."

Immigration "broadened the definition of what schools ought to be about."

Marvin Lazerson
Education Historian,
University of Pennsylvania

Progressive educators, academics, and race-relations experts introduced school programs to reduce racial, ethnic, and religious tensions and incorporate minorities on equal terms into the American mainstream.

Interculturalists talked about "our history" and "our American way of life" and how various immigrant groups contributed to that collective notion.

But pluralism had its limits.

Some interculturalists pushed to affirm cultural diversity; others wanted simply to acknowledge it and keep the affirmation muted lest it disrupt national unity.

In 1945, Stewart Cole, the director of a group promoting intercultural education, warned: "National cultural unity must not be jeopardized by an exaggerated development of the forces of cultural diversity."

The intercultural movement foreshadowed another shift of the pendulum, spurred by the civil rights movement of the 1960s. With the push for "multicultural" education, schools again would have to confront tensions surrounding assimilation, unity, and diversity.

The Language Debate

The civil rights movement was a turning point, pushing American society and its schools to address inequities among the poor and racial and ethnic minorities—and, eventually, language-minority students.

A slew of court rulings and federal laws securing equal access to school programs focused attention on the needs of immigrant and non-English-speaking children. Special programs were designed to help youngsters who, in the inelegant jargon of the experts and bureaucrats, were labeled "limited English proficient," or LEP.

The debate over language instruction for LEP students, however, is not a new one.

Contemporary bilingual programs, in which students learn some academic subjects in their native languages, bear some resemblance to German-language programs in such heavily German cities as Cincinnati and Indianapolis from the mid-19th century to the early 20th century. The programs were offered largely as a means of luring German immigrants away from parochial schools, which often taught in German.

Such programs were not without their critics. In 1870s St. Louis, the district offered a German-language kindergarten and offered German study in the elementary grades.

Opponents, especially the Irish, denounced such classes as costing too much, interfering with the regular curriculum, and threatening the standing of the English language.

The anti-German sentiment incited by World War I ended whatever was left of the early language accommodation in schools.

But in the past quarter-century, two

U.S. Supreme Court rulings have radically reshaped the school landscape for LEP and immigrant children.

In its 1974 decision in *Lau* v. *Nichols*, the court held that the San Francisco schools had to offer special help to enable LEP students to participate equally in school. In its argument to the high court, the San Francisco district reflected the view of many schools at the time, says Peter Roos, a civil rights lawyer based in that city.

"The kids had to adapt to the school, not the other way around. The argument then was there's no obligation to adjust in any way the district's educational program," which was designed for English-speaking "Anglo" students, Roos says.

Then in 1982, the Supreme Court ruled in *Plyler* v. *Doe* that schools could not deny illegal-immigrant children a free public education.

In California, the state most heavily affected by immigrants, voters approved a ballot initiative in 1994 to deny illegal immigrants access to most public benefits, including a free education, and another in 1998, to virtually eliminate bilingual education from the state's public school classrooms. The first measure has been shot down in the courts; the second is being carried out while legal and political battles continue.

So, as the 20th century draws to a close, immigrants again are making their presence felt in the United States and pushing questions to the fore: What does it mean to be an American? What is it immigrants should be assimilating to? And on whose terms?

Such questions are immediate ones for Chicago's Hibbard Elementary. Black-and-white photographs and stories of several students and their families who have immigrated to the city's Albany Park neighborhood hang in the school hallway.

In addition to promoting diversity with its "Changing Worlds" project, Hibbard plans to use the project to make the curriculum more relevant to its mostly immigrant population.

"We highlight the different cultures, but yet we're always promoting patriotism and talking about what it means to be American," says Roquel Landsman, Hibbard's curriculum coordinator. "We're promoting tolerance. It's not 'us and them' at this school. We're all 'them' here." ∎

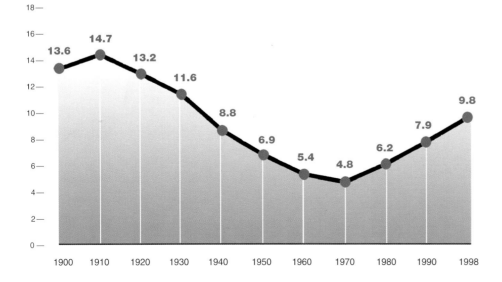

TRACKING THE TIDE

Percent of the U.S. population that is foreign-born.

13.6	14.7	13.2	11.6	8.8	6.9	5.4	4.8	6.2	7.9	9.8
1900	1910	1920	1930	1940	1950	1960	1970	1980	1990	1998

SOURCE: U.S. Department of Commerce.

Inclusion of the Disabled

For much of the 20th century, the practice of educating disabled students in regular schools and classrooms was exceedingly rare, almost unheard of. Today, it's a common occurrence—and a sign of how far students with disabilities have come.

Yet there's further to go, advocates for such students say. What is now called "special education" has made remarkable gains in the past 10 decades, but the next fight—the one for full educational equity for the disabled—will carry over into the 21st century.

"The passage of [the Education for All Handicapped Children Act in 1975] was about getting the doors open and acknowledging that kids were supposed to be in school," says Judith E. Heumann, the U.S. Department of Education's assistant secretary for special education and rehabilitative services.

By Joetta L. Sack

"Today, there's a whole higher level of expectations for the kids," she adds.

The groundbreaking federal law adopted nearly a quarter-century ago guaranteed a free, appropriate education for all students with disabilities. From then on, schools began to experiment with "mainstreaming" by placing disabled students in the same classrooms and facilities as their nondisabled peers. Later, mainstreaming evolved into "inclusion," which holds that students not only should be placed in regular classrooms whenever possible but also that they should be engaged there, as well, in the same curriculum and activities as their classmates.

During these years, the focus of special education increasingly has expanded beyond the more obvious physical and mental impairments to subtler—and more controversial—handicaps such as learning disabilities.

THE 'FEEBLEMINDED'

In the 19th century, and into this century, children who were blind, deaf, paralyzed, deemed mentally defective, or otherwise impaired were often considered a family burden best kept out of sight.

Compulsory-attendance laws began to change that picture around the turn of the century. Schools were flooded with thousands of new students, and policy-

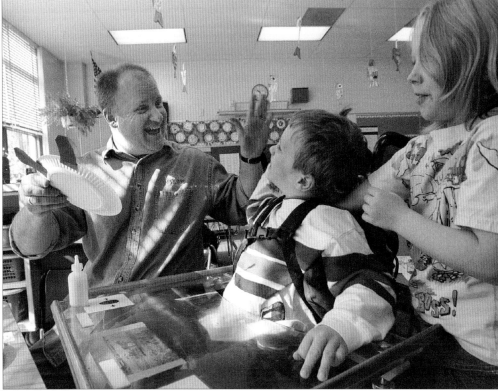

Benjamin Tice Smith

makers sought ways of dealing with children who seemed not to fit the mold.

In 1911, New Jersey mandated that school boards establish separate classes for "mentally retarded" children—an undefined category that included most mental, emotional, and learning disabilities—and other states soon followed.

It wasn't long before the "feebleminded" became perceived as a threat to society. In 1917, the famed psychologist and researcher Lewis M. Terman wrote: "Feeblemindedness has always existed, but only recently have we begun to recognize how serious a menace it is to the social, economic, and moral welfare of the state."

The move to segregate such students led to the growth of institutions and special schools.

Although first created in the 1800s by reformers who wanted to educate youngsters routinely shut out of regular schools, many of the institutions for the mentally disabled offered little, if any, instruction and instead served as de facto warehouses for children.

Over the course of decades, the system for educating disabled students came to be a hodgepodge, says Margaret J. McLaughlin, the associate director of the Institute for the Study of Exceptional Children at the University of Maryland. How a youngster was schooled often de-

At Zachary Taylor Elementary School in Arlington, Va., students with disabilities, such as Chris Clem, spend almost all of their days in regular classes. Chris' classmate, Britney Gill, is giving teacher Rod Baer a helping hand.

First lady Eleanor Roosevelt visits Jack Whelan, a student at the Weightman School for Crippled Children in Washington, in 1937.

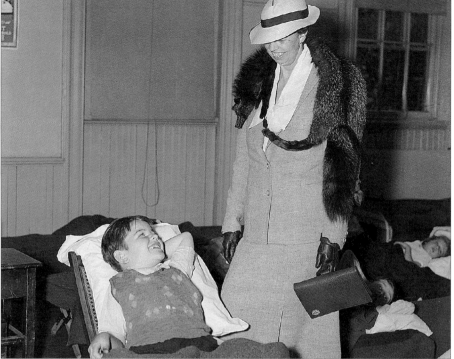

Corbis-Bettmann

pended on the philosophy of the state or the local district toward students with handicaps.

Special schools for the blind, deaf, and orthopedically disabled, or "crippled," were established, and, while they offered better educational services than the institutions for mentally impaired children, they generally still weren't on a par with the schools serving mainstream students.

TURNED AWAY

Perhaps no high-ranking education official better exemplifies the changing face of special education—or is a more fervent advocate for including students with disabilities in regular classrooms—than Heumann, who has been confined to a wheelchair since contracting polio as an infant. Her firsthand experiences began in the early 1950s when her parents tried to enroll her in kindergarten at the public elementary school in her middle-class Brooklyn neighborhood.

Because of her wheelchair, she was turned away. The district sent a teacher to her home for a few hours each week. "If you were lucky, you were getting a little home instruction," Heumann, now 51, recalls of the climate in the New York City schools at the time.

Fourth grade was the first time she saw the inside of a classroom, after her parents navigated a tough admissions screening for a special class for students with cerebral palsy. The class was in the basement of the local elementary school, completely separate from the classes for other youngsters. At the time, no student in the special class had entered high school.

Heumann, however, went on to attend a public high school and later graduated from Long Island State University with a bachelor's degree and earned a master's from the University of California, Berkeley. She also went on to found the World Institute on Disability, which she says was the first research institution devoted entirely to disability issues. She joined the Education Department as an assistant secretary in 1993.

The roots of the breakthrough law now called the Individuals with Disabilities Education Act can be traced to the 1950s, when the movement against racially segregated schools that culminated in *Brown* v. *Board of Education* inspired disability-rights advocates. Many of them were parents of children with handicaps.

At the same time, investigations of the grim conditions in some of the institutions for mentally retarded children came to light. In 1958, the first federal law addressing special education, the Education of Mentally Retarded Children Act, was passed, giving funding for the training of teachers for mentally retarded children. That was followed by the Elementary and Secondary Education Act in 1965, which provided funding to improve the education of disadvantaged children, including the disabled.

Two court cases, *The Pennsylvania Association for Retarded Citizens* v. *The Commonwealth of Pennsylvania* and *Mills* v. *Board of Education* in the District of Columbia, both decided in 1972, further laid the legal groundwork for the rights of disabled students.

FEDERAL STRATEGY

As Judith Heumann and others fought local school boards and states in the early 1970s, the members of some national education groups began to meet monthly to talk about how students with disabilities might be included in regular schools, says William Healey, a special education professor at the University of Nevada, Las Vegas.

While they hadn't intended to write a major federal law ensuring that disabled students have the right to a "free and appropriate public education," the end result was the Education for All Handicapped Children Act.

The legislation, passed with bipartisan support in 1975, was based on a variety of state laws that had been adopted in the early 1970s, as well as court cases, says Lisa Walker, who at the time was an aide to the Senate Education and Public Welfare Committee, which drafted and pushed through the Senate version of the law. Walker is now the executive director of the Education Writers Association.

The EAHCA did not fully go into effect until 1978, and states showed considerable reluctance to accept it, she says. "Many states already had their own legislation and didn't see why they needed it," she remembers.

All states eventually signed on, however. And, today, while many states balk at what they see as inadequate federal funding for the special education services that Congress has mandated, none has seriously threatened to withdraw from the IDEA, the successor to the EAHCA.

That's not to say, though, that every tension has been eliminated. Schools and lawmakers are still debating the appropriate means for disciplining disruptive disabled students, and the federal mandate has contributed to a backlash among school administrators and taxpayers, who see rising special education costs sapping local budgets. Some critics question whether special education is worth the enormous financial investment—more than $5 billion in federal dollars alone in fiscal 1999—when nondisabled students are also in need.

Preparing regular education teachers to educate the students with disabilities who are now included in their classrooms poses another challenge. Complicated, as well, is defining "disability." Some argue that labels such as learning-disabled and attention deficit/hyperactivity disorder are so ambiguous that they sweep too many children into special education. Others charge that parents actively seek such labels for their children to get special services.

But for the most part, the battles have paid off for disabled students, most researchers agree. And, with new research and more experience with inclusion, special education is constantly evolving.

"We've achieved a great deal," says McLaughlin of the Institute for the Study of Exceptional Children. "But we could still go a lot further in inclusion for kids." ■

EMERGING RIGHTS

- The first federal law addressing special education, the Education of Mentally Retarded Children Act, was passed in 1958. It authorized funding to train teachers for children who were considered mentally retarded.

- The Elementary and Secondary Education Act followed in 1965. It authorized federal aid to improve the education of disadvantaged children, including students with disabilities.

- Section 504 of the Rehabilitation Act of 1973 bars discrimination against the disabled in any federally funded program and specifically requires appropriate education services for disabled children.

- In 1975, the Education for All Handicapped Children Act was passed, prompting states to experiment with mainstreaming disabled students. The law, which guarantees a "free, appropriate public education" for all disabled students, is now known as the Individuals with Disabilities Education Act. The law has been amended several times, most recently in 1997.

- The Americans With Disabilities Act, passed in 1990, bars all forms of discrimination against the disabled.

Growth in the Garden

The first public school built in Garden City, Kan., has been a mirror of sorts throughout the 1900s, reflecting the town's shifting demographics and needs.

Garden City, Kan.

The land, a patchwork of brown punctuated by irrigated green, bears witness to the stubborn determination of this town's settlers to carve out an existence in a desertlike corner of the High Plains. Despite the naysayers—and an average annual rainfall of just 18 inches—residents learned to bend the land to meet their needs.

They dug irrigation ditches to siphon water from the Arkansas River. Then they used pumps, first powered by windmill, later by gasoline or electricity. Eventually, deep-well turbine pumps allowed farmers to tap the Ogallala Aquifer below the earth's surface, and improved irrigation methods made this

Lydia Smith

Garfield's student population has gone through as many changes as the school's architecture. The original 1886 school, left, burned in 1901. Today's building, above, is the school's fourth incarnation.

By Lynn Schnaiberg

Finney County Historical Museum

corner of southwest Kansas one of the nation's most productive agricultural areas.

Many say it is that same relentless spirit that has kept the town's first public school open for more than a century. First built in 1886, Garfield has occupied four buildings—two of which were leveled by fire.

But both the community and the school have had to bend to the needs of new settlers, triggering indelible changes that some have embraced and others have accepted grudgingly as the price of progress.

With few exceptions, Garden City has been a growing community, weathering more boom than bust. The cash crop of choice over the century has shifted from sugar beets to such grains as milo, corn, and alfalfa that are used to feed livestock. Lured by a burgeoning cattle-feeding industry, beef-packing plants set up shop in town. By the 1980s, existing plants expanded, and new ones moved to town, eliminating the need to ship cattle to urban plants for butchering.

The plentiful jobs brought Hispanic and Southeast Asian workers to town. Many of the newcomers are transient; many are poor. Many do not speak English well or at all. The town's demographic shifts have been reflected even more dramatically in the schools.

From 1980 to 1990, the Garden City school district grew by 45 percent, from 4,500 students to 6,600. Now, the district enrolls 7,700 students. In 1991, Garfield became majority minority; a few years later, the district followed suit.

Whom the school has educated and how it has done so has shifted through the years. And, always, Garfield has been reshaped by events and changes in the community.

For a time, Garfield was the only school in town, serving grades 1-12 in a community with a population of 2,500 in 1886. Now, the city's population hovers near 25,000, and Garfield serves just a piece of the district's K-4 enrollment.

It's clear that Garfield's modern-day mission includes much more than just teaching the three R's. Today, the school provides a safe place where immigrant children can master a new language and eases students and their families from their homelands to the heartland.

"It's not Dick and Jane and Spot anymore," says Garfield Elementary School Principal Willis Pracht. "It's a whole different ballgame."

A high log fence circled the yard of Northside School, which opened its doors

in 1886 and later would be rechristened Garfield. Students had to enter the school through stiles, fashioned to keep livestock away from what was considered one of the area's finest brick buildings.

The eight-room, two-story building housed grades 1-8 on the first floor and grades 9-12 on the second. The school was overcrowded when it opened—a trend Garden City educators would find repeated throughout the 1900s.

"The new school building Monday presented the appearance of a beehive, the children literally swarming there, all anxious to resume their studies," the local newspaper reported just after the school opened. "The different apartments are full to overflowing, some of the teachers being obliged to place benches in the aisles to accommodate their pupils."

Before residents voted to tax themselves to build the school, some families paid $1.25 a month per child to attend "subscription" schools held for three- or four-month terms in private homes and churches.

Just barely into the 20th century, Garden City's first public school went up in flames, the result of a basement fire of unknown origin. School board members found room to continue classes in places like the Colored Baptist Church and the courthouse.

When the school reopened in 1902, it carried the last name of President James A. Garfield, who had been assassinated in 1881. Some local residents had fought under him when he served as a Union general in the Civil War.

While Garfield quickly filled up, it is unclear how wide a swath the school cut through Garden City's school-age population. What's recorded as Garden City's first high school graduating class in 1888 numbered five. By 1911, there were 24 graduates, and the city moved grades 9-12 out of Garfield to a separate high school.

The 1911 Sugar Beet, the high school annual, lists teachers in the subjects of English and German, history and Latin, domestic science and art, and mathematics and science—a far cry from Garden City High School's current thick course guide that includes landscape architecture, desktop publishing, and industrial technology.

Laws requiring school attendance and regulating child labor were in place early in the century, but both included plenty of loopholes.

The 1922 Annals of Kansas recorded "deplorable" child-labor conditions in the sugar beet industry, which took root in Garden City and surrounding Finney

County in the late 1800s and continued into the 1950s. "Scores of children between the ages of 6 and 14 were compelled to work in the fields," it said, "and many never attended school."

In addition to growing crops such as wheat, farmers across the Midwest—many of German descent—were drawn to the area to farm the sugar beets. Mexican migrant laborers, some of whom were already in the area for railroad jobs, helped thin, hoe, and harvest the beets, which fed the demand for refined sugar.

Like other young men from his homeland who eventually settled here with their families, Hesiquio Rodríguez came from Michoacan, Mexico, to lay and repair track for the Santa Fe Railroad about the turn of the century.

One of his daughters, Cipriana Rodríguez, who also goes by Sue, still lives in the tree-enveloped family home that sits so close to the railroad tracks that the ground under the house rumbles when trains pass. Her sister, Felisa Guadian, lives across the street.

The sisters recall attending Garfield off and on during the years they worked the beet fields with their father to keep the family of 10 afloat.

The Rodríguez family formed part of the beginnings of a small Mexican community in Garden City whose numbers would dip during the Great Depression and pick up again after World War II.

While schools in larger Kansas cities were closed to Mexican children until the late 1910s or early 1920s, Garden City's were open. But by most accounts, not many Mexican-American children made it to school consistently, and, for those who did, school was not always an accommodating place.

Both 84-year-old Rodríguez and 77-year-old Guadian recall falling quickly behind.

"We all worked, and then we'd come back into school and they'd be on the last page of the book," Guadian says.

Learning English was a struggle. Local histories tell of children being held back for years because they did not have the English skills to move on. When the city's minority population started growing in the late 1970s, Guadian worked as a bilingual aide in Garfield and other Garden City schools.

"I could remember myself what those kids were going through," she says. "I wish I had that kind of help when I was young, but it just wasn't there."

By 1950, just 18 Mexican-Americans

Lydia Smith

had graduated from Garden City High School since the century began, according to one researcher. Neither Guadian nor Rodríguez finished high school. But, Guadian notes with pride as she and her sister flip through a family scrapbook, all seven of her own children did.

If Garfield was not quite ready for students like the Rodríguez sisters back then, the sheer number of immigrant children and the children of immigrants years later would prove too big to ignore. And Garfield would have to bend.

Lydia Smith

To this day, 74-year-old Katherine Hart remembers the Oliver Wendell Holmes poem she memorized for class in the 1930s.

"Have you heard of the wonderful one-hoss shay,
   That was built in such a logical way
   It ran a hundred years to a day,
   And then, of a sudden, it—ah, but stay ..."

By the time Hart attended Garfield, the school had lost two more grades, 7th and 8th, and the district was offering kindergarten.

School at Garfield in the 1930s to mid-

century, by most accounts, was a tightly scripted affair. Some student desks had shifted from wood to metal, but they remained in tidy rows. If students misbehaved, they received the dreaded "swats" with the paddle.

Garfield students typically began their day with the Pledge of Allegiance and a short prayer. A 6th grade Kansas reader from 1926 offers "the great classics," which include works by Lord Byron and Nathaniel Hawthorne, as well as the "Odyssey" and the Bible.

In a 1952 manual, Garden City schools Superintendent J.R. Jones offered parents a few examples of the way elementary school had changed since the days they were in school: "In our day we sat, we memorized and recited. ... In our day,

Above: Sue Rodríguez, left, and her sister Felisa Guadian both attended Garfield when they weren't working in the fields. Both Rodríguez and Guadian recall falling quickly behind. "We all worked, and then we'd come back into school and they'd be on the last page of the book," Guadian says.

Left: "It's not Dick and Jane and Spot anymore," says Garfield Elementary School Principal Willis Pracht. "It's a whole different ballgame."

Pedagogy and penmanship often were overshadowed by events outside Garfield, such as the Depression in the 1930s, with World War II close behind.

the teacher was pretty much a dictator. ... School for us used to be dull and tiresome." But with the changing times the superintendent described, students were expected to learn from the teacher, other students, and from textbooks or whatever other materials were available.

But pedagogy and penmanship often were overshadowed by events outside Garfield, such as the double whammy of dust storms and the Depression in the 1930s, with World War II close behind.

Pauline Joyce, 76, who taught 5th grade at Garfield in the early 1940s, recalls damp sheets hanging in the classroom windows in an attempt to block the "black blizzards" that could transform day into night.

"It was very frightening; it just enveloped us like a heavy snowstorm. You couldn't see at all," Joyce says of the drought-induced dust storms.

The Depression had a direct impact on Garfield. Its third building, constructed in a U-shape around the 1902 building that eventually was razed, went up in 1937 with the help of federal Public Works Administration money. In 1936, the county had urged voters to approve the bond issue needed to secure federal aid for Garfield—and help provide jobs for some of the 400 families on the public-aid rolls.

The Second World War set off a critical labor shortage that spilled over into the teaching force, enabling people like Joyce to teach without full credentials. Garfield played host to air-raid-warden classes, and, eventually, the war would furnish students with a cafeteria, tucked into barracks across the street.

Local histories tell of ladies' clubs in the 1930s preparing lunches for children who came to school without them or who could not go home for the noon meal. But it was only after President Harry S. Truman inaugurated the federal school lunch program in 1946 that large numbers of children here regularly ate a meal at school.

Garfield teachers and alumni from the 1930s, '40s, and '50s remember a tight-knit, solidly middle-class neighborhood institution where most children walked to and from school, most went home for lunch, and nearly everyone knew everyone else.

Most people didn't bother to lock their doors until 1959, when the Clutter family was murdered in their home in neighbor-

ing Holcomb. Many here say the event, which inspired Truman Capote's 1966 book *In Cold Blood*, marked a loss of innocence of sorts in town.

Those teachers and alumni don't remember much racial and ethnic diversity in the classroom, though Garden City's schools have always opened their doors to the town's Hispanics and its small black population; today, about 2 percent of the district's students are black.

Hart gently fingers a black-and-white photo of a dozen children proudly holding up their artwork on Garfield's front steps.

"I know all these little kids. I went all through school with them," says Hart, whose father, a doctor, brought the family to Garden City when she was 6 weeks old. "I think we were a pretty easy bunch to teach. The schools are certainly dealing with more urban-type issues than when we were there." She touches the photo again. "It's just a sign of the times."

The sign outside Garfield School's current building declares the campus a drug-free and gun-free school zone. It's a not-so-gentle reminder that Garden City is not living in the past.

Garfield's third home was reduced to a shell in 1975 in a fire set by three boys (the oldest was age 12), giving rise to the modern building Garfield occupies today.

Brick storefronts and the State Theater on Main Street a few blocks from the school mirror the images frozen in vintage postcards from the 1950s in the local historical museum.

And the streets still turn from asphalt to brick around Garfield in what was once the center of town.

But Susie Carabajal's 1st grade class feels a world apart from the memories of such longtime residents as Katherine Hart.

The student names on Carabajal's door include Jesus, Noemi, Oscar, and Candelaria. One cluster of children reads on squares of carpet on the floor, while another sounds out syllables with a bilingual teacher's aide at the front table.

A U.S. flag hangs above the blackboard, its red and white stripes filled in with the Pledge of Allegiance in Spanish: "Yo le

doy mi lealtad a la bandera de los Estados Unidos de America. ..."

About a third of Carabajal's students never went to school before coming to Garfield. Most arrived not speaking English. Many were born in El Salvador, Guatemala, or Mexico or have parents who were.

Of Garfield's 340 pupils, 81 percent are members of minority groups—overwhelmingly, Hispanic. Nearly 200 students are learning English as their second language.

The school provides breakfast to about half its students and lunch to about three-quarters—most for free or at reduced prices because so many families fall below the federal poverty line.

The rapid-fire turnover at the two beef-packing plants in town, which together employ nearly 5,000 workers and many Garfield parents, contributes to high student turnover.

In the front office, Gail Koehn, 45, herself a Garfield graduate, talks through a translator with a parent gripping a green John Deere baseball cap in his hands.

"So this was the address up to this weekend, right?" she asks gently. "And the new one?"

Garfield's office sees so many ins and outs that Pracht says the joke now is, if you've been here over the weekend, you're a bona fide Garden City resident.

Garfield, like schools across the country, was shaped by the rise of the civil rights movement and the push to make schools better serve all students.

In the 1960s, with new federal money available to serve disadvantaged students, Garfield was part of the district's remedial-reading program. Some here point to the program as an early way of coping with youngsters who were struggling with English as a second language.

Garden City's first Hispanic mayor since the turn of the century took office in 1973. It was not until 1974 that the schools began a formal program to address the needs of students who spoke a language other than English. And it was a rocky road, says Linda Trujillo, who oversees migrant, immigrant, bilingual, at-risk, English-as-a-second-language,

Lydia Smith

and homeless programs for the district.

"We really didn't know what we were doing. It was all brand-new," she says.

In 1980, a Garden City group called the Mexican-American Committee for Education filed a class action against the district, charging that it gave Hispanic students short shrift.

While the two sides eventually were able to hammer out a deal, the district initially fought the group's demands for bilingual programs. By most accounts, the experience was a painful one for the community.

"There was a lot of resistance to the bilingual notion, myself included," says Horace Good, Garden City's superintendent from 1969 to 1984. "I had to yield and give in."

"People in the community said English is our language, and you learn it just as soon as you can, however you can," says John Dickerson, who worked in the district from 1952 to 1978 as a teacher and administrator. "There was a sense of 'Well, why do we have to do this? It seems like everything worked OK before,

so why change it.' "

At the same time, Garden City was becoming more ethnically diverse more quickly than ever. Southeast Asians—a small but conspicuous presence in town since the mid-1970s, when local churches resettled Vietnamese refugees—started to arrive in search of jobs.

And the beef-packing plants began to attract a stream of newcomer Hispanics with roots throughout Central America.

To cope with the enrollment boom, the district built three more elementary schools in the 1980s; Garfield shed its 5th and 6th grades as the city grew.

Garfield has bused children since the 1970s, when many families with children moved out of the old town center to newer neighborhoods. Fields once full of prairie grasses today hold trailers at one end of the economic spectrum and, at the other, subdivisions of sprawling homes.

Since 1980, Spanish-speakers in need of language help have been bused to Garfield so that the district can better concentrate its scarce bilingual and ESL resources on a few elementary campuses. Students who

Susie Carabajal teaches 1st grade at Garfield Elementary. "The parents all want to know how are the kids doing in English. Forget reading or math or any of that. It's English," Carabajal says.

While Garden City shares, in microcosm, some of the problems of a Chicago or a Los Angeles, it is still very much a place that relies on the land.

speak Vietnamese, Laotian, or German dialects—a result of German Mennonite farmers' moving here from Mexico—are mostly in other schools.

"It's been quite an adventure," says Pracht, 46, who grew up in a central Kansas town of 3,000. "And in some ways, I think we're still a bit shellshocked by it all."

While Garden City shares, in microcosm, some of the problems of a Chicago or a Los Angeles, it is still very much a place that relies on the land and what it produces. But farming is now agribusiness; it takes fewer people and more money and training to farm.

It's hard to overstate the impact that meatpackers like IBP Inc. and spinoff industries have had on Garden City. The district two years ago hired a liaison to improve communications between IBP and the schools.

And it was the fast-paced demographic change wrought in large part by the plants' plentiful low-skill jobs that drew a team of researchers here as part of a Ford Foundation project on immigration in the late 1980s.

The city took the researchers' recommendations to heart, setting up a multiracial board to keep the city informed on diversity issues. Garden City celebrates Beef Empire Days, but it also celebrates Tet, the Vietnamese Lunar New Year, and the Mexican holiday Cinco de Mayo.

The Ford researchers' report documented two Garden Cities: one for newcomers and one for more established residents. The schools are one of the places where the groups mix the most. Seeing the community's changes in such stark terms made them somehow more real, Pracht says.

"I think some people didn't even realize what we'd become," he says. "We needed someone else to hold up a mirror. And frankly, some folks didn't like what they saw."

Born in 1929, Frank Schmale, a former city commissioner and mayor, likes to say he never got far in life: For six decades, he lived and worked within three blocks of the house where he was born and raised,

two blocks from Garfield.

His father, who came to the United States from Germany at 14, farmed wheat and sold land to other farmers who wanted to make a home here.

But Schmale says he's not so fond of all the transformations he's seen in town over his 69 years.

"This is a city now, nothing like when I was growing up," he says wistfully. "It just seems these new folks want us to change to their way instead of them changing to our way. ... I read how we're a model city and all that. But it's just too much change."

Teachers say Garfield's mission today reflects Garden City's social and economic realities. Many families have two working parents. Some parents get home from the beef-packing plants at 6 a.m.; others leave for their shifts at 6 a.m.

The bookshelf in Jean Dubbs' office is lined with titles on stress reduction, anger control, self-esteem, and grief management. A poster in the counselor's office gives children the top 10 reasons to say no to drugs. Dubbs, who has worked as a counselor in the district for 14 years, says problems that she used to see at the junior-high level now have trickled down to elementary school.

About a third of Garfield's children are in single-parent households, and about 40 percent of Garfield parents have less than a high school education—parents like Araceli Castro.

Castro, 29, attended school in El Salvador until 6th grade. The family came to Garden City four years ago so her husband could take a job on the cattle slaughter floor, which pays a better wage than the job he had picking vegetables in Northern California.

Castro says that it was hard for her to adapt to life here but that her three children have blossomed.

"I came here, and I thought, oh no, it's so flat. I didn't know if I could get used to it. But I see that the children, they really are comfortable here," Castro says in Spanish, watching her 4th grader at a classroom computer during a family-literacy night and book giveaway at Garfield. "For them, this is home."

First grade teacher Carabajal embodies how Garfield has bent to its new population.

"Working with the families to adapt here—not just the kids—is part of my job. It can't not be," says the 26-year-old teacher. She knows firsthand what many of her students are going through. Carabajal grew up in Ulysses, Kan., as a first-generation U.S.-born daughter of Mexican immigrant parents. Like many of her students, she played the role of family translator at the bank, the post office, and the doctor's office.

"The parents all want to know how are the kids doing in English," Carabajal says. "Forget reading or math or any of that. It's English."

But Garfield delivers much more than a second language. Students in the 4th grade classroom tote plastic bins filled with books and supplies from one cluster of tables to another to work in rotating stations on math, communications (previously, reading, spelling, and writing), science, and social studies. Add to that human sexuality, character education, behavior curricula, and gang prevention.

Pracht drives through town in a red pickup, past the strip mall that houses the Lamkee Noodle House and Panaderia Real bakery. He turns into one of the seemingly endless trailer parks sprawled around the edges of town. He points to the blue letters MCB—for "master criminal boys"—spray-painted onto a garbage dumpster.

Later, he slows to point out what's left of the sugar beet factory. Its red brick facade bears witness to the factory's 1906 founding and a different age for Garden City and Garfield. Today, a plumbing wholesaler occupies much of the building.

"Yes, we have to teach math and reading. Being instructional leaders—that's all great and good," he says, as he waits for a cargo train to pass. "But sometimes that's so far down the totem pole for us it's not even funny." ■

Access to Education: The Changing Meaning Of a Continuing Challenge

A perspective by Ellen Condliffe Lagemann

This is a discouraging moment to be writing about access to education in the United States. In a rush to raise standards, colleges and high schools seem to be pushing students out their doors rather than bringing them in. For the first time since such statistics have been collected, the United States has fallen behind most other industrialized countries in its high school graduation rates. How could we have allowed that to happen?

The meaning of access to education has, of course, changed over time. During the early history of this country, really until the late 19th century, access to education meant little more than acquiring the right to attend a public school. For white Americans, increasing access to education had primarily to do with hiring enough teachers and building enough schools so children could go to school relatively easily. White women were generally barred from formal education after the early years, but many of them surmounted the constraints of gender through informal means. For free African-Americans in the North, schooling was available usually in segregated schools. For enslaved black Americans, however, there simply was no access to formal schooling until after the Civil War. Then, with an energy that bespoke a people's long-suppressed hunger for education, local groups within African-American communities in the South, supplemented by aid provided by Northern Protestant missionary groups, began to establish the facilities that would begin to offer access to education to all students of color.

The meaning of access to education became more complicated at the end of the 19th century. Then, leaders in education like President Charles W. Eliot of Harvard University began to talk and write about what we today call the selective function of education.

Recognizing that there were significant inequalities in American society, Eliot came to believe that the country's long-standing commitment to equality could be sustained only if equal chances for advancement were offered to everyone through the public schools. This belief was rooted in his sure sense that different people had different abilities, and that schools could effectively identify talent and match people to careers based on those. In an 1897 essay in *Outlook* magazine, Eliot claimed that "the vague desire for equality in a democracy has worked great mischief in democratic schools. There is no such thing as equality of gifts, or powers, or faculties, among either children or adults."

From that belief, it was but a short step to suggesting that sorting should be an important part of what "democratic schools" do. If access to education had once pertained merely to the availability of schooling, from now on it would also pertain to the content of schooling, to whichever track your given "powers" opened to you.

Eliot did not merely advocate that schools assume a selection function they had not previously fulfilled; he also worked diligently and effectively to institutionalize that view. Losing the National Education Association as an effective medium thanks to challenges mounted by women teachers, Eliot and other college presidents instead sought to advance their cause through newly created philanthropic foundations like the Rockefellers' General Education Board and the Carnegie Foundation for the Advancement of Teaching.

With Eliot as its first board chairman and Henry S. Pritchett as its president, the Carnegie Foundation became a powerful lobbyist for a pyramid-like system of educational institutions that linked schools to colleges and colleges to professional schools while also differentiating among elite and less elite institutions, the elite being those with the most and best resources. In addition, through its frequent and widely disseminated reports—the best-known having been the Flexner Report on medical education—the Carnegie Foundation helped popularize an ideology that could rationalize the kind of educational system it was helping to build. Based in ideas having to do with merit, objectivity, and professionalism, this ideology made belief in the fairness and appropriateness of sorting according to tests of academic ability and achievement a commonplace of 20th-century American life.

Obviously, this was not an entirely new belief at the turn of the century. Among others, Thomas Jefferson had enunciated it a century earlier. What was new was that the meritocratic ideal was becoming institutionalized in practice. Earlier schools, colleges, and professional schools had not been articulated in a system, let alone in a hierarchical system that screened students out at every level.

By the beginning of the 20th century, then, access to education was no longer a significant issue in terms of the general availability of schooling, though many people continued to choose to go to school for only a relatively few years. Thanks to the linkage between education and selection that had developed, the questions of import having to do with access to education were increasingly ones concerning the amount and kind of education one could gain entry to. Could one win a seat in the academic as opposed to the vocational or general track in high school? If so, could one also gain access to college? To the right college? And the best professional school? Those questions were central to many of the important educational developments of the 20th century: to the establishment of the College Board and then the Educational Testing Service; to James B. Conant's efforts in behalf of the comprehensive high school; to passage of the GI Bill and later the various education acts of Lyndon B. Johnson's administration; and to the 1954 decision in *Brown* v. *Board of Education* and all that would flow from it.

Because education and selection were now linked, equality of educational opportunity became an important matter for reformers, civil rights leaders, and policymakers at every level of government. If life chances were to be distributed through school accomplishment, fairness required that all children have equal access at the start

of the race. For a long time, it was assumed that this merely required equal inputs into education in the form of numbers and qualifications of teachers, numbers of textbooks, laboratories, and libraries, and the like. Then, in 1966, James S. Coleman's massive survey of equality of opportunity in the nation's schools, which had been mandated by the Civil Rights Act of 1964, demonstrated that equal "inputs" did not necessarily result in equal "outputs." The testable achievement of black and white children was not equal even when their schools, which tended still to be segregated throughout most of the country, were more or less equal in resources. Undermining cherished beliefs about the power of schooling to advance equality as well as about the malleability of schooling to relatively simple reforms, the Coleman Report and the subsequent studies it stimulated changed the meaning of access to education yet again.

After the Coleman Report, access to education came increasingly to be tied to results. Equal access now required not only that one have a chance to go to school and to enter a track for which one was suited by ability, but also that one leave school having gained as much as one's classmates regardless of race, class, sex, or physical handicap. In pursuit of this new and enlarged conception of access to education, scholars of education began to unravel the little-understood "black box" of education—what it is that actually goes on inside schools and classrooms that helps or hinders teaching and learning. The growth in knowledge during the more than 30 years since Coleman's survey appeared has been impressive. From studies of effective schools and teacher behavior to current efforts to foster teachers' communities and design experiments based on principles derived from cognitive science, a great deal has been learned about what is required to grant all students access to education in the post-Coleman sense of the term.

Especially impressive when one remembers that there have been drastic declines in support for research from both public and private sources, the research record of the past 30 years promises possibilities for equalizing education that are unprecedented. So does the commitment to high standards and opportunities to learn for all students that governors, business people, and education leaders have articulated in

recent years. Even if that commitment is still more rhetorical than real in terms of results, it is tremendously important to have linked equity and excellence by acknowledging that all children can achieve at high levels.

And yet, despite these auguries of progress, we are graduating fewer young people from high school than Finland, Norway, Poland, South Korea, the Czech Republic, France, Germany, Canada, and Ireland. Why is that?

I would venture a bet that the problem is a result of at least two factors. The first has to do with the growing and changing inequality outside of schools, which some social scientists call the new inequality. This is a situation in which increasing numbers of people are unable to work their way out of poverty because the employment prospects of workers with limited education have deteriorated so severely. While the past two years have shown some improvement, the long-term trends indicate declining wages and rising levels of unemployment for workers with no more than a high school education.

These problems are particularly striking among African-Americans in urban areas. There is evidence that they are caused by discrimination among employers as well as by poor educational preparation in urban schools and geographic distance between inner-city workers and jobs springing up in the suburbs. The new inequality means that poverty and hardship are the most likely future prospects facing many young people who do poorly in school.

Kids are smart; many find going to school an alienating and demeaning experience. Why persist if the people around you are poor, struggling, and going nowhere? Why believe the system will work better for you? Given the circumstances in which too many Americans live, it may well be that access to education will now require interventions in the labor markets that can help young people sustain their hopes that success in school will actually have a payoff, first, in admission to college, and then, in a good, secure job that offers a chance for advancement.

The second factor I believe is relevant to sustaining progress toward equal access to education has to do with our long-standing ambivalence about education. Americans love to talk about the importance of education. Most American presidents would like to be known as an "education president." However, in the face of such sentiments, we continue to pay our teachers miserly salaries that, in some instances, are less than those paid to sanitation workers, and we blame teachers for the crisis in our schools rather than praising them for serving on the front line. To become a teacher in the circumstances many teachers face is heroic; to remain a teacher should make one eligible for sainthood.

Our ambivalence is also evident in our unwillingness to acknowledge that education no less than agriculture, highway construction, medicine, and space discovery requires significant levels of research and development. As the President's Panel on Technology noted last spring, we are failing our schools when we spend less than 0.1 percent of every education dollar on research.

American ambivalence toward education has made it woefully difficult to actualize access in what I have called the post-Coleman sense of the term. It has undermined our capacity really to deliver on the belief that *all* children should be given an education sufficiently powerful to allow them to achieve parity with their peers regardless of their group or ascriptive characteristics. Whatever side one takes in the ongoing debates about whether and how money matters in education, common sense should tell you that education is starved for the resources it needs to offer all children: adequate school buildings and equipment; well-trained, -paid, and-respected teachers; support staffs with loads that make it possible for them really to help students and their parents with the myriad school and nonschool problems that confront them; administrators who have the knowledge, skill, and authority necessary to be powerful instructional and community leaders … the list could go on endlessly.

The Coleman Report told us there was not a simple relationship between inputs and outputs in education. It did not say that resources are irrelevant. Deployed according to a constantly revised, research-based strategy for improvement that is understood and supported by parents, school staff members, and community leaders, resources can help teachers foster learning in ways that produce results. Superintendent Anthony Alvarado showed that in District 2 in New York City. Despite that, we do not give schools the resources they need to grant equal access to *all* children. Our ambivalence about education leads us, on the one hand, to expect too much of

schools, and, on the other, to support them inadequately. Unless we can face and overcome that ambivalence and all that has fed it, including complicated attitudes about race and social class, access to education in the United States will remain unequal and will become more and more constrained relative to that available to young people elsewhere in the industrialized world.

Some would say that the problem today is not finding ways to realize a conception of access to education that has expanded and become more generous and difficult to achieve over the years. I disagree. To accept such a retreat would be myopic because we live in a world where returns to knowledge and skill in global markets require that more and more Americans, indeed *all* Americans, become well enough educated to go on being educated for the rest of their lives. Instead of retreat, therefore, we need to renew the determination to

equalize access to education that sprang in earlier times from recognizing that in a democratic society such as ours, the deficit of one is a deficit for all.

Equal access to education has been a central aspiration of this country at its greatest moments in history. Moving forward toward ever-fuller conceptions of what access means remains essential to our well-being as a society. ■

Ellen Condliffe Lagemann is the president of the National Academy of Education and a professor of history and education at New York University in New York City. Her most recent book is John Dewey's Defeat: The Contested Role of Scholarship in Education.

Our ambivalence about education leads us, on the one hand, to expect too much of schools, and, on the other, to support them inadequately.

rites of passage

Americans' perceptions of children and youths have long been in flux. Early in the century, Victorian ideals of childhood coexisted with the hard realities of child labor; meanwhile, the concept of "adolescence" as a distinct stage of life was just beginning to emerge.

By the 1920s, the modern "comprehensive" high school was forming, and it would define the teenage years as no institution before had done.

Indeed, throughout the 20th century, the place of young people in American society and its schools continued to evolve. Today, teenagers and their younger siblings exert enormous influence on the nation's economy and popular culture.

Students arrive at the Anacostia (Md.) High School prom in 1953.

Photo by Corbis-Bettmann

Corbis-Bettmann

A Time and Place for Teenagers

High school has been an evolving institution, slowly bending
to the ever-changing world of adolescence.

By
Bess
Keller

High schools and adolescence grew up together. Before the modern high school took shape in the 1920s, hardly anyone thought about "adolescents" as a defined group.

Young people, for the most part, were simply "children" until at some point in their teenage years they left school, married or got a job, and joined the world of adults.

In *Middletown*, Robert S. and Helen Merrell Lynd's 1929 study of Muncie, Ind., the terms even for high school students are "children" or "boys and girls"—not "adolescents" or "teenagers." The notion of a distinct age group, the members of which were more like one another than they were like children or adults, was only just taking hold.

Not that the older generation hasn't always heaped hopes and fears on the rising one, expecting it both to carry on what adults value and avoid their mistakes. Teenagers reflect what we are and suggest what we will become—with all the energy of youth. No wonder that adults have often wrung their hands over teenagers, sounding alarms that to later generations seem quaint.

"The growing custom of steady dating among teenagers is a matter of concern to educators, parents, and teenagers," fretted the staff of the *Ladies Home Journal* in 1949. "Psychologists say it can have a permanent emotional effect on teenagers that makes later marriage anticlimactic."

The emergence of the term "adolescence" gave adults a repository for their strong feelings about the teenage years. By the 1920s, the changes in young people wrought in adolescence by biological and social forces might have resembled those of an earlier time, but there was a new spotlight on them.

Likewise, by that decade, an institution was forming that would define the teenage years like no other: the new "comprehensive" high school concerned with the problems and talents of the vast majority of adolescents, instead of a privileged few.

By the early part of the 20th century, school people and policymakers had begun to distinguish between education that would prepare students for college and schooling that would prepare them for the workplace and life. Earlier, secondary education in most public and private schools had been organized around academic disciplines. Tough mental training was thought to be good preparation for any respectable future, from running a dry goods store to attending Yale.

But as more students from working-class families found their way to high school, the schools added classes in "manual training" and eventually linked whole sequences of courses to jobs. In the same building, then, students could receive either a general education or a specific one, something like an apprenticeship.

Most high schools today fill much the same mold. These large schools, populated by a diverse group of teenagers, seem quintessentially American. And now as then, they are places where students can variously broaden their horizons, slip through the cracks, fraternize with "the wrong types," or tune out their surroundings in a haze of alienation.

TRADITION VS. CHANGE

High school has become a venerable institution. Like any institution, especially a long-standing one, it is liable to distraction from its mission.

Some of the serious questions being asked about high schools at the end of the century reflect this concern:

Are many high schools so large because that size offered the best chance for a good education? Or because such schools provided more and better-paid jobs for specialists and administrators, who in turn favored big schools? Or because taxpayers require less costly operation achievable through economies of scale?

Are high schools too often boring for the "average" student because the best teachers teach the high achievers? Or because savvy, affluent parents demand a top program for their children?

Is the high school day broken into 50-minute blocks because teenagers learn better that way or simply because that's how it has always been done?

"The rituals of high schools, whatever their shortcomings, appeal to many people who suspect that substantial reform would undo the essence of teenhood," suggests "Breaking Ranks," a 1996 report on high schools from the National Association of Secondary School Principals.

Tradition for tradition's sake and vested interests have surely shaped American high schools. But democratic impulses and genuine understanding of youth have played their roles, too.

Like any modern marriage, the match between high schools and adolescents needs more than occasional work. Largely to the degree that the schools have grasped important things about teenagers and their times, they have served them.

When high schools have viewed adolescents as an alien life-form, and when they have failed to respond to changes in the world teenagers inhabit, they have done less well.

SHIFTING DEMANDS

Once, in this country, it was relatively easy to tell when childhood ended. A boy abandoned his knickers for long pants and took up adult work, or left to find his fortune; a girl married or left home or both.

But as the 19th century closed, more children enjoyed for a longer time the protected status of childhood, in part because the industrialization and commercialization of work favored formal education, and in part because more families could afford to extend their material support.

Educators and policymakers were reconsidering the nature of secondary schooling. They took their cue from everyday life, arguing that schools should pre-

pare students for the workplace.

Meanwhile, teenagers got, if not their own institution, their own place. By 1924, the high school in Muncie, for example, had become "the hub of social life" for the town's young people, according to the Lynds, who spent more than a year studying the community.

To gauge the relative importance of the classroom and extracurricular activities at the school, the Lynds examined yearbooks from 1924 and 1894. Both books allocated the most space to class data, but athletics came second in 1924, while faculty and courses had occupied that position in 1894. In addition to team sports for boys, a swarm of school clubs vied for attention, the most prestigious of which were unofficial versions of college and adult fraternities and sororities.

Not surprisingly, many teenagers cited their social life as the thing they liked best about school, and the Lynds observed many of the common social features and rituals of teenage life associated with high schools today: classrooms and hallways humming with chatter and primping, annual banquets, "school spirit," athletic heroes, and school publications.

CHANGING FASHIONS

Not long ago, I quizzed my mother about two portrait photographs taken around the time she graduated from high school in 1935. "You dressed up for the pictures?" I asked.

When Harry S. Truman, last row, fourth from left, graduated from Missouri's Independence High School in 1901, teenagers weren't even considered a distinct group. The modern conception of "adolescence" wasn't established until later.

Corbis-Bettmann

The Kobal Collection

When James Dean, right, and Sal Mineo appeared in the 1955 hit movie "Rebel Without a Cause," their characters appealed to American teenagers, who were beginning to feel alienated from their parents' world.

"Oh, no," she replied. "That's what you wore to school every day—silk stockings, high-heeled shoes, silk dresses. You wanted to look grown-up."

She added that "it was only later, in college, that I wore saddle shoes, skirts, and sweaters." By then, fashions had changed; the "bobby-soxers" of the 1940s—the first "teenagers"—were about to be born.

In fact, the 1930s were probably the last decade when the dress of high school students might be mistaken for that of their teachers. From that decade onward, with most teenagers now brought together as a group in high school, students started looking to each other rather than their elders for style—and eventually for much, much more.

In a sense, the trend had begun earlier, when the years around puberty first came to be considered as distinct from both the adult world and childhood. Following the publication in 1904 of *Adolescence*, an encyclopedic treatment of the psychology of teenagers by educator and psychologist G. Stanley Hall, that period began to be widely known as "adolescence."

The notion had roots in the 19th century, as various experts pondered the impact of urbanization and industrialization on children around the age of puberty. Those years, they declared, were a dangerous time of life that needed careful watching. They doubted that children could navigate the shoals of adolescence by merely observing adult models. And they were especially leery of "precosity"—adult experience too soon. So adolescence was a time to protect teenagers from a hard world and their own confusion.

But how many years does adolescence comprise?

That question was not settled in the popular mind until the 1920s, when educators began to equate adolescence with secondary school attendance. From that time hence, "adolescence" was most often taken to extend to 18 or 19 years old.

In *Elmtown's Youth*, A.B. Hollingshead built upon the foundations laid by *Middletown* and other studies, looking notably at the issue of social class among adolescents in a Corn Belt community of 6,000. His study, conducted in 1941 and 1942, foreshadowed some of the problems of adolescence that emerged in the postwar period and that have drawn so much attention since then: smoking, drinking, and sexual activity. In 1941, many of Elmtown's male adolescents indulged in all three, but even a common activity like drinking was hidden from adults—and many adults winked to avoid seeing it.

But Hollingshead's book primarily explored the links between social class and the lives of the town's teenagers. Perhaps most important, it exposed class—determined by the parents' position in the town's social structure—as the best predictor of who would go to high school and who would graduate. The book gave a sad picture of dropouts before the word was in use.

Hollingshead told, for example, an anecdote about two teenagers who ran afoul of a new rule at their high school: Any tardy student—no excuses accepted—was to be sent to detention.

When Kathy, the daughter of a prominent middle-class family, skipped detention to get her hair fixed for a dance at the country club the next evening, the principal mildly reproved her. The day Kathy was scheduled for detention, her mother had talked "casually" with the school superintendent's wife.

Things went differently, however, for "Boney," the son of a laborer at the local fertilizer plant, after he committed the same offense. The principal shoved him into the building, grabbed him by the collar, and as Boney fought, hit him with the heel of his hand. The superintendent slapped him, and eventually the two administrators shoved Boney out the door. "You're never coming back until you bring your father," yelled the principal. Back in his office, the superintendent said, "That boy is a troublemaker. ... Look at the gang he's running with."

LIMITED OPPORTUNITIES

Overwhelmingly, Hollingshead discovered, students from the top rungs of the

The Emergence of Teen Fashions

Corbis-Bettmann

[1] **1900s.** In the early part of the century, teenagers typically dressed for school in clothing that mimicked styles worn by adults.

[2] **1920s.** Even as the concept of adolescence began to emerge, students continued to go to school in adult fashions. For these girls in 1925, that meant dresses and high heels.

[3] **1940s.** Though the dressed-down look was more associated with the next generation, these girls wore dungarees to an outdoor dance in New York City's Central Park in 1946.

[4] **1980s.** Shock value goes a long way in setting teenage trends, and by the mid-1980s the look known as punk was showing up on street corners and in classrooms.

Corbis-Bettmann

Corbis Hulton-Deutsch Collection

Corbis-Bettmann

social ladder were in school. But only six out of 10 working-class teenagers of high school age and a dismal one out of nine poor teenagers were in school.

As *Elmtown* illustrated, poor adolescents and their parents regarded a high school education as not worth the trouble and expense, and educators and solid citizens alike compounded that view by making school life different for students according to their backgrounds.

Compared with their middle-class counterparts, poor and working-class students received harsher discipline, lower grades, and less help from teachers. They were shut out of extracurricular activities by social networks that didn't include them, as well as a lack of money, transportation, and time.

To school authorities in Elmtown, the dropouts seemed invisible. They insisted that the compulsory-attendance law was enforced and that the "few kids" who weren't in school were either country people—whose parents didn't believe in education beyond 8th grade—or past their 16th birthdays.

Neither was true. In fact, almost three-quarters of the young people who had withdrawn from school did so before they were 16.

All this coexisted with the view, prevalent not only in Elmtown but also across the nation, that a high school diploma reflected a young person's capacity to hold a white-collar job. The diploma had become a mark of middle-class respectability, and those without it often paid a price in opportunity.

Concern that poverty and discrimination can narrow chances for success in school has not gone away. Indeed, high schools have long been criticized as providing an inferior education to minority students, sometimes through the mechanism of tracking. Today, Hispanic students do not graduate from high school at nearly the rate of black or white students, and black students have only recently caught up with whites.

By the 1950s, a solid majority of teenagers were earning high school diplomas. And not only the proportion, but also the number of students kept rising as baby boomers flooded schools during the '60s and '70s. Before the pace slackened in the 1980s, the nation's public schools had seen eight decades of growth.

GENERATION GAP

Up on the screen in a darkened movie house, the camera pans over acres of new, low-slung houses in the California sunshine. "Nice homes, very respectable," intones actor Gig Young.

Then comes a shot of "Dawson High School"—where full-skirted girls and tie-wearing boys carrying books under their arms flood the steps after the final bell. "Nice kids, well-clothed," Young tells the audience.

"But beneath the surface—trouble, plenty of it."

This short preview was made to promote "Rebel Without a Cause," the 1955 hit movie that spoke to a generation of young Americans who were beginning to feel alienated somehow from the world of their parents. The film presaged the upheavals to come in the youth culture of the 1960s and quickly made its charismatic star—James Dean, dead later that year at age 24—an icon of teenage confusion and angst.

The movie, according to its makers, asks the question "What makes kids from nice homes" act like "slum kids"?—racing cars, getting drunk, arming themselves with knives, running away.

The answer seemed to be: their neglectful, confused, and ineffectual parents. Parents drove teenagers to turn to each other for emotional sustenance, forming—as the preview says when the trio of characters played by Dean, Natalie Wood, and Sal Mineo appears— "makeshift families."

In the early part of the century, middle-class adolescents, at least, had generally turned a conforming and acquiescent face to the older generation. Teenagers' pastimes, like their taste in music and clothes, often resembled those of their parents: clubs, dances, and movies.

In the '40s, when advertisers and merchandisers popularized the word "teenager," adolescents thrilled to the same swing music that got adult feet tapping. The older generation showed some exasperation at bobby-soxer fashions and fads fueled by the spending money of postwar prosperity, but adults could reassure themselves that at bottom adolescents shared their values. When teenagers transgressed, they kept it under wraps.

'A CULTURAL MINORITY'

But by midcentury, things were beginning to change. Holden Caulfield, in J.D. Salinger's 1951 novel, *The Catcher in the Rye*, hinted at the turmoil to come when he declared war on everything "phony."

By 1955, when "Rebel Without a Cause" exploded onto the scene, teenagers had started to become incomprehensible to adult onlookers. Dean's angry performance touched a nerve: Even "nice kids" from "nice homes" could pose a threat.

As if to confirm their parents' suspicions, teenagers' taste in clothes began to reflect working-class style—leather jackets and blue jeans. And their musical preferences drew from even lower down the social scale: African-American rhythm and blues. Soon there was raucous rock 'n' roll. And crime committed by teenagers was on the rise: The rate has tripled since World War II.

Most adults still thought adolescents should be protected, but there was more of a feeling that teenagers also were to be feared.

Economic forces soon tapped into the emerging teenage culture, speeding the process that was pulling adolescents away from adults.

What started out as a group demarcated primarily by age and secondarily by class had developed its own styles, rituals, and entertainment. By the early '60s, sociologist Herbert J. Gans, in a study of Levittown, N.J., could write: "Teenagers are a cultural minority like any other." But, he scolded their parents, "whereas no Levittowners expect Italians to behave like Jews, most still expect teenagers to behave like children."

ERA OF TURMOIL

In October 1969, a high school in Syracuse, N.Y., with a country club image was the scene of a riot. When the principal tried to stop it, he was clubbed and went to the hospital with a fractured skull. The rioters were mostly working-class or poor black students, who had recently been moved to the school under a desegregation plan, and a group of their friends.

The origins of the melee were traced to an incident in which members of an all-white fraternity at the high school had told several black students to "get out of our school."

Soon after the riot, 600 students and their parents—black and white—met to discuss the situation. Black students and teachers generally said the school was pervaded by racism. Their white counterparts talked of fear and territoriality. The next year, the school closed 10 times because of violent clashes.

Those events, described by Gerald Grant in his 1988 social history of the school, *The World We Created at Hamilton High*, were far from unique. High schools all over the country, like colleges, were turbulent in the late '60s and early '70s.

Corbis/Charles Harris, Pittsburgh Courier

NEW PROBLEMS, NEW MISSION

By the '70s, high schools had come to seem increasingly out of step with the informality, openness, and tolerance that many students celebrated (and flaunted) in their lives away from school.

As schools struggled to re-establish order, they also were expected to shoulder much of the burden of creating a society with opportunity for all. As their mission evolved, high schools added social services to handle the needs of a student body that had grown more mixed in terms of race, language, and disabilities.

"In many ways, what happened in the late '60s and early '70s was a long-overdue questioning of the schools," education historian Robert L. Hampel says. Many high schools emerged from the '70s with an atmosphere that Hampel, a professor at the University of Delaware, calls "mellow."

They accorded students more rights, thanks in part to court rulings. And they sought students' cooperation, not their unswerving obedience. Groups of students that had been neglected began to receive more attention.

Meanwhile, the problems with which schools had to deal mounted. During the '70s, the age at which young people first had sex dropped significantly. The increasing availability of contraception and legal abortion made sex less risky for girls, while the media provided ubiquitous reminders of sexual pleasure. Yet despite the availability of birth control, the birthrate for unmarried teenagers climbed (and didn't stop climbing until the 1990s).

Drug use among high school seniors, as measured by the proportion of those who reported they had used illegal drugs in the past month, rose from 31 percent in 1975 to 37 percent in 1980.

Adults, meanwhile, divorced in record numbers in the '70s and '80s, often creating less stable environments for their offspring. During those same decades, the rate of adult crime went up, and adult confidence in the institutions of society went down. If teenagers seemed to be having a rough passage, so were many of their parents.

NEED FOR REALIGNMENT

With the nation wearying of social conflict, peace had returned to most high schools by the end of the '70s. But the

Suits and dresses were the fashion at this hop in Pittsburgh in 1962. But teenagers' tastes in clothes were beginning to change. Before long, a casual bluejeans look would prevail at most social occasions.

Mary Beth Tinker and her brother, John, were suspended from North High School in Des Moines, Iowa, in 1965 after they wore black armbands to class to protest the Vietnam War. The students sued, claiming that their First Amendment rights had been violated. In 1969, the U.S. Supreme Court agreed, ruling that schools do not have the right to silence student expression simply because they disagree with the students' viewpoint.

"In many ways, what happened in the late '60s and early '70s was a long-overdue questioning of the schools."

Robert L. Hampel
Education Historian,
University of Delaware

peace, the more relaxed atmosphere, and the fairer shake for more students came at a price.

The tolerant high school also tended to be value-neutral, and as high school offered more things to more people, achievement suffered.

In the 1980s, a flurry of national reports decrying the state of schools drew attention to the problems.

In many schools, students who in another generation might have dropped out found that the path of least resistance was simply to tune out. Many did only the minimum needed to get a diploma—or to win admission to college.

But for those who wanted it, there was usually good teaching far removed from old-fashioned drill and textbook memorization. There were sports and activities that would teach them as much as many classes. And there were teachers and students alike who valued high-quality work.

But if they didn't want it, the institution didn't care, as portrayed in the 1985 book *The Shopping Mall High School: Winners and Losers in the Educational Marketplace,* by Arthur G. Powell, Eleanor Farrar, and David K. Cohen. That seminal book uses the metaphor of the shopping mall to describe schools full of choices about what courses to take, what degree of rigor to seek, what path to follow, but little guidance about what choices are the most worthwhile.

Hampel—whose *The Last Little Citadel: American High Schools Since 1940* emerged from the same highly regarded study as the Powell-Farrar-Cohen book—is speaking almost as much of high schools today as those of 20 years ago when he says: "Engagement is often optional. It's there if you want it, but you don't have to, and the burden is on you to pick and choose."

'ON THEIR OWN'

It has always been hard for adolescents to balance the autonomy they crave with the experience they lack. And now as in earlier times, teenagers from poor or troubled families suffer more than the rest.

Still, many experts agree that there has been no harder time in the past 100 years—with the possible exceptions of the Great Depression and World War II—to be a teenager.

Patricia Hersch, a journalist who spent three years befriending eight teenagers in suburban Reston, Va., to write her 1998 book *A Tribe Apart,* pleads with adults to get past their stereotypes and their fears of young people and to see the adolescent's

world as it is.

Ten years ago, Hersch contends, that world was "a circumscribed portion of childhood—a place to stop in-between, a place to stay before becoming an adult." Issues like drugs, divorce, and vandalism a decade ago were "surrounded by a sense of the unusual." Not so today, according to Hersch. The dividing line between "good kids" and "bad kids" is blurred. "Good kids" engage in many of the same behaviors as "bad kids"—sexual intercourse even before the high school years, lying to parents, cheating on tests, illegal drinking—but they do so less frequently.

Other observers, Hampel among them, question whether the statistics on teenagers today justify the message that the news is bad and probably getting worse. He says the sharp rise in risky behaviors may have come more than 25 years ago, after the sexual, political, and social upheaval of the 1960s and early 1970s, but before most of the statistics were routinely collected. He points to "facts that should be more frightening" than the trend lines for teenage drinking, suicide, dropping out, and out-of-wedlock births—all of which have dropped or leveled out.

He worries instead about the prevalence of part-time jobs, peer pressure to do no better than moderately well in school, and hours spent watching television.

The historian Grace Palladino, the author of *Teenagers,* a 1996 history of 20th-century adolescents in the United States, also counsels against a crisis mentality. She contends that teenagers without a talent for schoolwork and a stable family risk a bleak future, but she notes that it has always been so. Such young people are, Palladino writes, "more or less on their own—as they have been ever since the rise of high schools a century ago."

SEEKING SOLUTIONS

Part of what could be better, many observers agree, is the fit between high school and today's adolescents. Grant has argued, much as Hersch did in her book, that a big part of what is missing in the lives of teenagers is sustained, meaningful contact with adults.

Without the chance to work alongside adults—in jobs or helping with child-rearing—teenagers often find them distant, and their own long period of dependency galling. Adults have compounded the problem, Hersch and others say, by giving in to the convenient and self-protective beliefs that adolescents no longer need or want adult connections and that

Corbis-Bettmann

they are not interested in contributing to their families or communities.

Grant, in a 1983 article in the journal *Educational Leadership*, suggested mandating a semester or a year of voluntary service for all high school students. In doing real-world work, he wrote, they "would have an opportunity to learn more by giving more, to develop other sides and aspects of themselves in a noncompetitive environment, to gain dignity and a heightened sense of self-worth by being useful to others, and to build a wider network of mentoring relationships with adults." The state of Maryland and some school districts have taken a step in that direction by including service requirements as part of the curriculum. Another 10 states encourage service by allowing districts to award credit.

A more radical proposal has come recently from Leon Botstein, the president of Bard College, who contends that the last two years of high school should be abolished. By that time in an adolescent's life, he argues, high school "becomes like a jail, holding them back, age-segregating them."

In his 1997 book *Jefferson's Children: Education and the Promise of American Culture*, Botstein notes that today's teenagers reach sexual maturity two or three years earlier than their counterparts at the beginning of the 20th cen-

tury. For educators not to recognize that fact, or the sophistication that modern communications and transportation have brought adolescents, is to shortchange teenagers, he says. "High school retards, misses a major opportunity to motivate young people," Botstein says. The greater freedom available to today's teenagers, while holding risk, also can inspire discipline and ambition.

Coupled with the reduction in the years of schooling (and the reconfiguration of elementary school, with high school including grades 7-10) would be a set of standards that must be met for a high school diploma.

Under Botstein's scenario, graduating teenagers would chose from among a community college, a four-year college, the job market, national service, and an array of vocational programs. Inner-city high schools would be converted into 24-hour educational centers and emergency shelters offering safe havens from drugs, violence, and street life.

Botstein does not underestimate the ambitious scope of the change he is suggesting, and many experts such as Hampel have serious doubts about the likelihood of major changes in an institution that has changed remarkably little in nearly 100 years.

"Orderly schools with tight discipline matter more to many people than orderly

thinking. And therefore change, which is neither tidy nor orderly, will probably continue to be slow and uneven," Hampel wrote in 1986.

Today, though, the historian says he would be at least a little less pessimistic about the prospects for meaningful change. He says he has been heartened by the sustained attention to education reform since the mid-1980s and by some of the improvements that have begun to take hold in high schools.

The 1996 NASSP report, "Breaking Ranks," contained surprisingly bold recommendations from a committee formed mainly of high school administrators. It called for an end to impersonal schools, the archaic system of academic departments, and a day divided rigidly into short segments. Instead, the educators envisioned schools of no more than 600 students, where each would have a "personal adult advocate" and where learning would take many more forms and use more computer technology than it typically does now.

But despite some optimism, Hampel worries that internal squabbling among educators and open battles in public will deflect attention from what should be the central concern of every high school.

All too often, adult agendas and moldy tradition prevail over the needs of students, he says. "The experience of being a teenager gets overlooked." ■

Changing Childhood

Corbis-Bettmann

These boys, workers in West Virginia mines in the early 1900s, were photographed by Lewis Hine, a sociologist who took up photography and documented the conditions under which children worked. Photographs such as those taken by Hine were used to help end child labor.

The ambivalence that people feel toward children can be heard in Linda Bird-Davies' voice when she talks about her career.

She began a family-child-care program in the mid-1970s so she could be at home with her daughter. Now, more than 20 years later, Bird-Davies is the director of a Los Angeles child-care center—part of an industry that has made it possible for parents to be separated from their children for long hours while they work.

By Linda Jacobson

It's a setting where young children—currently viewed as resilient and independent—have been forced to adapt to the fast-paced schedules of families in the '90s. But it's one in which Bird-Davies says she sometimes feels sorrow when she knows a child just wants to be with his or her mother.

The truth is, Americans' feelings about children and their place in society have always been mixed. In the introduction to his 1982 book *The Rise and Fall of Childhood*, C. John Sommerville, an associate professor of history at the University of Florida, writes: "We do not seem to know exactly how we feel about children."

At the close of the 20th century, a confluence of changes—social, economic, technological—has led many authors and child-development experts to warn that the very concept of childhood is in danger. Youngsters are scooted off to daily programs, bombarded by electronic media, and saddled with increasing responsibilities.

"Children are much more mature, and their parents treat them that way," Bird-Davies says.

In the preface to the 1988 revised version of *The Hurried Child*, David Elkind, a professor of child development at Tufts University, writes: "Our new conception of children and youth is epitomized in the metaphor of the Superkid. Like Superman, Superkid has spectacular powers and precocious competence even as

an infant. This allows us to think that we can hurry the little powerhouse with impunity."

As the Victorian era was coming to a close in the early 1900s, children were depicted through artwork and advertising as innocent, almost angelic creatures to be pampered and protected from corrupt influences.

For the more advantaged classes, that idealistic image often held true, says Robin Love, a child-development professor at San Jose State University who teaches a course on the changing notions of childhood in the 20th century.

But the early 1900s were also an era of child labor. Such labor played a major part in the Industrial Revolution, and it was widely assumed that children over the age of 9 should be working and contributing to the family income. Before 1920, children from poor and immigrant families, some as young as 3, worked in mills and factories as long as 10 hours a day.

Ultimately, the increasingly widespread use of a modern medium of communication—photography—helped alert the public to the abuses of child labor and strengthened the hand of reformers who sought to curtail such practices.

"The faces staring out from magazines and newspapers were shocking contradictions to what had become the mainstream American definition of childhood. Neither healthy, nor innocent, nor happy, they must have seemed not to be children at all," writes Mary Lynn Stevens Heininger in *A Century of Childhood: 1820-1920.*

The end of child labor and the spread of compulsory-education laws were part of a movement to preserve childhood as a special time in life. Organizations devoted to children's issues were founded, among them the Child Welfare League of America in 1921 and the National Association for the Education of Young Children in 1926.

As a result of such efforts, a separate justice system for juveniles, child-protection laws, and even playgrounds emerged.

Ironically, at the end of the century, states and communities are again rethinking the way they handle juvenile offenders: Now, the prevailing sentiment is that minors who have committed violent crimes should be subject to the same laws and receive the same punishments as adults.

A SCIENTIFIC APPROACH

The early 20th century also saw the beginning of the child-study movement and acceptance of the belief that children should not all be held to one standard of development.

Religious influences—viewing children as either inherently evil or inherently innocent—gradually were overshadowed by more secular and scientific approaches to childhood, says Martha Minow, a law professor at Harvard University and one of the creators of a course there that examines the role of children in society.

Throughout the first two decades of the century, a variety of measurements were created to gauge children's development, both physical and psychological. And research on child development rapidly splintered into different schools of thought.

Sigmund Freud, the founder of psychoanalysis, made popular the idea that the problems of adults could be traced to their childhood years.

Of Freud, Sommerville writes: "Childhood was not, in his view, simply a con-

Fighting Childhood Disease

In 1900, the average American could expect to live 47.3 years. Diphtheria, measles, and whooping cough killed thousands each year, and most victims were children. By the 1960s, vaccinations had those contagious diseases under control. In fact, child-mortality rates have decreased about 60 percent since 1960 among children ages 1 to 9, and 43 percent among children ages 10 to 14. Americans now live an average of 75.8 years, and injuries are the most common cause of childhood death.

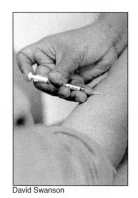
David Swanson

POLIO: Polio was called the last of the great childhood plagues. The first large U.S. outbreak of polio, which attacks nerves in the brain and spinal cord, was in the summer of 1916; 27,000 people were paralyzed and 6,000 died. Epidemics continued to occur throughout the country each summer, with the most serious in the 1940s and 1950s. A field trial in 1954, involving 1.8 million children and financed primarily by the National Foundation for Infantile Paralysis, proved that a killed-virus vaccine developed by Dr. Jonas Salk prevented polio. He became a national hero when the results were announced in 1955, and a campaign to inoculate all children followed. In 1961, a live-virus vaccine developed by Dr. Albert Sabin was licensed. Sabin's vaccine was administered on a sugar cube soaked in liquid, eliminating the need for trained professionals to administer shots. In a few years, polio was virtually eliminated in the United States.

MEASLES: Before 1963, when a vaccine was first used in the United States, there were about 500,000 reported cases and 500 deaths each year from measles, which is caused by a virus. Most deaths were among children younger than 5. Measles reached a low point of fewer than 1,500 cases in 1983 but has since risen to more than 18,000 cases in 1989 and 27,000 in 1990; most of them were in young children who had never been vaccinated.

MUMPS: Mumps is caused by a virus similar to the influenza virus, and usually involves fever, headache, and swelling of the glands under the jaw; fatalities associated with mumps are rare. A live-mumps vaccine was licensed in 1967.

RUBELLA (German Measles): Rubella is a viral infection that can occur in children and adults. In pregnant women, the virus can cause birth defects. A vaccine was first licensed in the United States in 1969; a more potent vaccine was introduced in 1979. Before the use of the vaccine in this country, most cases of rubella occurred in children ages 5 to 9. In 1990, more than 1,000 cases of rubella were reported in the United States.

DIPHTHERIA, TETANUS, AND PERTUSSIS (whooping cough): The DTP vaccine, which protects against diphtheria, tetanus, and pertussis—all once-fatal childhood diseases—has been widely used in the United States since 1945. Since 1980, fewer than five cases of diphtheria—which can lead to paralysis, pneumonia, and heart failure—have been reported each year in the United States. Tetanus, also known as lockjaw, enters the body through a break in the skin. On average, 50 to 100 cases of tetanus are reported each year in the United States, mostly among adults. Pertussis, a very contagious disease that affects the lungs and airways, can lead to pneumonia, brain damage, and death. The number of pertussis cases reported each year in the United States varies between 1,000 and 4,000; infants are at the highest risk.

SOURCES: U.S. Centers for Disease Control and Prevention, *Contagious and Non-Contagious Infectious Diseases Sourcebook,* and U.S. Department of Health and Human Services.

venient time for establishing 'good' behavior patterns; rather, it was the most fateful part of life. The neuroses that troubled his patients in Austria seemed always to go back to their earliest years."

The increasing prestige accorded what were seen as scientific approaches to child development was reflected, too, in the influence of another school of child-rearing—behaviorism. The belief was that children, almost like Pavlov's dog, could be conditioned to behave a certain way. Parents were advised by psychologists such as John B. Watson to keep their babies on a strict feeding schedule. Early toilet training was encouraged, while affection, rocking, and cuddling were not.

In the early decades of the century, the federal government weighed in for the first time with the establishment of the Children's Bureau, which was housed in the U.S. Department of Labor, and the publication of a manual called *Infant Care*. The 1914 document was intended to provide mothers with practical information on such topics as child health and nutrition, but it also emphasized strict routines and rules.

Greater attention was being paid to hygiene, sanitation, and routine health examinations. Documents such as the "Children's Charter," from the 1930 White House Conference on Child Health and Protection, spoke of providing children with "pure food, pure milk, and pure water."

A reaction was building, meanwhile, to the cold and inflexible methods of child-rearing practiced by so many parents early in the century. It was a generation raised on those methods that, as its members became parents themselves, embraced wholeheartedly the much different advice of Dr. Benjamin Spock. His *Baby and Child Care*, first published in 1946, told parents to eschew rigid methods and trust their own instincts. Spock was later criticized as being too permissive—some even blamed him for the youthful rebelliousness of the 1960s—but today's parents still turn to updated versions of his international best seller for counsel.

Embedded in this trend, which Sommerville calls "the liberation of children," was the message that childhood should be fun and that children should be allowed to enjoy it.

PARENTING ADVICE GOES COMMERCIAL

The publishing success and celebrity status enjoyed by Spock point out another aspect of child-rearing: While advice for parents has always been available, in the 20th century it became a commercial enterprise. A bewildering array of books and magazines—spouting a variety of opinions on how to "parent"—now lines bookstore shelves. Many of the current recommendations on child-rearing, Minow notes, are "child centered," meaning that the child's viewpoint is considered vital.

But Kay Hymowitz, a contributing editor of *City Journal*, a magazine published by the Manhattan Institute, argues that giving children a lot of freedom to make decisions and being concerned about their self-esteem have created in the 1990s what she calls "egotistical" children.

Hymowitz, who released the book *Ready or Not: Why Treating Children as Small Adults Endangers Their Future—And Ours* last fall, says that what used to be, in the 19th century, an obsession with protecting children began to shift in the 1950s and 1960s to the opposite extreme, with parents being unable to restrain their children. While "people don't like bratty kids," she says, Americans think that precociousness in young children is cute and often encourage, for example, an early interest in the opposite sex.

CHANGING DEMOGRAPHICS

Changes in the structure and well-being of families have had, of course, a significant effect on children. For one, children are simply more likely to live long enough to become adults.

In 1900, children had only a 79 percent chance of living past age 15, sociologist Peter Uhlenberg points out. By 1979, those chances had increased to 98 percent.

"As infant mortality has declined, childhood has become a more clearly differentiated stage of life, and families have increasingly focused upon children and emphasized the nurturance of children," Uhlenberg says in a chapter called "Death and the Family" in the 1985 book *Growing Up in America: Children in Historical Perspective*.

With child-labor laws in place, fathers typically became the sole breadwinners. Americans left behind farming jobs and moved to cities for work, writes Donald J. Hernandez in an article on changing demographics published in a 1995 "Future of Children" report from the David and Lucile Packard Foundation.

And while oral contraceptives were not available until the 1960s, the family-planning movement grew throughout the century. By 1930, the average number of children in a family had dropped from seven to only two or three.

NURSERY SCHOOL

By 1940, most children over the age of 7 were enrolled in public school. But the history of organized programs for younger children is far more complicated.

During the early part of the century, babies and young children were predominantly cared for by their mothers, except in the case of poor mothers who needed to work. Most child-care arrangements were informal.

But "day nurseries," operated by charity groups, also were available. Emily D. Cahan, the author of *Past Caring: A History of U.S. Preschool Care and Education for the Poor, 1820-1965*, estimates that there were 700 day nurseries in the United States by 1916. She also documents the substandard conditions under which many of those programs operated.

The nurseries eventually attracted critics, who said that children should not be separated from their mothers. That sentiment contributed to the rise of "pensions" that many states paid to lower-income mothers to keep them at home with their children and out of the workforce.

Nursery schools, which served as a type of laboratory for the child-study movement, were started in the 1920s and 1930s. And kindergartens, developed by the German teacher Friedrich Froebel in the 1830s, began to spread through the United States in the early part of the 20th century.

While such influential figures as Froebel, the Italian physician Maria Montessori, and the Swiss psychologist Jean Piaget are best known for their theories on education, they have also shaped the way society in general views and treats children.

It was Froebel who emphasized that children learn through play. He introduced the idea of teachers as "facilitators," instead of authoritarians.

Child-size tables, chairs, and cups—now common in many homes with young children—can be traced to Montessori in the early 1900s. In the 1920s, Piaget identified stages of development that children go through as they move from exploring the world with their senses to understanding abstract concepts.

WOMEN IN THE WORKFORCE

Experts often point out that the fields of early-childhood education and child care have developed simultaneously, but with little connection between the two.

The United States faced its first major child-care dilemma during the Second World War: With millions of fathers in the military, many mothers confronted the decision of whether to stay home or go to work in defense factories.

Simply being a mother was patriotic enough, the nation's leaders stressed. Still, tens of thousands of women placed their children in special wartime child-care centers operated by the federal government and went to work.

While most of those centers closed in the years after World War II, the end of the war didn't necessarily mean the end of demands for child-care services.

Between 1940 and 1960, Hernandez writes, the number of homes with mothers and fathers both working increased significantly. The economic benefits of being employed, combined with escalating divorce rates and an increase in never-married mothers, led to a greater need for child care, and the demand for organized programs is expected to grow in the 21st century.

Since 1975, the percentage of working mothers has increased dramatically, according to the Labor Department's Women's Bureau. In 1975, 47.3 percent of mothers with children under 18 were in the labor force. In 1998, the figure was 72 percent.

And current U.S. Census Bureau figures show that more than 10 million children under 5—about half the children in that age group—are either in child care or have parents who are seeking child care of some sort.

It's a trend that the media, even women's magazines, largely ignored until publications like *Working Mother* came on the scene in the late 1970s.

But now, child care and educational programs for young children have become major political issues at the local, state, and federal levels.

Growing interest in brain development, combined with changes in welfare policy, have led many states to expand child-care and preschool programs. The issue has also received more attention as women seek more flexible work schedules that allow them to balance their home and job responsibilities.

In *Images of Childhood*, published in 1996, Maris A. Vinovskis notes that movements that focus on children often begin with efforts to address poverty. A 20th-century example is Head Start, the popular federal initiative that began as a summer program for low-income children in 1965 and has grown to a full-

Corbis-Bettmann

year, and in some cases full-day, program serving about 800,000 children.

While research on the effectiveness of Head Start has been mixed, many Americans have come to view early education as an essential part of the childhood experience and a necessity for future success in school and life.

'ELECTRONIC BABYSITTER'

Another place youngsters came to spend more and more of their time was at home—in front of the television set. And almost from the time TV was introduced into American households in the late 1940s, the effects of the "electronic babysitter," the "boob tube," the "vast wasteland" on children have been a near-constant subject of national worry and debate.

Throughout the latter part of the 20th century, parents have had to confront such issues as violence, profanity, and sexual explicitness on television as well as the sheer number of hours their children watch.

In the 1993 book *Children and Television: Images in a Changing Sociocultural World*, TV is described as a part of the American household that competes with traditional means of socialization, such as the family, school, and church.

And concerns have been raised over how children are portrayed on television and through the media in general. Advertising images of teenage girls wear-

President Lyndon B. Johnson greets children in Washington in May 1965 to celebrate the beginning of the federal Head Start program.

ing makeup and dressed in alluring fashions have once again helped create a concept of children as "miniature adults," as they were viewed through much of history.

Cultural and societal changes—not just working mothers, but significant levels of drug use, sexual activity, and violence among children and teenagers—have led many experts and social critics to argue that the lines between childhood and adulthood have been irrevocably blurred.

But it's not just negative influences that have robbed children of their special childhood years, says Elkind. The efforts of parents and the practices of schools can also force children to grow up too fast.

In *The Hurried Child*, Elkind writes that pushing children into sports and other activities at a young age, as well as emphasizing reading skills during the preschool years, can create children who are overloaded with adultlike decisions. And schools, by pushing more demanding curricula and testing into lower and lower grades, may actually be harming children, he contends.

CHANGING IMPRESSIONS

But children aren't the only ones influenced by technology and the information age. Adults' impressions of children have shifted because of the media, says Cynthia Scheibe, the director of the Center for Research on the Effects of Television at Ithaca College.

For one, educational television programs—especially "Sesame Street"—have raised expectations of what children should know when they enter kindergarten, Scheibe says.

And news reports—often disturbing accounts of violence and drug use by young people—also shape adults' views of children, says Lillian Brinkley, the principal of the Willard Model Elementary School in Norfolk, Va., and a 38-year veteran of education.

But while sensational cases often make it seem as if children are out of control, Brinkley says that hasn't been her experience. Students wind up in her office for the same reasons they did 30 years ago—fighting, name-calling, setting off the fire alarm.

While the society children live in has changed dramatically, "there is still that line that runs down the middle," Brinkley says. "As filled as their world is with all kinds of things, they still want to know that there is someone there to provide some direction for them." ■

Benjamin Tice Smith

Children at the White House

In roughly 10-year intervals throughout the 20th century, the White House has brought together prominent academics, physicians, social workers, community leaders, and others to address issues involving America's children. Whether the country was at war or at peace, prosperous or in an economic slump, each White House conference reflected the challenges facing children at the time. Some of the presidential gatherings were catalysts for significant and enduring reforms in child welfare, while others produced few lasting results.

1909: White House Conference On Dependent Children

This first conference, chaired by President Theodore Roosevelt, was the brainchild of James West, a young lawyer and presidential appointee who had been raised in an orphanage in Washington. Roosevelt intended the two-day conference to examine the needs of destitute and neglected children, and it

helped pave the way for a federal agency devoted to promoting child welfare. The Children's Bureau was started in 1912 and remains today as part of the U.S. Department of Health and Human Services. It primarily focuses on foster care, adoption, and child-care standards.

1919: White House Conference On Child-Welfare Standards

President Woodrow Wilson had proclaimed 1918, while the United States was at war in Europe, the "Children's Year" to try to inspire support for safeguarding American children during a time of national peril. The Children's Bureau organized the conference to set minimum standards for children's health and welfare. Guests from other countries joined more than 200 American participants, including social workers, pediatricians, public-health nurses, economists, judges, and parents. The panelists' recommendations helped steer legislation setting standards for child labor and employment, child protection, and medical care for infants and mothers. Recommendations from the gathering laid the groundwork for maternal- and child-health programs under the Social Security Act passed by Congress in 1935.

1930: White House Conference On Child Health and Protection

In the midst of the Great Depression, as child advocates were working overtime to care for increasing numbers of impoverished children, President Herbert Hoover saw a national conference as a way to build public support for children's services and laws designed to protect young people. The president tapped the secretary of the interior to be chairman and the secretary of labor to act as vice chairman. The event was financed with $500,000 in leftover funds from the First World War. More than 1,200 participants divided into 138 committees to review subjects such as pediatric-health services and education and training. The committees' reports combined to form the first national "Children's Charter," which laid out the rights of children to attend schools that were "safe from hazards, sanitary, [and] properly equipped," to be raised in safe

environments, and to be provided with proper medical care. The conference has been credited as being a catalyst for advances in pediatric medicine. The charter—endorsed by Hoover—set in motion employment protections that eventually would shield underage workers from exploitation on the job.

1940: White House Conference On Children in a Democracy

The fourth White House conference focused on all of the country's children, not just those who were poor. With World War II already under way in Europe, President Franklin D. Roosevelt charged the 700 or so conferees with considering "how a democracy can best serve its children and how children can be helped to grow into the kind of citizens who will preserve democracy." Though the 1940 recommendations were modest compared with those of previous conferences and called for no new programs, the gathering itself may have helped provide momentum for subsequent federal action. In 1941, the U.S. Supreme Court declared the Fair Labor Standards Act constitutional, making its child-labor provisions the permanent standard of protection for children.

1950: Midcentury White House Conference on Children and Youth

The theme of the midcentury conference—understanding child development—reflected the significant gains in research on human development and child psychology during that period. President Harry S. Truman's White House gathering brought together more than 4,800 participants, 500 of them younger than 21. The diverse group of professionals, students, pediatricians, labor leaders, and others examined ways of fostering children's mental and emotional health. The conference endorsed the need for research in developmental psychology, the importance of early intervention to promote healthful lifelong habits, and the virtues of leisure time for building children's social skills. After this conference, several governors convened similar state-level meetings.

1960: Golden Anniversary White House Conference On Children and Youth

In a time of material abundance, scientific discoveries, and breakthroughs in technology, President Dwight D. Eisenhower used this conference to address people's growing interest in children's values. The conference, attended by 11,000 people, examined the role of family, religion, community, and government in children's lives. The conferees focused on the emerging problems of juvenile delinquency, school failure, and illicit drug use by youths that many said symbolized a moral decline. Though 670 recommendations emerged from the conference, none formed the basis for enduring nationwide action.

1970: White House Conference On Children and Youth

The 1970 conference on children, chaired by President Richard M. Nixon, focused on such topics as the effect of racism on young people, family neglect and abuse, juvenile justice, and child care. The well-attended gathering, which included state leaders, was a springboard for several national social and educational initiatives. The meeting helped build public support for the idea of a U.S. Department of Education and helped promote initiatives to prevent child abuse. After the conference, Nixon proposed an expansion of child-care services. But just a year later, in 1971, he vetoed the Comprehensive Child-Development Act, which would have

laid the foundation for a national network of child-care centers.

1980: White House Conference On Families

Changing trends in the family was the theme of the conference called by President Jimmy Carter. Conferees considered how cultural and social changes, such as an escalating divorce rate and the growth of single-parent households, affected children. The participants also looked at how economic circumstances had fostered certain migration patterns—from rural to urban, and urban to suburban communities—during the 1970s and how the increased mobility had affected young people. The leading areas of concern included the availability of child care, the quality of education, the availability and quality of health care, and work discrimination. At the conclusion of the conference, Carter called on each state governor to designate a coordinator to address children's issues.

1997: White House Conference On Child Care

Citing the importance of the first three years of a child's life, President Bill Clinton focused on the importance of child care in the latest White House conference on children. Child-development experts, medical professionals, and directors of local programs met to share scientific findings on how children learn and how best to provide enriching care for them. Of the five initiatives Clinton proposed at the meeting, an effort to reduce the number of uninsured poor children was perhaps the most significant. In 1998, Congress approved a children's health-insurance bill that extended coverage to 3 million previously uninsured children through an expansion of Medicaid.

—JESSICA PORTNER

SOURCES: *The Story of the White House Conferences on Children and Youth*, the U.S. Department of Health, Education, and Welfare, 1967; *Highlights from Past National Conferences on Children and Youth*, White House, 1981.

Hollywood Goes to School

Hollywood has an insatiable appetite for heroes and villains, and it's found plenty of both in the classroom. More realistic portrayals of school life in the 20th century are harder to come by. The difficult, sometimes tedious work of teaching and learning doesn't translate quite as easily to the big and small screens, even when producers try.

But Hollywood is in show business, not education policy, and many of the classroom-related movies and television shows described here are as entertaining as they come.

■ By Mark Walsh

URBAN SCHOOLS

Urban schools are almost invariably depicted as war zones. In *Class of 1984* (1982), a B movie that might be more deserving of a D, a mild-mannered music teacher becomes a vigilante against gang members. Fast-forward to the *Class of 1999* (1990), in which security guards wear Darth Vader-like masks and the "department of educational defense" uses teacher-robots to take on the gangs.

A similar theme pervades *187* (1997), in which teacher Trevor Garfield (Samuel L. Jackson) is driven to kill gang members and ends up dead himself. The screenplay

■ *Cooley High.*

■ Michelle Pfeiffer in *Dangerous Minds.*

was written by a former teacher who thought too many Hollywood school movies ended on unrealistically upbeat notes.

But there are optimistic urban school movies, from *Up the Down Staircase* (1967), in which 1960s urban hoodlums learn to appreciate Dickens, and *Cooley High* (1975), which has a promising message for an all-black high school in Chicago.

In *Dangerous Minds* (1995), the classroom vulgarities would have shocked even the hoods from *Blackboard Jungle*. But ex-Marine LouAnne Johnson (Michelle Pfeiffer) uses martial arts demonstrations and candy bars to turn her students on to poetry.

TEACHERS

Hollywood teachers are heroes—usually. They are idealistic. They battle the principal and other cynics and doubters. They question whether they can go on, but in the end, they make a classroom breakthrough and sign up for another year.

In *Blackboard Jungle* (1955), the prototypical American film of the genre, Korean War veteran Richard Dadier (Glenn Ford) faces a class of boys who make his life hellish. He is mugged, his wife is harassed, and his colleague's priceless record

■ Glenn Ford in *Blackboard Jungle.*

collection is smashed. He is ready to quit, but he goes back to his education school professor for re-inspiration. In the climax, a student pulls a knife on him, but some of the other boys help squelch the violence. Despite one-dimensional characters, it is the classroom movie against which all others are measured.

A dedicated teacher is also the focus of *Good Morning, Miss Dove* (1955), with Jennifer Jones as an elderly educator who recalls a lifetime of shaping the lives of her students.

In *Stand and Deliver* (1987), based on a true story, Jaime Escalante (Edward James Olmos) is one movie teacher who takes on the system and wins. Confronted by skeptical test authorities, his Latino students ace an Advanced Placement calculus test not once, but twice.

More typical is the teacher who defies conventions and pays a price, such as John Keating (Robin Williams)

■ Robin Williams in *Dead Poets Society.*

in *Dead Poets Society* (1989). His romantic notions about engaging the minds of his boarding school boys butt up against tradition. He loses his job, but at least he gets his students to stand up on their desks and recite, "O Captain! My Captain!"

STUDENT LIFE

In the 1920s and 1930s, America's image of schoolchildren was shaped in part by Hal Roach's Our Gang movie shorts. The gang, also called the Little Rascals, engage in their memorable mischief in titles such as **Bored of Education** (1936). In the Andy Hardy series (1937-46), teenage life is "swell"; MGM won a special Oscar for representing the "American way of life."

How things had changed by the 1980s and '90s. In **Risky Business** (1983), Joel Goodson (Tom Cruise) helps run a prostitution ring for a "future business leaders" club project. A stoned Jeff Spicoli (Sean Penn) has pizza delivered to class in **Fast Times at Ridgemont High** (1982).

Director John Hughes helped define the 1980s with such movies as **Sixteen Candles**

■ The Little Rascals.

■ *Hoop Dreams.*

(1984), **The Breakfast Club** (1985), and **Pretty in Pink** (1986), which all feature smart, sassy teenagers in affluent suburban settings.

One of the most realistic depictions of student life is in 1994's **Hoop Dreams**, a project that started out as a short documentary about playground basketball and turned into a three-hour-plus window on urban public schools, suburban Catholic schools, and dashed expectations.

PRINCIPALS

In the movies, the school principal (or vice principal or headmaster) is often bumbling (Mr. Rooney in **Ferris Bueller's Day Off**, 1986), villainous (the Catholic school principals in two obscure but poignant films, **The Chocolate War**, 1988, and **Heaven Help Us**, 1985), or pedantic (Mr. Wameke in **Blackboard Jungle** and Mr. Rivell in **Teachers**, 1984).

But school leaders have also played heroic roles. In the sentimental **Boys Town** (1938), Father Flanagan (Spencer Tracy) gets through to even the toughest delinquents in his school.

In **The Principal** (1987), Mr. Latimer (James Belushi) is a failed suburban classroom teacher

■ Spencer Tracy in *Boys Town.*

■ Joe Clark, right, is portrayed by Morgan Freeman in *Lean on Me.*

turned inner-city principal who takes on gangs and uncaring teachers.

And **Lean on Me** (1987) tells the true story of the autocratic Joe Clark (Morgan Freeman), who wields his trademark bullhorn and baseball bat and locks fire doors to keep drug dealers and other miscreants from the halls of his school. With the troublemakers gone, the rest of the students pass a basic-skills test that keeps the school accredited. The bad kids apparently all transfer to the troubled schools in other movies.

TELEVISION

In the half-century history of television broadcasting, classrooms have been the setting for many shows, but only a few memorable ones. (Many shows didn't last more than one season.)

Among the first were **Mr. Peepers** (NBC, 1952-55), with Wally Cox as a shy science teacher, and **Our Miss Brooks** (CBS, 1952-56), with Eve Arden as a wisecracking English teacher who was always trying to snag science teacher Mr. Boynton as a husband. Arden was so popular she received offers to teach in real schools.

■ Eve Arden in *Our Miss Brooks.*

In **Mr. Novak** (NBC, 1963-65), James Franciscus played a likable, fresh-faced English teacher working in a Los Angeles high school, with Dean Jagger as the dignified principal.

In **Room 222** (ABC, 1969-74), teacher Pete Dixon (Lloyd Haynes) at Walt Whitman High School dispensed lessons about history, tolerance, and sensitivity.

Welcome Back, Kotter (ABC, 1975-79) is recalled disapprovingly for its racially and ethnically stereotyped student "sweathogs," but the show also had a sweet disposition and a great theme song.

The Simpsons (Fox, 1989-) isn't just about school, of course, but the episodes at Springfield Elementary are the most biting satire of public education anywhere. The sign outside the school on parent-teacher night says: "Let's share the blame."

■ Bart of *The Simpsons.*

Team Players

By Kerry A. White

F oul.

That's how historians sum up high school sports in the early 1900s, when students, outsiders, and, above all, chaos governed the games.

Before school officials took control, competition was virtually unstructured. There were few eligibility requirements for players, inadequate rules to ensure fair play, and scant or no precautions taken to safeguard athletes.

Nothing barred coaches—often school alumni or students from nearby colleges—from playing on the teams they coached, and no rules stopped outsiders, including older, paid athletes, from joining in especially fierce competitions. With few safety measures in place, thousands of preventable injuries and numerous deaths befell high school athletes each year.

"In the first decade of this century, there were some very, very unsavory things going on in high school sports," says Dick Kishpaugh, a sports historian and author in Parchment, Mich.

"Though teams used school names as if they represented their high schools, schools didn't set policy, players did. ... Serious injuries were common, gamblers arranged games," and shady recruiting practices were the norm, Kishpaugh says.

Football was especially popular, and brutal, at the turn of the century. Mass formations, gang tackling, and spearing—using the top of the head to plow into opponents—were mainstays of the game.

By about 1910, as enthusiasm for both participating in and watching organized sports was growing, so were problems associated with competition. Around that time, school sports had gotten so out of control, so dangerous and embarrassing, Kishpaugh says, that "schools realized they had to get in on the act."

Principals began to issue game rules. They improved safety by barring unnecessarily risky plays, required athletes to wear safety equipment, and mandated that players be bona fide students. They began to set guidelines for recruiting players and rules to prevent players from shopping for schools. And for the first time, principals began questioning the prevailing win-at-all-costs mentality of sports and contemplating athletics' educational mission.

"Everybody but the schools had been running high school sports, and though colleges had gotten serious about sports—the [National Collegiate Athletic Association] was established in 1906—high

High school sports have matured from virtual free-for-alls to community institutions.

The Sauk Center (Minn.) High School basketball team may have used the school's name, but few teams in 1910 were governed by school rules.

Photo courtesy of Corbis/Minnesota Historical Society

It didn't take long for interscholastic sports to become as much a part of the American school experience as reading, writing, and arithmetic.

schools didn't follow until some time later," says Joan S. Hult, a professor emeritus and sports historian at the University of Maryland College Park. "But going into the 1920s, principals began saying, 'If we're going to run this world, let's make it educational.'"

Yet, even as schools began to clean up their sports programs and formalize interscholastic competition, complications persisted because school rules and philosophies weren't always in sync. Principals began to organize local associations that rallied around agreed-upon policies and principles. But soon, as teams began to travel greater distances for games, competition hitches arose from disparate rules and regulations.

To further standardize high school sports, whole states began to form athletic associations, which in 1923 organized under the newly established National Federation of State High School Athletic Associations. Today, as the National Federation of State High School Associations, the organization guides high school athletic programs and co-curricular activities in the 50 states and the District of Columbia.

Once the states began to organize school sports and the federation was formed, interscholastic sports became an institution, as much a part of the American school experience as reading, writing, and arithmetic. School sports also became a centerpiece—and in many regions, the sole rallying force—of small towns and communities. Team mascots were chosen, and whole new clubs and activities—booster clubs, marching bands, cheerleading squads—formed to support and salute high school teams.

High school sports grew so strong over the years that losing streaks, occasional scandals, wars, even the Great Depression could not shake fans' allegiance. Just around the time that lights first came to high school gridirons and baseball diamonds, in fact, the Depression hit. But in many places, souring economic times had little effect on gate receipts: High school football, basketball, and baseball games, like the Hollywood movies of that era, were among the nation's remaining affordable diversions.

Interschool rivalries gave locals something to cheer or grouse about unrelated to their financial woes.

"Most schools maintained a pretty good audience from the 1920s on," Kishpaugh says. "For cheap entertainment during the Depression, you couldn't beat [high school] games or the movies."

That's not to say that budgets weren't tight. High school sports, like just about everything else, faced deep cuts through the Depression and World War II. Some competition, especially games that involved extensive travel, was trimmed back; other games were suspended altogether.

But loyalty toward high school teams, especially in football, basketball, baseball, and track and field, was basically unwavering. In most small towns, those sports dominated small talk, and winning teams have been glorified to this day. Sports came to define schools to the public, overshadowing all other activities, academics included.

In his 1941-42 study of young people in a typical Midwestern town, *Elmtown's Youth*, sociologist A.B. Hollingshead wrote: "Extracurricular activities without spectator appeal or broad public relations value, such as girls' athletics, student government, and departmental clubs, receive little active support from the [school] board or community. ...There is far more public interest in the football and basketball teams than in all other high school activities combined. The team has come to be a collective representation of the high school to a large segment of the community. Business, professional, and working men not only expect but also demand ... winning teams."

Most school administrators would agree—and many lament—that such an observation rings true more than half a century later.

"A great football or basketball season can completely excite a community, almost to the point of hysteria," says Gene Buinger, who has served as a coach, teacher, and school administrator in several sports-crazed districts and today is the superintendent of the Bibb County, Ga., system, which includes Macon. Before taking his post there, Buinger was the superintendent of schools in Odessa, Texas, the town featured, rather harshly,

Corbis-Bettmann

Corbis-Bettmann

in H.G. Bissinger's best-selling book on the Permian High School football team's 1988 season, *Friday Night Lights*.

"In a small town, where there are no professional sports teams, people's allegiance has tended toward their high school teams," Buinger says. "And if you have a good football or basketball season, the pride students feel for their school carries over into the community.

"Though you hope for some balance, it's been athletics, not academics, that has tended to shape the community's view of a school," he says, adding: "There's an old adage among high school principals that you need a graduate degree and a winning football team to make it, and that's not so overblown. You feel the pressure."

While the demand for winning teams has remained a constant, high school sports' educational mission has continued to evolve, and today, competition has come to be viewed as a means of instilling the importance of determination and discipline in the players—skills and understanding that will carry over to the classroom and, eventually, the workplace.

U.S. schools are the only ones in the world to tie sports so closely to academics. Elsewhere, schools and sports typically remain separate institutions with distinct goals.

"School sports have a unique purpose, to keep young people focused on schoolwork, and to emphasize citizenship, teamwork, respect, and honesty," says Robert F. Kanaby, the sixth executive director of the national high school federation. "We want young athletes to become better people, not just better players."

The typical student athlete, he says—and studies confirm—tends to perform as well or better academically than his or her nonathlete peers and is more likely to steer clear of depression, alcohol and drug abuse, and pregnancy.

But athletes' behavior and academic achievement are, of course, not always stellar. And while school officials over the years may have encouraged athletes to stay out of trouble and keep their grades up, there were no laws dictating what sort of student could or couldn't play sports until 1984, when business magnate Ross Perot persuaded lawmak-

Above: Junior high school students play baseball in spring 1942 in Washington. For many African-Americans, chances to play school sports were limited by segregation. Where schools were integrated, athletic competition often forged close bonds between black and white players.

Left: Girls have had sporadic outlets for competitive sports since the turn of the century. But it wasn't until the passage of Title IX in 1972 that many high schools began to offer a variety of interscholastic athletic opportunities for female students.

A growing body of professionals—coaches, one or two athletic directors, physical trainers, even legal advisers—works to keep the average sports program afloat.

ers in football-mad Texas to adopt a policy barring students with failing grades from competition.

The Texas policy was dubbed "no-pass, no-play," and nearly 30 states and many districts have put similar restrictions on the books since, many of which extend to students participating in all co-curricular programs. Critics argue that such rules are too punitive and haven't worked to push students to work any harder in school. As a result, some policymakers already have begun to soften such requirements.

Through the 20th century, virtually every aspect of school sports programs has steadily expanded. A few choices have multiplied to many, including more specialized diversions such as synchronized swimming, archery, water polo, and ice hockey. And as the offerings have grown, so have the staffs that manage them.

"For years, the standard was three sports taught by three coaches—all male," says Art Taylor, the associate director of the Center for the Study of Sport in Society at Northeastern University. "Everything's changed."

Nowadays, a growing body of professionals—a legion of coaches, one or two athletic directors, physical trainers, even legal advisers—works to keep the average high school's sports program afloat.

Much of the growth in interscholastic athletics can be credited to Title IX of the Education Amendments of 1972, the federal law prohibiting sex discrimination in schools accepting federal funds. The law, says Judith C. Young, the executive director of the National Association of Sport and Physical Education, "has brought the most obvious and extensive change to high school sports," by forcing schools to broaden their roster of sports and, at least as the law is written, to open up as many athletic opportunities for girls as for boys.

Participation surveys illustrate school sports' expansion and the steady gains in the number of female athletes over the past three decades: Some 6.4 million high school students participated in interscholastic sports in the 1998-99 school year—about 2.6 million, or 40.6 percent, of them girls, according to the national federation. Those figures compare with about 4 million student athletes, 294,000, or 7.4 percent, of them girls, in 1971, the first year the federation conducted its participation survey.

Though Title IX opened up unprecedented chances for female athletes, school-age girls and women had been competing in sports all along. Opportunities to play basketball, volleyball, tennis, field hockey, and other sports had been in place since the turn of the century through intramural sports and outside clubs. And those programs expanded over the years.

"Women have always had competitive outlets; they were just outside the school systems," says Hult, the sports historian. "Women didn't want the same scene as men, which was already so corrupt," she says. With no power over or position in male sports, she explains, they wanted control of girls' sports, so they started their own organizations.

The game rules and the settings for those early girls' teams—what Hult calls the "underground varsity"—were drastically different from what they were for boys. Girls' basketball, for example, was played on a half court, and men were banished from the gym during games. In some regions, female players couldn't play two consecutive quarters and were checked regularly for signs of overexertion.

Despite the kid gloves, Hult disputes the implication that the women who played in those early leagues were at all sluggish. "When women had the chance to play competitive sports," she says, "they played vigorously."

Eventually, faced with girls who had sufficiently developed their athletic talents to perform as well as or better than their male counterparts, some schools began adding girls to their otherwise all-male team rosters. In California, so many girls were running, swimming, diving, and playing tennis and golf with the boys, according to William W. Russell, the executive director of the California Interscholastic Federation from 1955 to 1980, that the state began to start or expand existing girls' sports teams in the 1960s.

"We were getting so many calls from principals asking if girls could play on boys' teams, I said, 'We've got to do something about the girls' program,'" recalls Russell. "If it's good for boys, we thought, then it's good for girls."

But California's effort to expand girls' sports was the exception. Nationwide, most schools didn't offer girls near the opportunities to play that boys had, and outside opportunities were limited. It wasn't really until the mid-1970s that female athletes began having a strong presence on high school campuses. By adding millions of young women to high school teams, Title IX helped dispel some of those early notions of a "weaker sex."

As in professional and college sports ranks, however, all is not equal for the young men and women who play high school sports.

Diana Everett, a former executive director of the National Association for Girls and Women in Sport, maintains that Title IX still has "a long, long way to go" to make high school sports equitable.

"We've made some great strides in women's sports, no doubt. But discrimination is still a huge problem in schools, and especially high schools," she says.

The story of African-Americans in high school sports is not entirely different from that of girls and young women. Like that of female athletes, African-Americans' experience depended heavily on local vagaries. But for blacks in segregated school systems, race was the factor in high school sports.

"If a black youngster in the North were lucky, he or she could go to a fairly decent public school where sports were a regular part of the extracurricular activities program," the late tennis champion Arthur R. Ashe Jr. wrote in *A Hard Road to Glory: A History of the African-American Athlete 1919-45*, published in 1988. "In the South, a black youngster would be lucky to finish the seventh grade before being forced by economic necessity to work. Even if he or she had the time, the imbalance of facilities was blatant."

Where schools weren't segregated, many say that race simply wasn't a big

Paul A. Souders/Corbis-Bettmann

factor. Russell, who played basketball for an integrated high school team in Santa Barbara, Calif., and later played on a college team, says that where he went to school and competed, "race never was an issue. High school teams played as if there were no color lines at all."

Thomas D. Hemans, the director of New York City's Public School Athletic League, was one of the few black basketball players for his team at Thomas Jefferson High School in Brooklyn in the early 1950s.

He looks back on his basketball-playing years fondly, and when asked, says no specific racial indignities from those times come to mind.

"In the regular school setting, people tended to be pulled toward their own ethnic group. And even today, that's still the case," Hemans says. "But when you have students on a team together because of their talent and working for a common goal, race is not a factor. We have a United Nations of teams here, and these kids are not interested in the color of each others' skin."

With the capability of school sports to help forge such friendships, as well as lay the groundwork for academic and per-

sonal success and draw communities together, there are few forces threatening the institution.

But some observers worry about the shenanigans of professional athletes who engage in "trash talk," disrespect coaches and game officials, and have run-ins with the law—all while earning millions.

One result of such examples has been escalating trouble on high school basketball courts and football fields, and more high school students—despite the million-to-one odds—who aspire to what seems an easy life of big money and big fame in the professional ranks. To counter such problems, some schools have scaled back or modified their athletic programs.

But to Taylor of the Center for the Study of Sport in Society, high schools shouldn't give up on sports because of the unsportsmanlike behavior of some athletes.

Because of their educational mission and understanding of what motivates young people, Taylor says, school officials have the power to stave off some of the problems and abuses that plague college and professional sports—and that's power they should use, he says. ■

Fans celebrate a score at a homecoming football game at Calvert High School in Prince Frederick, Md., in October 1995. High school sports teams have become a unifying force in communities across America.

The Social Determination Of Childhood and Adolescence

A perspective by David Elkind

What a difference a hundred years makes. The promise of a golden era of childhood and adolescence with which we began the 20th century has not been kept. To the contrary, at the end of this period, we now mourn what Neil Postman has called the "disappearance of childhood." It is particularly ironic that, as we leave the teen centuries, we have all but forsaken the teen years.

This century began with the celebration of the stages of childhood innocence and adolescent immaturity, with an appreciation for the wide range of normal youthful behavior, and with the provision of ample spaces for children and youth. At the end of this era, the stages of innocence and immaturity are challenged, the range of normality for children and youth has narrowed, and space for young people has shrunk. During the same period, the stages of adulthood have been heralded, the range of normality for grown-ups has vastly expanded, and adult recreational spaces multiplied exponentially. A century that began with the pre-eminence of pediatrics ends with the veneration of geriatrics.

This extraordinary change in our generational positions mirrors the equally dramatic social, economic, political, and technological alterations that have been the hallmark of the 20th century. While it is not possible to detail these changes here, I would like to try to elaborate briefly on the generational reversals with regard to stages, normality, and space. For purposes of discussion, and ease of presentation, I will present the differences more starkly than they are in fact. Also, while I am presenting the contemporary scene as less favorable to children and youth than the earlier time, I neither want to mythologize the past nor demonize the

present. There were many awful things done to children and youth in earlier times, and there are many good things happening to children and youth today.

Nonetheless, it does seem to be the case that, in the United States at any rate, the needs of adults are now weighted more heavily than those of children and youth. Just the reverse seemed to be the case at the start of the century.

■

The Stages of Development. Many different historical forces converged to give prominence to the stages of childhood and adolescence around the turn of the century. Charles Darwin's theory of our human, as opposed to our divine, origins allowed us to interpret children's behavior from a natural, rather than from a moral, perspective. Sigmund Freud's theory of infantile sexuality, which stressed the importance of the early years for personality formation, added to the prominence accorded this age period. The separation of the social sciences from philosophy and the emergence of child psychology as a scientific discipline also made their contribution. The publication of G. Stanley Hall's two-volume work *Adolescence* in 1904 and his founding of the *Journal of Genetic Psychology* served to formalize this field of investigation.

In the early decades of this century, a number of writers elaborated for parents the stages and phases of child development. But it was John Dewey who translated this developmental material into an overall progressive philosophy of education. The essence of Dewey's position derived from his functionalism. Education had to be practical, to prepare young people for the society they are living in now, not for the societies of long ago. Moreover, he insisted that education should be developmentally appropriate, geared to children's interests, abilities, and levels of understanding. Like the Founding Fathers, Dewey believed that education was essential for preparing individuals to live in a democracy. This added to the

importance attributed to the student years.

The significance attributed to childhood and adolescence was reinforced by the invention of the intelligence test by Alfred Binet and Theodore Simon in 1905. Testing quickly caught on in America after Lewis M. Terman translated the Binet Scales and published them as the Stanford-Binet. Group tests of intelligence were soon developed and used both in the schools and the armed services. One consequence of group and individual mental testing was the finding that the IQ peaked at age 18 (reiterated by the psychologist David Wechsler as recently as 1958). This added to the importance attributed to the years of childhood and adolescence and to the dismissal of the adult years—now regarded as a period of waning mental powers and creativity. In the first half of this century, therefore, childhood and adolescence were regarded as more important than adulthood.

After World War II, however, the imbalance of the weights accorded childhood and adulthood was progressively reversed. The causes were many. The 1960s social movements, in behalf of equality for African-Americans, women, and other minorities, were inappropriately extended to children and youth. This group too was regarded as being deprived of its human rights and opportunities. Implicit in this assumption was the belief that children were competent enough, and adolescents sophisticated enough, to demand these rights. As a result, the legal system changed its emphasis from protecting children to protecting children's rights. In schools, for example, this often resulted in the dismissal of truant officers for not using due process.

The recent advent of child-friendly technologies, such as television, VCRs, and computer games, added to a new perception of child competence. The increased number of sexually active teens (in response to the new social acceptance of premarital sex) along with extensive teenage drug use (coincident with the introduction of rock music) gave credence to a new perception of adolescent sophistication. The schools have accepted these new perceptions of competence and sophistication and are committed to sex and drug education even at the elementary school level.

The social sciences have added their weight to these altered perceptions. Many contemporary child psychologists challenge the validity of developmental stages and have devised experimental techniques to demonstrate that children can do things earlier than the developmentalists had described. Psychiatrists, too, now dispute the views of Freud and Erik Erikson and argue, for example, that adolescence is a transition period no different from any other.

These new perceptions of childhood competence and adolescent sophistication are reinforced by the growing number of divorced, two-parent-working, and single-parent families that are constrained to place children in one or another form of child care or, in the case of adolescents, to leave them home alone. Parents have to assume that young people are mature enough to cope with these experiences. Schools have also accommodated to these new family configurations. Full-day kindergartens are a child-care initiative, as are before- and after-school programs in both elementary and secondary schools.

On the other side of the ledger, a new appreciation of adult development is well under way. Psychologists acknowledge that they made a mistake when they

argued that intelligence peaked at age 18. It was a problem of sampling. In fact, they now say, some facets of intelligence continue to increase through the 60s, and there may be a second period of creativity in the 80s. As the life span lengthens, there is a growing appreciation of the stages of adulthood as described in best-selling books such as Gail Sheehy's *Passages* (1976) and Judith Viorst's *Necessary Losses* (1986). In addition to works on

The needs of adults are now weighted more heavily than those of children and youth. Just the reverse seemed to be the case at the start of the 20th century.

There are fewer and fewer places for young people just to congregate with friends, a necessary and developmentally important adolescent activity.

"midlife crises," there are now books on the stages of divorce, of remarriage, and of death. It is distressing that as we have come to recognize and to appreciate the stages of adult development, we seem ready to deny them to children and youth.

The Breadth of Normality. A similar shift can be observed with respect to normality. At the end of the 19th century, a new image of childhood appeared. It was the result of many social forces, including the new humanitarian ethos and the secularization of society. The exploitation of children was looked upon as an evil, and the belief in the child as embodying "original" sin was abandoned. Children came to be seen as mischievous but harmless. Adolescents were regarded as immature and involved in challenging escapades— regarded as a testing of adult authority normal to that age period. As a consequence of these views, both children and adolescents were allowed a great deal of latitude in their behavior.

On the other hand, adult behavior in the early decades of the 20th century was extremely constrained. There were social taboos against premarital sex, against divorce, against working mothers, and against single parenting. The moral restraints reached an extreme with the passage of Prohibition and all of its amoral consequences. There was also censorship in the guise of the Hayes Office, which ensured that profanity was kept off the radio and nudity and overt sexual activity off the motion picture screen. Up until midcentury, adults were afforded only a narrow latitude of behavior.

After midcentury, however, the balance with respect to normality reversed as well. For many different reasons, we have progressively narrowed the range of normality for children and adolescents. In part, this was the result of new diagnostic methods that were more sensitive than those used in the past. In part, it was the new acceptance of children with special needs within our classrooms, and in part, it is the increasingly stringent demands for academic achievement. The positive benefits of providing for children with special needs have been more than offset by a focus on diagnosing deviance. And this has been made even more unfortunate by the movement away from an understanding and appreciation of

normal development.

A personal illustration may help to make the point. When I first entered the profession, more than 30 years ago, I began as a school psychologist in Boston, working for the state of Massachusetts. In one 1st grade classroom I visited, I noticed a boy running about, talking to his friends and teasing the girls. I told the teacher I thought he was, using the terminology of that day, "hyperactive" and in need of evaluation. She laughed and replied, "Oh, no. He's all boy, he'll get over it." Today when I visit a 1st grade classroom and observe similar behavior, I am told the child has attention deficit/hyperactivity disorder, and might have to be put on Ritalin. Certainly, some children do have ADHD and may benefit from Ritalin, but too many children are being misdiagnosed.

The range of normality has been narrowed for adolescents as well. Increasingly, youthful offenders are being tried and incarcerated as adults. In some states, the age of statutory rape has been lowered. The range of normality has narrowed in other facets of adolescent life as well. Young people who attended trade and technical schools were, in the early decades of this century, accorded considerable respect and admiration. Today, thanks to the enormous value placed upon academic achievement, those young people who attend vocational schools are derogatorily called "vokies."

If the range of normality has narrowed for children, it has expanded for adults. Many behaviors that were once taboo are now acceptable. Premarital sex is now socially acceptable and the stuff of TV programs such as "Friends" and "Seinfeld." Likewise, divorce is socially acceptable and commonplace. Two-parent-working families and single parents (there are now 13 million) are the rule rather than the exception. Two people living together without marriage (cohabitation) is the fast-growing living arrangement in our society. The range of normality for adults has expanded just as that for children and youth has narrowed.

The Provision of Space. We can observe similar changes with respect to space. At the beginning of the century, there were many spaces for children. Basements, for example, were often the preserve of the young and were a place where they could play pingpong, build models, or just hang out and read comic books. Vacant lots were plentiful, and young people congregated there to play their own games of marbles, kick-the-can, or hide-and-seek. These neighborhood spaces were safe, and parents did not hesitate to tell their children to "go out and play." For adolescents, there were malt shops and soda fountains as well as large movie theaters with dark balconies where young people could begin their initial sexual explorations.

For adults, there were many fewer spaces. Most families did their serious shopping "downtown" in the department stores. While there were ballparks and bowling alleys and movie theaters, these were spaces that adults often

shared with young people and that were not exclusively their own. For many parents, the home and the back yard were their major spaces for everyday living and recreation.

Once again, things have changed since the middle of this century. In our fast-developing communities, vacant lots are often hard to come by. Now, many houses are built without basements or with basements that are outfitted as "family rooms." If there is a spare room, it is often a computer or exercise room shared by all. The prevalence of fast cars and roadways, along with worries about abduction, have made parents fearful of allowing children to go out on their own. In response to these considerations,

children are often sent to lessons or to participate in organized team sports where there is always adult supervision. In our elementary schools, playgrounds are used less today than in the past, in part because of insurance concerns and in part because of the belief that the time is better spent in instruction.

The spaces for adolescents have vanished as well. Malt shops and soda fountains in drugstores are a thing of the past, as are large movie theaters. And though malls have proliferated, young people are not always welcome in these spaces. There are fewer and fewer places for young people just to congregate with friends, a necessary and developmentally important adolescent activity.

At the same time, there has been an explosion of space for adults. The availability of affordable cars and superhighways has made national travel easy and convenient. Malls have proliferated, and there are now too many places to shop. New restaurants, health clubs, tennis clubs, and golf courses are being built to accommodate the growing number of adults who participate in these activities. In addition, huge arenas are being built around the country to house the ever-growing number of adults who attend a variety of sports events. In sum, the spaces for adults are expanding while those for children are shrinking.

The social determination of childhood and adolescence is evident in the reversed fortunes of the two generations over the past century. On every measure that we have—health, education, and welfare—children and adolescents are doing less well today than they did even a quarter of a century ago. To be sure, the scene is not entirely dismal. There is much greater acceptance today than there was in the past of children with disabilities and of children from different cultures and ethnic backgrounds. Our schools now

make special provisions for these children, which they did not do even a quarter of a century ago. Nonetheless, the overall picture is bleak and one that seems to benefit adults over children and youth.

It is not necessary to give up all of the gains that we have made as adults to even the balance between the generations. All that is needed is the will. It would not be that difficult to reinvent the stages of childhood and adolescence, to broaden the range of normality for children and youth, and to provide new, safe spaces for the young to play and to congregate. Now that we grown-ups have realized the benefits of recognizing the stages of adulthood, we should find it in our hearts to once again value the stagewise development of children and youth. ■

David Elkind is a professor in the Eliot-Pearson department of child development at Tufts University in Medford, Mass. His books include The Hurried Child *(1981) and* Reinventing Childhood *(1998).*

struggle for integration

L ike a sharp knife slicing through the heart of 20th-century America, Brown v. Board of Education of Topeka *divides education in the past 100 years into two distinct eras. The decades before the U.S.* Supreme Court's historic 1954 ruling saw the creation and tenacious defense of a system of racial separation in public schools in the Southern and Border States.

That system, along with widespread but less formal segregation elsewhere, relegated millions of black children to an inferior education. The years since the Brown *decision record the often-bitter struggles to end segregation and to ensure a good public education for children of all races.*

A student steps off a school bus in Lamar, S.C., in 1970 as a National Guardsman looks on. The widespread adoption of mandatory busing for desegregation during the 1970s sparked protests and even violence in some communities.

Corbis-Bettmann

In Black and White

Though the *Brown* decision in 1954 opened the door to equal education for students of all races, desegregation continues to be a sharply disputed issue.

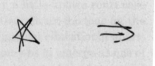

struggles of the next 100 years.

Pleading poverty, the Augusta school board had shut down the public high school for blacks. The city's African-American residents fought the move all the way to the nation's highest court. *Cumming* v. *Richmond County Board of Education*, as it was known, marked the first time the U.S. Supreme Court had directly confronted the issue of racial discrimination in the schools.

By Caroline Hendrie

Coming just three years after the famous 1896 ruling in *Plessy* v. *Ferguson*, which upheld a Louisiana law requiring "separate but equal" rail cars for blacks and whites, the Geor~~gia~~

~~schoolchildren deserved the same educa~~tional opportunities as anyone else.

But that was not to be. In a decision issued shortly before the new century dawned, the court instead affirmed Augusta's right to eliminate public secondary education for black children while maintaining it for whites.

The upshot, Harvard University desegregation scholar Gary A. Orfield says, was

that "within three years of *Plessy* it became apparent that the 'equal' part of 'separate but equal' would not be enforced."

For African-Americans, says J. Morgan Kousser, a historian at the California Institute of Technology, "it meant fairly clearly that the national door to equality in the schools was closed."

VICTORY PROVES ELUSIVE

That door, as it turned out, would stay shut for more than half a century.

In the intervening decades, racial separation and inequity were to become deeply embedded in the nation's developing public education system, despite the protections ostensibly afforded blacks in the post-Civil War amendments to the U.S. Constitution. This segregation was enforced by law in the Southern and Bor~~der states, and by circumstance and cus~~

~~schools unconstitutional—the obstacles to~~ acting on that principle seemed daunting. And the Supreme Court possessed no magic wand to wave them away.

As a result, the court chose simply to proclaim, as Richard Kluger writes in *Simple Justice*, his 1976 book on the *Brown* case, "that segregation was wrong." As for what to do about it, he adds, the court elected to "rely on the

best instincts of the American people to figure out how to eradicate the practice."

Nearly half a century later, whether the nation has yet figured out how to do that remains a matter of impassioned debate.

For some analysts, the job was essentially done when communities were forced to dismantle systems that required blacks, solely on the basis of race, to attend schools that were separate and usually inferior.

But for others, the goal was a much broader one: to ensure blacks and other minorities lasting access to a high-quality, integrated education that had been denied them for generations because of their color.

If judged by that broader standard, much of the public and many experts now believe that the campaign to desegregate the schools that unfolded haltingly and sometimes violently after the *Brown* decision has fallen far short of its goals.

The history of school segregation and desegregation in this century has been complicated by a lack of consensus on what those words mean.

"There are very many different definitions, and they have changed over time," notes David J. Armor, a research professor at George Mason University who helps districts win release from court-ordered desegregation plans.

At the heart of these evolving and often conflicting meanings has been a debate over what constitutes illegal segregation and what schools must do to remedy it.

Myriad related questions have arisen

as courts and communities have struggled to define and redefine desegregation:

• What is in the best interest of minority students—desegregation, integration, or equal educational opportunity—and just where do those objectives intersect?

• How do you know a desegregated school when you see it—by its overall racial balance, by the racial composition of classes and programs, by the relative achievement of students? By all of the above, or none?

• How far must systems go to erase the tangible and intangible effects of segregation and how should those effects be identified?

• Does remedying the harms of segregation of blacks or other minority groups justify racial distinctions that may disadvantage other groups?

• And how do you define desegregation as whites become scarce in many systems and constitute a smaller share of the increasingly diverse U.S. population?

Such questions have figured prominently in guiding politicians, educators, courts, and communities during the long struggle to integrate the nation's schools.

And they are helping shape the nation's response to a question that has become inevitable as the 20th century draws to a close: Where do we go from here?

CHALLENGE HAS DEEP ROOTS

From Colonial times until the early

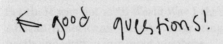

← good questions!

suffering educational discrimination, nor in protesting it. The first lawsuit directly challenging school segregation arose in Ohio in 1834, according to Kousser, a professor of history and social science at Caltech.

During the 19th century, nearly 100 court cases from 20 states and the District of Columbia challenged segregation or racial discrimination in schools. In the North, blacks won a majority of those cases, contributing to a wave of state laws, starting in 1855 with a Massachu-

When Augusta, Ga., shut down its all-black high school, many displaced students continued their educations at local private academies, such as the Paine Institute. The U.S. Supreme Court in 1899 affirmed the school board's right to deny secondary education to blacks in Cumming v. Richmond County Board of Education.

Courtesy of J. Morgan Kousser

orbis-Bettmann

Charles Hamilton Houston left his position as dean of the law school at Howard University in 1934 to fight racial discrimination with the NAACP. Above, in 1939, Houston appears before the board of education in the District of Columbia to protest the barring of black singer Marian Anderson from the auditorium of Central High School.

ington to attack racial discrimination for the NAACP on several fronts, including education.

Two years later, a former protégé of Houston's at Howard who had been essentially donating his services to the NAACP came on board full time. In Thurgood Marshall, the association gained a champion who would eventually lead it to historic victories in the Supreme Court, before himself breaking the color line on the court by becoming its first black justice.

From 1933 through World War II, the NAACP focused on two types of education lawsuits: challenging the exclusion of blacks from public graduate and professional schools, and attacking the practice of paying black public school teachers significantly less than their white counterparts.

In the late 1930s, those efforts began to pay off. In 1938, the Supreme Court found Missouri's failure to provide a law school for blacks unconstitutional, holding that the legitimacy of segregated institutions "rests wholly upon the equality" they offered the separated groups.

And in 1939, the high court let stand a ruling that struck down race-based differentials in teacher pay in a case from Norfolk, Va.

Despite those victories, inequities in graduate programs remained pervasive as the United States emerged from the Second World War. A sizable racial gap in teacher salaries in elementary and secondary schools also persisted in most Southern states.

"In the university cases, litigating equality in fact proved to be extremely time-consuming," writes Mark V. Tushnet in *The NAACP's Legal Strategy Against Segregated Education, 1925-1950.* "[I]n the salary cases, school boards developed methods of perpetuating unequal salaries for black and white teachers in which the criterion of race was submerged enough that successful attacks would be difficult."

setts law that prohibited segregation in public schools.

In the South, of course, matters were very different. Separate and unequal schools for whites and blacks—those lucky enough to attend school at all— were required by law throughout the first half of the 20th century.

In *An American Dilemma*, Gunnar Myrdal's landmark 1944 treatise on the plight of black Americans, the Swedish economist described the state of black public education in the South as marked "by miserably poor standards all around."

"[A] complete lack of schools in some rural areas, an insufficient number of schools in other areas, a grave lack of equipment, a lack of enforcement of the truancy laws for Negroes, an inferior quality of teacher training, [and] differential payment to teachers" were just some of the conditions he cited. "As a consequence, Negro children come out of their school system—both elementary and secondary—very poorly educated."

NAACP SETS THE STAGE

Around 1930, the National Association for the Advancement of Colored People, which had been founded in 1909, began laying the groundwork for what eventually would blossom into a multipronged legal attack on Jim Crow education.

In 1934, Charles Hamilton Houston left his position as the dean of the Howard University law school in Wash-

PRESSURE MOUNTS

Up through World War II, the NAACP had taken on few challenges to the unequal school facilities in the Southern and Border states. After the war, however, pressure to contest those conditions grew as African-American parents increasingly became fed up with worn-out textbooks and ramshackle schools.

Still, finding plaintiffs willing to bring such suits was difficult, and there were conflicting views on how to proceed. A critical issue was whether the NAACP Legal Defense and Educational Fund, which had been formed in 1939 to handle the association's litigation campaign, should lend support to the kind of suits that had occasionally succeeded in winning better facilities within the context of segregation. NAACP strategists generally insisted on challenging the dual system of educating blacks and whites rather than pleading for better—but still separate—facilities.

At midcentury, the NAACP reached a turning point.

In June 1950, the Supreme Court issued decisions in two university cases on the same day, one involving the state law school in Texas and the other concerning graduate education programs in Oklahoma. The court declined in both cases to overturn the separate-but-equal doctrine established by *Plessy*. But in finding the programs that states offered blacks unconstitutional, the justices stressed that it was not just physical resources but such intangible qualities as a school's reputation and a student's chances to interact with classmates that determined whether the education offered blacks was in fact equal.

Buoyed by those rulings, Marshall and his staff decided the time was finally ripe for "an all-out attack" on segregation, from kindergarten through college.

BATTLE IS JOINED

In the ensuing months, the battle opened on no fewer than five fronts.

Starting in early 1951, the NAACP coordinated lawsuits that directly challenged segregated schools in four states and the District of Columbia. By midsummer, lower-court judges had handed down rulings adverse to the plaintiffs in three of the cases: *Bolling* v. *Sharpe* in Washington; *Briggs* v. *Elliott* in Clarendon County, S.C.; and *Brown* v. *Board of Education* in Topeka, Kan. In March 1952, a three-judge panel followed suit in the Virginia case of *Davis* v. *School Board of Prince Edward County*.

Finally, the following month, fortune smiled on the NAACP with a ruling in a pair of companion suits in Delaware, the only place where the challenges proceeded in state court. In *Belton* v. *Gebhart* and *Bulah* v. *Gebhart*, Judge Collins Seitz ordered the plaintiffs admitted to

Their Day in Court

Selected U.S. Supreme Court rulings affecting school segregation:

■ 1896 *Plessy* v. *Ferguson*

Upholds an 1890 Louisiana law requiring railroads to provide "equal but separate accommodations for the white, and colored races," thereby sanctioning state-imposed segregation. The ruling becomes the key legal underpinning of racial segregation in the public schools.

■ 1899 *Cumming* v. *Richmond County Board of Education*

Rejects a bid by blacks to force the Augusta, Ga., schools to end secondary education for whites until the district restores it for blacks. The ruling, the first school segregation case to reach the high court, allows for wide disparities in the quality of education afforded blacks and whites in the South.

Corbis-Bettmann

Chief Justice Earl Warren wrote the high court's opinion in Brown.

■ 1908 *Berea College* v. *Kentucky*

Upholds a state law prohibiting integrated classes for blacks and whites, in a case brought by a private college with a tradition of mixed-race education.

■ 1927 *Gong Lum* v. *Rice*

Affirms a Mississippi district's right to require a Chinese-American girl to attend a segregated black school, rejecting her bid to attend the school for whites.

■ 1938 *Gaines* v. *Canada*

The first challenge to racial discrimination in graduate programs to reach the high court. Declares unconstitutional Missouri's failure to provide a law school for blacks. Establishes that the legitimacy of segregated institutions "rests wholly upon the equality" they offer the separated groups.

■ 1948 *Sipuel* v. *Board of Regents of the University of Oklahoma*

Citing the *Gaines* ruling, the court directs the state to provide a legal education to a black student denied entry to its all-white law school. The state slaps together a school for blacks, a response that the high court refuses to overturn.

■ 1950 *Sweatt* v. *Painter*

Finds that a hastily contrived law school for blacks in Texas is unconstitutionally inferior and orders the white law school to admit the black plaintiff. A decision issued the same day in *McLaurin* v. *Board of Regents of the University of Oklahoma* strikes down an elaborate set of rules physically segregating a black student from whites in a graduate education program. Citing harm caused by intangible as well as physical inequalities, the rulings prefigure the demise of state-sanctioned segregation.

■ 1954 *Brown* v. *Board of Education of Topeka*

Unanimously declares that segregating elementary and secondary students by race violates black children's constitutional right to equal protection of the laws. Seen by some scholars as the high court's most far-reaching ruling ever, the May 17 opinion arose from cases in four states (Delaware, Kansas, South Carolina, and Virginia). The same day, the court invalidates school segregation in the District of Columbia on the grounds that it violates black students' rights to due process. The court defers judgment on implementing its ruling.

■ 1955 *Brown* v. *Board of Education of Topeka*

Brown II orders districts in the original cases to make a "prompt and reasonable start toward full compliance." The ruling obligates local school authorities to overcome obstacles to desegregation "with all deliberate speed" and directs federal district judges to oversee the process. Also stresses that constitutional principles cannot be sacrificed "simply because of disagreement with them."

■ 1958 *Cooper* v. *Aaron*

Rejects a bid by the Little Rock, Ark., district to delay desegregation because of the upheaval surrounding the opening of its high school the year before to a handful of black students. "[L]aw and order are not here to be preserved by depriving the Negro children of their constitutional rights," the justices unanimously rule. Regarded as a blow to Southern resistance.

■ 1964 *Griffin* v. *Board of Education*

Rules that Prince Edward County, Va., one of the districts involved in *Brown*, can no longer avoid integration by keeping its public schools closed, as it had done since 1959. Also affirms a decision blocking tax breaks and tuition grants used to subsidize private schools for whites.

■ 1968 *Green* v. *New Kent County School Board*

Declares in a Virginia case that districts that operated "dual systems" for blacks and whites have a duty to eliminate racial discrimination "root and branch." Says districts must dismantle segregation in student assignment, faculty, facilities, staff, transportation, and extracurricular activities—which become the "Green factors" used by courts to gauge whether a district had met its obligations to desegregate.

■ 1969 *Alexander* v. *Board of Education*

Overturns an appeals court ruling that gave 33 Mississippi districts more time to come up with plans to desegregate. The unanimous ruling says districts must end their dual systems for blacks and whites "at once and to operate now and hereafter only unitary schools."

■ 1969 *United States* v. *Montgomery County Board of Education*

Upholds the use of numerical quotas for the racial balancing of school faculty in a case arising in Alabama.

■ 1971 *Swann* v. *Charlotte-Mecklenburg Board of Education*

Authorizes mandatory busing, redrawn attendance zones, and the limited use of racial-balance quotas as desegregation tools. Holds that individual schools need not reflect the districtwide racial balance but that districts bear the burden of proving that any one-race schools do not result from discrimination. In one of three related rulings issued the same day, the justices strike down a North Carolina anti-busing law that prohibited race-based student assignment .

■ 1972 *Wright* v. *Emporia City Council* and *United States* v. *Scotland Neck Board of Education*

In separate rulings issued the same day, the court rejects bids to carve out new school districts in Virginia and North Carolina. In both cases, the districts would have had enrollments with a greater ratio of white students than in the desegregating districts they were leaving.

■ 1973 *Keyes* v. *Denver School District No. 1*

The court holds a district liable for intentional segregation even though it had never required separate schools by law—extending the duty to desegregate beyond Southern and Border states. A majority also finds that discriminatory acts affecting some neighborhoods or schools create a legal presumption that the whole district should desegregate. The justices say Hispanics should be counted with blacks in determining whether a school is segregated.

white schools on the grounds that segregation as practiced in Delaware was unconstitutional.

"For the first time, a segregated white public school in America had been ordered by a court of law to admit black children," Kluger observes in *Simple Justice*.

Still, even Seitz stopped short of striking down segregation as such. Only the U.S. Supreme Court, he concluded, could overrule itself on that critical issue.

The chance to do that soon presented itself. Between June and November of 1952, the high court agreed to hear appeals in all five of the cases. The four state cases became known collectively as *Brown* v. *Board of Education*, which took its name from Oliver Brown, the lead Topeka plaintiff, who sued on behalf of his daughter Linda.

Following oral arguments in December 1952, it was clear that the justices were anything but united on whether to take the momentous step of overturning *Plessy*. So they deferred a decision, directing both sides in June 1953 to prepare for a second round of arguments in the fall.

In the interim, President Dwight D. Eisenhower named Gov. Earl Warren of California to take over as chief justice after the death of Fred Vinson Jr. The new chief justice was to succeed where his predecessor had failed in forging consensus on a fractured court.

On May 17, 1954, after hearing rearguments the previous December, Warren announced the court's unanimous opinion.

In the four state cases, the right of black children to equal protection of the laws, enshrined in the 14th Amendment in 1868, was violated by segregated public schools. And in the District of Columbia, which did not fall under the equal-protection clause, such schools violated the right to liberty guaranteed by the due-process clause of the 5th Amendment.

Citing the court's 1950 decisions in the university cases, the *Brown* opinion held that the intangible deprivations of opportunity arising from segregation at the graduate school level applied "with added force to children in grade and high schools."

"To separate them from others of similar age and qualifications solely because of their race," the ruling stated, "generates a feeling of inferiority as to their status in the community that may affect their hearts and minds in a way unlikely to ever be undone. . . . We conclude that in the field of public education the doctrine of 'separate but equal' has no place. Sep-

Corbis-Bettmann

John W. Davis and
Thurgood Marshall
squared off in the 1952
and 1953 arguments
that led to the Brown
ruling.

arate educational facilities are inherently unequal."

'ALL DELIBERATE SPEED'

The door to equality had swung open.

But left hanging by the celebrated decision was the question of exactly how the thousands of school systems that separated children by race were to go about bringing them together.

Before answering it, the Supreme Court asked for another round of arguments. Finally, a year and two weeks after the opinion that has come to be known as *Brown I*, the justices issued a decision that cast aside the NAACP's plea for a one-year implementation deadline. Instead, they sent the cases back to lower courts with instructions to require the defendants to admit the plaintiffs "to public schools on a racially nondiscriminatory basis with all deliberate speed."

The lower courts were authorized to consider communities' desires to proceed "in a systematic and effective manner," but not to allow disagreement with its ruling to excuse inaction.

While the justices failed to specify in *Brown II* just what they meant by nondiscrimination, the NAACP at the time described it as the elimination of all considerations of color in the operation of the schools. In time, however, the organization's views, as well as those of subsequent Supreme Courts, were to change as it became clear that policies that were color-blind on their face could in fact per-

petuate segregation.

Today, in the twilight of the legal crusade to desegregate schools, whether the *Brown* rulings should be read as outlawing race-conscious school policies, or as in fact requiring them to achieve racial bal-

← an enduring question

In the 21 states that allowed or required segregated schools, the *Brown* decisions were greeted with a mixture of alarm, disdain, resistance, and grudging compliance. In general, the backlash was mildest in the Border states, where some communities made a quick start at desegregating schools. Deep in the heart of Dixie, it was a different story.

The spirit of what was called "massive resistance" in such states was captured in a "Southern Manifesto" issued by a majority of the region's congressional delegation in 1956. In it, the legislators pledged "to resist enforced integration by any lawful means." States also passed anti-integration laws that took such actions as denying public money to integrated schools and erecting barriers to black students hoping to transfer to white schools.

A showdown came in Little Rock, Ark., in September 1957, when Gov. Orval Faubus dispatched the National Guard to the city's Central High School to prevent enrollment of a handful of black students.

After a meeting with Eisenhower, Faubus relented. But three weeks later,

■ 1974 *Milliken* v. *Bradley*

In the first major curb on the expansion of desegregation, the 5-4 ruling strikes down a plan to merge the Detroit schools with 53 largely white suburban districts. Cites a lack of evidence that those districts were guilty of intentional segregation and orders a new plan confined to the city, where enrollment was more than two-thirds black. Makes it harder for courts to order city-suburban desegregation plans to counteract the concentration of minorities in the cities.

■ 1976 *Pasadena City Board of Education* v. *Spangler*

Reverses a ruling requiring this California district to adjust attendance zones annually to preserve court-ordered racial ratios. A lower court had ordered that no school have a majority of any minority group, a directive with which the district fell out of compliance after one year.

■ 1977 *Milliken* v. *Bradley*

Authorizes courts to require remedial education programs as an antidote to past segregation, in a decision known as *Milliken II*. Upholds a ruling directing Detroit and Michigan to split the cost of programs in four areas: reading, in-service teacher training, student testing, and counseling. Opens the door to broader use of remedial programs and extra funding for racially isolated schools.

■ 1979 *Columbus Board of Education* v. *Penick* and *Dayton Board of Education* v. *Brinkman*

Upholds mandatory busing in two districts in Ohio, saying school officials had perpetuated segregation, to varying degrees, by their actions and inaction since the *Brown* decision. In dissent, future Chief Justice William H. Rehnquist says the rulings so blur the line between *de jure* and *de facto* segregation that the only way urban districts could avoid court-ordered busing, given residential segregation, was to get rid of neighborhood schools.

■ 1982 *Washington* v. *Seattle School District No. 1*

Strikes down a state anti-busing initiative passed by voters after Seattle voluntarily adopted a desegregation plan involving extensive cross-town busing.

■ 1982 *Crawford* v. *Board of Education*

Upholds an amendment to California's constitution that prohibited state judges from ordering busing for integration in the absence of a violation of the U.S. Constitution. The amendment followed a state supreme court order requiring Los Angeles to desegregate on the grounds that it was obligated under the state constitution to attack *de facto* segregation.

■ 1991 *Board of Education of Oklahoma City* v. *Dowell*

Stressing that court orders to desegregate were designed to be temporary, the ruling says federal judges should lift such decrees if districts have complied with them in good faith and remedied past discrimination "as far as practicable." Court allows the district to return to neighborhood schools.

■ 1992 *Freeman* v. *Pitts*

Authorizes courts to relinquish supervision over some aspects of a district's desegregation-related obligations, such as extracurricular activities, while retaining it in others. Also grants judges leeway to consider issues beyond the "Green factors" in assessing whether districts should be declared unitary.

■ 1995 *Missouri* v. *Jenkins*

Says a Kansas City magnet school plan aimed at luring whites amounts to judicial overreaching. The 5-4 ruling says neither the goal of attracting whites nor substandard test scores in the city justifies the plan. Justice Clarence Thomas, the court's only African-American, says in concurrence that the plan reflects an assumption "that anything that is predominantly black must be inferior."

pro-segregation protesters battled police outside the school. The president promptly federalized the state's National Guard and sent in additional troops to restore order.

If Little Rock showed Washington's willingness to wield a stick to squelch resistance to desegregation, a development some eight years later demonstrated the value of using a carrot.

In 1965, Congress passed the Elementary and Secondary Education Act, providing the first federal aid program for local school districts. Because the Civil Rights Act of 1964 had barred racial discrimination in programs receiving federal funds, the law suddenly provided a powerful incentive for complying with *Brown*.

"Schools were faced with the threat of not getting the money," Tushnet says. "So they capitulated and started genuine desegregation."

REAL PROGRESS DEMANDED

Into the 1960s, the Southern courts and communities inclined to comply with *Brown* generally had interpreted the ruling as demanding little more than lifting explicit policies that required separate schools.

In the absence of clear-cut guidelines from the high court, districts tended either to adopt "freedom of choice" plans allowing biracial enrollments or to draw neighborhood school boundaries that encompassed both black and white students. In reality, such plans afforded little genuine integration, as most students stayed in schools where their race predominated.

In 1968, the Supreme Court for the first time explicitly stated that the test of a school district's desegregation plan was its effectiveness at producing mixed-race schools.

In a Virginia case, *Green* v. *New Kent County School Board*, the justices held that formerly segregated systems have an affirmative duty to eliminate racial discrimination "root and branch." And the duty applied not only to enrollment, but also to faculty, staff, transportation, extracurricular activities, and facilities. Those soon became known as the six "Green factors," and were later used by courts to gauge whether a district had met its obligations to desegregate.

Three years later, the court took its mandate for affirmative integration a giant step further in a case from Charlotte, N.C.

Noting that lower courts had proceeded largely by "trial and error" since *Brown*, the court set out in *Swann* v. *Charlotte-Mecklenburg Board of Education* to provide more specific guidelines. The result was an endorsement of aggressive steps to overcome the residential segregation so common in urban areas, including cross-county busing, redrawn attendance zones, and pairing of city and suburban schools.

In upholding busing, which was highly unpopular politically, the justices concluded that the ban on court-ordered busing in the Civil Rights Act of 1964 did not apply in cases of former state-imposed segregation. "Desegregation cannot be limited to the walk-in school," the court held.

In *Swann*, the court also authorized racial quotas for student assignment, though the decision said such quotas should be considered a starting point and not rigid requirements. It also held that not every school had to reflect the districtwide racial mix or adjust its ratios annually to offset demographic changes.

Despite the latter qualifications, the message *Swann* sent was that school systems must achieve as much racial mixing as possible and that busing was an important tool for achieving that goal. The ruling set off a wave of busing plans throughout the South. In many cases these plans fueled white flight from core cities. But they also yielded greater racial mixing in many Southern schools.

DIVIDING LINE BLURS

Starting with the *Brown* decision, the Supreme Court consistently distinguished between segregation due to a law or other official act—*de jure* segregation—and the *de facto* segregation arising from forces that are ostensibly beyond school system's control, such as private housing choices. And it held that only the former is forbidden.

But in the years after the *Swann* ruling, the line between the two began to blur.

An important step in that process came in 1973, when the Supreme Court for the first time extended the duty to desegregate to a district outside the Southern and Border states where schools had not been segregated by law.

Though Denver had never had an official policy of separating the races, the court found in *Keyes* v. *Denver School District* that the Colorado district was nevertheless guilty of *de jure* segregation. Because school officials had taken steps over the years that contributed to the isolation of blacks in some schools, the court held that the whole district should desegregate.

> "Schools were faced with the threat of not getting the ⟨...⟩ desegregation."

Mark V. Tushnet

Author of *The NAACP's Legal Strategy Against Segregated Education, 1925-1950*

White students block the school doors in Little Rock, Ark., in 1957.

AP/Wide World

"While the *Keyes* decision left the *de facto-de jure* distinction alive in theory, it had much less practical significance," Armor writes in *Forced Justice,* his 1995 book on desegregation law, "because few school districts at that time could meet a burden of proving that they had not contributed to housing segregation or had not intentionally adopted a neighborhood school policy."

As the *Keyes* decision opened the door to court-ordered desegregation outside the South, it soon became clear that Northern communities could be just as unwelcoming as their Southern counterparts.

In Boston, a federal judge's busing order in June 1974 turned some neighborhoods—and their schools—into battlegrounds. The turmoil and violence included assaults on busloads of black children by rioting rock-throwers, in-school stabbings, and clashes between police and protesters of both races. The exodus of whites from the city school system in the mid-1970s has never been reversed.

A Turning Point in Detroit

The same year that Judge W. Arthur Garrity Jr. handed down the Boston ruling that so enraged anti-busing forces, the Supreme Court delivered the integration movement its first major setback since the pre-*Brown* era. By a vote of 5 to 4, which revealed an enduring philosophical split on the court, the justices in *Milliken* v. *Bradley* struck down a plan to merge the Detroit schools with 53 largely white suburban districts.

Holding that "school district lines may not be casually ignored or treated as a mere administrative convenience," the court ordered a new plan confined to the city, where student enrollment was by then more than two-thirds black.

The district responded with a plan that featured partially state-funded compensatory programs for students in overwhelmingly black schools. In 1977, the Supreme Court upheld the plan, prompting broader use around the country of remedial programs and extra funding for racially isolated schools as a remedy for illegal segregation.

In a strongly worded dissent, Justice Marshall predicted that the nation would ultimately regret allowing "our great metropolitan areas to be divided up each into two cities—one white, the other black."

Integration advocates have concluded that the ruling had precisely this effect,

Challenging the U.S. Conscience

By Caroline Hendrie

As the United States waged war in Europe against fascism, a leading European intellectual issued a clarion call for America to mount a similar battle on the homefront: a crusade against racism. Published in 1944, Gunnar Myrdal's *An American Dilemma: The Negro Problem and Modern Democracy* was never a best seller. But its influence on U.S. opinion-makers was profound.

By underscoring the contradiction between American democratic ideals and their betrayal by the accepted realities of racial segregation and subordination, the book represented a forceful challenge to the national conscience.

"Its very size, range, and completeness made its findings seem almost inarguable," writes Richard Kluger in *Simple Justice*, his 1976 history of the struggle against school segregation that culminated in *Brown* v. *Board of Education.*

Coming a decade before the Supreme Court's historic 1954 decision, the book became instant fodder for the lawyers from the NAACP Legal Defense and Educational Fund who were chipping away at state-sanctioned segregation. And that the high court took notice of it was undeniable: *An American Dilemma* was one of a handful of social science works cited by the justices in a famous footnote to the *Brown* decision supporting their conclusion that segregation damaged black schoolchildren.

An American Dilemma was the product of a two-year research study commissioned by the Carnegie Corporation of New York and overseen by Myrdal, a Swedish academic who went on to win the 1974 Nobel Prize in economics. Dozens of researchers contributed to the project, and Myrdal received substantial writing assis-

by making it far harder to address segregation in the many metropolitan areas where blacks and other minorities are concentrated in cities and whites in the suburbs.

"Rejection of city-suburban desegregation brought an end to the period of rapidly increasing school desegregation," Orfield writes in his 1996 book *Dismantling Desegregation.* And because it "slammed the door on the only possible desegregation strategy for cities with few whites," Orfield argues, "it shifted the attention of urban educators and civil rights lawyers away from desegregation and toward other approaches for helping minority children confined to segregated and inferior city schools."

courts, the social sciences, and the politi-cal arena have pushed desegregation policy in a number of new directions.

Desegregation cases continued to be filed and won in communities across the country well into the 1980s. But at the same time, desegregation plans that had been adopted years earlier were modified in many districts, often to de-emphasize compulsory busing in favor of voluntary options such as magnet schools and "controlled choice." These trends were fueled by evidence that desegregation was contributing to white flight and thereby frustrating efforts to achieve racial balance.

Segregation within schools, rather than between them, also emerged as a problem. Black students and other minority youngsters attending schools that were racially balanced overall routinely found themselves in less challenging courses.

Meanwhile, many districts that had ted desegregating years earlier saw r cases wind down, and in some in-ces end altogether.

s districts sought an end to court rsight, educators and judges were ed to grapple with questions that had persisted since *Brown*: What standards should be used to determine whether a

tance from two close collaborators. The result was exhaustive analysis that surveyed the social, political, educational, and economic plight of African-Americans, with special emphasis on the South.

'VICIOUS CIRCLE' OF BIAS

Myrdal concluded that blacks were victims of a caste system that had been perpetuated since slavery by a "vicious circle" of discrimination.

"White prejudice and discrimination keep the Negro low in standards of living, health, education, manners, and morals," Myrdal argued in the book. "This, in turn, gives support to white prejudice. White prejudice and Negro standards thus mutually 'cause' each other."

But as he surveyed America a decade before *Brown*, Myrdal saw unmistakable signs of change. As World War II rekindled the nation's pride in its democratic traditions, he predicted that the "American creed"—a deep belief in equality, freedom, justice, and opportunity—

Corbis-Bettmann

would triumph over racial bigotry in a generation.

Myrdal, who died in 1987, came to see his prediction as overoptimistic. But 30 years after *An American Dilemma*'s publication, he regarded the "great progress" that had been made as evidence that America was moving "in the right direction" to solve its great dilemma. ■

In 1944, Gunnar Myrdal published An American Dilemma, *a book based on a two-year research project looking at the conditions under which African-Americans lived in the United States.*

district is free of discrimination? And how should districts maintain racial balance once a court has declared them "unitary," a legal term meaning they have eradicated the dual system of black-white schooling?

In 1976, the Supreme Court addressed the latter question in a ruling that suggested that achieving racial balance was more of a temporary obligation than a perennial one. In *Pasadena City Board of Education* v. *Spangler*, the court held that the California district did not need to readjust its attendance zones each year to preserve court-ordered racial ratios.

WHEN TO CALL IT QUITS

Whether schools should be required to maintain racial balance indefinitely emerged as a central issue in several high-profile cases during the 1980s.

In 1986, for example, the Supreme Court let stand a ruling that allowed Norfolk to return to neighborhood elementary schools after being declared unitary,

even though it meant that some schools in the southeastern Virginia city would become overwhelmingly black. In Austin, Texas, a federal appeals court permitted a similar move, rejecting the argument that the restoration of neighborhood schools was discriminatory.

But in Oklahoma City, an appeals court blocked the district's plan to reinstitute neighborhood schools, many of which would have been more segregated. That case yielded a major Supreme Court ruling in 1991 that gave new guidance to lower courts on the issues of unitary status and districts' continuing obligations after achieving it.

In *Board of Education of Oklahoma City* v. *Dowell*, the high court gave its blessing to the return to neighborhood schools, stressing that desegregation decrees were designed to be temporary. And it established two new criteria for deciding when such orders should be ended: whether the district has complied in good faith, and whether it has remedied past discrimination "as far as practicable."

As one of three dissenting justices,

Thurgood Marshall argued that desegregation orders should remain in effect so long as "any condition that perpetuates the message of racial inferiority" persists, including racially imbalanced schools. It was his last word in a school segregation case before retiring from the bench. Exactly 40 years had passed since he had launched the historic lawsuits intended to abolish segregated schooling forever.

COURT'S ROLE DECLINING

Since *Dowell*, two more Supreme Court decisions have echoed its message that the federal courts are getting out of the business of desegregating schools. In 1992, the justices in *Freeman* v. *Pitts* warned against overstating the consequences of "past wrongs to the black race." In that case from DeKalb County, Ga., they argued that the causes of segregation—including demographic change—may be beyond the reach of the courts, and that restoring local control of the schools is of utmost importance.

Then, in 1995, a divided court decreed in *Missouri* v. *Jenkins* that a judge had gone too far in ordering an ambitious desegregation plan in Kansas City, Mo., designed to woo suburban whites to inner-city magnet schools.

The majority labeled the plan an end run around the ban on unjustified inter-

The ruling was a big win for Missouri, which had been found jointly liable for segregation in the city schools and had been footing much of the bill for the plan for a decade. It set in motion the state's recent exit from its desegregation obligations in Kansas City and a broad scaling-back of the unusually extensive magnet program there.

The *Jenkins* decision marked the first and only time Justice Clarence Thomas has participated in ... brand predominantly black schools inferior, Thomas urged abandonment of the view that "blacks cannot succeed without the benefit of the company of whites."

"Given that desegregation has not produced the predicted leaps forward in black educational achievement, there is no reason to think that black students cannot learn as well when surrounded by members of their own race as when they are in an integrated environment," he wrote. "[B]lack schools can function as the center and symbol of black communities, and provide examples of independent black leadership, success, and achievement."

DISILLUSIONMENT ABOUNDS

Such views are nothing new. Ever since the NAACP took aim at segregation, there have been strong African-American voices in favor of seeking educational excellence for black schools rather than integration with whites.

Once desegregation was under way, moreover, the debate resurfaced.

Starting in the mid-1970s, a schism has existed in the social science community—as well as the political arena—over whether desegregation has been as beneficial as its proponents suggest in such areas as student achievement and reduction of racial prejudice.

This division has coincided with the perception among many blacks that they paid too high a price for desegregation. After all, it has often meant the busing of black children out of their neighborhoods at a younger age, in greater numbers, and for longer periods of time than white children.

A poll of black and white parents released in 1998 by Public Agenda and the Public Education Network found that eight in 10 black parents considered it important that their children's schools be racially integrated, as did nearly seven in 10 white parents.

But 68 percent of the black parents polled said the nation had pursued the goal of integration in the wrong way, and just 55 percent supported busing to achieve better racial balance. Nearly three-quarters said schools had neglected instructional quality in the quest for integration.

Scholars debate the reasons for such mixed feelings toward desegregation. The education historian Diane Ravitch, for one, views the multiplicity of views as evidence "not of a dissolution of the movement for black equality but of the success of the social revolution initiated by the *Brown* decision."

But the Harvard University sociologist Charles V. Willie takes a dimmer view.

"Blacks have been betrayed," he says. "Whites took the concept of integration and hijacked it. Furthermore, they dropped the educational components that blacks had assumed would go hand in hand with integration. It was like turning to the fox that had been caught stealing the chickens and then saying, 'Fox, develop a plan to secure the chicken house.' "

SUCCESSES AND FRUSTRATIONS

Mr. Willie's disappointment is shared by many.

"The century-long perspective is that there was a struggle to achieve integrated schools, and it has ended without integration having been achieved," says Tushnet, a constitutional historian at Georgetown University and a former law clerk to Justice Marshall. "It's been

Benjamin Tice Smith

Corbis-Bettmann

essentially a failure."

Like Tushnet, Theodore M. Shaw of the NAACP Legal Defense and Educational Fund sees the relevance of school desegregation receding in the political, legal, and educational realms.

"I think most people, regardless of race, do not think of desegregation as an important goal," says Shaw, the defense fund's associate director-counsel. "It's thought of as being a '60s-type, touchy-feely, somewhat naive, liberal sentiment, but it doesn't have any real place in the hard reality of the '90s. And I think that that's a shame."

Indisputably, African-Americans as a whole are better off educationally at century's end than in 1900. Yet scholars and educators disagree over how much of their gains can be attributed to desegregation. And as the stubborn achievement gap between black and white students underscores, in many respects they still have a long way to go.

Still, some who survey the distance between principle and practice say the story cannot end here.

Efforts to make the ideals of *Brown* a reality may have been thwarted and gone awry, they believe, but that doesn't mean such attempts should be abandoned.

There remain plenty of successes to celebrate—such as the archipelago of sparkling magnet schools that dot the nation's cities—and it is these triumphs that many integration advocates believe should be showcased and replicated.

If not, they predict, the nation may well lose the progress it has achieved and slide back toward a more segregated and unequal tomorrow.

"In American race relations, the bridge from the 20th century may be leading back into the 19th century," warned a 1997 report on school resegregation by the Harvard Project on School Desegregation, headed by Orfield. "There is no evidence that separate but equal today works any more than it did a century ago." ■

South Boston (Mass.) High School in September 1974.

Left: Theodore M. Shaw of the NAACP Legal Defense and Educational Fund speaks with reporters outside the U.S. Supreme Court in 1995. Shaw was representing Kansas City children in a desegregation case before the court.

Beyond the Common Battleground

I t takes just one look at the San Francisco schools to see that desegregation reaches far beyond black and white.

The city district made national headlines in 1999 after agreeing to stop using race and ethnicity in assigning students to schools.

The tentative deal is an effort to settle a 1994 lawsuit brought by Chinese-American students and their parents to get out from under a 1983 racial-balance plan championed by the city's African-American community.

By Lynn Schnaiberg

While the groups may disagree about the best way to keep the schools free of discrimination, it's clear that both have long struggled with desegregation issues.

Beginning in the late 19th century, San Francisco's Chinese-American community pushed for the right to attend the same schools as whites, rather than separate schools for "Mongolians."

A MULTIRACIAL ISSUE

And in places like Minneapolis, communities are trying to find a multiracial solution to a multiracial problem. In that Midwestern city, a racially mixed group is negotiating with the state over two lawsuits, one filed in 1995 by the NAACP, the other in 1998 by a group of Hmong and Hispanic parents. The suits charge that state and Minneapolis-district policies have segregated students by race and socioeconomic status, denying them an adequate education.

"Policymakers here clearly recognize it's no longer just a black-white issue," says John Shulman, a lawyer for the local chapter of the National Association for the Advancement of Colored People.

Throughout the century, Hispanics, Asian-Americans, and American Indians have fought for equal treatment in the nation's schools. Where the South historically has been ground zero for black-white segregation, for Asian-Americans, it has been the West, especially California; for Hispanics, particularly Mexican-Americans, the Southwest has served as the central battleground.

Those battles have not produced a long roster of U.S. Supreme Court decisions; most were decided in lower courts.

And though segregation of Asian-Americans and American Indians was enforced by law in some places, for Mexican-Americans it was usually by local circumstance and custom and was rarely uniformly applied, historians say.

BEYOND THE *BROWN* CASE

Mexican-Americans were successful in court battles to strike down school segregation in Arizona, California, and Texas even before the Supreme Court declared it unconstitutional in the 1954 *Brown* v. *Board of Education* ruling.

Often, school officials argued that Mexican-Americans, a large presence in states along the border between the United States and Mexico since the turn of the century, had to be taught in separate schools or classrooms because of their limited English skills and intermittent school attendance as the children of migrant workers.

Hispanics had moved from the "other white" category in court cases in the 1940s into a distinct minority group with a pattern of past discrimination, like African-Americans, by the 1970s. Unlike blacks, however, Hispanics today tend to be viewed as an ethnic group that includes individuals of various r

In California's landmark *Westminster School District* can-American parents in 19 that their children and other descent" in a number of Orange districts were segregated in violation of the U.S. Constitution's promise of equal protection. No state law specifically required or permitted local districts to mandate separate "Mexican" schools, they said; state segregation laws applied only to "nonwhite" races.

U.S. District Judge Paul J. McCormick agreed in a 1946 decision in favor of the parents. Upheld by the appeals court a year later, *Mendez* marked the end of *de jure* segregation in California and became a catalyst for school desegregation rulings across the Southwest.

In Texas, for example, historians say *Mendez* influenced a federal district court ruling in 1948 in *Delgado* v. *Bastrop* that marked the beginning of the end of legal school segregation.

More than 20 years later, how Hispanics would be viewed in the eyes of the courts took center stage in the federal district case *Cisneros* v. *Corpus Christi Independent School District*. The court was asked to apply the principles of *Brown*, which meant treating Mexican-American students for desegregation purposes as a separate, identifiable minority group. For the first time, in 1970, a court officially agreed.

Guadalupe San Miguel Jr., a history professor at the University of Houston, says that the *Cisneros* ruling "introduced a new group into the national desegregation process." Federal courts now had to consider Mexican-American students in determining whether a school system was "unitary"—freed of vestiges of past discrimination.

But conflicting federal appeals court rulings pushed the issue to the Supreme Court in *Keyes* v. *Denver School District No. 1*. In a case originally filed by blacks in Denver, the high court in 1973 affirmed that Hispanics should be counted with blacks in determining whether a school was segregated.

Even as civil rights leaders hailed *Keyes* as a victory, Hispanic advocacy groups began turning away from the courts and desegregation battles and began looking to state legislatures—and bilingual education—for remedies for educational inequality, San Miguel says.

At the end of the 20th century, desegregation scholars such as Harvard University's Gary A. Orfield say that while historic progress made by blacks toward integration is slowly eroding, even more dramatic is the rising segregation of the nation's fast-growing Hispanic population.

SCHOOLING FOR ASIAN-AMERICANS

Throughout the 19th and 20th centuries, the United States sometimes banned, other times simply restricted, immigration from Asia. Most Asians who made it to the United States in the first half of the century landed on the West Coast, many of them settling in California, especially San Francisco. And they were not always made to feel welcome.

In the 1976 book *All Deliberate Speed*, Charles Wollenberg describes a study of San Francisco's Chinatown launched by city officials in 1885 at a time of "anti-coolie" sentiment. They concluded that although many of the 722 children living there were American-born, the public schools should be closed to them to "defend ourselves from this invasion of

Duane Braley/Star Tribune

Mongolian barbarism."

In the same year as the study, the California Supreme Court upheld a lower court's finding that San Francisco had no legal basis for excluding Chinese students. But days later, the legislature passed a law allowing districts to establish separate schools for "Mongolians." San Francisco and other communities did exactly that, though in some places small numbers of Chinese went to racially mixed schools, and even in San Francisco, segregation policies were applied unevenly.

Unlike the Chinese experience, California's Japanese attended regular public schools at the turn of the century. In 1906, when San Francisco officials told Japanese students to attend the separate Chinese school, Japanese families filed suit. After intervention by the federal government, which wanted to avoid a diplomatic crisis with Japan, San Francisco agreed to drop its segregation policy.

By 1910, about 41,000 of the nation's 72,000 Japanese lived in California. After a new phase of anti-Japanese sentiment emerged amid the nativism of the World War I period, the California legislature in 1921 gave districts the authority to segregate the Japanese. But some historians suggest that relatively few

districts actually set up separate schools.

The most dramatic school segregation of Japanese-American students, however, came at the hands of the U.S. government, not California lawmakers. Two months after the United States declared war on Japan on Dec. 8, 1941, the federal government moved 110,000 Japanese-Americans from the West Coast into detention camps. Almost overnight, the government had to educate more than 25,000 Japanese-American children, setting up tar-paper schools behind barbed wire.

When the camps shut down in 1945 as World War II ended, Japanese-American children returned to integrated schools.

In 1947, with the appellate court ruling in *Mendez*, *de jure* segregation in California formally came to an end, though historians say it had fizzled out for Asian-Americans earlier.

But the 1994 case brought by Chinese-Americans in San Francisco shows that Asian-Americans continue today as part of the desegregation debate. And though study of Asian-American school segregation centers on California, the 1927 Supreme Court ruling in *Gong Lum* v. *Rice* is an early instance in which the issue surfaced elsewhere. In that case, the high court affirmed a Mississippi district's right to require a Chinese-

Protesters dance and beat drums to disrupt a Minneapolis school board meeting in March 1998 over what was being called a return to racial segregation in the district's schools. Such protests continued at board meetings throughout the spring; police were called to maintain order at a session in late May 1998.

In 1921, the California legislature gave school districts the right to segregate Japanese-American students in a period of growing nativism in the United States. That sentiment continued to grow, and just two years later, a Hollywood residents' group began a campaign to force Japanese from the

American girl to attend a segregated black school, rejecting her bid to attend the school for whites.

BIRTH OF THE BIA SCHOOLS

Over the century, the task of educating American Indian children gradually has shifted from the federal government to the states. In part because many districts refused to admit Native American children early in the century, the U.S. government set up schools for them through the Bureau of Indian Affairs.

In *Piper* v. *Big Pine* in 1924, the California Supreme Court established the right of Indian children to be admitted to state-supported rather than federal schools, ruling in favor of a 15-year-old Indian girl's right to attend her local public school. Although the court didn't challenge the "separate but equal" doctrine, the *Piper* decision didn't result in large numbers of segregated public schools for Indians, according to Wollenberg.

Gradually, by offering financial incentives, the federal government persuaded districts to accept Native Americans in regular, integrated schools. In 1935, California stripped its school code of the authority to segregate American Indians born in the United States.

As a result of shifting federal policy, the 1950s marked a major migration of Indians from rural and reservation areas to urban centers and their schools. American Indians have been active in desegregation efforts in such cities as Minneapolis.

But in general, says William Demmert, an associate professor of education at Western Washington University, the Indian community tends not to see the BIA school system as racially segregated. Instead, he says, it is viewed as a political arrangement, based on the unique relationship between sovereign tribes and the federal government.

And some experts have argued that desegregation plans in the regular public schools only exacerbate Indian students' isolation.

"They know if they scatter into the public school system, the schools are not prepared to serve their needs," Demmert says. "And until they are, many see a continuation of the bureau schools as vital." ■

Corbis-Bettmann

Echoes of the Coleman Report

With little fanfare, President Lyndon B. Johnson's Department of Health, Education, and Welfare released a two-volume report on July 2, 1966. That report, *Equality of Educational Opportunity*, is now widely regarded as the most important education study of the 20th century.

"I don't think there's anything close to it," says Albert Beaton, who helped analyze the report and its surveys of 570,000 students and 60,000 teachers as a researcher for the Educational Testing Service. "It changed the way we thought about the whole issue of equality of educational opportunity," says Beaton, a professor of education at Boston College and the director of its Center on Testing.

By David J. Hoff

Instead of proving that the quality of schools was the most important factor in a student's academic success—as its sponsors had expected—the report written by the sociologist James S. Coleman of Johns Hopkins University found that a child's family background and the school's socioeconomic makeup were the best predictors.

Civil rights advocates were skeptical of the data at first because the report's official summary suggested that the data showed schools had no effect on achievement, says William L. Taylor, a noted school desegregation lawyer who was the staff director of the U.S. Commission on Civil Rights in 1966.

A better summary of the findings, from Gordon M. Ambach's perspective, is: Family and socioeconomic backgrounds are so important that it's difficult for schools to overcome them.

Ambach, now the executive director of the Council of Chief State School Officers, participated in a Harvard University project that reviewed Coleman's data for three years after their release.

Eventually, social scientists and civil rights leaders found pieces of the Coleman Report that supported their beliefs. Frederick Mosteller and future U.S. Sen. Daniel P. Moynihan, the Harvard professors who led the review project, wrote in a 1973 book that their analysis of the Coleman Report found that desegregation would help "somewhat" in raising achievement. But they also recommended welfare programs to supplement poor families' income.

Civil rights champions also discovered similar data when they reanalyzed the report, Taylor says. "The data ... supported the notion that racial isolation was harmful," he says of the civil rights commission's 1967 review of what is commonly called the Coleman Report. "The part of it that troubled civil rights groups the most was the idea the schools don't matter."

Coleman also found that:

• American schools of the 1960s were thoroughly segregated, regardless of region. Eighty percent of white students attended schools that were at least 90 percent white, while 65 percent of black children went to schools that were at least 90 percent black.

• African-American children's achievement levels were lower than their white peers' from the start, with the gap growing throughout their school careers.

• Per-pupil spending accounted for a negligible difference in student achievement, and school facilities had little impact.

Coleman, who later moved to the University of Chicago and who died in 1995, noted in a 1975 report that school desegregation encouraged "white flight" from cities and failed to integrate schools. In a controversial study in the 1980s, he concluded that Roman Catholic schools do a better job teaching than public schools do.

Echoes of the Coleman Report could still be seen in research some 30 years later. For example, a 1997 evaluation of the federal Chapter 1 program—now called Title I—reiterated the finding that a school's socioeconomic background is a strong determinant of its students' achievement.

The study, conducted by Abt Associates under a contract with the U.S. Department of Education, found that children from high- and middle-income homes were also at a disadvantage if they attended schools populated predominantly by low-income children.

Yet, the lasting impact of the Coleman Report may be its focus on student achievement, Mosteller and Moynihan wrote in 1973: "Henceforth no study of the quality of education or the equality of educational opportunity can hope to be taken seriously unless it deals with educational achievement or other accomplishment as the principal measure of educational quality." ∎

Corbis-Bettmann

More than 30 years ago, sociologist James S. Coleman found that family background and a school's socioeconomic makeup are the best predictors of a student's academic success. The Coleman Report is now widely considered the most important education study of the 20th century.

Years of Entrenched Inequality

Growing up in Tulsa, Okla., in the 1920s, the historian John Hope Franklin attended the city's "separate schools." As cut off as he was from his white peers, though, Franklin was by no means unaware of how his segregated schools stacked up.

For student productions requiring a sizable stage, he remembers, youngsters from his all-black high school sometimes borrowed the white school's auditorium. At those times, the disparities in the two facilities were on full display.

"It was not at all ambiguous to me," says Franklin, a professor emeritus at Duke University and the chairman of the advisory board for President Clinton's Initiative on Race. "I knew we were disadvantaged. I felt it."

By Caroline Hendrie

For at least half a century, the better part of America's black students experienced a similar feeling.

Throughout the Southern and Border states, the schools reserved for blacks were impoverished cousins in an educational family that itself was none too prosperous. As a whole, the region's educational system fared poorly in most national comparisons, but its black schools fared far worse than the rest.

"The system of segregation, far from being a burden, was a convenient means of economizing at the expense of Negro children," Louis R. Harlan noted in his 1958 book *Separate and Unequal: Public School Campaigns and Racism in the Southern Seaboard States 1901-1915.*

By early in the 20th century, the inequalities that were to persist for decades in the segregated South were well-entrenched. In schools for blacks, teachers' salaries were far lower, buildings were typically rickety, and equipment was paltry.

Not only were African-American schools in session fewer days per year, but black children in rural areas also were routinely absent to work in the fields. High schools for blacks were often nonexistent.

In 1909-10, the average school term for black students was 101 days in the 11 former Confederate states and Kentucky, a full 17 days less than the average for whites.

"It was not reasonable to suppose that the Negro children were so smart that they could learn as much as white children while going to school for a much shorter period of time each year," Henry Allen Bullock wrote in his 1967 book *A History of Negro Education in the South: From 1619 to the Present.*

SALARY GAP DRAMATIC

Discrepancies in educators' salaries were no less glaring. In 1928-29, for example, white teachers in the 11 former Confederate states earned a typical monthly salary of more than $118, but black teachers received less than $73. And in some states, the disparity was far greater. In South Carolina,

Corbis-Bettmann

A teacher reads to pupils attending an all-black school in Uno, Va., in 1947. White students attended a school in nearby Orange.

black instructors' salaries were less than a third those of whites.

Most of those African-American teachers, moreover, were themselves products of inadequate schooling. During the 1930s, a third of the black teaching force in the South had not even completed high school, Stephan and Abigail Thernstrom reported in their 1997 book *America in Black and White: Race in Modern America.*

On the facilities front, black students in the South attended schools that were typically worth less than a quarter of those of whites. Given such gaps, it is not surprising that the bottom lines of black and white schools' budgets were grossly unequal.

By the late 1920s, per capita spending on black students throughout the South averaged about a third that spent on whites, according to Bullock. And in some states, the picture was even bleaker. Alabama,

Louisiana, and Mississippi each invested more than five times as much in their white students as in blacks, while South Carolina spent more than 10 times as much.

The disparities began to narrow in the 1940s, as courts began signaling that Southern states would have to start addressing the "equal" half of the "separate but equal" doctrine.

In response to lawsuits—or to head them off—many Southern states began raising spending on black students at a faster pace than for whites.

By the 1949-50 school year, a survey of six states in the Deep South found that per-pupil spending in black schools stood at 65 percent of that for whites, up from 41 percent a decade earlier.

Efforts to close the gap accelerated as the NAACP Legal Defense and Educational Fund launched an all-out assault on segregated education. In 1951-52, per-pupil spending for blacks in those six states had climbed to nearly three-quarters of that in white schools, according to the Southern Education Reporting Service, a Nashville-based agency that is now defunct.

The U.S. Supreme Court's 1954 *Brown* v. *Board of Education* decision striking down segregated schooling served as a further spur to equalization, as states sought to forestall desegregation.

BITTERSWEET MEMORIES

As black Americans look back at segregated schools from a greater and greater distance, some say it is important to remember the good things that happened in them—despite their manifold disadvantages.

Franklin recalls outstanding black teachers who expressed unwavering faith in him and his classmates: "They spent a lot of time making us feel that we were somebody—that despite the inequalities that existed that we were as good as anybody else."

Franklin regards the educational segregation that shaped his youth as "a bittersweet kind of thing."

"On the one hand, it protected us from antagonisms and hostilities of people who didn't want to be with us," he observes. "On the other hand, it deprived us of equal opportunities, equal facilities, equal everything." ∎

'Doll Man'

The lawyers who waged war against Jim Crow schools in the early 1950s turned for ammunition to the social scientists of their day—none more prominently than Kenneth B. Clark.

Debate still swirls around the role of the New York City-based social psychologist in the cases that culminated in the *Brown* v. *Board of Education* decisions in 1954 and 1955. Known as the "doll man" for his research using brown and white dolls, Clark became a lightning rod for criticism from supporters as well as opponents of the historic rulings. Still, his role in marshaling evidence and mobilizing a cadre of like-minded social scientists set the stage for desegregation litigation for decades to come.

By Caroline Hendrie

The collaboration in the *Brown* cases was a forerunner of similar partnerships that yielded starring roles for social scientists as expert witnesses, desegregation planners, and court-appointed monitors in cases across the country.

"This was a watershed," says Mark A. Chesler, a professor of sociology at the University of Michigan who has studied the role of social scientists in school desegregation cases. "There was a partnership created here that was semi-institutional."

The partnership began as lawyers for the NAACP Legal Defense and Educational Fund prepared their challenges to segregated schools in four states and the District of Columbia in 1951. The No. 2 man at the fund, Robert L. Carter, began looking for scientific evidence that segregation damaged black children.

His search led to Clark, then a 36-year-old professor at City College of New York. In the 1930s and 1940s, Clark and his wife, Mamie, had used dolls and crayons in conducting research on the racial self-concepts of young black children in Northern and Southern cities.

In the now-famous tests, the Clarks asked black children ages 3 to 7 to choose dolls based on such criteria as which one was white, which was "Negro," which one they would like to play with, which one they considered nice, and which was "bad." They found that more than three-quarters of the children were color-conscious, and that some 60 percent "preferred the white doll or rejected the brown doll."

In the crayon tests, the researchers asked black children, ages 5 to 7, to color pictures in shades that corresponded to their own skin tones. They found that about one in six children with medium- or dark-brown complexions chose white or a color such as green or blue.

Yet in both the doll and coloring tests, the Northern black children were found to be more likely to express preference for white skin than Southerners and to display more "emotional turmoil" over the issue.

Those latter findings helped convince some critics that Clark had twisted the facts to show that segregated Southern schools were detrimental—a charge he staunchly denied. Critics also argued that because the children were so young, it was unlikely that school segregation was the crucial factor in their views about race.

LAWYERS SKEPTICAL

From the beginning, not all the lawyers for the black schoolchildren were enthusiastic about Clark. "[H]is dolls were the source of considerable derision, and the social-science approach itself was viewed as unlikely to sway the justices," Richard Kluger writes in *Simple Justice*, his 1976 book on *Brown* v. *Board of Education*.

Still, Clark testified in the Delaware, South Carolina, and Virginia cases that were consolidated with *Brown*, though not in the Kansas case for which the decision was named. When the cases reached the U.S. Supreme Court, Clark and two colleagues produced a "Social Science Statement" arguing both that state-sanctioned segregation was harmful and that obstacles to desegregation were surmountable.

The defense fund ended up appending the statement, signed by 32 other social scientists, to the brief it submitted in the consolidated *Brown* case in 1952.

The NAACP's strategy paid off on May 17, 1954, when the high court's decision overturning school segregation acknowledged the evidence presented by the social scientists. The justices quoted at length from a lower court's finding in the Kansas case that segregation damages black children mentally and educationally. The high court said the finding was "amply supported by modern authority," then cited a list of seven social-science works—a report by Clark first among them. The footnote became, in Kluger's words, "one of the most debated in the annals of the court."

After the 1954 ruling, Clark continued his involvement by helping the defense fund prepare for arguments on the implementation of the decree. ∎

Corbis/Robert Maass

The role of social psychologist Kenneth B. Clark in the historic Brown v. Board of Education *rulings is still debated, but his collaboration in the case set the stage for future desegregation cases. In deciding the* Brown *case, the justices cited evidence presented by social scientists, Clark among them.*

At the Crossroads

When the U.S. Supreme Court ruled against segregation in 1954, Prince Edward County, Va., shut down its schools rather than mix races. Today, its schools are among the most integrated in the nation.

By Debra Viadero

Farmville, Va.

Red, white, and blue signs marking historic Civil War sites are as common as stop signs amid the rolling farmlands of this southern Virginia community. The war took its last official gasp in and around this county. The final big battle of the war, fought 20 minutes east of here at Sayler's Creek, killed more than 3,000 Confederate stalwarts. And Robert E. Lee and Ulysses S. Grant spent the night in Farmville, the Prince Edward County seat, before heading to Appomattox Court House 28 miles away for the formal surrender.

Nearly 100 years later, the white people of the county were still tilting at some of the same windmills. This time, the enemy was the U.S. Supreme Court.

A school desegregation case that originated here was one of the five decided by the high court on the watershed day in 1954 when it handed down its ruling in *Brown* v. *Board of Education of Topeka*. But rather than bend to the will of the court as the other communities eventually did, Prince Edward County closed

Prince Edward officials opened a new all-black Moton High School in 1953 but shut it down with the rest of the county's schools in 1959.

Photo by Richmond Newspapers

Students lured the principal away from school on a ruse, ordered their teachers to keep out of the way, and walked to the county courthouse.

its public schools—and kept them padlocked for five long years. Now, with the curtain about to drop on the 20th century, the residents of the county have at long last finished fighting.

White students have trickled back into the public schools, making them among the most integrated in the nation.

And the school system, once deemed the worst in the state, is now widely considered to be among the best in this rural corner of the Old Dominion.

"Prince Edward County is the success story of the five cases that were decided with the *Brown* v. B*oard of Education* decisions," *Newsday* reporter Timothy Phelps concluded after visiting all five communities in 1995. "The same community that treated its black children like so much trash is now a model for the nation."

~

On a grassy triangle of land at the portal of this town sits Robert R. Moton High School. From the tip of this inverted triangle, a visitor can take one of two roads.

One road—Griffin Boulevard—is named after the Rev. L. Francis Griffin, the local minister who sustained the black community's long drive to integrate its public schools. The other fork is Main Street. It leads to the city's Mayberry-like downtown, the stamping grounds of the white politicians and merchants who fought so hard to keep white and black students apart.

The symbolism is fitting. For this cheery-looking, red-brick schoolhouse was the focal point for the desegregation battle that divided the community for decades. On a spring day in 1951, 16-year-old Barbara Johns, a niece of the civil rights leader Vernon Johns, led her fellow students on a daring walkout from the all-black Moton High. The students lured the principal away from school on a ruse, ordered their teachers to keep out of the way, and walked the half-mile up Main Street to the county courthouse. There, they demanded a school just as good as the one the white students had

at nearby Farmville High School.

By all accounts, the students had a convincing case. Moton High School was built in 1939 to accommodate 167 students. But, by 1950, 450 students were cramming into the building each day. Teachers held classes on the stage, elsewhere in the auditorium, even in a school bus. To meet the demand, the county had erected three tarpaper buildings—the students called them "shacks"—on the school grounds. The buildings, which gave Moton the appearance of a poultry farm, leaked when it rained. In the winter, the students seated next to the stoves that heated the shacks sweltered, while their classmates a few feet away shivered.

Vera J. Allen

Students attending Moton High School in the early 1950s stand in front of one of the tarpaper buildings erected to alleviate crowding.

"Sometimes, the coals would pop out, and someone would have to scoop them up and throw them back," says Edwilda Allen Isaac, 61, who was an 8th grader at Moton at the time of the walkout. "In biology, we had one frog that we had to share, and our books were discards from Farmville High School."

The building had no cafeteria. For lunch, Isaac remembers, students could pick up a carton of milk and a cinnamon roll on the stage in the auditorium.

The students walked out because their parents' repeated efforts to persuade county school officials to build a new black high school didn't seem to the teenagers to be working. Lawyers for the

National Association for the Advancement of Colored People, called in soon after the walkout, agreed to take on the case if the students would ask for integrated schools, rather than settle for a separate, new building.

Two years later, the county, acceding to the students' original demand, opened a modern high school for black students three miles south of town. By then, however, the wheels of justice were already turning toward integration. Less than a year later, on May 17, 1954, the Supreme Court, in its *Brown* opinion, which included the Prince Edward County case, would declare school segregation unconstitutional.

Five more years of delays and courtroom skirmishes would ensue before the Prince Edward County board of supervisors voted against funding its public schools on June 2, 1959. The board wrote:

"The action taken today by the board of supervisors of Prince Edward County has been determined upon only after the most careful and deliberate study over the long period of years since the schools in this county were first brought under the force of federal court decree. It is with the most profound regret that we have been compelled to take this action. ... The school board of this county is confronted with a court decree which requires the admission of white and colored children to all the schools of the county without regard to race or color. Knowing the people of this county as we do, we know that it is not possible to operate the schools of this county within this principle and at the same time maintain an atmosphere conducive to the educational benefit of our people."

It would take five more years and another Supreme Court decision to reopen the public schoolhouse doors.

Fearful for their daughter's safety, the Johns family sent Barbara to live with her uncle Vernon in Montgomery, Ala. Except for summers spent at the family farm, she never returned to stay before

her death in 1991.

Isaac, who was a friend of Barbara Johns' younger sister, was one of the student leaders called upon by Johns to help lead the strike that day in 1951. Isaac's 83-year-old mother, Vera J. Allen, remembers how her family first learned of the news.

"My husband was downtown, and a man said, 'Didn't I see your daughter walking with that group going downtown? Why don't you go and pull her out?' My husband said, 'Well, I didn't put her in,'" recalls Allen, who was a visiting teacher in the black school system at the time. "We were scared to death."

When Allen's teaching contract came up for renewal the following year, the county declined to renew it. She spent the next few years working first in the Wayne County, N.C., school system and then in the Caroline County, Va., schools. She commuted home on weekends, where her husband was running the family funeral home and raising the couple's two teenage daughters.

Allen came back to Farmville to stay in 1960, eventually becoming assistant to the superintendent of the Prince Edward County school system. Now retired, she is helping spearhead a community-wide campaign to transform the old Moton school into a civil rights museum. The group is about halfway toward its goal of raising the $300,000 needed to buy the property from the county.

"People always ask, 'Why didn't you leave?' We had a family business and a home," Allen says. "In those days, getting a home was quite an achievement."

The Allen girls—Edwilda Isaac and her sister, Edna Allen Bledsoe, 60—managed to graduate before the schools closed. They went on to out-of-state colleges. Both are teachers themselves now. Isaac teaches band at the public middle school, and Bledsoe is on the faculty at Longwood College, a state institution in downtown Farmville.

Younger black students, though, were forced to scramble for an education. Some never returned to their hometown.

Rita Moseley, who was 12 when the schools closed, stayed home for two years until a Girl Scout leader urged her mother to find a way for her to continue her schooling. The American Friends Service Committee, a Quaker group that found school placements for a few of the older black children, sent Moseley to live with a white family of educators in Blacksburg, Va., so that she could attend an integrated public school there.

"It was very frightening. I had never left home before—not even to spend the night

Benjamin Tice Smith

with anyone—and I had to leave my family and friends," says Moseley, 51.

Even now, decades later, the pain is fresh. Moseley, like other adults whose educations were disrupted by the school closings, cries as she tells her story. Blacksburg is roughly a three-hour drive from Farmville, but to the young, fearful girl, "it seemed like 1,000 miles away."

When federal money was channeled into the county in 1963 to set up free schools for black students, the elderly mother and daughter who had taken Moseley in offered to pay her college tuition if she would stay. In Blacksburg, Moseley had turned out to be a stellar student, earning the highest grades in her class.

"But I couldn't [stay in Blacksburg]," she says. "I wanted to be with my family again."

Back at school in Farmville, Moseley was eager to see old friends and classmates. She quickly found, however, that half of them were gone.

A few white community leaders at one point had offered to raise money for separate, private schools for blacks. But the offer was widely regarded with suspicion, and only one student applied.

Consequently, most of the students Moseley yearned to see that day had missed out on schooling altogether dur-

Vera J. Allen and her daughter Edwilda Allen Isaac visit the building that housed the all-black Moton High School. Edwilda Allen was an 8th grader at the school in 1951 when students walked out, demanding facilities on a par with those at the town's all-white high school.

The white children were bused to makeshift classrooms in churches, stores, and homes throughout the county.

ing the long lockout. In their late teens and early 20s at that point, they felt too old to go back to school.

Anna Harrison cried, too, when her mother packed her off on a train and sent her to live with a brother in New York City at the start of the school closings.

"I wasn't used to being in a big city," says Harrison, who was 14 at the time and had to shop, cook, and keep house for her brother. "When I came back, I saw the chains on the school door, and I felt like I was cheated. I never knew my older sisters and brother. I made up my mind if I ever had a family, they would stay together regardless."

Harrison earned failing grades her first semester at the integrated high school she was attending in New York. She hoped her marks would persuade her mother to let her come back home.

"But the guidance counselor—Mrs. Cosby—at my school, said, 'No, you can do it. Your parents sent you here, and you must do it,'" Harrison, now 56, recalls. She followed the counselor's advice and earned a diploma.

"If you were to listen to everyone from that time, they'd have a different story, and it's like a quilt," says Penny Hackett, 42, who spent 1st grade attending school in a neighboring county. "To each person in their lives, it meant something different, and we all know quilts are handed down from family to family. They mean something."

To get to school, Hackett and her brothers traveled each morning to a great-uncle's roadside market. There, a white teacher from neighboring Appomattox County picked them up and took them with her to school.

"If she had errands to run after school, we had to duck down in our seats because we were not supposed to be transported across county lines," Hackett recalls.

The hiding and the separation ended for good in 1964. In that year, an authority no less than the U.S. Supreme Court, ruling in *Griffin* v. *Board of Education*, ordered the public schools back into operation.

All three women are now part of the school system that once rejected them. Hackett teaches art at Prince Edward County High School in the same building first erected to replace Moton. Moseley, a parent of two of the school's graduates, is the school secretary, and Harrison is a substitute teacher.

Harrison's youngest daughter, Dwauleka, a 10th grader at the high school, has never known the educational

Edward H. Peeples

The Worsham Academy for Whites was one of the private schools opened in Farmville after Prince Edward County closed its public schools, rather than integrate them.

hardships her mother endured. Dwauleka is a B student who plans to go to college and major in physical therapy or sports medicine. And most of her classes, she has found, have been pretty evenly divided along racial lines.

Dwauleka recalls having felt the sting of prejudice in school only once. It came in a 9th grade mathematics class in which a handful of white students sat apart from the rest of the class, never speaking to Dwauleka or her black classmates.

But more than half of Dwauleka's own friends are white. She knows most of them from the basketball, softball, and

volleyball teams she plays on, and she sees them outside school as well.

"I just mix with everybody," Dwauleka says. "I have a couple of black friends who say, 'You're always hanging around those white people.' It doesn't really bother me." And if her mother's experience has taught her anything, she says, it is to get an education herself. Because, her mother has told her, once you have an education, no one can ever take it away from you.

∿

In many ways, white students, too, were victims of the school closings. But by September 1959, the white community had established Prince Edward Academy, a private school system extensive enough to serve some 1,500 white children, writes Bob Smith, whose 1965 book, *They Closed Their Schools*, chronicles the Prince Edward saga. The white children were bused to makeshift classrooms in churches, stores, and homes throughout the county. As adults, some still recall the feeling of peering inside the windows of locked public school buildings and wishing they could be inside.

By 1961, the private school system's founders had raised enough money to build the academy's first permanent structure, an upper school building set on a sprawling campus just outside town.

"If you were on the inside, you could see this thing was going to drag on and on," says Robert Taylor, the only surviving founder of the private school. "I had three children at the time, and something had to be done."

Now 79 and in ill health, Taylor lives in a spacious brick colonial surrounded by a cream-colored picket fence. The house, built by the contracting company he owns, sits on a hill above town. A son and daughter live just steps away.

His great-grandfather died in the Civil

War, just a month after joining the Confederate army. And Taylor recounts casualty numbers from the war and unjust tariffs imposed on the South as clearly as if they had happened yesterday.

To him, the county's desegregation battle, like the great war itself, was a matter of states' rights.

"At that time, people hadn't quite knuckled under to the federal government all over the country like it is now," he says in a slow, drawling baritone. "We were selected—I think primarily by Senator [Harry Flood] Byrd [Sr.]—to carry the torch on this thing." The late Democratic U.S. senator, an ardent segregationist, had tried to organize a campaign of "massive resistance" throughout the state. Only Prince Edward County held fast.

But Taylor concedes he also very much opposed desegregation himself.

"Black children with a 7th grade education did not have any more education than 4th or 5th grade white children," he says. "If we had done it gradually and brought children up so they could get to a par, I don't think there would've been a problem. But look at what you're graduating now, and you've got this social promotion going on."

His own children and grandchildren all went to private schools, most of them graduating from Prince Edward Academy. Taylor eventually became the chairman of the academy's board.

But if his thinking hasn't turned around in the 40 years since the school closings, the school he helped found is at least trying to transform itself.

With its 60-acre campus and California-style school buildings, Prince Edward Academy, under a new name, these days serves 600 students—less than half the original enrollment—in prekindergarten through 12th grade. And those students, once primarily from Prince Edward, now come from 13 Southside Virginia counties.

Dropping enrollments nearly caused the school go under in the early 1990s. Taylor rescued it with a call to J.B. Fuqua, a wealthy Atlanta businessman with whom he had grown up in the nearby village of Prospect. Fuqua initially put $10 million into the school with the proviso that it be remade into a "model school of excellence for rural America."

"When he said a 'rural model of excellence,' he also meant to open the school to everyone who qualifies," says Carolyn Culicerto, the academy's communications director. Its leaders at the time seized on the opportunity, changing the mascot and school colors almost overnight and

Benjamin Tice Smith

rechristening the school Fuqua Academy after its benefactor.

But the sudden transition proved rocky at first. To set it right, J.B. Fuqua four years ago lured Ruth S. Murphy, a public school administrator from North Carolina, to take over as the school's president. Murphy instituted block scheduling and an open-governance policy, holding school board meetings in public and enlisting the advice of her faculty in decisionmaking. She introduced multiage classes in the early grades so that children could progress at their own rates, and she opened up the school's summer pool memberships to the wider Farmville community.

"Diversity strengthens a school community," Fuqua's rewritten mission statement reads, "and should be embraced."

Currently, 5 percent of Fuqua's students are members of minority groups. The faces of black and white students smile out from the school's promotional brochure. And Murphy has accepted an invitation to join the board of the Moton museum project.

"I never thought that I was walking into a hotbed of racism," she says, noting that the school's first African-American

Steve Wall, left, the publisher of the Farmville Herald, *sends his children to integrated public schools, though his grandfather led the fight against integration when he owned the paper. Editor J. Kendrick Woodley III is a leading booster of the project to turn the old Moton school building into a museum.*

When James Anderson became superintendent of the Prince Edward County schools, blacks made up more than 90 percent of the enrollment.

student was admitted back in 1984. "I think times have changed, but we needed to be able to articulate that."

Times are also changing at the *Farmville Herald*, the newspaper whose cigar-chomping owner, J. Barrye Wall Sr., once led the crusade against integration here. He died in 1985.

His long-haired, 43-year-old grandson, Steve, now publishes the paper in the same unrenovated brick building it has occupied since its 1890 founding. Another grandson, Bidgood, runs a new radio station next door and sits on the county board of supervisors.

Although Steve Wall graduated from Fuqua when it was still known as Prince Edward Academy, his own two children attend the public elementary school here.

"We went to all the local schools and studied the elementary program," he says. "It was done strictly on the basis of what was best for my children."

Unlike his grandfather, the younger Wall leaves most of the editorial writing at the paper to his editor, J. Kendrick Woodley III. Woodley, who keeps a volume on the Beatles in his second-story office and wears a "WWJD" bracelet—shorthand for "What Would Jesus Do?"—has been a leading booster of the Moton museum project.

When the paper first got wind of now-discarded plans by the county to sell the Moton High property to a commercial developer, Woodley sat down at his keyboard and unleashed an impassioned editorial.

"If we're going to tear down the former R.R. Moton High School," he wrote, "let's go ahead and tear down Independence Hall, too, and dump the Liberty Bell in the river."

Woodley also sits on the project's board of directors. For his efforts in support of the museum, the black community two years ago gave him a plaque that he displays near his desk.

He sees the museum project as an exemplar of improving race relations in the county. Bringing together the town's black and white communities, Woodley says, "has been a kind of mission for me."

"You feel like there's something worth accomplishing here, and this is the world in microcosm," says the bearded editor, 41, who came to the paper right after graduating from Hampden-Sydney College, a Presbyterian school for men, six

Courtesy of First Baptist Church of Farmville

Ministers James S. Williams, left, David T. Shannon, and L. Francis Griffin in 1967. Griffin was active in leading the black community's push to integrate the schools.

miles down the road from Farmville. "And, if this is the world in microcosm, and you can help bring about this coming together, then there's hope for bringing larger parts of the world together."

A statue of a Confederate soldier stands outside Farmville United Methodist Church. Inside, the Rev. Sylvia S. Meadows, the associate pastor, also talks about racial unity as a personal mission.

Like many of the students who went to the "white" school, Meadows, 44, never suspected there was anything unusual about her schooling.

"When you grow up going to an all-white school, you just assume that everybody white goes to an all-white school,"

she says. "I didn't know what racism was when I was a child. But I do now."

She graduated from Prince Edward Academy in 1974, a popular student who was twice named to the homecoming queen's court. Four of her early elementary school years, however, were spent in private classes in the basement of the church that now employs her.

Though her own family never expressed any racist sentiments, Meadows remembers hearing a few jokes about blacks from schoolmates. But those comments were rare, she says, and in the years since she left the academy, she has heard black colleagues make jokes about whites, too.

"I can remember some things that were scary," Meadows says, sitting in the quiet of her dimly lit church office. "I can remember my parents getting a phone call in the middle of the night to come to a local bank and get grants for tuition at the private school. Maybe my spirit sensed there was evil there."

To skirt a court order against using public money for private schools, county leaders at one point in the crisis arranged to open up local banks at midnight, minutes after the order had expired, in order to distribute tuition grants to local families before a judge could reimpose the order later that morning.

Robert Taylor, who confirms this story, says the school and some of the parents were later ordered to repay the money.

Meadows' perspective on the desegregation conflict broadened when she got a job as a teacher's aide in the predominantly black Prince Edward County school system in the late 1970s. She found students eager to be educated and black teachers whose work inspired her. She stayed on and became a teacher herself and then a guidance counselor in the public schools.

Now, in her second career, as a minister, Meadows finds that her lifetime journey has taken her almost full circle. She currently is a doctoral student at the school of theology at Virginia Union Uni-

black institution where she is often the only white student in her class. And, last November, when a communitywide Thanksgiving Eve service was held at Moton High School, Meadows gave the sermon.

Her own daughter, Lacy, an 8th grader, has also known what it feels like to be the only white student in class. But for Lacy, who has spent her entire school career in public schools, the feeling has been less unnatural.

"When you get out in the real world, you have to know how to get along with people of all races anyway," she says matter-of-factly.

Meadows is awaiting a transfer to another church outside the county. But in her remaining months at the largely white Farmville United Methodist, she plans to, as she puts it, "proclaim what needs to be heard here" to dispel some of the mistrust that some whites and blacks still harbor toward one another. Healing those old wounds has, to her, become a calling.

"I had a dream once that I was on a hill, and there was arguing going on, and it was between a black person and a white person," she says. "Someone was getting ready to either hit the black person with a stick or shoot them, and in my dream, I jumped in front of them."

The desegregation conflict here, however, was as remarkable for its lack of violence as it was for its longevity. One night soon after the black students' strike, a cross was burned on the grounds of Moton High School. By day, though, county residents maintained a veneer of courtesy toward one another as they shopped and worked side by side. These were families that had known one another for generations.

When, under President John F. Kennedy, the federal government set up a program for Farmville's school-less youths with money from the U.S. Office of Economic Opportunity, Robert Taylor and Francis Griffin headed it together. Griffin, who was the pastor of First Baptist Church, grew up three blocks from Taylor.

Taylor credits the long-deceased civil rights leader with helping to prevent the violence that racked so many other communities torn by racial conflict. He says Griffin always informed the sheriff when demonstrations were planned. U.S. Attorney General Robert F. Kennedy and the Rev. Martin Luther King Jr. came to town, and their visits passed peacefully.

Others also did their share to ensure peace. Rita Moseley waited years to tell

Benjamin Tice Smith

her own two children about the school years she had missed growing up. To do so any earlier, she feared, might embitter them toward their white neighbors and schoolmates.

"I blame the government—not the people themselves," says Anna Harrison. "They [the government] had the power to get those doors opened."

Given his own deep roots in rural Southside Virginia, James M. Anderson Jr. became the natural choice to lead what was at first a virtually all-black school system into the modern age of integration.

Anderson, who is white, was born and bred in neighboring Buckingham County. He believes the black community wanted him for superintendent of schools because his reputation had preceded him. The white community, reluctantly going along, trusted his heritage.

In Buckingham County, where Anderson had been the high school principal, the honor of valedictorian traditionally

James M. Anderson Jr. came to Prince Edward County in 1972 when only 7 percent of the system's students were white. When he retired 25 years later, the schools' racial mix reflected that of the county. He says that by ignoring the competition and improving the schools, he was able to integrate the district without violence, busing, magnet schools, or federal programs.

The bigger challenge for the school system today is poverty. More than half the students come from families that qualify for free- or reduced-price lunches.

went to the student with the highest grade point average. Under his watch, the recognition, which came with a chance to speak at graduation, went to a black student for the first time in 1969.

When Anderson's superintendent heard the news, he called the principal and asked him to reverse his decision because the student had come to Buckingham Central High School as a transfer student.

The determined principal pointed out that the previous year's valedictorian, a white, had also been a transfer student. No one had complained then.

The African-American student, the superintendent countered, had made all her good grades in the black school. Not so, the principal politely retorted.

If you persist in this course of action, the superintendent finally said, neither he nor any county officials would attend the graduation ceremony.

"At commencement, we had two completely empty rows," Anderson, 66, recalls. No superintendent, no school board member, no county supervisor came to the ceremony.

"I just could not, in all conscience, sleep at night to do that injustice to that young lady," he says of the superintendent's request.

Anderson also bucked the status quo by permitting his white high school baseball team to play the black Prince Edward County High School team in 1970 when few other schools would. He remembers that the Prince Edward team showed up wearing mismatched uniforms, most of the pieces hand-me-downs from Hampden-Sydney College. A good-sized crowd had come for the game, too, and Anderson surmises they were expecting to see a match with Prince Edward Academy, the private school.

Anderson's actions finally landed him in a paper-shuffling job in the county school system, where he sat until a Prince Edward County school administrator invited him to apply for the $15,000-a-year post as superintendent.

When he came to Prince Edward in 1972, only 7 percent of the school system's 1,850 students were white. When he retired 25 years later, the racial mix in the student population almost exactly reflected county demographics. Now, of the system's 2,700 students, 58 percent are African-American, and 41 percent are white. The remaining 1 percent is a mix of other minority groups. Moreover, 90 percent of the county's school-age children attend the public schools.

The bigger challenge for the school system today is poverty. More than half the county's public school students come from families poor enough to qualify for the federal free- or reduced-priced lunch program. Many of them are likely the children of the county's "crippled generation," the term coined for the students whose educations ended when the school doors were locked.

If there is any other vestige of segregation now, black community leaders say, it likely lies in the district's programs for gifted students, with whites far outnumbering blacks. But school officials, aware of the imbalance, say the problem is that too few black parents refer their children to the program. Officials also say they are working to correct the situation.

Even in the school system's top job back in the '70s, Anderson found himself on the outside looking in, just as he had as a Buckingham County principal. When he presented his first budget request to the county board of supervisors, the chairman asked him, "Why don't you run your schools like ours?" By "ours," Anderson explains, the chairman was referring to the private school.

At the time, the state had just passed a law requiring school systems to provide a base level of funding. Meeting that base the first year, Anderson recalls, required a 48 percent increase in school funding.

So he spent much of the next few years battling for money to renovate old schools and build new ones to stem overcrowding. He says one elementary school, built without walls on the inside, became so congested that a visitor opening the door to the shell-like structure had to step between student desks to enter the building.

A turning point came in 1979, when Longwood College closed its campus school, which had served the children of faculty members from both Longwood and Hampden-Sydney. When it shut down, more than half its former students enrolled in the public school system. By then, a new president of Hampden-Sydney, Josiah Bunting III, had also arrived in town and was sending his own children to public school. With so many prominent, highly educated whites enrolling their children in the public schools, other white families may have figured the education there must be all right.

Anderson is proud of the fact that the demographic transformation of Prince Edward County's schools came without violence, busing, magnet schools, or federal programs.

His idea was simpler: Ignore the competition and improve the schools.

Besides improving regular instruction, he took care to ensure that the schools offered something for everyone. Under his watch, foreign-language offerings in the district's one high school and one middle school expanded from Spanish and French to include Latin, Russian, Japanese, and German.

Extracurricular activities sprouted like dandelions at the high school, making it the envy of some students in neighboring counties. These days, Prince Edward High School offers everything from literary journals and debate clubs to tennis and golf teams. And its yearbook attests to the fact that, by and large, those teams and clubs include students of both races.

But Anderson knew he had reached his goal when the county board of supervisors unanimously granted his request to spend $5 million to renovate the high school—a job that was completed just last summer. His work done, Anderson retired in 1997.

A seventh-generation Southerner himself, Anderson says he understands the sentiments that led Prince Edward's leading residents to take the stand they chose four decades ago. His own grandfather was a Confederate soldier.

"I will defend to the last breath his having fought for the Confederacy because of the question of states' rights," says the superintendent.

But when his grandfather left the army, Anderson also proudly notes, he got a job teaching in a one-room school for black students. ∎

Desegregation And the 'American Dilemma'

A perspective by Robert W. Peebles

Nearly half a century has passed since the landmark *Brown* v. *Board of Education* decision of the U.S. Supreme Court in 1954. Much has been written about school desegregation, and an abundance of resources exists on the topic. This 50-year slice of history demonstrates the beauty and the beast of the American character as we struggle to comply with the law, the Constitution, and what Gunnar Myrdal called "an American dilemma."

What have we learned over this period? Where do we stand today? Race issues continue to plague this nation, and social class is closely entwined with race as families decide whether to move or remain within public schools, one of the greatest equalizing institutions in our history.

Following the *Brown* decision, the civil rights movement that grew during the Kennedy and Johnson administrations sparked initiatives that protected rights guaranteed by the constitutional amendments adopted after the Civil War. Indeed, the failure of the Founding Fathers to recognize the basic equality of human beings in the final draft of the U.S. Constitution set the course of future events shown most dramatically by that tragic war. To this day, we remain seriously divided and frustrated by racial issues.

We have learned that some earlier assumptions about race and schools were erroneous. For example, we mistakenly believed that the South would have far more difficulty than the North in desegregating schools. Yet once the initial period of protest passed, highlighted by policies of "massive resistance," Southern states began to comply with the law more readily than many Northern school districts. Not that it was easy. Only with the power provided by the Supreme Court's 1971 decision in the Charlotte, N.C., busing case (*Swann* v. *Charlotte-Mecklenburg Board of Education*) did a broad-based, serious approach to desegregation become policy in Southern school districts. Despite living for generations under Jim Crow laws, thus establishing racially segregated schools de jure, the South acquiesced and proceeded to desegregate its public schools.

By contrast, the Northern states developed their own segregated patterns resulting in de facto segregated schools, particularly in cities and surrounding suburbs. Public schools were left to their own means of complying with the law. They lacked a well-planned, coordinated approach that included housing policies devised by public and private coalitions along with political leadership.

Vast numbers of people—adults and children—were emotionally affected by desegregation. It made a profound impression upon individual lives and families, on all of us.

The relative calm and blandness of the 1950s were deceptive. While the Levittowns and other housing for World War II veterans were being built, discrimination was rampant and contributed significantly to the racial separation characterizing the rapidly growing suburbs. A *New York Times* story in December 1997 commemorating the 50th anniversary of Levittown cited a housing code stipulating that buyers of Levittown houses had to be Caucasian. During the 1960s, lawsuits were being prepared claiming discrimination and denial of opportunity rights. Meanwhile, the United States was digging itself into an

> Vast numbers of people—adults and children—were emotionally affected by desegregation. It made a profound impression upon individual lives and families, on all of us.

The problems that remain for a substantial segment of the black population are of a different, far more complex order—one of economic class.

ever-deepening, bloody war in Vietnam that divided America in many ways.

We now see disturbing and discouraging trends relating directly to school desegregation. Recent Supreme

Court decisions have supported lower-court rulings that weaken or destroy previous gains made in attempts to integrate public schools.

What caused the school desegregation effort to deteriorate? Why did the enthusiasm for it dissipate? Progress was being made for nearly two decades following the *Brown* decision. A report by the U.S. Commission on Civil Rights published in June 1973 bears this out.

Following a year of investigation, the commission documented several encouraging, even promising findings. For example, evidence showed, it said, that desegregation had improved the quality of education. This positive finding pointed to curricular improvement and specific training of teachers and administrators to heighten awareness of race issues and sensitivities. Innovations led to different approaches to learning, team teaching, and more flexible scheduling of classes. The report provided no information regarding test results, but test scores were not reported by ethnic categories until the 1980s.

In conclusion, the commission wrote: "It is time to emphasize what unites us as Americans, rather than what divides us." Mind you, this report came nearly 20 years after the *Brown* decision.

"Separateness is inherently unequal"

was the essence of that decision. Recognizing shocking inequities, and driven by ideological zeal, a coalition of individuals and institutions representing racial and ethnic diversity generated a movement that profoundly affected American society. Between 1960 and 1980, a moral fervor paralleling that of causes like abolition, Prohibition, and feminism swept across this land. Many leaders of the school desegregation movement were heroic, some naive.

For a book I am writing, I am interviewing participants in the school desegregation efforts in four cities where I have had firsthand experience. Two are large (Boston and Pittsburgh), and the others smaller (Alexandria, Va., and Louisville, Ky.). These participants have stories to tell. The fact that their memories are still vivid speaks to the emotion they felt then and retain today. I hope to discover why our country moved backward toward resegregation and positions that are similar to the "separate but equal" doctrine of *Plessy* v. *Ferguson*.

My interviews to date—of school administrators, mayors, community leaders, and members of boards of education—convey a clearer and more accurate understanding of what happened. They reveal perceptions and subtleties of each community's unique experience. The voices are mixed and far from harmonious. As André Gide said, "There can be no harmony if the whole choir sings in unison."

As I hear the participants from Boston, for example, flesh out their experiences and review those wrenching times, a quarter of a century disappears quickly. Few know or remember that the chief justice of the United States, Earl Warren, in 1954 cited Boston as a city that had eliminated segregation—in 1855. Digging into what happened in Boston's history in the 1970s, when U.S. District Judge W. Arthur Garrity Jr. ordered the city to desegregate its public schools, I find a shattered mosaic filled with so many pieces that it is difficult to perceive the entire picture. Like a Tolstoy novel, it has numerous characters, each playing a role as the narrative unfolds. And, as with accident eyewitnesses, they often disagree.

Kevin White, Boston's mayor during the 1970s, had his political career destroyed over the busing issue. "Busing tore up Boston, not really the issue of desegregation," he says. "It is rare to have an entire city have … a nervous breakdown." The former mayor attributes the tumult more to fear than to hatred. But Ruth Batson, a civil rights leader who grew up in a segregated housing project in Boston and now heads her own educational foundation, recalls events differently: "I truly felt we were going to succeed, but I underestimated the hate. How do you get past that? People just don't know enough of the facts."

Judge Garrity, who was approaching 80 when I spoke with him and was serving as a judge for the U.S. District Court for Massachusetts, disputed the "facts" of the Boston desegregation story as described by the late J. Anthony Lukas in his 1985 book *Common Ground*. Lukas described the compelling saga of three Boston families involved in the city's upheaval.

"Don't get me started on Lukas," the judge said. "Not that I didn't like him. He was a talented writer. But he wasn't accurate, and I believe he had his story already written in his head before he started to write. It's like a novel with deliberately drawn characters playing roles he designed for them." Apparently, the judge added, the journalist and author wanted to paint him "as a 'lace curtain' Irishman with Yankee Brahmin pretensions." Not true, Judge Garrity averred.

In retrospect, recalls Paul Parks, a former Massachusetts secretary of education, Boston's desegregation plan was doomed from the start. "What they did was to take two very poor white communities, Charlestown and South Boston, and pair them with the very poor, black community of Roxbury, then ask these people to handle one of the most difficult, complex social problems in the country," he says. "You can't ask poor people to share. When those buses came into South Boston—Irish Catholic South Boston—it was much more a matter of losing their community than anything else. They had very little to share."

Says Thomas W. Payzant, Boston's schools superintendent since 1995: "I don't think there was any other way to begin desegregation following the *Brown* decision than to physically move kids by busing. In hindsight, and I want to emphasize hindsight, we should have concentrated much earlier on the educational quality of schools and achievement standards. We missed an opportunity, and this was a mistake. To most parents, the bus ride wasn't the issue."

Charles V. Willie, an African-American professor of education at Harvard University who was raised in the South, has been actively involved with Boston's schools and desegregation plans since 1974.

The current trend to return to separateness disturbs him. "I understand it," he says. "Many blacks have been disillusioned and feel betrayed, especially those who took huge risks. Still, it was important to require white schools to desegregate, even though it meant much greater disruption to black families. We tend to overlook the accomplishments of desegregation."

What has been accomplished? Actually, a lot. Before the 1960s, we had what amounted to an apartheid system in our country similar to South Africa's before Nelson Mandela's amazing revolution. American schools were legally segregated in the South, truly a comprehensive apartheid arrangement. And in the North, particularly in major cities, schools were de facto segregated. These cities are in some cases, such as Washington, Baltimore, Detroit, and several others, beyond any realistic hopes of desegregation. Has the struggle failed? To my mind the answer is no, but the problems of urban public schools remain enormous.

Thurgood Marshall: American Revolutionary, Juan Williams' biography of the late U.S. Supreme Court justice, reveals interesting insights on this topic. Justice Marshall's critical role as a lawyer in the 1954 *Brown* decision is well-known, but the other dimensions of his personality and character will shed more light on the historic story of race segregation in American society. The book establishes convincingly, for example, that Marshall believed in integration. Separatist arguments never persuaded him—indeed, they irritated him. He was steadfast in this opinion, and his influence shines through the years of debate and struggle over school desegregation. Not that numerous racist episodes affecting him were lacking, including the embarrassing 10 months taken in 1961 by the Senate Judiciary Committee, then headed by Sen. James Eastland of Mississippi, to confirm his appointment to the U.S. Court of Appeals for the 2nd Circuit.

Marshall's unwavering belief in integration had enormous, albeit more quiet, power as desegregation began to take hold across the country. His concentration on legal strategy as opposed to militancy, and his arguments based on the Constitution, made the difference and accomplished changes once unimaginable.

Now, with the emphasis on quality schools in neighborhoods, the cause of desegregation has moved more to the background. To predict the future of school desegregation is hazardous. But has any other issue commanded more attention, stirred more emotions, and affected more people in our country? What other issue of the 20th century has taken longer to resolve? Is it resolvable? ∎

Robert W. Peebles is a retired schools superintendent who headed urban districts in Massachusetts, Connecticut, and Virginia. Since retiring, he has advised several large metropolitan school systems, including those of Louisville, Ky., and Charlotte, N.C., on desegregation issues. He lives in Alexandria, Va., where he is completing a book on early efforts to desegregate the schools.

the great debate

The energy and optimism that radiated from the United States as it strode confidently into the 20th century found a perfect outlet in the multifarious movement known as progressivism.

Under the progressive banner, a busy nation rooted out corruption in business and government, crusaded for social change, and sought better lives for its poor citizens.

In education, progressives saw a golden opportunity. They were convinced they could build a democratic society full of informed, active citizens while at the same time freeing American schoolchildren from the tyranny of dull, numbing lessons.

But the wave of educational innovations that followed soon brought cries that schools had strayed too far from their primary mission.

The ensuing debate between the progressives and those who called for a return to academic tradition struck at the heart of both the purpose and practice of schooling. And it continues today.

Progressives strove to create schools that would stimulate and challenge youngsters. But critics charged that many of the reforms diverted schools from high standards and academic studies, as shown in this 1940 cartoon that appeared on the cover of The American School Board Journal.

Illustration reprinted from The American School Board Journal, July 1940

Reprinted from The American School Board Journal, July 1940

Tugging at Tradition

The progressive movement offered educators a fresh, 'child centered' approach to learning. Its critics say it took schools far away from their primary mission.

The students' baggy jeans and Doc Martens shoes are distinctly late-20th-century. And no one would mistake the well-worn sofas and movable tables in these classrooms for the nailed-down desks of an earlier era. But much of the philosophy behind the 300-student Francis W. Parker Charter Essential School in Devens, Mass., would be sweetly familiar to its namesake.

Often referred to as the "father of progressive education," Parker first came to prominence in 1873 as the superintendent of the nearby Quincy, Mass., school system.

By Lynn Olson

At a time when public schools were dominated by recitation, memorization, and drill, Parker advocated placing the child at the center of education and building schools around their students' motivation and interests. Under the Quincy System, as it came to be called, textbooks gave way to magazines, newspapers, and materials developed by teachers. Students learned geography by exploring the local countryside. And they studied an integrated curriculum that stressed learning by doing and expression through the arts.

The modern-day Parker School similarly aspires "to move the child to the center of the education process," according to its mission statement. The students, age 12 and older, progress at their own pace, following personal learning plans that are jointly crafted by the students, their parents, and their teachers. Movement from one "division" to the next is based on demonstrated performance, primarily through "exhibitions" and long-term projects.

Small classes and an advisory system enable teachers to know their students well. And the teachers design—and revise—the curriculum to reflect students' interests and needs and to promote engagement.

"It's kind of radical, in a sense, because it's so different," says Kaitlin LeMoine, a 15-year-old student, "but it's really nice to be here. You kind of run on your own motivation."

Her ingenuous comment nicely captures a century-old debate in American education between two schools of thought, often referred to as "progressive" vs. "traditional." This "Great Debate," as some have called it, has waxed and waned with bitter intensity throughout the 20th century. And it is no less heated or closer to resolution today than it was in the beginning.

At its simplest level, one could say it's a

← this sounds great!

tion's cultural heritage and one designed to preserve it.

Progressive education, for example, has often been associated with more active learning, cooperative planning by teachers and students, a greater recognition of individual differences, attempts to relate learning to "real life," and efforts to broaden the school's mission to address health, vocational, social, and community issues.

But to summarize the debate in such pat phrases is a gross oversimplification. Historically, educational progressives, as well as their conservative counterparts, have come in all shapes and sizes. And what has been viewed as "progressive" in one era has become hopelessly retrogressive in the next.

In practice, notes Larry Cuban, an education historian at Stanford University, good schools can be found on both sides of the pedagogical and philosophical divide. And most teachers employ a hybrid of instructional practices that he has dubbed "conservative progressivism."

To Cuban and others, the debate over progressive and traditional ways of teaching is really front language for much deeper questions about why we have schools and what we believe about children and the nature of child rearing. Such questions, rooted in the nation's changing political and social context, have been ed in this country since its inception. answers to them help define who we as a nation, which explains, at least in , the moral fervor of the argument.

formal education is the playing field on which society vies over values," says Theodore R. Sizer, the writer and education reformer who is a co-principal of the Parker School and a leading proponent of modern-day progressivist thought. "And it's deeply charged because those of us who have children care deeply."

The debate is a fundamental one that "arises from different views of human nature," he argues. "To put it in sort of classical, early-19th-century terms, some people believe that children are born with original sin, and you have to beat it out of them, literally or figuratively. Others think that children are Rousseauean little flowers that are going to bloom each in its own way. And, boy, those are two quite different views."

ROOTS OF PROGRESSIVISM

As the late Lawrence A. Cremin observed in his 1961 history *The Transformation of the School*, progressivism in education sprang from a much larger social and political movement in the first two decades of the 20th century.

It was an era of unprecedented industrial and urban growth. In 35 years, from the Civil War's end to the turn of the century, America remade itself from a nation of farms and small towns into an urban, industrial empire.

Wealth became concentrated among a handful of corporate giants, such as the financier John Pierpont Morgan, the oil magnate John D. Rockefeller, the steel king Andrew Carnegie, and the railroad baron Jay Gould. And much of that wealth was built on the backs of laborers, many of them immigrants, who were swarming daily into the cities.

The most famous voice to come out of the progressive movement in education was the philosopher and educator John Dewey, whose voluminous writings spanned more than half a century.

Dewey arrived at the University of Chicago in 1894 at the height of a great railroad strike, which ended when President Grover Cleveland dispatched federal troops to Chicago on the grounds that the strikers had interfered with the mails and interstate commerce.

By 1900, Chicago's population had grown to nearly 1.7 million from half a million in 1880—the vast majority of that growth fueled by immigrants and their children.

How to reconcile this massive industrialization with the welfare and freedom of individuals became a topic of pressing concern. Muckraking journalists exposed corruption in education and municipal government and the plight of the urban poor.

Settlement workers such as Jane Addams agitated for better working conditions, improved city services, and an expanded social mission for the schools.

Progressive politicians such as Gov. Robert M. La Follette of Wisconsin sought to curb the excesses of modern capitalism by regulating industry and commerce, emphasizing concern for human over corporate welfare, and placing the scientific expertise of the university at the service

← you could say that...

through World War I had their program for the school. Humanitarians of every stripe saw education at the heart of their effort toward social alleviation."

From the outset, the movement was marked by a "pluralistic, frequently contradictory character," Cremin wrote. "Throughout its history, progressive education meant different things to different people, and these differences were only compounded by the remarkable diversity of American education."

MULTIPLE STRANDS

Historians have identified at least three strands of progressive education that grew from a common root and that were often intertwined.

The "pedagogical progressives" included Parker, who moved from Massachusetts to Chicago in 1883—first to run the Cook County Normal School and later to head his own independent school. They favored more informal, student-centered classrooms; more active, interdisciplinary

While superintendent of the Quincy, Mass., public schools in the late 1800s, Francis W. Parker advocated a more child-centered approach to education that later became known as the Quincy System. Parker is now often referred to as the "father of progressive education."

Corbis-Bettmann

Teachers College, Columbia University

learning; and schools of a more humane character.

Parker and many of his contemporaries had gone on pilgrimages to Europe. There, they were influenced by European Romanticism and by the ideas of such scholars as Friedrich Froebel, the inventor of the kindergarten, and Johann Pestalozzi, who advocated bringing education into harmony with the natural development of the child. These "child-centered progressives," as they were later called, wanted schools to fit the interests and inclinations of children, not vice versa.

Leading advocates of child-centered pedagogy in the United States included G. Stanley Hall, the president of Clark University in Worcester, Mass., and the author of *Adolescence*, a groundbreaking 1904 treatise. He promoted an image of children as creative beings to be nurtured, rather than disciplined, shaped, and controlled. Particularly in the early elementary grades, children should be encouraged to draw, paint, and sing; to engage in social activities; and to learn through experience.

In 1918, William Heard Kilpatrick, a self-described "interpreter" of Dewey, wrote an influential, 18-page article titled "The Project Method." In it, Kilpatrick, a professor of education at Teachers College, Columbia University, urged schools to abandon their traditional passivity for projects that would have a more lasting influence on children by engaging them with "wholehearted purpose." Such projects could range from producing a newspaper, to organizing a play, to solving a geometry problem. The *Teachers College Record* eventually would distribute some 60,000 reprints of the monograph.

Like Dewey, Kilpatrick believed that learning took place only when students had internalized what they had gained through experience and practiced it in their own lives. He argued that the "fundamental error" of school systems was that "they began with fixed and set subject matter, when they should have begun with the student's present interests, purposes, abilities, and needs."

A silver-haired, charismatic speaker, Kilpatrick would teach more than 35,000 ~~students during his 30 years at Teachers~~

← yes yes yes

THE 'RECONSTRUCTIONISTS'

While the child-centered progressives were concerned primarily with students' inner development, the "social progressives" envisioned a larger role for schools. They believed schools in an industrial society must assume many of the functions increasingly abandoned by home and community and work to fashion a more egalitarian order.

Social progressivism came to greatest prominence during the Great Depression, when a group known as the "social reconstructionists" urged a more militant role for schools. Led by such Teachers College professors as Dewey, Kilpatrick, George S. Counts, Harold Rugg, John L. Childs, and Bruce Raup, they protested the evils of laissez-faire capitalism and dared the schools to build a new social order.

The group published its own journal, *The Social Frontier*. But in the late 1930s, it lost many of its members when the more radical faction urged schools to practice social indoctrination and suggested that class warfare was the only road to a better society.

Robert M. Hutchins, the chancellor of University of Chicago and the founder of the widely used Great Books program, would later argue that the movement failed because the schools couldn't promote a revolution with which the vast majority of Americans disagreed.

"A revolution cannot be brought about through the conscious inculcation of revolutionary doctrine in the schools," Hutchins wrote in *The Conflict in Education in a Democratic Society,* published in 1953.

The social reconstructionists fell out of favor in the period shortly before and after World War II, as the nation was gripped with anti-Communist fervor. But its legacy still can be seen in the provision of health and other social services through the schools and in attempts to engage schools in community issues.

THE 'ADMINISTRATIVE PROGRESSIVES'

In contrast to the social progressives, the "administrative progressives" were less concerned with ameliorating society than with helping students adjust to it.

Led by such men as Edward L. Thorndike, a professor of education at Teachers College, and Ellwood P. Cubberley, a Stanford education professor, they sought to use new advances in scientific measurement and testing to bring greater efficiency to schools. That, they believed, would in turn enable schools to cope with an influx of poor and immigrant students.

Administrative progressives sought to "equalize" educational opportunity by providing each student with a curriculum best suited to his or her interests and abilities. The goal was to prepare students for their places in society.

Dewey once criticized the administrative progressives as attempting to "perpetuate the present order, with at most an elimination of waste."

Yet it was the ideas and techniques of the administrative progressives that proved most immediately useful to schools. Such practices as more frequent use of standardized tests, a curriculum differentiated for vocational and college-bound students, and the grouping of students by levels of ability addressed the pressing need to organize education along more rational lines in the face of rapid, often overwhelming growth in enrollment.

One of the most common tools of the administrative progressives was the survey, in which a group of educational experts would study a local school system, point out its faults, and leave behind recommendations for change. During the period from 1910 to 1919, the Stanford historian David B. Tyack points out, at least 67 such surveys of city school systems were published. From 1920 to 1927, there were 114.

Indeed, while experts continue to argue about the ultimate impact of the pedagogical progressives, the influence of the administrative progressives was profound and lasting. Much of it remains in the school bureaucracies of today.

Of the varied branches of progressive education, administrative progressivism "was the one that really took," says Tyack, "because it got built into structures." Its ideology, he explains, "was finding the right niche for the right person, and not some broader notion of raising everybody to the same high level."

HEYDAY OF THE MOVEMENT

By 1919, when the Association for the Advancement of Progressive Education was formed, the progressive movement was already pushing and pulling in different directions.

School districts like Gary, Ind., were rethinking their use of time and space both to save money and to engage children in a range of academic and nonacademic pursuits.

In Denver, Houston, and St. Louis, educators were revising their curricula along progressive lines. Meanwhile, some of the most pedagogically innovative progressives abandoned the public schools entirely to form independent schools. Those schools—such as the Dalton and Lincoln schools in New York City and the Marietta Johnson School of Organic Education in Fairhope, Ala.—served a primarily white, upper-middle-class clientele, and were more concerned with nurturing individual potential than with improving society at large.

By the 1940s, the historian Diane Ravitch argues in *The Troubled Crusade: American Education 1945-1980,* progressive ideas were no longer referred to as new or modern, but simply as "good educational practice."

Regional accrediting agencies and state evaluators judged schools by progressive criteria, such as whether classes were teacher- or student-dominated and whether students helped plan the curriculum. By 1938, the Association for the Advancement of Progressive Education—renamed the Progressive Education Association—had grown to 10,440 members.

From 1932 to 1940, the organizat conducted its famous Eight-Year Study which some 30 schools or districts exp mented with changes in the second curriculum. Students from the exp mental schools, which actually var.... widely in their practices, received waivers to enter colleges or universities since they did not have traditional college-preparatory courses or transcripts.

To evaluate the impact, graduates of

Faculty and students pose on the steps of Earl Hall at Teachers College, Columbia University, in 1914. Dean James Earl Russell is seated in the center of the first row. Beside him are education professors William Heard Kilpatrick, second from right, Edward L. Thorndike, third from right, and John Dewey, third from left.

"Proponents of virtually every progressive cause from the 1890s through World War I

I'm intrigued!

the school.

Lawrence A. Cremin
The Transformation of the School

participating schools were matched with college classmates of similar ability and background from more traditional high schools.

The evaluation, under the leadership of Ralph W. Tyler of the University of Chicago, concluded that among the 1,475 matched pairs, graduates of the experimental schools earned slightly higher grade point averages, received slightly more academic honors, seemed to possess a higher degree of intellectual curiosity and drive, and participated more often in organized student groups, among other characteristics. Moreover, the graduates of the most experimental schools showed the greatest differences along those lines.

Today, proponents of progressive education still point to the study as a vindication of their ideas. But many of the schools involved in the initiative soon fell back on more traditional practices once the foundation money that had underwritten the venture dried up. Moreover, the loss of foundation support placed the PEA in a precarious financial position that contributed to the organization's demise in 1955.

The 'Life Adjusters'

At the time the Eight-Year Study was under way, what many saw as a much more pernicious version of curriculum reform was sweeping the country under the banner of progressive education.

Its roots could be traced to the 1918 publication of *Cardinal Principles of Secondary Education* by the National Education Association, which had formed in 1857 as an organization of educational leaders, most of them school administrators. (The organization did not create a separate department for classroom teachers until 1912 and did not actively begin to recruit rank-and-file teachers until after 1916.)

Cardinal Principles was as much a creature of the administrative progressives' search for social efficiency as it was of new concepts in pedagogic practice. The study argued that schools should take their cues from the needs of society and from adult activities, rather than from the traditional academic disciplines. It urged schools to focus on "fundamental processes" such as worthy home membership, vocation, and use of leisure time. And in keeping with the administrative progressives, it advocated separate curricular tracks for students of different interests and abilities.

In 1944, that utilitarian view of educa-

tion was reiterated in the NEA's publication *Education for All American Youth*, which continued to downplay the role of subject matter.

The low point came in 1945, with the birth of the "life adjustment movement," a virtual parody of Dewey's notion of preparing students to address society's

← YAY!

...remaining 60 percent, according to the theory, needed school training of a more practical character to prepare them for the problems of daily life.

In 1947, U.S. Commissioner of Educa-

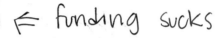

← funding sucks

The Backlash

The life-adjustment courses of the late 1940s and early 1950s added fuel to the criticism of progressive education that had been building since its inception.

Even Dewey had criticized his colleagues and disciples, though often in such polite and muted tones that they failed to notice. In 1938, in his last book, *Experience and Education*, Dewey denounced the excesses of child-centered pedagogy for proceeding simply on the basis of "rejection, of sheer opposition" to what had gone before.

"I am sure you will appreciate what is meant when I say that many of the newer schools tend to make little or nothing of organized subject matter of study," he wrote, "to proceed as if any form of direction and guidance by adults were an invasion of individual freedom, and as if the idea that education should be concerned with the present and future meant that acquaintance with the past has little or no role to play in education."

But Dewey's critiques were nothing compared to those mounting from outside, especially during the height of the life-adjustment fad.

Foremost among the attackers were laymen Mortimer Smith and Albert Lynd, two former school board members; the historian Arthur Bestor of the University of Illinois; Chancellor Hutchins of the University of Chicago; and a Navy vice admiral, Hyman G. Rickover. These critics lambasted the schools for deni-

grating academics and for trying to address society's ills at the expense of an intellectual focus.

In all too many cases, Smith contended, the child-centered school had become the "child-dominated school," without goals and aims and which turned out ...dents who lacked a sound moral com...s. While "neopedagogues palaver ...re and more about the 'real needs' of ...ngsters," chided Lynd, "the pupils are ...ning less and less."

...onically, given the egalitarian foundation of the progressive movement, these critics also attacked the life adjusters for maintaining social stratification. By failing to give youngsters from less advantaged backgrounds access to a common academic curriculum, they ...rged, schools helped perpetuate the ...tus quo.

Progressive education became regres... education," argued Bestor, a graduate ...he progressive Lincoln School in New ...k City, "because instead of advancing, it began to undermine the great traditions of liberal education and substitute for them lesser aims, confused aims, or no aims at all."

"The West was not settled by men and women who had taken courses in 'How to be a pioneer,'" he wrote in 1953 in *Educational Wastelands*. "I for one do not believe that the American people have lost all common sense and native wit so that now they have to be taught in school to blow their noses and button their pants."

Such criticism came amid the Korean War and the anti-Communist sentiment fueled by the House Un-American Activities Committee and Sen. Joseph R. McCarthy of Wisconsin. By January 1949, China had fallen to the Communists, and in September 1949 the Soviet Union exploded its first atomic bomb.

"In the McCarthy era, there was an indiscriminate charge of communism for anyone who was associated with progressive causes," says Herbert Kohl, a senior fellow at the Open Society Institute in New York City. "What happened was that the progressives were basically either driven underground or fired or, very often, those who survived were driven out to the suburbs, where progressive ideas fit much more with the creative ideas of parents who wanted their kids to be upwardly mobile."

By the time the Soviets launched Sputnik I, the first man-made earth satellite, in the fall of 1957, the progressive movement was in deep trouble. The nation quickly embraced a call for more mathematics, science, and foreign-language instruction and tighter discipline in the schools. Admiral Rickover, in particular, praised the European systems of education and urged Americans to pay more attention to their gifted and talented students.

Even without Sputnik I, Cremin believed, progressivism would have died of its own weight, battered down by factions, distortions, loss of popular support and understanding, and an inability to change with the times. "The surprising thing about the progressive response to the assault of the '50s is not that the movement collapsed," he wrote, "but that it collapsed so readily."

Both critics and proponents credit the movement with two lasting effects. On the positive side, schools had become much more humane and informal places by midcentury than they had been in 1900.

But the increased expectations that the progressives placed on schools to solve societal problems also made them vulnerable to criticism and charges of failure.

A TEMPORARY RESURGENCE

The political and social winds in the United States shifted once again in the late 1960s and early 1970s. And a new generation of activists discovered—or, more often than not, reinvented—progressive thought and practices.

In the mid-1960s, a succession of angry young educators wrote best-selling memoirs about their teaching experiences, primarily in highly segregated, inner-city classrooms. James Herndon, John Holt, Herbert Kohl, and Jonathan Kozol railed against the imposition of subject matter without any attempt to relate it to students' experiences or to the upheavals in society.

They derided the meaningless routines, dehumanizing discipline, and lock-step schedules of many schools; denounced unbridled authoritarianism and the schools' role in perpetuating social inequities; and waxed eloquent over their own attempts at innovation.

Those books and the political and social ferment of the times helped revive educational practices that echoed those of the first quarter of the 20th century, including project-based learning, narrative report cards, individual and small-group instruction, student involvement in choosing activities, a more flexible use of space, and integrated curricula. "Open education," a relaxed style of elementary schooling that incorporated many of those

a return to Jefferson's ideals and plans ←

Corbis-Bettmann

practices, was popular from the late 1960s to about 1975.

Some leaders of this neoprogressive movement, such as Vito Perrone, who was then the dean of the University of North Dakota's New School of Behavioral Studies in Education, were well-versed in progressive history.

But in general, lamented Cremin and others, the new progressives were "notoriously atheoretical and ahistorical ... with the result that boundless energy has been spent in countless classrooms reinventing the pedagogical wheel."

Looking back, Kohl, whose book *36 Children* chronicled his early teaching experiences in New York City, agrees.

"I did not read John Dewey until after I'd formed most of my educational ideas," he says. "We had to reinvent progressivism, but without either a historical perspective or knowing that a lot of the materials and things that we felt we were creating for the first time were already there."

Unlike the earlier progressive movement, this temporary resurgence soon ran up against the back-to-basics movement of the late 1970s and the imposition by many states of minimum-competency tests to ensure that high school graduates had achieved mastery of basic reading, writing, and math skills. The new pro-

Hyman G. Rickover, a Navy vice admiral, speaks at a 1960 gathering of the Mayor's Committee on Scholastic Achievement in New York City. Rickover was among those who criticized child-centered schools, saying such schools tried to address the ills of society at the expense of academics.

gressivism had little uniformity in either definition or practice, asserts Cuban, who compares its meteoric rise and fall to a "streak across the sky."

IN RETREAT?

Since the 1970s, the political and educational climate in the United States has generally been chilly for progressive thought and practice. Increases in course requirements, a reliance on standard[...] tests, and the rise of the academic-s[...] dards movement have often made it [...] cult to pursue innovations along the l[...] of Dewey, Kilpatrick, and others.

But that does not mean that progres[...] theories and practices have disappeared. Far from it. The voluntary national standards for mathematics, proposed by the National Council of Teachers of Mathematics, reflect many progressivist ideas. They draw heavily on "constructivist" psychology, which holds that students must construct meaning from experience, an idea with clear echoes of Dewey.

In 1984, Sizer formed the Coalition of Essential Schools—a group of high schools dedicated to reforming themselves along largely progressive lines. And in the late 1980s, it appeared that progressive ideas would even influence policy from the bottom up. Through a project known as Re:Learning, Sizer worked with the Education Commission of the States to craft state-level policies that would be supportive of better practice in the schoolhouse.

Hundreds of schools continue their adherence to progressive approaches. And a new generation of schools serving substantial proportions of poor and minority students—such as the Urban Academy, Central Park East, and El Puente in New York City—have revived the idea of marrying progressive pedagogy with issues of social justice.

But today, many progressives like Sizer are operating at the margins of the education system: in charter schools, alternative schools, and schools of choice that have some freedom from the dominant, central-office-driven culture.

"I think, at the moment, we're deeply ambivalent toward progressive education," says Patricia Albjerg Graham, the president of the Spencer Foundation, which underwrites educational research.

DEBATING THE LEGACY

Today, educators and historians still quarrel about the legacy of the progres-

sive movement. Many of the ideas that teachers now take for granted—movable furniture, working with students in small groups, the provision of social and medical services in schools, and integrated curricula—can be traced directly back to progressive roots.

"I think the best thing that one can attribute to progressive education is usually the methodology," says Ravitch, a senior research scholar at New York University who has written books critical of progres-

very true ⟹

practice, argues that while such changes have been significant, they hardly represent the sweeping reorganization of classrooms and pedagogy that progressives envisioned. Even at the height of the progressive movement, he asserts, most teachers embraced a hybrid form of "teacher-centered progressivism," in which lectures and "teacher talk" still predominated.

While a core of progressive teaching practices won a foothold in elementary classrooms between the two World Wars, it never reached anywhere near a majority of teachers and had only a minimal influence on the high schools.

"What progressive education showed us was that with gifted teachers and students from families and communities committed to education, you could provide a fabulous education," Graham says. "What it also showed us is that with less gifted teachers and with children from families and communities that were not supportive of education, it could be terrible.

"At its best, it was very, very good. And at its worst, it was awful."

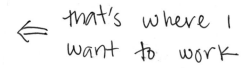 ← *that's where I want to work*

by the administrative progressives, [...] sistant to progressive pedagogy. Fifty-minute classes, 180 students a day at the high school level, teacher isolation, and college-admission decisions driven by test scores and course requirements all work against interdisciplinary, hands-on, individualized instruction.

Second, a web of social beliefs about what constitutes "school," based on teachers' own experiences, tends to dis-

courage innovations in practice. Nancy Sizer, Theodore Sizer's wife and the other co-principal of the Parker School, sees that every day. "What makes Parker less than perfectly progressive is just the same old problem," she says. "Scratch a well-meaning teacher, and you will find someone who feels nervous if his or her kids don't 'know enough.' And that means enough calculus and enough biology and enough Spanish. So we're always pulled the other way."

Finally, as Dewey himself admitted, "a system of education based upon living experiences [is] a more difficult affair to conduct successfully than it is to follow the patterns of traditional education."

Teachers in progressive schools, observes Linda Darling-Hammond, a professor of education at Stanford, need extensive knowledge and skill to teach both students and subjects well. They need to have a firm grasp of their disciplines, understand child development, and know how to mesh the two.

Theodore Sizer agrees. "It is much easier to run a highly controlled school—tell students what to do all the time, don't give them any running room, and teach to the test," he says. "It's much harder to say that the purpose of school is for each kid to know her own running room. And it's much harder to say we care how kids operate when we're not looking."

The strongest criticisms of progressive education continue to focus less on its pedagogy—which even such critics as E.D. Hirsch Jr. concede may be effective in some instances—than on the diminution of subject matter. Hirsch, a professor of English at the University of Virginia, has proposed a common core of knowledge that all students should learn to function in a democracy. He has been particularly critical of what he sees as the denigration of knowledge.

"Political liberals really ought to oppose progressive educational ideas because they had led to practical failure and [...] ter social inequity," he wrote in 1996 [...] *he Schools We Need and Why We [...] 't Have Them*. Instead, he laments, [...] anti-subject-matter principles of pro[...] ssivism have demonstrably triumphed [...] american schools."

'THESE THINGS CYCLE'

Yet Sizer—like Dewey before him—argues that students need both process and content. Even when students are learning thinking skills, they have to be thinking about *something*.

The question is, in part, one of bal-

Courtesy of Jonathan Kozol

ance—an eternally elusive goal.

Visit a Parker classroom, and you'll find students debating philosophical essays on freedom vs. determinism in preparation for studying about World War II. Visit one of Hirsch's Core Knowledge schools, and you are likely to see students working in cooperative groups and creating dioramas or plays about the ancient Greeks or Egyptians.

"At its best, the progressive movement had this notion that all children can learn if only the situation was sufficiently flexible and creative and open and interesting," Kohl says. "Now, there's a real contradiction that emerges: Does that sacrifice content?"

He argues that it does not. "But I do believe that there is a process part of the progressive movement as it emerged in the '60s," he adds, "in which process and feeling overrode content, really to the detriment of kids."

As for himself, Kohl says he has "moved much more to the point of saying it's necessary for kids to know the Bill of Rights and the Constitution."

Many of the elements of the current movement for higher academic standards, he believes, can be adopted by progressives: "I think the real difference is say-

ing, look, once we decide on the kinds of things that kids really need to know to survive, we don't believe they can be coerced to know them. We also don't believe there's one way to learn it."

Kohl's comments underscore how hard it often is to divide educators neatly into progressivist vs. traditionalist camps. "Our traditional approach, in order to increase the population in school, has been to change the curriculum and hold th pedagogy constant," says Graham of th Spencer Foundation. "Now we are tryin to reverse that by holding the curricu lum constant, but marrying conservativ content to progressive pedagogy."

But despite the search for a middle ground, few believe the century-long debate between progressives and traditionalists is over. "I actually think it's a pretty good debate to have," says Graham. "It's about diversified pedagogy and the civic purposes of education and the value of traditional knowledge."

Meanwhile, progressives with a long historical view, like Sizer, say they won't give up the fight. "These things cycle, and you just have to hang on," he says. "It's pretty hard to hang on when you get pounded all the time, but that's the nice thing about having been trained in history." ∎

debate means that we're striving for improvement!

While a teacher in Boston in 1965, Jonathan Kozol joined protests against segregation in public schools. He was one of several young educators in the mid-1960s who wrote memoirs about their teaching experiences that were sharply critical of prevailing school practices.

Dewey: The Era's Misunderstood Giant

John Dewey has been called the "most influential writer on education" and the "greatest philosopher" this country has produced. He's also one of the most misunderstood, oft-quoted, and least-read educational commentators of the progressive era.

"Dewey, in fact, is an icon who was picked up for better or for worse on all sides of most debates," says Ellen Condliffe Lagemann, a professor of history and education at New York University. One reason for Dewey's complicated reputation is simply that he lived so long—from 1859 to 1952—and wrote so copiously during a period of enormous change.

By Lynn Olson

"That's part of the problem of Dewey," argues Diane Ravitch, a senior research scholar at NYU. "He wrote so much over so many years. Forty years later, the schools didn't look the same. So people always had a choice: Do you pay attention to the Dewey of 1902 or the Dewey of 1938?"

STARTING WITH THE CONCRETE

Born in Burlington, Vt., to a modest, middle-class family—his father ran a grocery business—Dewey graduated from the University of Vermont and then taught high school in Pennsylvania for three years before earning a graduate degree in philosophy from Johns Hopkins University.

He moved from there to the University of Michigan and then to the University of Minnesota before settling in Chicago in 1894 to chair both the philosophy and pedagogy d...

solid goal! ⟹

...putting thought into action: primarily, by confronting problems that arise while engaging in activities that interest them. He advocated that education start with a child's interest in concrete, everyday experiences and build on that understanding to connect with more-formal subject matter. At the Lab School, children participated in experiences drawn from community life and occupations.

The school's curriculum was built around themes, such as "progress through exploration and discovery," which were supplemented by specific work in languages, mathematics, the fine and industrial arts, science, music, history, and geography.

Dewey also saw schools as engines of democracy in which children would learn citizenship through practice. In them, children would form the habits of

University of Chicago

John Dewey founded the Laboratory School of the University of Chicago in 1896 while serving as the chairman of both the philosophy and pedagogy departments.

mind that would enable them not only to live in society but also to improve it.

In 1899, his first major book on education, *The School and Society*, attempted to spell out the relationship between the education of the young and the development of an intelligent citizenry.

DENSE AND DIFFICULT

Dewey's writings touched on the arts, politics, and nature, as well as education. But while he was prolific, his writing was dense and often difficult. In *The Transformation of the School*, Lawrence A. Cremin wrote of the "frequently discussed problem of Dewey's style, described by Irwin Edman as 'lumbering and bumbling,' by Justice Oliver Wendell Holmes as 'inarticulate,' and by William James as 'damnable; you might even say God-damnable.'"

Dewey, people often said, lived in the present. The slim, mustachioed scholar was supportive of young people and eager to listen to their concerns, but reluctant to indulge in his own reminiscences. His lectures at Columbia University were delivered in a slow—some said meditative—cadence. "His classes were well attended," said one observer, "but the lectures were not well listened to."

Still, William Heard Kilpatrick, one of the most popular lecturers at Teachers College from the 1910s to the 1930s, would describe Dewey as his "master." In his biography of Kilpatrick, who also lived to the ripe age of 93, John A. Beineke quotes from Kilpatrick's diaries: "'I feel in some measure that I am best qualified of those about here to interpret Dewey. His own lectures are frequently impenetrable to even intelligent students.'"

Scholars continue to argue about which of the two men had more influence on progressive educational practice, and whether Kilpatrick faithfully interpreted Dewey's ideas or misconstrued them. In his biography of Dewey, Robert B. Westbrook argues that "much of what critics (then and now) attacked as aimless, contentless 'Deweyism' was in fact aimless, contentless 'Kilpatrickism.'" But in *And There Were Giants in the Land*, Beineke asserts: "That Dewey ever disavowed Kilpatrick, even indirectly, would be difficult to prove."

Some scholars blame Kilpatrick more than anyone else for what they view as the denigration of subject matter. But Ravitch places the onus on Dewey. "If you look at all of the things that are happening in American education that are anti-intellectual," she says, "there is a line that takes you back to John Dewey, and there is no escaping it."

'Thorndike Trumps Dewey'

Dewey's most direct attempts to influence practice were when he ran the Lab School, which he left in 1904. During his eight years at the elementary school, "Dewey began to develop a very promising approach to scholarship in education," Lagemann says. "Unlike most people, he wasn't sitting in a university office studying education, he was doing it with kids and teachers and trying to work out problems of practice."

In her forthcoming book, *John Dewey's Defeat*, Lagemann argues that in leaving the University of Chicago for Columbia in 1905, Dewey essentially ceded the field of education research to Edward L. Thorndike and other "administrative progressives." Those scholars thought research should be conducted in the university; that researchers should not be a part of schools, other than to test students; and that they could generate laws of learning for a primarily female teaching force to carry out. In Lagemann's view, "Thorndike trumped Dewey."

"I think it is fair to say that Dewey did not speak out as strongly as we might wish he had about some of the excesses of progressivism," Lagemann continues. Nonetheless, "I don't think you can blame the excesses of progressivism on Dewey."

Dewey's interest in the present moment was both a strength and a weakness. It gave his ideas tremendous vitality, but also made them hard to interpret in a later age.

"There were many John Deweys," says Patricia Albjerg Graham, the president of the Spencer Foundation. "The needs of American education from the time he started writing in the 1880s until the 1950s changed dramatically."

Today, she argues, much of what Dewey said that retains its value has been forgotten.

"What's been lost in the current discussions about education," Graham says, "is Dewey's powerful idea ... that if you're going to have a democratic society, you have to have an educated populace. And that an educated populace not only needs to know how to read, write, add, and subtract, but they have to know how to live together and to recognize that as a value." ■

← sweet!

Charles Moore/Black Star

Students work in an open class at Fargo Elementary School in Fargo, N.D., in 1971. The relaxed schooling style, a British import, began catching on in U.S. schools in the late 1960s.

Open to Innovation

On May 3, 1971, *Newsweek* magazine's cover story explored the "joy and excitement" of an educational movement that had burst into the national consciousness with the publication of Charles E. Silberman's *Crisis in the Classroom*.

Like numerous other critics writing at the time, Silberman decried what he saw as the repressive, grim, and joyless character of many classrooms. The antidote, he believed, was to be found in "open education," a relaxed style of elementary schooling imported from Britain that in the late 1960s had begun to capture the attention of American educators.

By Ann Bradley

"In hundreds of grade schools, the familiar sight of children seated at measured rows of desks, studying from standardized textbooks and listening to a teacher's precise directions, has disappeared," *Newsweek* reported. "Instead, children wander through their cl_____ writing, writing."

Open education enjoyed the spotlight from 1967, when the writer Joseph Featherstone praised the practices of the British primary schools in *The New Republic*, until about 1975, when mounting criticism and declining SAT scores ushered in an era of attention to basic skills.

The 1970 publication of Silberman's book—the product of years of research subsidized by the Carnegie Corporation of New York—catapulted open education into the mainstream. Architects began designing "open space" schools for suburbs across the nation, although the buildings' configurations were not necessarily related to their pedagogical practices.

Process of Learning

Never precisely defined, open education typically stressed giving children choices and plenty of opportunities to experiment and get their hands dirty in classrooms full of books, animals, and art supplies. Teachers monitored pupils' __rk, rather than dictating what they __uld study and learn. Curriculum and __lt authority were played down. The __cess of learning—rather than the __wledge acquired—was the goal.

__s a movement, open education in the United States was clearly rooted in the political and social tumult of the times.

← education → democracy

It quickly became a cause for its adherents—many of them young teachers who had questioned authority in objecting to the Vietnam War and who shared a reluctance to impose their wishes on students.

A number of open-style schools sprang up in minority communities in big cities, where educators and parents were looking for alternatives to the traditional schooling that left many children behind.

"It was a radical time, and a radical critique of U.S. society was emerging," recalls Featherstone, today a professor of education at Michigan State University. "It was open education, the Beatles, peace, and civil rights."

Proponents of open education, or what Featherstone prefers to call "democratic education," were somewhat mystified with architects' embrace of open-space schools.

Many of the cavernous buildings proved unpopular both with parents and with teachers, who promptly tried to use bookshelves to erect private spaces.

The closest link between physical space and educational methods, in fact, was made by Lillian Weber, an influential New York City educator who used an "open corridor" arrangement to link a handful of elementary classrooms and a hallway in a Harlem school.

The biggest influence on open educators was Jean Piaget, the Swiss philosopher and psychologist, who wrote extensively starting in the 1920s until his death in 1980 about children's thinking and the stages of their intellectual development. Open educators, like other advocates of progressive education before them, also drew on the writings of John Dewey to make the case for children's active engagement in their own learning.

SCIENCE STUDY'S IMPACT

Many of the links between Britain and the United States were forged by educators involved with the Elementary Science Study, a federally funded project in the early 1960s that created a new science curriculum for elementary schools. Its 56 units on various topics were designed with the idea that children should "do" science with real materials, not just read about it in textbooks.

Part of the impetus for open education, in fact, stemmed from the science educators' frustration that the new ESS curriculum was such a poor match for the typical classroom, which tended toward verbal and abstract instruction, the education historian Diane Ravitch writes in *The Troubled Crusade: American Education 1945-1980.*

The federal government blessed open education with money for open-style programs in 10 cities; the initiative, called Follow Through, was for elementary children who had participated in the Head Start preschool program. State education departments, among them those in Massachusetts, New Jersey, New York, and Vermont, allocated money for open education. And teacher-training programs—such as those at Harvard University, Lesley College, and Wheelock College in Massachusetts—embraced its tenets.

In North Dakota, where just 41 percent of elementary teachers had bachelor's degrees in 1968, the state launched an ambitious teacher education project based on the philosophy. The New School of Behavioral Studies in Education, housed at the University of North Dakota in Grand Forks, trained teachers in open-education methods while sending young faculty members out to take their places in schools.

The project's goal, *Newsweek* said, was "to launch an all-out assault on educational convention by producing a radically new breed of elementary teachers."

"The central idea was to have kids leave school believing they were historians, mathematicians, and scientists," says Vito Perrone, now the director of teacher education at Harvard University, who ran the North Dakota program. "So that they had really internalized these subjects and internalized knowledge in a very large way and could actually do something with it."

POLITICAL AGENDA

As interest in open education grew, its proponents began to extrapolate its promise for young children to the upper grades and, indeed, to society at large.

Silberman of *Crisis in the Classroom*, an editor at *Fortune* magazine who left journalism to promote open education, elevated it from a pedagogical approach, Ravitch writes, "into an ideology about children, learning, and schooling that was intended to revive society and the quality of life in America."

Open education was partially a "political agenda" aimed at making classrooms responsive to children of all races and income levels, agrees George E. Hein, a retired professor at Lesley College who worked on the Elementary Science Study.

But the movement fell prey to charges of excessive zeal among its true believers, which helped undermine its credibility. Eventually, it was blamed for a rise in youth crime and a drop in test scores, even though the number of schools that embraced open education was very small.

"It was very threatening to hierarchical, highly structured school systems to give more freedom and responsibility to teachers," Hein says, "and, in turn, to children."

As the principal of open-style schools in New Haven, Conn., and Newton, Mass., Roland S. Barth experienced both the promise and the pitfalls of open education. Barth, now a retired Harvard professor of education, was fired from one school after the faculty bitterly divided over open education.

He wrote a doctoral dissertation attempting to define open education, which he calls a "polarizing concept" for

Corbis-Bettmann

Corbis-Bettmann

parents and teachers. Parents, who had little choice over where to send their children, resisted change in the familiar institution of school. And some teachers balked at open education's informality.

"I took over a school as principal where the previous principal had been run out of town over this issue, and the faculty and parents were badly divided over which side would win—workbooks or gerbils," recalls Barth, who wrote the book *Run School Run* about that experience in Massachusetts. "It was a kind of either-or notion in a lot of schools."

INFLUENCE STILL FELT

In retrospect, Barth wishes open educators, who were opposed to giving students letter grades, had paid more attention to evaluating children's work. The movement promoted written commentaries about students' performance, which were too taxing on teachers, he argues.

Open education also exaggerated the failings of traditional classrooms, Barth says, while poorly executed open classrooms could degenerate into sloppiness or worse.

Despite its short life, open education's legacy is still seen in schools.

Many primary-grade classrooms closely resemble the physical setup of open classrooms, with book corners and plenty of materials for exploring science and mathematics. Curriculum materials in all subjects give students the opportunity to get their hands, and not just their minds, around a topic.

In the past 25 years, Featherstone says, schools have made "astonishing" gains in encouraging children to write and in using good literature—two major features of open educators' agenda.

And at the high school level, says Perrone, echoes of open education live on in the small high schools in New York City and other cities that attempt to connect students to the community, to involve them in projects, and to foster understanding and not just factual recall.

But open education's most significant contribution, Featherstone believes, was its promise of creating top-quality schools for low-income children.

"To me, the most exhilarating thing was the opening up of the possibility that schools for poor kids could start to be decent," he says. "That was a vision that was hammered out in those years, and I don't think it has disappeared." ∎

Above: In New York City in 1966, students attend the wall-less Public School 219.

Left: Advocates of "open education" were greatly influenced by the theories of Jean Piaget. The Swiss philosopher and psychologist wrote extensively about the stages of children's intellectual development.

The 1950s: Progressives Under Fire

During the 1950s, progressive education was ridiculed by both laymen and university scholars who accused the schools of abandoning traditional studies in favor of "life adjustment" courses and child-centered pedagogy.

Excerpts compiled by Senior Editor Lynn Olson

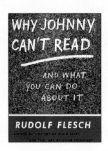

take to it at once. If you use a common-sense approach, you try again and again, exert a little patience, and after some time the child begins to learn. But if you are a 20th-century American educator, equipped with the theory of "readiness," you drop the whole matter instantly and wait until the child, on his own, asks to be taught. Let's wait until he's 7—until he's 8—until he's 9. We've all the time in the world; it would be a crime to teach a child who isn't "ready."

Educational Wastelands: The Retreat From Learning In Our Public Schools

1953 / by Arthur Bestor (1908-1994), a professor of history at the University of Illinois.

Reprinted with permission from University of Illinois Press.

The economic, political, and spiritual health of a democratic state depends upon how successfully its educational system keeps pace with the increasingly heavy intellectual demands of modern life. Our civilization requires of every man and woman a variety of complex skills which rest upon the ability to read, write, and calculate, and upon sound knowledge of science, history, economics, philosophy, and other fundamental disciplines. These forms of knowledge are not a mere preparation for more advanced study. They are invaluable in their own right. The student bound for college must have them, of course. But so must the high school student who does not intend to enter college. Indeed, his is the graver loss if the high school fails to give adequate training in these fundamental ways of thinking, for he can scarcely hope to acquire thereafter the intellectual skills of which he has been defrauded. ... Progressive education became regressive education, because instead of advancing, it began to undermine the great traditions of liberal education and to substitute for them lesser aims, confused aims, or no aims at all.

Why Johnny Can't Read: And What You Can Do About It

1955 / by Rudolf Flesch (1911-1986), an author and an advocate of the phonics method of reading instruction.

Reprinted with permission from HarperCollins.

When you get to the subject of "readiness," you approach the holy of holies, the inner sanctum of the whole "science" of reading. In each of the fat tomes on how to teach reading, pages and pages are filled with profound discussions of what makes a child ready for reading, when does he get ready, how to tell whether he is or not, how to speed him up or slow him down, what to do with him before he gets ready, how to instill readiness, how to make it grow, how to use it, treat it, protect it, diagnose it, improve it, ripen it, and direct it. Deep mystery covers this whole recondite subject, and work has been going on for decades to explore its inner recesses. ... If ever there was an example of reasoning in a vicious circle, this is it. You take a 6-year-old child and start to teach him something. The child, as often happens, doesn't

The Conflict in Education In a Democratic Society

1953 / by Robert M. Hutchins (1899-1977), a former chancellor of the University of Chicago.

Reprinted with permission from HarperCollins.

If we can ever find out what the educational system should do, I am sure we shall discover that it will be so difficult as to demand all the time and attention we can give it. It follows that whatever can be learned outside the educational system should be learned outside it because the educational system has enough to do teaching what can be learned only in the system. The words of Sir Richard Livingstone should be written in letters of fire on every schoolroom wall: "The good schoolmaster is known by the number of valuable subjects he declines to teach." Even if driving a car, understanding plumbing, and behaving like a mature woman are valuable subjects, they can be, and therefore should be, learned outside the educational system.

Education and Freedom

1959 / by Hyman G. Rickover (1900-1986), a vice admiral in the U.S. Navy.

Reprinted with permission from Dutton.

Dewey's insistence on making the child's interest the determining factor in planning curricula has led to substitution of know-how subjects for solid learning and to the widespread tendency of schools to instruct pupils in the  minutiae of daily life—how to set a table correctly, how to budget one's income, how to use cameras, telephones, and consumer credit—the list is endless. Add to this that Dewey insisted the schoolroom must mirror the community and you find classrooms cluttered with cardboard boxes, children learning arithmetic by keeping store, and education stuck in the concrete and unable to carry the child from there to abstract concepts and ideas. Our young people are therefore deprived of the tremendous intellectual heritage of Western civilization which no child can possibly discover by himself; he must be led to it.

The 1960s: The New Progressives

During the 1960s, a new group of critics cried out against the social inequities and the dull, mindless coursework they saw in the public schools. This group of largely youthful critics resurrected—or reinvented—many of the progressive practices of an earlier era.

How Children Fail

1964 / by John Holt (1927-1985), an author, educator, and social critic.

Reprinted with permission from Perseus.

Children are subject peoples. School for them is a kind of jail. Do they not, to some extent, escape and frustrate the relentless, insatiable pressure of their elders by withdrawing the most intelligent and creative parts of their minds from the scene? Is this not at least a partial explanation of the extraordinary stupidity that otherwise bright children so often show in school? The stubborn and dogged "I don't get it" with which they meet the instructions and explanations of their teachers—may it not be a statement of resistance as well as one of panic and flight? ...

We encourage children to act stupidly, not only by scaring and confusing them, but by boring them, by filling up their days with dull, repetitive tasks that make little or no claim on their attention or demands on their intelligence. Our hearts leap for joy at the sight of a roomful of children all slogging away at some imposed task, and we are all the more pleased and satisfied if someone tells us that the children don't really like what they are doing. We tell ourselves that this drudgery, this endless busywork, is good preparation for life, and we fear that without it children would be hard to "control." But why must this busywork be so dull? Why not give tasks that are interesting and demanding? Because, in schools where every task must be completed and every answer must be right, if we give children more demanding tasks they will be fearful and will instantly insist that we show them how to do the job. When you have acres of paper to fill up with pencil marks, you have no time to waste on the luxury of thinking.

Death at an Early Age

1967 / by Jonathan Kozol (born 1936), an author, educator, and social critic.

Reprinted with permission from New American Library.

I noticed this one day while I was out in the auditorium doing reading with some children: Classes were taking place on both sides of us. The Glee Club and the sewing classes were taking place at the same time in the middle. Along with the rest, there was a 5th grade remedial math group, comprising six pupils, and there were several other children whom I did not know about simply walking back and forth. Before me were six 4th graders, most of them from the disorderly 4th grade and several of them children who had had substitute teachers during much of the previous two years. It was not their fault; they had done nothing to deserve substitute teachers. And it was not their fault now if they could not hear my words clearly since it also was true that I could barely hear theirs. Yet the

way that they dealt with this dilemma, at least on the level at which I could observe it, was to blame, not the school but themselves. Not one of those children would say to me: "Mr. Kozol, it's too noisy." Not one of them would say: "Mr. Kozol, what's going on here? This is a crazy place to learn."

36 Children

1967 / by Herbert R. Kohl (born 1937), an author and educator, now a senior fellow at the Open Society Institute in New York City.

Reprinted with permission from New American Library.

I put an assignment on the board before the children arrived in the morning and gave the class the choice of reading, writing, or doing what was on the board. At no time did any child have to write, and whenever possible I let the children write for as long as their momentum carried them. Time  increasingly became the servant of substance in the classroom. At the beginning of the semester I had tried to use blocks of time in a predetermined, preplanned way—first reading, then social studies, arithmetic, and so forth. Then I broke the blocks by allowing free periods. This became confining and so I allowed the length of periods to vary according to the children's and my interest and concentration. Finally we reached a point where the class could pursue things without the burden of a required amount of work that had to be passed through every day. This meant that there were many things that the class didn't "cover"; that there were days without arithmetic and weeks without spelling or my dear "vocabulary." Many exciting and important things were missed as well as many dull things. But the children learned to explore and invent, to become obsessed by things that interested them and follow them through libraries and books back into life; they learned to believe in their own curiosity and value the intellectual and literary.

The Way It Spozed To Be

1968 / by James Herndon (1927-1990), an author and educator.

Reprinted with permission from Heinemann.

Grouping by ability, formerly anathema in the district, has caught on. We group them high, low, and average in math and science. ... Below that we've tried "remedial" classes, and above that, "enrichment." (The remedial kids complain that they ain't 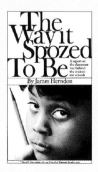 learning nothing but that baby stuff, and the enriched that they do the same thing as the other kids, just twice as much of it.) We "experiment" a lot. We teach Spanish experimentally to everyone, then drop it experimentally. We experiment with slow learners ... with core programs, team teaching, with "innovative" programs. These programs, being only "experiments," remain on the fringe of things; the general curriculum, not being an experiment at all, isn't affected by them.

A Blueprint for Change

By David J. Hoff

Gary, Ind.

James M. Piggee sorts through his keys. He tries one. Then another. Then a third.

A tall, distinguished man with a neatly trimmed gray beard, he is hunched over the padlock that secures the auditorium at Horace Mann High School, where he is the dean of students.

Today, as on most days at Horace Mann, the auditorium is empty, and school officials have chained its two doors to keep potential vandals away. Once upon a time, such a scene would have been unthinkable. When Piggee went to school in the 1940s and 1950s across town at the then-all-black Roosevelt School, the auditoriums in Gary's schools were open and actively used all day.

They were, in fact, central—figuratively and literally—to what may have been the 20th century's longest and most thorough experiment with progressive education. The district's "platoon system," or work-study-play program, made the schools here internationally famous—and sometimes infamous. More than any other public school system, Gary applied the ideas of the country's most celebrated and debated educational thinker, John Dewey.

In doing so, the city's schools relied on their auditoriums for a range of academically and socially challenging activities almost

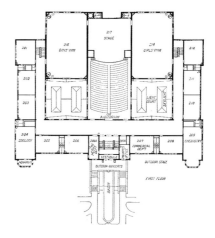

John Dewey's ideas came to life behind the doors of the Gary, Ind., schools.

Left and above: In the heyday of the Gary, Ind., school district's "platoon system," auditoriums played a central role, both academically and physically, as shown in the floor plan above for the Froebel School.

Facing page: The Froebel School's auditorium as it appears today.

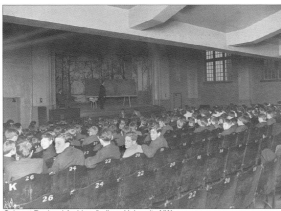

Calumet Regional Archives/Indiana University NW

Opening photo by Benjamin Tice Smith

The auditorium was "a speaking and listening chamber and laboratory. It was one of the outstanding features of the platoon system."

around the clock.

"The Gary auditorium is the nub of school both day and night," Hazel Harrison, a teacher at the Benjamin Franklin School, wrote in a 1927 book the Gary district published about its auditorium program.

"It was our daily bread—a speaking and listening chamber and laboratory," YJean Chambers says over a recent lunch while recalling her 12 years as a student and 26 years as a teacher in the Gary schools. "It was one of the outstanding features of the platoon system."

Horace Mann High—which opened in 1927, when the platoon system was at its height—is a relic of that era, a symbol of the Gary school system's historic self.

Dating back to the beginning of the Gary public schools in 1906, pupils from 1st grade through 8th grade spent at least one hour of the school day in an auditorium. Older students could take the class as an elective. They sang, gave lectures, questioned one another's presentations, put on plays, viewed films, and recited poetry.

They sometimes were divided into smaller groups for lessons in diction, speech, or music appreciation.

At night, they often returned with their families.

On some evenings, parent-teacher groups met. On others, families paid 10 cents each to watch the latest Hollywood movies.

In the rooms beyond the auditorium, students learned arithmetic, spelling, and other academic subjects; practiced their skills in shops and laboratories; and played in swimming pools and gymnasiums—experiencing work and study and play every school day.

The Gary schools had adjacent parks, zoos, and, for a while, a farm where youngsters harvested crops. The front lawn of the Horace Mann School included a pond, Piggee remembers.

Throughout the day, students learned to sew, type, and cook. Young chefs and future homemakers applied their knowledge by cooking in the school cafeteria, while students learning printing skills produced school materials, including a 1928 pamphlet describing the work-study-play approach to prospective teachers.

But it was the auditorium where everything came together, according to several accounts of what was widely known as the Gary Plan.

Chambers—like Piggee, a graduate of

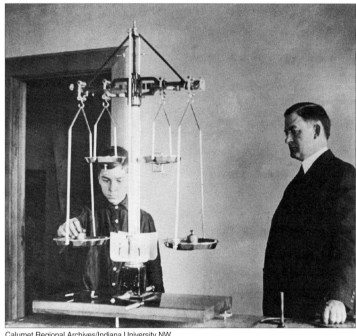

Calumet Regional Archives/Indiana University NW

Gary schools Superintendent William A. Wirt watches as a student works in a science lab in 1911.

the Roosevelt School, where she was in the Class of 1939—remembers that every auditorium had a diagram shaped like a wheel. The spokes listed academic and vocational subjects taught at the school. The hub named speaking, listening, music, and the arts. Underneath, she recalls, it read: "All learning is trans-

← THIS IS WONDERFUL

northwestern Indiana, about 30 miles from Chicago, was transformed from vacant land into a city in a matter of a year or so. In 1906, one writer said, Gary had "only wastes of shifting sand dunes, dot-

ted here and there with clumps of scrub-oak trees and broken in places by swamps." But after U.S. Steel Corp. built a plant there that year, as well as housing for its employees, the area became an industrial center and company town, named for the chairman of the corporation. By 1912, its population was 40,000.

In 1907, the city's leaders selected an idealistic educator named William A. Wirt as their superintendent of schools.

Wirt had studied under Dewey at the University of Chicago and had begun to use some of his ideas as the superintendent in Bluffton, Ind. But until he arrived in Gary with the challenge of building a school system from the ground up, Wirt hadn't had the chance to thoroughly apply Dewey's philosophy, with its emphasis on activity-based learning and the school's role in the community.

In a memoir stored in the archives at the Gary campus of Indiana University, Margaret Cook Seeley recalls that her schedule at the Emerson School—one of several Gary schools that taught students from kindergarten through 12th grade—was divided into the following one-hour periods:

8:15: Arithmetic and spelling
9:15: Gym
10:15: History and geography
11:15: Lunch
12:15: Nature study
1:15: Auditorium and music
2:15: English and writing
3:15: Art

e schedule was typical for 1st gh 8th graders in Gary during the three decades in which Wirt led the city's schools.

The work-study-play system included three one-hour periods on academic material; one or two, depending on the age group, in physical education; one or two in special activities, such as art; and one in auditorium, according to the 1928 pamphlet that described the program to prospective teachers.

The approach also was called the platoon system because each K-8 class was split into two sections. While Margaret Cook and her classmates attended an academic class, such as arithmetic or spelling, a separate section at the same grade level participated in some form of activity-based learning, such as nature study or auditorium. (Auditoriums throughout Gary would hold three classes at a time.) Later, the sections switched places.

Even the youngest children in the K-12 schools changed classes every hour, switching from room to room. Jessie MacLennan, a teacher in the Gary schools from 1926 until 1972, remembers making molds in the school foundry and caring for farm animals as a student at the Emerson School before she graduated in 1924.

On Saturdays, Wirt opened the schools for remedial work or for play periods. And throughout the summer, 65 percent of students attended classes. Some came for makeup work; others studied to move ahead of their age groups.

The schedule also encouraged students to learn outside school.

Once a week, children could choose to leave their schools to attend religious education at the churches of their choice. Pauline Bennett, a 1931 Roosevelt graduate, had to hurry to get to her church class. "You had to run or else you'd be late," she says.

And Marie Edwards, a 1934 Horace Mann graduate, was excused from her second gym period to take piano lessons off campus.

Beyond that, when a Gary school collected entrance fees for special events, such as movies shown in the auditorium, it spent the money on artwork for the walls, ultimately accumulating enough to be considered a museum, say Edwards and MacLennan, who both returned to the Gary schools to teach.

"Wirt's notion was not only to afford each child vastly extended educational opportunity—in playgrounds, gardens, libraries, gymnasiums and swimming pools, art and music rooms, science labo-

Benjamin Tice Smith

and isn't that what school should be about?

book on progressivism in American education.

Wirt's philosophy was based in educational theory, but the superintendent's desire for economy and efficiency and his belief in the superiority of capitalism also played a strong role. In his extensive writing about the program in reports, pamphlets, and journals, Wirt emphasized that the Gary Plan grew from economic concerns, as much as educational ones, according to historians Ronald D. Cohen and Raymond A. Mohl.

The emphasis on applied learning grew from Dewey's teachings, but the efficiency of having large groups of students performing or lecturing in the auditorium, cooking in the cafeteria, or learning outside reduced the need for classroom space, and, therefore, the tax burden on the growing city.

"The limited resources of the School

YJean Chambers decided she wanted to be a teacher after giving an extemporaneous speech as a 1st grader at the Roosevelt School.

so everyone's happy!

Students were required to follow Robert's Rules of Order in auditorium meetings. "Little ones even would learn how to run a meeting."

Town and the overwhelming size of the school obligation to be met led to a most careful investigation and study of school plant economy," Wirt wrote in a report to the Gary Town Council in 1909. The document is cited in *The Paradox of* gressive Education: The Gary Plan Urban Schooling, a 1979 book by Co and Mohl. "The purpose of the schoo ministration has been to secure not an efficient school plant but the most economical and efficient plant."

In little time, the Gary Plan became internationally renowned.

John Dewey himself and his daughter, Evelyn, praised it in their 1915 book *The Schools of To-morrow.*

MacLennan, Edwards, and other students recall streams of visitors from throughout the United States and even foreign countries. (Today, Japanese scholars remain fascinated by the Gary Plan and its impact in their country in the 1910s and 1920s, Cohen said in an interview. At least one researcher from Japan has traveled to the Midwestern city to study the system.)

In 1914, John Purson Mitchel, the new mayor of New York City, toured the Gary schools and decided that Wirt's model would solve his school system's problems with overcrowding.

The city hired the Gary superintendent as a $10,000-a-year, part-time consultant and instituted the work-study-play program in 32 schools in Manhattan, the Bronx, and Brooklyn. But the progressive ideas weren't embraced in New York as they were in Gary, according to *The Great School Wars*, Diane Ravitch's 1974 history of the New York City schools.

Protestant and Jewish leaders complained about allowing Catholic children to attend church instruction during school hours. Newspapers criticized the

Gary Plan as easier than the traditional academic program it replaced. And the school leadership was determined to provide "a seat for every child" in a self-contained classroom—a goal counter to

gram in 10 of the schools experimenting with it.

While Ravitch portrays opposition to the Gary Plan as a grassroots movement, Cohen and Mohl write that the riots and streams of anti-Gary propaganda were organized by Tammany Hall, the New York City political machine that Mitchel had ousted in 1913

after winning the mayor's office.

Regardless of the cause, the Gary Plan died in New York as soon as Judge John F. Hylan, the Tammany candidate, trounced Mitchel and two others in the 1917 election. The school system spent $300 million on construction over the next eight years, but still did not have enough seats for every child, Ravitch writes.

The defeat in New York did little to curtail interest in Gary. By the late

1920s, more than 200 cities in the United States adopted some portion of the work-study-play program, Cohen notes in his 1990 history of the Gary school system, *Children of the Mill: Schooling and Society in Gary, Indiana, 1906-1960*. Detroit and Portland, Ore., among others, adapted Wirt's ideas in their schools.

"Few other communities remained totally unaffected by its innovations," according to Cremin.

Visitors to any of the eight so-called unit schools—ones that included students from kindergarten through 12th grade—built during the Wirt era were likely to find the auditorium first. From the front door, they'd walk up a half-flight of stairs and end up across the hall from the centrally located room. (Even today, a guest looking for the principal's office at Horace Mann High wanders toward the auditorium before being directed to the basement.)

On a recent tour of the Horace Mann building, James Piggee unchains the doors to the room. Unlike the multiple-use cafeteria-auditoriums in more recently built schools, this auditorium is magnificent. The 600 or so seats slope upward, giving every audience member a clear view of the wide and deep stage. The floor is carpeted, and the auditorium seats are upholstered in burgundy—the product of redecorating in the 1980s, Piggee says.

Behind the stage, stairs lead up to two floors of classrooms. YJean Chambers says that's where students used to go for small-group music or speech instruction while a larger group would stay for auditorium activities. Today, those rooms

Calumet Regional Archives/Indiana University NW

Visitors to the district came to learn about the Gary Plan in the early decades of the 20th century. The district received attention both nationally and internationally. And even today, Japanese scholars remain fascinated with the impact the plan had on their country in the early 1900s.

are never used.

In *The Auditorium and Its Administration*, published by the school system in 1927, Edna Arnold Lockridge outlined how she divided a 50-minute class period in the school's auditorium: listening to music on "the Victrola" (five minutes); announcements (three minutes); music appreciation or chorus (20 minutes); calisthenics (two minutes); speeches, drama, or films with audience response (20 minutes).

Lockridge encouraged students to lead all portions of the class. During the chorus, those who played musical instruments accompanied the choir. Lockridge assigned other students to direct the choir. Still others led the brief exercise session.

During the final 20 minutes, Lockridge and other auditorium teachers led a potpourri of activities. One day, a local minister spoke about Abraham Lincoln; on another, the school principal talked about effective study habits. On April 7, 1925, at the Beveridge School, the secretary of the local YMCA lectured on the theme: "Be a Capitalist and Be Religious."

Some days, the teacher would show a movie for an hour. The 1927 book suggested a series of travel films, nature films such as "Our Feathered Aviators" or "Why Elephants Leave Home," or movie versions of "Macbeth," *Uncle Tom's Cabin*, or other classic literature.

Teachers might discuss current events or encourage young children to tell stories. They also might hold committee meetings, where students were required to follow Robert's Rules of Order.

"Little ones even would learn how to run a meeting," says Hylda Burton, a 1926 graduate of the Froebel School, who taught in auditoriums throughout the city from 1928 until the school system discontinued the program in 1955. She later taught 2nd grade in Gary until she retired in 1971.

During an extemporaneous speech in an auditorium session, YJean Staples, now YJean Chambers, chose her career path.

As a 1st grader, she volunteered to tell a story to her auditorium class, she says. Her classmates listened intently, laughed, and applauded as she told them about Goldilocks and the three bears.

And when she finished telling her story, she decided she wanted to teach in that room as an adult.

Benjamin Tice Smith

And she did teach in the Roosevelt School's auditorium for 10 years before the district shut down the mandatory, hour-long program and replaced it with electives.

Like Chambers, many other children graduated from the Gary schools with stage presence.

The list includes Karl Malden, an Oscar winner for his supporting role in the 1951 film "A Streetcar Named Desire" and the star of the 1970s television show "The Streets of San Francisco"; Alex Karras, the former National Football League all-pro who became a television actor and producer; Charles O. Finley, the insurance salesman who owned the Oakland A's baseball team in the 1970s; and Hank Stram, a Super Bowl-winning football coach and later a broadcaster.

(Possibly the most famous Gary natives—the singer Michael Jackson and his siblings—missed out on the glory days of the city's school system. Chambers, however, remembers turning the Jackson Five and its preschool lead singer away from a high school talent show until the sponsors decided to let them in.)

Jessie MacLennan, left, and Hylda Burton stand outside Gary's Emerson School, MacLennan's alma mater. Two years after she graduated in 1924, MacLennan started teaching in the Gary schools, where she worked until 1972. Burton graduated from the Froebel School in 1926 and taught in the district from 1928 to 1971.

Some elements of Wirt's plan remained in place. But by the end of World War II, the work-study-play program was "only a shadow of its former self."

All those people knew how to speak clearly, organize their thoughts, and entertain an audience, the advocates of the Gary Plan say, because they spent an hour a day in the auditorium.

In a 1996 newspaper interview, Karras—who graduated from the Emerson School in 1953—said his transformation from football player to actor had its roots in the Gary system.

"The great thing about my hometown—I always say this; Karl [Malden] always says this, too—is that we went to a school where, if you were a football player and you chose to act in the drama class, that was perfectly OK. There was no 'I'm a football player, what would I do with those dudes?' So we were able to go back and forth as actors and football players. I loved athletics and it kept me off the street, kept me busy, but what I liked most was drama," Karras told an interviewer from *The Times* newspaper in nearby Hammond, Ind.

After leaving her teaching position at Roosevelt High School in 1971, Chambers became a professor of speech and theater at Purdue University's campus in Hammond. She later won a seat on the Gary school board.

From the dais during meetings, she says, she and her colleagues judged parents' speeches. If the adult spoke with proper diction, enunciated words, and presented a coherent argument, they whispered to each other: "Pre-1955."

If the parent fidgeted, mumbled, and failed to make a persuasive argument, they'd say: "Post-1955."

"We could tell," she remembers. "It was so obvious. It really was."

"The Gary graduate could speak clearly," Edwards, the 1934 graduate of Horace Mann, says. "I've noticed the difference since it's been ended," she says of the auditorium program. Edwards taught at Gary's Lew Wallace School for 21 years

and later became the district's supervisor

← such a valuable skill set!

and adding new schools to the system, including Horace Mann.

In the 1930s, the Great Depression left the Gary district, like most school systems, cash-strapped. Still, Wirt managed to start Gary College, based at the Horace Mann School. College classes met in the K-12 school's classrooms in the late afternoon and evening, and the college

Calumet Regional Archives/Indiana University NW

The Froebel School in Gary, Ind., included a nature-study room with an attached greenhouse.

grew to become Indiana University Northwest, Gary's branch of the state university.

At several points during the decade, Wirt halted evening or Saturday activities to save money, according to Cohen, the Indiana University historian.

Wirt remained Gary's superintendent until his death at the age of 64 in 1938. Teachers announced his death in the auditoriums in the city's 21 schools, according to the reports in the March 11, 1938, edition of *The Gary Post-Tribune*. His body lay in state in the auditorium of the Emerson School.

Three years after the architect of the Gary Plan died, the school board started

to make gradual changes.

nuary 1941, three schools experi- d with keeping 1st graders with me teacher all day; 2nd and 3rd s stayed in the same classroom 80 t of the time.

hat fall, the school board abandoned the platoon system for 4th through 8th graders. The school day for kindergarten to 3rd grade shrank to six hours. Other grades were in school seven hours and 15 minutes, compared with eight hours every weekday under Superintendent Wirt.

Some elements of Wirt's plan—such as auditorium, home economics, and music—remained in place. But by the end of World War II, the work-study-play program was "only a shadow of its former self," Cohen writes in his 1990 book.

The platoon system—and the auditorium program with it—finally ended in 1955.

That year, consultants from the Public Administration Service, a Chicago nonprofit group, noted that while portions of Wirt's plan had been abandoned, nothing had been developed to replace it.

The lack of coherence could be seen in the consultants' finding that eight schools still enrolled children in grades K-12; in the rest, grade-level groupings varied from K-3 to K-8. The report recommended that the system be divided into K-6 schools, junior high schools, and three-year high schools. The proposal was phased in over the next 13 years, Cohen writes.

And the report suggested that the platoon system be abandoned completely. By then, Cohen observes, auditorium and physical education classes were the only vestiges of Wirt's original vision.

The changes meant that Hylda Burton left the auditorium in 1956 for a self-contained 2nd grade classroom. The speech and theater lessons Y.Jean Chambers taught in Roosevelt's auditorium became electives.

Today, Gary's schools face the problems encountered by many urban school systems. Its 19,500 students, most of whom are African-American, live in poverty in higher proportions than students in just about any other U.S. city. The property-tax base has been undermined by the "white flight" of the 1950s and 1960s, as well as a continued lack of economic development.

U.S. Steel—now named USX—continues to run its steel mill on the lakefront, but it's smaller than the ones from the company's Gary heyday. A Sheraton hotel stands abandoned just two blocks from the mill. An apartment building across the street from Horace Mann High School has been boarded up since Piggee, the dean of students, arrived 27 years ago.

Still, Gary's schools are recognized as beating the odds in some ways. In 1995, the system won a performance-based accreditation from the state based on its scores on the Indiana Testing for Educational Progress and its plans for improving those scores, an unusual accomplishment for an urban district. Benjamin Banneker Elementary School, the city's magnet school, has been named a "Four-Star School" by the state for placing its students in the 75th percentile on the state tests several years running.

Yet, many of the remaining graduates of Wirt's system aren't satisfied. If they were running the schools, things would be different. Speech, theater, and music—electives in most schools today—would be mandatory if Chambers, Burton, and other Gary alumni had their way.

Those studies would be at the center of the curriculum, much as the topics and skills taught in the original auditorium program were at the heart of the work-study-play program.

"I would be sure somehow to insert the speech, music, [and physical education] curriculum more fully into what we're doing. I would stop these things they do called language arts. I'd go back to teaching grammar, how to parse sentences, and parts of speech," YJean Chambers says.

Benjamin Tice Smith

"And then I would have speech—all the way through, I would have speech. I would build a curriculum all the way from K through 12 called speech. I would inject that … into everything," she says.

Over tea one afternoon in their friend Hylda Burton's apartment, Marie Edwards and Jessie MacLennan dream about reforming a school system.

"If some of us had enough nerve, we'd go to a place like Gary, Indiana, and re-institute the Wirt system," Edwards says.

"It would be good," MacLennan interrupts to add.

"Anytime you get three people together who went to the Gary schools during those years, they start talking about how we need [Wirt's work-study-play plan] now," Edwards finishes.

But at Horace Mann High School, the pool is used only once a year for a nine-week physical education elective. The pond that graced its lawn is a parking lot. And the doors to the auditorium—once the centerpiece of the school day—are almost always chained and padlocked. ∎

James M. Piggee, the dean of students at Horace Mann High School, sits in the school's redecorated auditorium. When Piggee attended Roosevelt High School in the 1940s and 1950s, auditoriums in the Gary district's schools were still the center of student life.

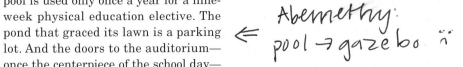

The Power and Peril Of Idea-Driven Reform

A perspective by Robert L. Hampel

In dreams begin responsibilities, as the poet Delmore Schwartz said. The educators profiled in these pages recounting the century's philosophical debates in education wanted to see their ideas take hold. They knew it might require a decade or more for schools to put the principles into practice. Stamina had to accompany passion. Publication often marked the start, not the end, of the work. One upshot is that many of the best-known books on education reform this century have one or more sequels where "implementation" is the story.

I put implementation in quotes because the word misrepresents what happens in reforms where ideas are central. Whenever broad concepts are at the heart of a coalition, the teachers who use them will adapt, not adopt, those notions. Each site is encouraged to interpret the ideas to suit local needs. A central staff will offer advice, host conferences, and generate materials to explain the concepts, but there are no models to imitate slavishly or detailed procedures to follow unswervingly. Idea-driven reform respects teachers and honors their ability to read, talk, and link theory with action.

Idea-driven reform is practical rather than quixotic in that other approaches rarely work. Cajoling schools with legislative mandates, shackling teachers with minutely scripted curricular packages, replacing staff with the latest technology: All have been tried and none went very far. Without honoring the wit and will of the people closest to students, new initiatives falter. The history of school reform indicates that agendas pushed down from above telling schools what to do eventually get set aside unless the teachers understand and endorse the ideas.

Yet sustained faculty conversation about important educational issues is as rare as it is crucial in most American schools. Doing takes precedence over talking, and isolation is more common than collegiality. What might seem an exception—the lengthy "self-study" done for accreditation—often promotes a checklist mentality. Do we have this or that? Can we match our programs with their guidelines?

Necessary for serious discussion of reform principles is a shift in school culture, a quest for what some writers call "reflective practice" in a "community of learners." Teachers like to quip that anyone can "talk the talk" rather than "walk the walk." But talking the talk is a big job in itself, too easily dismissed as pointless "philosophizing."

To converse thoughtfully takes time and effort. Although few reform principles are abstruse, they are not simple or self-evident. They convey more than "try something different," which is how some teachers construe membership in a national network— permission to do something, anything, new. As an ideology, reform principles are not as open as a psychologist's projective test, a Rorschach with no right answers. Nor are they as narrow as a specific instructional strategy—an ideology is not a script to follow, package to buy, or program to install.

What often happens is that people and principles get equated. Schools join reform networks, but individuals carry out the changes, especially at the start, when "whole-school change" is still far away. Particular teachers, or groups of teachers, emerge as the staunchest advocates. Their words and deeds seem to be one and the same as the beliefs of John I. Goodlad, John Dewey, whomever.

That confluence can be helpful. Without the example of an articulate and respected colleague, the core ideas and their manifestations in action are elusive, more abstract, and harder to grasp.

But what if the vanguard teachers are not the school's best teachers? In school improvement initiatives, the leaders usually volunteer. Eagerness to participate, not pedagogical excellence, is what the vanguard shares, and the two traits are not always synonymous. Rejecting old methods does not guarantee success with newer ones (just as acceptance of old ways does not ensure failure with new ways). So it becomes easy for an observer to leap from, "That 5th grade team is struggling," to, "E.D. Hirsch's ideas stink."

The conflation of people and principles helps explain why in many schools a measure of progress is the conversion of individuals who had been holdouts. That is, the willingness of a previously indifferent or ornery teacher to join a team, chair a committee, create interdisciplinary units, or participate in others ways is heralded as evidence that the ideas are spreading. However, the recruits sign on for many reasons, some only remotely related to educational principles. Snaring a second planning period, teaming with an old friend, protecting curricular turf, and other motives can overshadow agreement with and understanding of the ideas driving the reform.

Even when excellent teachers with honorable motives join and lead the way, the cadre may not have strong organizational skills. Little in their background equips them for the sudden responsibility of overseeing school change. So sometimes their stewardship seems naive and improvised. For instance, in the late 1980s, in networks keen on "restructuring" schools, many teacher-leaders were remarkably wary of structure. Meetings would lack ground rules, evaluation would be postponed, budgets wouldn't be balanced, and so on. As a result, some colleagues stayed away because they equated the project's ideas with chaos, even when the problems were simply the predictable and well-intentioned fumbling first steps of inexperienced teacher-leaders.

It is not an easy task to read, discuss, and use the ideas in the major books on education. Unlike a university seminar, it is hard to establish one interpretation as better than another. Who in the faculty is privileged to do so? There are few teachers who know the concepts so deeply that they can call attention to unthoughtfulness, misinterpretations, and other lapses in the conversations. Those who do may hold back for fear of sounding preachy and bossy.

In place of debate, teachers often try something new, tell colleagues it worked well, and no one then pushes to see if in fact the innovators performed as well as advertised. Colleagues congratulate each other for their willingness to experiment.

That generosity is sensible strategy early on, when it is vital to win allies. At the beginning, why risk offending anyone by insisting on this or that point of view, especially if teachers have heard there is no model to copy? There may be enough tensions and conflicts within the school without pouncing on each other's comments in meetings. But the price of the peace is lack of practice in the rigorous analysis and questioning that the principles themselves usually press teachers to do with their students.

Without frank, collegial discussion of

The history of school reform indicates that agendas pushed down from above telling schools what to do eventually get set aside unless the teachers understand and endorse the ideas.

the reform ideas, teachers are prone to stress part of a concept and overlook or reject the rest. For example, the popular "less is more" aphorism is often oversimplified. It is easy to envision "less" but much harder to see how less can be more. How can one Shakespeare play possibly offer more than three? Doesn't the state test require coverage, not depth? Won't our students botch their Advanced Placement exams? Without conversation and discussion, each question can become an exclamation point, an easy excuse to reject less-is-more. A major challenge for school reformers is to take away the easy excuses (especially the popular "But we already do that!") without insulting anyone.

American schools have long been polite places where no one confronts anyone else too directly. Teachers who disagree with policies complain in private and ignore the policy in practice. Administrators congratulate themselves on their accomplishments without seeking evidence of success or failure from those they know to be skeptical. Those schools that consistently paper over areas of disagreement hardly ever build educational programs that truly develop their students' potential.

Schools that do engage in rigorous discourse have many advantages that increase and persist over time. The climate of the school becomes more professional, centered around dialogue about teaching and learning. Those usually labeled as resisters can win the regard of their peers because of their ability to ask the most difficult questions. In turn, the resisters find legitimate avenues for involvement. All staff members feel relieved they can speak openly instead of covertly, and they begin to see that direct conversation, straight shooting, can improve their capacity to work with students.

There is no reason why the landmark books on education cannot find a wide audience, both within schools and outside. The books and reports cited in *Lessons of a Century* broadcast familiar aspirations for schools. They set forth hopes and dreams shared across the country. Many sold well for that reason—they expressed yearnings deeply felt but not fully developed or forcefully articulated by parents and citizens.

A key reason why most of the major works are accessible is their attentiveness to life in classrooms. They are full of painstaking descriptions of teaching. The canonical works are not philosophical treatises or arcane research disconnected from everyday life in schools. It is a literature of exhortation based on close observations, including a large amount of autobiography. It is thus surprising whenever anyone dismisses the works as "theory" or "educationese." The opposite charge—not enough theory undergirding the anecdotes and testimonials—would be more appropriate.

Readers also value the moral outrage in many of the books. The popular autobiographical accounts by John Holt, George Dennison, Jonathan Kozol, James Herndon, and others in the 1960s pilloried schools for the poor, and celebrated idealistic teachers who persevered inside dreary urban schools. To a man like the social critic Paul Goodman, pedagogical change should have gone hand in hand with a transformation of the entire culture. On the other hand, educators have occasionally been the target of the indignation. Arthur Bestor and other critics of progressivism were forever sputtering over the excesses of the "life adjustment" movement at midcentury. Recently, there have been fewer books marked by indignation, but they still appear, sell well, and arouse strong feelings, as Kozol's *Savage Inequalities* demonstrated.

One group of writers who carry on the tradition of impassioned observations on schooling is journalists. We need a good history of 20th-century journalists' commentary on schooling. They produced portraits of schools before qualitative research became fashionable, lacing their descriptions with blunt criticism. Books by Benjamin Fine, Martin Mayer, Peter Schrag, Fred and Grace Hechinger, and Charles Silberman are indispensable for understanding what it felt like to teach in schools between 1945 and 1970.

Recent books by the journalists Samuel Freedman, Tracy Kidder, Thomas French, and Patricia Hersch provide what is too often missing in research from the academy: the perspectives of students. Usually, the journalists profile between six and 15 students, and astonishing variety stands out more than any commonalities. Within the same school, kids with utterly different lives are side by side. Often they move within social groups totally separate from other social groups. The journalists' accounts caution against across-the-board reform proposals that minimize or ignore the inescapable fact that kids differ.

If there are books *about* students, it is rare to find books and reports that are *for* students. Where in these pages celebrating the century in education are passages addressed to adolescents? In contrast to reformers' focus on other adults, the corporate appeal to the youth market is direct and intense. The incentives are immediate and substantial—magazines, movies, music, and other after-school pursuits yield billions. The commercial messages are pervasive, beguiling, and thoroughly anti-intellectual. If marketing departments can reach and hold teenagers, why can't educators and students develop equally sophisticated campaigns on behalf of better schools? I hope that in our 2099 review of the 21st century in education, there will be many books excerpted that target the only people who can sustain school improvement, the students in our schools. ■

Robert L. Hampel is a professor and the interim director of the school of education at the University of Delaware in Newark. His books include The Last Little Citadel: American High Schools Since 1940 *(1986) and* Kids and School Reform *(1997), with Patricia Wasley and Richard Clark.*

evolving curriculum

A mericans may get swept up in debates over education finance, school safety, and the latest classroom technology. But throughout the 20th century, their attention has never strayed far from what lies at the very heart of schooling: the curriculum.

What society chooses to fill children's minds with generates a degree of passion that few other issues in education can match.

So, too, does the matter of who decides what students should be taught. Here, the country has seen a historic shift. Teachers, administrators, and school board members still wield considerable clout, but increasingly, state boards of education, legislators, and governors are exercising their prerogatives over subject matter and how it is taught.

The core curriculum of reading, writing, and arithmetic has long since been expanded to meet the changing demands of the nation. On the brink of a new century, educators continue to deliberate over what knowledge schoolchildren will need to conquer new challenges.

Parents, educators, and politicians have long debated what students should learn in American schools—and how they should be taught.

Photo by Corbis

Corbis

The State of Curriculum

Over the course of the century, decisions about what America's children study have shifted from the schoolhouse to the statehouse.

By Kathleen Kennedy Manzo

At the dawn of the century, Highland Springs Elementary School was akin to thousands of other one-room schoolhouses that dotted the American landscape. Inside the roughly hewn structure near Richmond, Va., a lone teacher toiled in relative isolation to provide basic lessons to more than two dozen students. She supplemented her own meager education with textbooks and the state course of study.

In the state capital to the west, Virginia's leaders, like many of their counterparts throughout the nation, were engaged in a passionate debate over the prospects for universal schooling, as they set out to redefine education for a new era.

Like the sunlight that sneaked through cracks in Highland Springs' wood siding, the modern conceptions that were emerging over what and how to teach a rapidly growing student population were barely brightening the daily routine of the classroom.

What the historian Herbert M. Kliebard describes as "the struggle for the American curriculum" was just beginning. That struggle—among scholars with conflicting philosophies about curriculum-making and teaching, and between local and state officials wrestling for control—would ebb and flow for decades.

Throughout the 20th century, the curriculum would become a national preoccu-

pation that would open up the classroom to greater scrutiny. It would at times unify the country in patriotic fervor, and at others, divide it in sectarian ferment. It was both the property held most dear by communities bent on determining what their children should learn and a medium for legislators and others seeking to correct societal ills.

The 1920s and 1930s would see an expansion and diversification of the curriculum to deal with a bulging high school population and to appease concerns over the economic realities of the day. In the 1940s and 1950s, the slackening of academic standards would come under attack as the United States vied with adversaries for military and technological superiority. In the wake of that criticism, the nation would redirect resources to improve math and science education. The civil rights and women's movements of the 1960s and 1970s brought demands for changes in curriculum and textbooks to give greater play to disenfranchised groups and to present the nation's history in a more critical light. By the 1980s, public worries about perceived "mediocrity" and global economic competition stirred a vast wave of state legislative action seeking more rigorous academic requirements.

On the eve of the 21st century, the struggle for the curriculum—being played out in the setting of state academic standards and measures for holding schools, teachers, and students accountable for meeting them—is no less fractious. Scholars, administrators, teachers, and parents are all bidding to leave their imprint. But

in the span of a hundred years, much of the control over what is taught has shifted from the schoolhouse to the statehouse—an often turbulent transition made reluctantly and grudgingly. State leaders, more than ever, are at the helm, still trying to fulfill the hope and promise for public education their counterparts were striving for a century ago.

MIND AS MUSCLE

As the 20th century opened, schools were free from state strictures on what was taught.

At Highland Springs Elementary, circa 1900, children huddled around a coal-burning stove reciting Longfellow's "Song of Hiawatha" and other memorized lessons. The strict discipline and tedious exercises that ruled those early school days scarred the memories of many youths.

"That one room was like a prison," recalled alumnus Leonard H. Rose for a writer who compiled the school's history in 1986.

Another former student remembered that in 1910, "teacher Bell Graham drilled and drilled the students in spelling."

Those sentiments in Virginia were echoes of a 1913 survey of young factory workers in Chicago, who said they preferred "factory labor to the monotony, humiliation, and even sheer cruelty that they experienced in school," Kliebard writes in *The Struggle for the American Curriculum: 1893-1958.*

That doctrine of "mental discipline"

maintained its stranglehold on most class-rooms into the early 1900s. Exponents of the theory, which shaped the curriculum throughout the 19th century, likened the mind to a muscle that had to be exercised in a precise and systematic way.

The philosophy "provided the backdrop for a regime in school of monotonous drill, harsh discipline, and mindless verbatim recitation," Kliebard notes in his 1986 book. "This may have gone on anyway, since the poorly trained and often very young teachers undoubtedly were at a loss to do anything else, but mental discipline provided them with an authoritative justi-fication for continuing to do it."

But a more progressive approach being advanced by the day's scholars was gain-ing favor in some school districts. Those scholars pushed for abandoning the auto-cratic classroom environment and the lec-ture-based instruction of previous decades in favor of more child-centered methods, in which children were encouraged to ask questions and suggest areas of content to explore.

Reading, writing, and arithmetic—which, along with Bible study, were the foundations of schooling in the 1800s—continued to fill up the school day. Other subjects, however, including nature study, literature, social studies, art, music, and manual training, were finding their way into many classrooms.

State education departments were feel-ing pressure from the experts to embrace the new philosophy. Yet, they were too overwhelmed by other tasks to push many changes in the classroom.

Those miniature bureau-cracies, usually headed by a superintendent, were dealing with a flood of requests to certify thousands of new school districts, as well as at-tending to their primary duty: gathering statistics on student enrollments and school financing.

Besides, even if the educa-tion departments had had the manpower, they were in no statutory position to over-see what was taught in schools. They did, however, encourage schools to use their respective states' courses of study—guides drawn up by most of them in the last half of the 1800s that outlined in varying detail the general objectives and broad goals for each subject. State administrators hoped the

courses of study would give teachers the necessary direction to organize the school day. Some of the guides merely cited the courses that were expected to be taught; others, though, led teachers through al-most every minute of the school day.

State officials dispatched county super-intendents and inspectors to assist and ex-amine local schools, but "since travel was by horse and buggy over poor roads, even the most diligent state official could not visit many schools in a single year," wrote Jim B. Pearson and Edgar Fuller in *Edu-cation in the States: Development Since 1900*, a massive 1969 report by the Coun-cil of Chief State School Officers on the history of state education policy.

What's more, those visits were usually devoted to financial affairs, and rarely cur-riculum concerns.

Largely then, curriculum decisions fell into the hands of local officials. Many states reported that state superintendents could not break the grip of local control and exerted minimal leadership in cur-riculum matters in the first two decades of the century. County superintendents were widely viewed with scorn and suspicion, and courses of study were mostly ignored by classroom teachers.

Michigan's superintendent, Delos Fall, said in 1901 that "each district board should specify the studies in local schools," according to *Education in the States*. Teachers were encouraged to follow a state manual and course of study—if the

One teacher taught several grades and several texts in this rural Grundy City, Iowa, classroom in the 1930s. As the years passed, decisions about what teachers would include in their lessons moved from the schoolhouse to state legislatures.

Corbis-Bettmann

district did not provide one.

Ultimately, with nearly 200,000 school districts in the United States by 1910, sometimes with dozens alone in a single rural county, the content and quality of instruction varied widely.

NEW YORK DIFFERENCE

Curriculum, however, was becoming increasingly important to state legislatures and state boards of education.

The vast social and political changes of the era pushed the stakes higher for public education. With the arrival of more and more children at the schoolhouse door in the first two decades of the century, many of them immigrants, quality became more of an issue. As the schools came to be viewed as vehicles for preserving American values and democratic ideals among a more diverse citizenry, educators and their professional organizations, whose numbers and influence were growing, were vigorously promoting plans for expanding public education.

"Policymaking in public education by then had gravitated from the locally based and part-time evangelists for the common school to a new breed of experts and professional managers, people who made education a lifelong career, created new fields of specialization, and sought to re-

Corbis-Bettmann

shape the schools according to the canons of educational science and business efficiency," David B. Tyack and Elisabeth Hansot write in *Policy Making in Education*, published in 1982.

The high school curriculum—shaped by college-entrance requirements—was of particular interest. The prestigious Committee of Ten, a group of college presidents that was convened by the National Education Association to recommend standards for college admissions, first questioned the relevance of rigid academic courses for the new cohort of students, most of whom would not advance to college. But the committee concluded, in its 1893 report, that schools should maintain a single academic curriculum for all students.

Officials in New York state believed they were doing just that. The state's examination system, begun in 1865 and administered by the board of regents, all but guaranteed that students in even the most isolated districts had access to a college-preparatory curriculum. In 1910, the education department issued a detailed, 256-page syllabus for elementary education.

Two years later, the state education department was enormous by all accounts, with a staff of 250 to supervise and inspect more than 10,000 school districts. Throughout the century, the regents provided syllabi and support services to help teachers prepare students for the rigorous end-of-course exams, though decisions about textbooks and instructional methods were still left to individual districts.

While intended for a small proportion of the high school population, the standards set by the regents' program raised the stakes for all New York students, argues Gordon M. Ambach, the executive director of the Council of Chief State School Officers.

"The influence of those exams over the 20th century has just been incredible, in my judgment, by way of ensuring that any place you went in rural or urban New York, you would have access to the array of courses required for a regents' diploma," says Ambach,

the commissioner of education in New York state from 1977 to 1987. "The exam system provided an opportunity for students to stretch themselves and reach for a higher goal. They raised the ante for teachers and students, parents and schools."

But the elite high school program, such as New York's and those promoted by the Committee of Ten, had its critics. They disagreed with the committee's view that "education for college *is* education for life."

The statistics supported their view. In New York, for instance, only one in 16 high school students in 1904 completed the four-year program. Today, about 40 percent of the state's students earn a regents' diploma.

PUSHING TEXTS

By 1910, the winds of change favored progressive ideals, and more state policy efforts became focused on curriculum matters.

In a great irony, such efforts were often aimed at the rural schools to bring them up to par with their far superior urban counterparts. In the countryside, local boards with their often bullying tactics wielded tremendous power over teachers and, ultimately, what they taught, Tyack observes in his 1974 book, *The One Best System: A History of American Urban Education*. Urban districts had already begun standardizing coursework, and by the 1920s, became leaders in curriculum development. But rural districts, which made up a majority of the nation's school districts, fought to maintain autonomy over instruction.

Many states found it an impossible task to enforce standards in thousands of tiny school districts, but most communities rejected recommendations that districts be organized into larger, more cohesive units. Reluctant to intervene in what communities staunchly defended as local decisions, states turned their attention toward the primary tool of the trade—the textbook—to standardize classroom practice.

Throughout the 19th and the early 20th centuries, teachers relied heavily on textbooks, as some still do today. Twenty-two states, most of them in the South, eventually adopted policies for purchasing texts. Such policies were intended to impose a standard course of study. In the process, they were also expected to take such decisions out of the hands of often poorly educated, unsophisticated teachers and put them into those of experts; combat uneven pricing, corruption, and unscrupulous practices common among publishers of the

Corbis-Bettmann

day; and reduce the problems associated with a highly mobile student population, according to Michael W. Apple, a professor of education at the University of Wisconsin-Madison.

One educator, reviewing Kentucky's state textbook-adoption policy in 1919, reported that, with such an ill-prepared corps of teachers, "the only hope was to place the best textbooks possible in the hands of the students," Apple writes in *Textbooks in American Society*, published in 1981.

In the Southern states, screening texts guaranteed that books that did not promote Southern culture—in such sensitive areas as race—would not find their way into schools.

The book-adoption policies, which laid out in meticulous detail the topics and historical events and figures to be covered, went a long way toward establishing states' authority over subject matter.

California had the most restrictive policy, making it a misdemeanor for a school official or teacher to use materials other than the approved texts. The state had even built its own printing plant in 1885,

at a cost of more than $500,000, and for a time hired its own writers to ensure that the textbooks would meet requirements at a minimal cost. Despite rampant criticism that the system was "reeking with fraud and dishonesty," and resulted in higher-priced, poor-quality texts, the state continued to publish its own books into the middle of this century.

HEALTH AND SAFETY

Even the most thoughtfully chosen textbooks, however, offered no guarantees for improving education. Early in the century, reformers were pushing for state policies to address "the 'bookish' curriculum, haphazard selection and supervision of teachers, voluntary character of school attendance, discipline problems, [and] diversity of buildings and equipment" that characterized the rural school, according to Tyack. So state leaders sought to address what the Stanford University scholar calls the "rural school problem" in other ways.

At loggerheads with local boards over administrative issues, such as the con-

Left: Students at Roosevelt High School in New York City study in the building's library. State officials started an examination system in 1865 that aimed to ensure that even students in isolated districts had access to a college-preparatory curriculum.

Above: Patriotism was a popular theme of many early classroom mandates. Children in San Juan Bautista, Calif., in 1942 assemble to march in a parade to show off the scrap metal they collected for the war effort.

Physical education classes became the norm in schools after the First World War raised concerns about troop fitness. Right, junior high school students in Pittsburgh test their climbing skills in gym class in 1950.

"As confidence in the schools seemed to diminish . . . state legislators began to interest themselves more in education affairs."

J. Myron Atkin
Dean, Stanford University
School of Education, 1979-86

solidation of districts and the supervision of teachers, states initially exercised their authority over turf outside the traditional curriculum or in those areas in which they were likely to meet with the least resistance.

In the waning years of the 19th century, many legislatures had begun mandating studies in physiology, for example. Under pressure from the Women's Christian Temperance Union, schools were ordered to teach about the ill effects of alcohol and drug use. Patriotism was another popular theme of many early mandates, such as a 1909 provision requiring the singing of "The Star-Spangled Banner" in Indiana classrooms. In 1925, another law in that state—similar to those being adopted elsewhere—called for the teaching of the state and U.S. constitutions.

When the First World War raised concerns about the United States' military preparedness and troop fitness, states began requiring physical education. From 1915 to 1918, eight states—California, Delaware, Illinois, Maryland, Nevada, New Jersey, New York, and Rhode Island—enacted physical education laws. Most other states followed suit in the ensuing years and in the decade leading up to World War II. The military-style curriculum that became the norm—including ropes courses and calisthenics—shaped gym classes for decades to come. Similarly, the Great Depression prompted many states to require economics classes.

World War I also brought into sharp relief the realization that schools were not meeting the needs of most students. Following the advice of experts who promoted the idea of educating for social efficiency—preparing students according to their likely paths, either to college or the workforce—states began dividing the curriculum into general education and vocational tracks. The Oregon superintendent of schools in 1913 hired two assistants to travel around the state to promote vocational courses. The state attracted national attention for its extracurricular-training program, which had 12,000 students enrolled in clubs for sewing, poultry raising, cooking and baking, farming, and other skills, Pearson and Fuller noted in the Council of Chief State School Officers' report.

By that time, states were beginning to rally around vocational education. Within a few years, most states had created home economics programs, and about half had established agricultural education.

In 1917, federal legislation that provided funding for agricultural, occupational, and home economics education made vocational education a standard in the high school curriculum. The additions were not without their critics, many of whom saw such classes as anti-intellectual and a means of limiting students' academic opportunities.

The popular notion that the teenagers flooding the high schools were less talented than previous generations of students guided educators in diversifying the curriculum, David L. Angus and Jeffrey E. Mirel contend in their new book, *Conflict and Curriculum in the American High School*. It was incumbent on the schools, reformers argued, to meet the needs of what the psychologist G. Stanley Hall had referred to earlier in the century as "the great army of incapables."

By the 1930s, the high school ranks had swelled to nearly 5 million. By the end of the decade, more than 7 million students, representing three-fourths of 14- to 17-year-olds, were seeking a secondary education.

GROWING INVESTMENT

As the Depression wore on, states were taking on more of the financial burden of running schools. Between 1920 and 1940, the states' share of education spending nearly doubled, to 30 percent of total costs, and would increase to 40 percent by 1950, according to Pearson and Fuller. With their investment in public education growing, states believed they had more of a stake in curriculum matters and began to play a more active role in determining what was taught.

From studies of educational programs in hundreds of districts—by curriculum pacesetters such as Ellwood P. Cubberley, Franklin Bobbitt, Charles Judd, and George Strayer—emerged new models for designing curricula.

The favorable results from revised programs in Denver and other cities gave states the impetus for more widespread reform and, in the 1930s, spawned a curriculum-revision movement.

Under the guidance of Hollis P. Caswell, a professor of education, and his colleagues at George Peabody College in Tennessee, now part of Vanderbilt University, the curriculum-revision movement marked the first time states had instituted comprehensive curriculum-development programs, according to *History of the School Curriculum* by Daniel Tanner and Laurel Tanner, published in 1990. Beginning in Florida and Alabama, and expanding to California, Kansas, Maryland, Michigan, New Mexico, and nearly all the Southern states, the movement had far-reaching influence, Daniel Tanner says. While the state courses of study addressed the content to be studied, those statewide curriculum programs aimed to improve instruction.

"State curriculum programs took the lead in making a highly important redefinition of the meaning of the curriculum," Caswell recalled in a 1930s-vintage paper, "Emergence of the Curriculum as a Field of Professional Work and Study." Prior to that emergence, "courses of study gathered dust on shelves," Tanner notes in his book.

States struggling to maintain education funding in the midst of the Depression looked to foundations—including the General Education Board, underwritten by the Rockefellers, and the Carnegie Corporation of New York—to supplement state start-up money for the revision programs.

Virginia Superintendent Sidney B. Hall enlisted Caswell in 1931 to lead what would become the most famous of all the statewide programs.

Caswell was to "set up a more modern approach to the teaching situation which should exist in the classroom … and bring educational practice up to the standards described by our best scholars in educational theory," according to a state summary of the program.

Following the precedent set in Alabama and Florida, also choreographed by Caswell, collaboration among administrators, teachers, scholars, and community members would emerge as the main component of the Virginia initiative. For the first time, the teacher's role in curriculum development was at center stage.

"Initially, all 17,000 teachers in the state were invited to join in a curriculum-study program, and according to Superintendent Hall's account, an incredible 15,000 joined the study committees that were formed and held in 1931-32," Kliebard writes. Teachers intimately involved in the process, the program's advocates argued, were more likely to implement the recommendations.

Teachers statewide formed study groups to discuss educational objectives, the place of subject matter in the curriculum, and ways of organizing instruction and measuring outcomes, among other topics. They were asked to record descriptions of their best work and list materials they found valuable.

Unveiled in 1934, Virginia's revised course of study was much different from those of previous generations. It was

organized around what were deemed the purposes of schooling: protection and conservation of life, property, and natural resources; production, distribution, transportation, and consumption of goods and services; exploration; recreation; extension of freedom; and the expression of aesthetic and religious impulses.

By 1937, Virginia officials had declared the elementary course of study a great improvement. State surveys found that nearly 85 percent of teachers were implementing some part of the program in their classrooms. The high school program progressed more slowly.

"Progress has been made in every direction and we believe our program is well on its way to successful fruition," Superintendent Hall wrote in 1939.

A MODEL CURRICULUM

As many as 31 states, many of them using the work in Virginia as a model, underwent similar curriculum revisions. The movement was hailed as a great example of what could be achieved when all the interest groups—under the direction of the

Corbis/Charles Harris; Pittsburgh Courier

state—worked together.

But critics have characterized the process as manipulative and undemocratic.

"The goals of the curriculum revision were never truly open for discussion," the education historian Diane Ravitch writes in *The Troubled Crusade: American Education 1945-1980.* "Despite the rhetoric about participation and cooperation, the outcome of curriculum revision was fixed-in-advance by the experts."

Teachers who did not follow the group were fired, she writes. The Philadelphia curriculum guide, for example, said that "if teachers refused to behave 'intelligently and cooperatively,' then 'protective measures' would be taken 'in the interest of the common welfare.' "

Regretably, Ravitch writes, the curriculum-revision movement "was not an effort to balance intellectual, social, and emotional needs, but a conscious attempt to denigrate the traditional notion of 'knowledge for its own sake' as useless and possibly worthless."

But Virginia Lewis Dalton, 85, remembers her first few years of teaching as an exciting time. Dalton, who started teaching at her alma mater, Culpeper High School, in a rural county north of Charlottesville, Va., in 1940 and later headed the state teachers' association, recalls that the innovations promoted through the state's new curriculum brought welcome relief from the drill-and-skill tradition.

The curriculum program "called on teachers to be more creative," Dalton says. "I was young, and I was excited about it. It gave [teachers] an opportunity to interact more with students rather than with textbooks."

Such endeavors, though, did not last long. By 1940, foundations discontinued subsidizing them, and World War II was beginning to divert the country's attention to more urgent issues of national defense and the preservation of democracy. What had been a flood of mail arriving at Teachers College, Columbia University, which had collected copies of more than 85,000 courses of study drafted by states and districts, turned into a trickle. And publication of new courses of study was halted by shortages of manpower and materials.

But the era's influence on the emerging field of curriculum development is evident, scholars say.

"It represented the curriculum field as coming into its own," says Kliebard, now a professor emeritus of curriculum and instruction at the University of Wisconsin-Madison.

For the first time, states hired numerous subject-area specialists and created curriculum laboratories to help districts

The Clash Over Evolution

By Steven Drummond

In some ways, the Scopes trial was about a lot more than the teaching of evolution in public schools. And in some ways, it ended up being about a lot less—a sideshow that obscured as much as it revealed real concerns among Americans about religious beliefs, science, academic freedom, and public education.

It was about Southern pride, civic boosterism, and majority rule. It was about massive egos, old grudges, media hype, the American Civil Liberties Union, Christian fundamentalism, Charles Darwin, and monkeys.

One thing it never was about, really, was John T. Scopes.

In March 1925, the Tennessee legislature passed a law making it a crime to teach evolution theory in public schools. The ACLU advertised in newspapers statewide, offering to defend any teacher charged under the new law.

Civic leaders in the mining and farming town of Dayton saw the notice and in it, a chance to win some attention for their rural backwater. Over sodas at a local drugstore, they pitched their idea to the high school's 24-year-old science teacher and football coach, and Scopes agreed to be the guinea pig.

A grand jury quickly convened and indicted the young teacher on a misdemeanor charge. As Edward J. Larson puts it in his Pulitzer Prize-winning 1997 book on the case, *Summer for the Gods,* "the show had begun."

Smelling opportunity, the populist orator William Jennings Bryan, a three-time Democratic nominee for president of the United States, leapt at the chance to join the prosecution.

"In a stroke," Larson writes, "the ACLU lost control of what it initially conceived as a narrow constitutional test of the statute. With Bryan on hand, evolution would be on trial at Dayton, and pleas for individuality would run headlong into calls for majority rule."

The entry of the Great Commoner brought another old warhorse onto the field. Clarence Darrow, the nation's most famous defense lawyer and a well-known foe of many Christian beliefs, joined Scopes' defense.

Essentially, Bryan and the prosecution sought not to attack evolution as a scientific theory, but simply to defend the right of a majority of the people in a state, through their legislature, to determine what could be taught in the public schools.

Scopes' defenders portrayed that line of reasoning as an attack on academic freedom and constitutional protections of freedom of speech and religion. They hoped to introduce lengthy scientific tes-

rewrite curricula. As a result of the Virginia experience, Caswell designed the "scope and sequence" chart, a variation of which is still widely used today to design curricula.

"It was a turning point in the professionalization of the field ... an advance in some respects in people's thinking about curriculum," Kliebard argues.

States, universities, and professional organizations responded to the new thinking with an abundance of publications to support teachers and administrators. The California education department, for example, produced a monthly guide for teaching science in elementary school from 1934 to 1941. Cornell University produced leaflets for science teachers.

RETHINKING 'ADJUSTMENT'

In the late 1930s, the New York board of regents, which had long exerted its influence on the high school curriculum through its rigorous examination program, conducted an extensive study of graduates and dropouts to determine the system's weaknesses. The "regents' inquiry" and other studies of the period revealed wide gaps in the curriculum's ability to meet the needs of all children.

By the mid-'40s, policymakers and researchers determined to make education more functional were pushing for a rewriting of the high school curriculum.

A study commissioned in 1945 by the U.S. Office of Education to study the fu-

timony in support of evolution theory.

After weeks of intensive pretrial buildup in newspapers and church pulpits nationwide, the trial began July 10, 1925, in the sweltering heat of a packed courtroom in Dayton.

Outside, in a scene that has become familiar to Americans of a later time, reporters, photographers, hucksters, opportunists, and the simply curious had descended.

"Dayton was having a roaring time," observed H.L. Mencken, the most famous newsman of the day. "It was better than the circus."

The basic facts were never really at issue. After several days of procedural bickering and speeches by the lawyers, the trial reached its dramatic conclusion on July 20. In a surprise move, Darrow called Bryan to the stand as a defense witness and skewered the aging politician with questions about his literal interpretations of biblical events.

Both sides emerged bloody from the encounter. Bryan's ignorance of scientific matters had been laid bare, yet many considered Darrow's questioning mean-spirited and its atheistic tone ultimately harmful to the evolution cause.

Though it made for excellent theater, the stunt did little to alter the outcome. The jury quickly convicted Scopes, who was fined $100 and faded into history. He died in 1970.

In legal terms, the spectacle had accomplished little, giving neither the rousing victory for fundamentalism

Corbis-Bettmann

and majority rule that Bryan had sought nor the platform for a defense of evolution that Darrow wanted.

But for a few weeks, it had focused public opinion on matters of science and education as nothing would again until the launch of Sputnik three decades later.

In 1987, the U.S. Supreme Court struck down a Louisiana law requiring that creationism receive equal time with evolution in science classrooms. Variations on the issue continue to play out in legislatures and school boards.

Five days after the Scopes trial ended, Bryan died in his sleep. Without him, the national debate over the teaching of evolution lost much of its fire, though the embers still smolder more than 70 years later. ■

Well-known as a foe of many Christian beliefs, Clarence Darrow, far left, joined the defense team in the 1925 trial of science teacher John T. Scopes, seated second from right.

ture of vocational education concluded that many schools were failing to design programs for the 60 percent of students who did not participate in either college-prep or vocational programs. Those students, according to Charles A. Prosser, who had helped draft the federal vocational education law three decades earlier, would benefit from "life-adjustment education." Such programs, which were later endorsed for all students, consisted of "guidance and education in citizenship, home and family life, use of leisure, health, tools of learning, work experience, and occupational adjustment," Ravitch writes.

Soon, regional conferences were organized to discuss the issue. The Office of

Education and nearly every major educational organization were uniting behind the idea of restructuring education for "functional" purposes.

Some of the solutions promoted during the life-adjustment-education movement of the late 1940s and early 1950s—such as courses on dating and the proper use of leisure time—bordered on foolishness, in the opinion of its many critics.

Less than a decade later, in the midst of the Cold War, the logic behind the de-emphasis of subject matter would be questioned as schools took much of the blame for the nation's perceived shortcomings. The United States' embarrassment at falling behind in the space race with the Soviet Union's launch of Sputnik I in 1957 forced schools to re-evaluate the curriculum.

As in 1917, the federal government felt compelled to respond to a national emergency by taking aim at the curriculum, according to Kliebard. The National Defense Education Act of 1958 called on the National Science Foundation to restructure curricula in mathematics, science, and foreign languages. The law was expanded in 1964 to include social studies and English.

States eager to qualify for the matching-grant program began concentrating more on those disciplines. The new money from Washington allowed state education departments to expand their staffs substantially and hire many more subject-area specialists. The legislation also led to the creation of federal regional laboratories to assist districts.

The NDEA represented "a massive entry by the federal government into curriculum matters that dramatically changed the political balance and the nature of the interplay among the protagonists in the struggle," Kliebard writes. "The way in which the curriculum of American schools was determined was never quite the same after that."

PROMOTING EQUALITY

As the civil unrest of the 1960s erupted, academic rigor took a back seat to educational equality.

"Amid the extreme social dissension of the late 1960s, the schools—because of their role in generating values and teaching ways of knowing—were directly affected by antiwar protests, the splintering of the liberal center, the rise of the coun-

terculture, the growth of racial separatism, and demands for 'relevant' curricula by everyone who wished to change society," Ravitch writes.

The growing demand for equality from those who were disenfranchised or discriminated against—African-Americans, other minorities, women, and the handicapped—was being played out in the courts and in Congress, further accelerating federal encroachment into education.

As those groups were granted more legal protections, they pushed to get their viewpoints into the classroom. The advocacy groups, as well as curriculum materials, promoted a more balanced curriculum that incorporated the contributions of all people—not just those of white males of Western European stock.

Many state legislatures followed the federal lead in trying to promote reform in school.

"Although education policy is a major responsibility of the state legislature, until the 1970s considerable authority in fact had been delegated to local school boards, with the state determining only a broad policy framework," J. Myron Atkin, the dean of the school of education at Stanford University from 1979 to 1986, wrote in a 1980 article in the scholarly journal *Daedalus*. "As confidence in the schools seemed to diminish ... state legislators began to interest themselves more in education affairs." Increasingly, Atkin noted, legislation greatly diminished local school administrators' and teachers' control over the curriculum.

Citizens' groups seeking more school accountability for what they saw as escalating costs and poor academic results, began exerting their own influence, leading

protests over the content of textbooks and educational experiments, such as "open education." Taxpayer revolts in California and Massachusetts—which reined in the local property taxes that paid for education—forced those states to take on an even greater responsibility for the schools. In more than 30 states, parents and community groups were ultimately successful in pressuring their legislatures to mandate minimum-competency testing of students, prompting a re-emphasis on the teaching of basic skills.

"By 1980," Ravitch writes, "there was no turning back to the days when local school boards were near-autonomous."

A year later, U.S. Secretary of Education Terrel H. Bell noted "a widespread public perception that something is seriously remiss in our educational system." To help find a remedy, he created the National Commission on Excellence in Education to study the problems of public schooling.

The commission's influential and controversial report, *A Nation at Risk*, released in April 1983, described a society that no longer dominated the international economy, and an education system confused about its purpose.

"The educational foundations of our society are presently being eroded by a rising tide of mediocrity that threatens our very future as a nation and a people," the commission concluded. "We have, in effect, been committing an act of unthinking, unilateral educational disarmament."

The report, with its urgent rhetoric, ignited an intensive new campaign to improve American education. Its authors crisscrossed the nation to aim a spotlight on schools. A flurry of public attention to the report prompted governors and other elected officials to take a more active role in education. Following the release of the report, then-Vice President George Bush invited governors to his summer home in Maine to discuss a course of action. Many states quickly enacted laws beefing up instructional time and graduation requirements.

Despite such action, the depth of discussion around curricular matters was disappointing, Ernest L. Boyer, the president of the Carnegie Foundation for the Advancement of Teaching until his death in 1995, said a year after *A Nation at Risk* was published.

"It has not led to a serious and creative look at the nature of the curriculum," Boyer told a reporter in 1984.

"Instead," he said, "states have simply been adding units along traditional lines, almost mindlessly, without asking what it is we ought to be teaching in them."

Six years passed before a national

Corbis/Ted Streshinsky

summit on the issues the commission raised took place. During that gathering in Charlottesville in 1989, governors and education leaders committed themselves to working toward a set of goals for the nation's schools. Among them were aspirations for all students to master challenging subject matter in core disciplines and for U.S. students to become "first in the world" in math and science achievement.

TAKING CHARGE

Later, many policymakers and educators, heeding the recommendations in *A Nation at Risk*, decided the country needed to translate those goals into academic standards spelling out what students should know and be able to do. The federal government provided several subject-matter groups with money to write what were described as voluntary national standards in such disciplines as English language arts, science, history, geography, civics and government, and the arts. So upset were many educators and lawmakers by the results of those efforts, particularly in history and English, that support for national standards has all but disappeared.

State officials, who had spurned all but the most cursory of roles in the development of curriculum at the beginning of the century, maintained that it was their responsibility—indeed, their very right—to define classroom content. All but Idaho and Iowa have set standards in at least one subject, and many are creating assessments and comprehensive accountability programs designed to ensure they are met.

State legislatures, citing a lengthy history of ineffective reforms, have taken a more aggressive approach aimed at improving classroom practice, which has remained relatively constant over the century, regardless of the intensity or extent of reform efforts, Larry Cuban writes in *What Teachers Taught: Constancy and Change in American Classrooms, 1890-1990.*

Virginia, once again, is influencing other states. Highland Springs Elementary School is but a memory. And the state has shaken off the spirit of "progressive education" that made it a leader of curriculum revision in the 1930s. Today, a traditional curriculum is the guiding force behind the state's academic standards. Held up as a national model, the Virginia standards, which outline in detail what students should learn at each grade level in every major subject,

John Phillips

have been declared clear and rigorous, though some educators argue that they're too prescriptive and sacrifice critical-thinking skills for the memorization of facts.

As with the reforms of decades past, the standards adopted in most states are voluntary. But policymakers believe they have found a way to force their entry into the schoolhouse: a system of rewards and sanctions based on how well students master the material.

The power of the purse has proved to be a strong motivator. Some states, like Kentucky and North Carolina, provide bonuses for teachers in schools that meet state expectations on tests. Another tack has been for states to withhold aid unless instructional materials for reading are used for phonics instruction or related professional development. Nearly two dozen states passed legislation with that requisite in the past few years. Though local officials and teachers still try to maintain autonomy, state leaders are knocking ever louder at the classroom door.

Putting it bluntly, the "abject failure" of locally controlled schools forced states to take a stronger stand, Gov. Gray Davis of California recently told a reporter.

"When you have an earthquake or natural disaster, people expect the state to intervene," said the Democrat, who championed an extensive package of education measures passed by the legislature this year. "Well, we have a disaster in our schools." ■

Above: In 1956, a student reads a California history text featuring American Indians on its cover. California developed the strictest of the state textbook-adoption policies, making it a misdemeanor for school officials or teachers to use materials that had not been approved for classroom use.

Left: In 1981, U.S. Secretary of Education Terrel H. Bell created the National Commission on Excellence in Education to study problems in public schooling. Its report, A Nation at Risk, warned: "The educational foundations of our society are presently being eroded by a rising tide of mediocrity that threatens our very future as a nation and a people."

The Race to Space

By
David J.
Hoff

On Oct. 4, 1957, the Soviet Union launched Sputnik I—the first man-made satellite to orbit the Earth—and with it a campaign to change K-12 curriculum in the United States.

With the American public caught unaware by its Cold War enemy's scientific prowess, the federal government for the first time made a major investment in curriculum development for K-12 classrooms. The hope was to train future scientists who would help this country reach the moon before the Communist empire.

With money from the National Science Foundation, academics started to rewrite curricula for physics, biology, chemistry, and mathematics. By the early 1960s, the campaign had spread into the social sciences. University scholars conducted hundreds of summer seminars showing teachers how to teach with the new materials.

In the 20 years after Sputnik, the NSF—an independent federal agency—spent $500 million on curricula and teacher development. Some science materials were well-received and widely used; derivatives of them are in classrooms today. But others—such as the "New Math" of the 1960s and a controversial 5th grade anthropology program called Man: A Course of Study—failed to take hold and led to Congress' curtailment of NSF curriculum projects in the late 1970s.

While the foundation has reclaimed a role in the precollegiate curriculum in the past 15 years, its involvement has never again reached the level it did during the heyday of the space race.

ELITIST CURRICULA?

After Neil Armstrong, in 1969, became the first man to set foot on the moon—thus winning the pioneering race for the United States—public support for federal curriculum initiatives waned. The populace no longer demanded wholesale changes in schools, says Peter B. Dow, who led the effort to write Man: A Course of Study.

But the education historian Diane Ravitch maintains that NSF projects failed because they were created by academic elites without enough help from teachers or everyday citizens.

A redesigned math curriculum that emphasized theory over process and a social studies program that taught other cultures' values that contradicted American mores may have made sense to professors in Cambridge, Mass., and Palo Alto, Calif., Ravitch says. But those ideas didn't sit well in mainstream America, she says, where politically ascendant conservatives and other detractors questioned whether schools should challenge cultural beliefs and established methods—a tension that has been rekindled with the academic-standards movement launched in the late 1980s.

The seeds for curriculum change had been germinating a few years before the Soviet Union launched Sputnik. Professors at the Massachusetts Institute of Technology, Yale University, and the University of Illinois started to investigate new ways of teaching math and physics.

In fact, the Physical Science Study at MIT first received NSF money in 1956.

But it wasn't until 1958, when Congress passed the National Defense Education Act, that the 8-year-old NSF began pouring money into curriculum development.

By 1975, the science foundation's catalog of active projects listed 15 for elementary schools, 12 for middle schools, and 34 for high schools. In many subjects, the foundation backed several efforts. In high school biology, for example, the NSF supported a comprehensive curriculum and a series of films, including ones on viruses, ecology, and social biology.

Typically, the agency would underwrite a group of academic experts and a limited number of teachers working through universities or nonprofit organizations to write a curriculum. In the case of the New Math, the money went to Yale University to support the School Mathematics Study Group, or SMSG.

Educational Services Inc.—a Cambridge, Mass., nonprofit group that later became known as the Education Development Center—won NSF grants for a variety of projects, including the Elementary Science Study and Man: A Course of Study.

IN THEORY

The academics leading the new curriculum charge started with the assumption that schools were not teaching the theory behind disciplines without which the nation could not produce rocket scientists. Mathematics taught in schools emphasized simple calculations used in consumer or business situations but never taught the principles behind arithmetic, geometry, or trigonometry, says SMSG The Making of a Curriculum, a 1965 book by William Wooten, one of the founders of the New Math project.

Likewise, the MIT project found that science textbooks dedicated too much space to simple functions such as how refrigerators and car engines work, while ignoring basic theory such as how waves travel, noted "The Government in the Classroom," a 1980 article by J. Myron Atkin in the journal Daedalus.

The goal for the two NSF-financed projects—and many subsequent ones—was to teach the basic principles by offering students experiences in learning by doing. With that background, the hope was that students could apply their knowledge in a variety of circumstances.

"We want to expose children to science by letting them do science, by working with actual materials and deriving from their own manipulations a feeling of mastery and understanding which can come in no other way," said a 1961 proposal for an elementary science curriculum that borrowed heavily in format and content from the ongoing physics project.

As a result, elementary pupils started learning about sets and number theories based on groups other than 10, rather than learning the mechanical procedures of arithmetic. High school physics students studied how waves travel in detailed and intricate experiments using tidal pools.

For Man: A Course of Study—known by its acronym, MACOS—the curriculum writers encouraged students to act as anthropologists, comparing how and why different cultures developed their values, tools, languages, and social organizations.

By 1975, 17,000 elementary schools in 47 states were using the MACOS curriculum, according to A Minor Miracle: An Informal History of the National Science Foundation by Milton Lomask.

But it's not surprising that some aspects of the curriculum raised hackles. One segment, for example, taught about Netsilik Indians in the Canadian Arctic and their practices of infanticide and mercy killing.

Such lessons became the target of critics' attacks. By introducing such topics as how the Netsiliks preserve their culture by killing unwanted babies and abandoning the elderly on icebergs,

Corbis-Bettmann

MACOS was teaching a "hippie-yippie philosophy," charged the Rev. Don Glenn, a Baptist minister who organized opposition in Lake City, Fla.

Glenn succeeded in his campaign to remove MACOS from the Columbia County public schools. Conservative activists also rallied in Phoenix and other areas, and then took their cause to Congress.

After a series of hearings and intense floor debates, Congress voted to halt funding for MACOS in 1975.

Some schools continued to use the anthropology program, despite the controversy. Without federal funding for the publication of its materials or the training of teachers, however, MACOS slowly faded from the scene.

"MACOS really succumbed to the attacks of the right wing," says Dow, one of its architects. "School districts are very sensitive to those attacks, so they just allowed it to fade away," contends Dow, now an adjunct professor of anthropology at the State University of New York College at Buffalo and the president of a nonprofit organization that links museums and schools.

The demise of MACOS occurred, he writes in *Schoolhouse Politics: Lessons From the Sputnik Era*, because the curriculum developers and the newly organized and politically powerful conservative parents had different objectives.

The intellectuals wanted to teach children to "think about human behavior in a new way" and to "question and explore their own preconceptions," he wrote in his 1991 book.

Parents, by contrast, "saw the course as a violation of the accepted ways of schooling children and a repudiation of social studies materials that promoted American values," Dow wrote. And, according to those values, "children should not be encouraged to question; they should be taught what to believe."

But the criticisms also involved fundamental questions about what children should learn and how they should learn it, Ravitch says. When her children took MACOS in the New York City public schools, she recalls, they were assigned projects such as writing a radio script about a salamander swimming upstream.

"They thought it was a lot of fun, but silly," she says.

Not only did the MACOS curriculum succumb; the new methods and ideas incorporated in the math project also failed to take hold in the classroom. Teachers and parents didn't understand the theories underlying the content, and the textbooks written for the courses failed to explain them clearly, says Ralph A. Raimi, a professor emeritus of mathematics at the University of Rochester, who is writ-

The Soviet Union's launch of Sputnik I in 1957 triggered anxiety that the United States would lose the space race to its archrival. The federal government responded by pouring money into new curricula in physics, biology, chemistry, and mathematics.

ing a history of the New Math.

"It never did take hold very deeply," he says. "There's a lot more inertia in school systems than you might think."

During the 1976-77 school year, fewer than 10 percent of school districts surveyed by NSF researchers were using math materials created with foundation grants. Thirty-seven percent said they had used SMSG or other NSF-supported curricula before then, the survey found.

Still, some echoes of the New Math, especially its emphasis on conceptual understanding, are seen in the standards published by the National Council of Teachers of Mathematics in 1989. While those standards were once widely accepted, they too are now the target of critics, who maintain they fail to teach such basic tasks as addition and multiplication.

SCIENCE ENDURES

While the NSF's mathematics and social science work failed to make the impact the authors had envisioned, its science curricula were more successful. In that same 1977 survey, the NSF found that 41 percent of secondary schools used at least one form of the foundation's science programs.

Gerald F. Wheeler, the executive director of the National Science Teachers Association, suggests that the most important legacy of the foundation's science initiatives was to make the subject a standard part of the elementary school curriculum.

What's more, just about any high school student who has taken physics in the past 30 years has conducted extended experiments of waves in a ripple tank—as designed by the MIT project in the 1950s,

Wheeler says. And materials crafted by the Biological Sciences Curriculum Study, another NSF-financed group, are used in many schools.

"There's been more staying power in the science projects," Wheeler says. "In their initial state, they're gone. But there's a lot of echoes that still exist."

In addition, a series of professional-development seminars to train teachers in how to use the curriculum fostered a cadre of leaders who are active today, says F. James Rutherford, the education adviser for the American Association for the Advancement of Science and the director of the NSF's education programs in the late 1970s.

A few years after the MACOS brouhaha, the Reagan administration arrived in Washington intent on cutting all NSF education programs. It almost succeeded, according to Rutherford.

But in 1983, the federally commissioned report *A Nation at Risk* gave rise to a new scare about the inadequacy of the nation's schools. And the foundation entered the curriculum-development field once again. But its commitment over the past 16 years pales in comparison with the burst of activity in the '60s.

In this decade, the NSF's biggest projects have been programs helping states and cities define what they want to teach in science and mathematics and build the policies to accomplish those aims—what are generally referred to as systemic initiatives. The programs aren't reaching teachers the same way that NSF projects did in their heyday—when the foundation paid for thousands of young teachers, including Rutherford and Wheeler, to spend six weeks of their summers learning new course materials.

In fiscal 1999, the NSF's education division will spend $120 million on its standards-based math and science reform programs and $36.8 million on the development of curriculum materials. It will pay $126 million for teacher training.

The $282.8 million total compares with the $124.8 million NSF spent at the peak of its education efforts in fiscal 1968. The 1968 spending would equal roughly $550 million in today's dollars.

"There's less investment in teacher preparation and curriculum development," Rutherford says. "It's dealing more with systems as a whole and policy issues.

"In the '60s, [NSF projects] just seemed to be everywhere," he adds. Science education "was the main topic of concern." ∎

In 1959, students at Stuyvesant High School in New York City demonstrate the action of waves in a ripple tank—a staple of physics classes since professors at the Massachusetts Institute of Technology began working on changes to U.S. science curricula earlier in the decade.

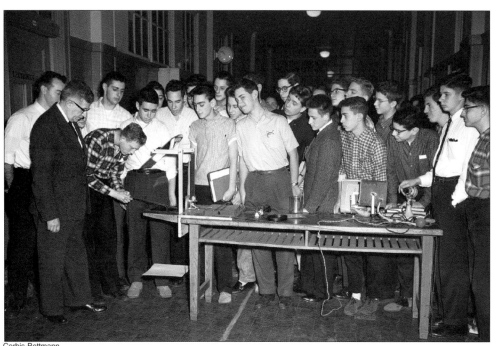

Corbis-Bettmann

Technology in the Classroom

I n a century that has worshiped scientific progress like none before, it's not surprising that technology increasingly has been seen as a powerful, transforming force in American public education.

Since 1900, nearly every technology that has affected the way knowledge is produced or disseminated has been offered to educators—simple projection devices and Victrolas in the 'teens, radio in the '20s, motion pictures in the '30s, television in the '50s, and computers and the World Wide Web in the '80s and '90s.

By Andrew Trotter

Those technologies all had their turns as a significant focus of attention in the education community. In its day, each has been the star subject of grant proposals, research on its educational effectiveness, and school investments in equipment purchases and professional development.

Technologies have been touted as ways to add dimensions to teaching and learning, whether by providing auditory or visual information, making material available to a larger group of students, adding interactive capabilities, individualizing instruction, or all of the above. They have been sent to schools and classrooms for more mundane reasons, too: to increase efficiency, lower costs, and reduce the need for teachers.

But for one reason or another—after a decade or so in the sun—most of the technological innovations drifted into the margins of school practice, to be used only occasionally or for peripheral activities by a few gung-ho teachers. Most didn't disappear, but they failed to achieve the impact for which they seemed destined.

One clue why comes from Emerson D. Jarvis, a former superintendent of schools in Fort Recovery, Ohio. An enthusiastic advocate of employing radio to broadcast lessons to classrooms, Jarvis wrote in *The American School Board Journal* in 1930 that radio was being used effectively in his state to supplement classroom teaching, update information in textbooks, and fill in gaps in teachers' knowledge; to expose students to the wider world; to foster thinking and listening skills; and to inspire students, among other benefits.

But tellingly, Jarvis began by warning that the cause of radio education would be hindered by two different groups: those educators who instinctively dis-

GELATIN and LIQUID MACHINES

Illustrated: Ditto D-44, newest electric automatic feed liquid type duplicator. Because Ditto leads, Ditto offers most advanced types of both gelatin and liquid duplicators.

DISCOVER NEW HORIZONS *With the New* Ditto

The American School Board Journal, March 1940

liked or distrusted technology, and the glassy-eyed enthusiasts who promoted their cause with hyperbole.

"One group is composed of those who are content to dispose of the subject with a shrug of their shoulders, or a wave of the hand," Jarvis wrote. "They dismiss the whole matter as impractical, visionary, and 'impossible.' The other group is made up of those who paint a picture of 20 to 30 years hence when, in their opinion, the classroom will resemble the classroom of today, with a blackboard, pupils, and a teacher's desk, but with one important factor missing: The teacher will be replaced by a loud-speaker."

The Ohio administrator finished by advising his readers, "Prudence and common sense will lead the experienced educator to take a position which is between these extremes."

The middle path that Jarvis was recommending was no easier to achieve for radio education, which largely fell by the wayside, than for most other forms of technology throughout the 20th century.

'INCREDIBLE CLAIMS'

Hyperbole has gone hand in hand with each innovation, says David B. Tyack, an education historian at Stanford University, who has written extensively about

Duplication machines were one of the less glamorous technologies to arrive in schools, but they had a lasting impact. Teachers used them to make multiple copies of everything from pop quizzes to permission slips and could create printed materials more timely than textbooks and more portable than blackboards.

In an Atlanta public school in 1926, students listen to a radio broadcast during a lesson on current affairs. Motion pictures, television, and computers have, in turn, followed the radio as technologies promising to revolutionize the classroom.

20th-century teaching practices.

"New technologies have been introduced to educators with incredible claims," he says. "People have made some very utopian claims for technology, as basically solving instructional problems and becoming a substitute for teachers."

Writing in the *School Board Journal* the same year as Jarvis, B.A. Aughinbaugh of Columbus, Ohio, for example, predicted that motion pictures would take schools up the evolutionary ladder from the printed word: "The motion picture is undoubtedly a timesaver and psychologists tell us that it is also a labor-saver, since it sets aside the difficult mechanics involved in reading and frees the mind for thinking."

Larry Cuban, another Stanford University historian of education, who wrote a book with Tyack about why educators have been slow to adopt technical advances, says the technologies that have been most successful in schools are flexible tools that have added functions to what teachers do already. He describes those technologies as having "hybridized" teachers' traditional activities and roles.

The mimeograph machine, for example, gave teachers a new way to distribute printed materials beyond the textbook. They could use worksheets or print off passages copied from books that weren't readily available for the whole class.

Other relatively unglamorous but successful technologies include the videocassette recorder and the overhead projector.

By contrast, long after telephones were common in homes, they failed to make much of an impact on schooling. Though phones had the apparent advantage of providing a direct communication link between teachers and parents, they violated two of the principles of the traditional classroom: It is a closed environment, and the teacher is nearly always engaged in direct supervision of students.

At least until the 1980s, school administrators weren't ready to consider a different arrangement, nor were many teachers demanding one.

Another relative failure was television. Educators first began experimenting with broadcasting courses to classrooms by television in the 1940s. One of the best systems, supported with grants from the Ford Foundation, was the instructional-television network used by the Hagerstown, Md., schools in the 1950s and '60s.

Many administrators at the time were interested in television as a way to handle swelling enrollments from the postwar baby boom without massive hiring of teachers.

Some teachers were dazzled by the medium's potential, says Peter Dirr, currently an executive at Cable in the Classroom. As a young teacher, he was introduced to educational television at a seminar at Fordham University in 1960, where he'd met some of the television industry's pioneers. "I was really struck by the [possibility of] reaching large numbers, so learners could benefit from a small number of good strong teachers," Dirr says.

But not too surprisingly, given the implications for their jobs, many teachers felt threatened by classroom TV, he says. And coordination of class schedules at different schools—necessary in the years before low-cost recording devices were available—proved a real hurdle.

Despite the impact television was having on the broader culture at the time, schools that had tried instructional television quietly phased it out when grants were no longer available.

Television didn't become teacher-friendly until the 1970s, when the VCR placed it under the teacher's control, Dirr says. "That's one of the themes of what we've seen in the second half of the century: When something is controlled centrally, and is imposed on people, people get their backs up," he says. "When it's put in their control and the quality is good, they use it."

THE TEACHER FACTOR

The success of educational technologies has ultimately depended on their acceptance by teachers, who generally enjoy autonomy in choosing the tools they use in their classrooms.

Cuban, a former superintendent, argues that technologies have failed when they have demanded too much of a departure from what teachers were already doing.

While some teachers may resist technology out of fear or laziness, others resist to safeguard their art, he says. They know how to create learning experiences that work using the traditional system, and they aren't convinced that adding a new element won't interfere with that process. They also have concerns other than instruction that they must deal with, such as keeping order and discipline among 25 or more children. Technologies that require teachers to direct

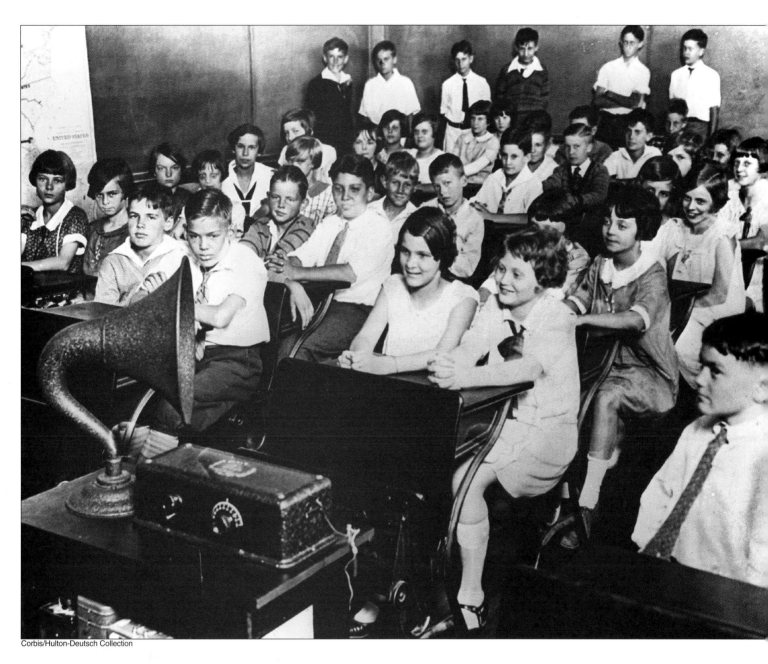

Corbis/Hulton-Deutsch Collection

their classrooms differently from what they're accustomed to will likely be adopted slowly, Cuban says.

Whether that slow evolution is "good or bad depends on whether you're an advocate or a skeptic," he adds.

POWER OF DIGITAL TECHNOLOGIES

As the century approaches its close, technology is a bigger part of schooling than it's ever been. Administrators are spending billions of dollars each year on hardware and software. Parents are demanding even more, saying it's critical for their children's future success in the workplace. And many educators who have experimented with digital technology say it can revolutionize the way students learn.

While the hype may seem familiar to those who have studied education throughout the 20th century, several historians agree that computers and the In-

ternet could mark a watershed in the use of technology in schooling.

In part, this is due to the nature of the technology itself. The World Wide Web gives students an unprecedented power to access information and communicate with people around the world.

In addition, computers and the Web can absorb and manipulate all the other technologies—images, films, and sound—that have gone before, notes Robbie McClintock, a professor at the Institute for Learning Technologies at Columbia University.

These multimedia capabilities may give today's digital technologies the flexibility and power to change schools that earlier classroom devices lacked, McClintock says.

Cuban agrees. "The digital technology is clearly more powerful, because of its interactive capacity, than any others— film, radio, TV. There's no question," he says.

What's more, digital technologies are

achieving a critical mass in the nation's schools, thanks in part to government investments at all levels, including the federal E-rate program, which provides discounts on telecommunications services to schools and libraries.

As a result, nine out of every 10 schools in the country now have access to the Internet, and schools have an average of one computer for every six students—a level of penetration far greater than radio, film, and television achieved during their heydays.

Digital technologies have also gained a firmer foothold in school budgeting, and in training and administrative routines, than their predecessors.

But Tyack points out that the Internet is still establishing itself and that the choices society makes about how the medium evolves will have a significant influence on education.

"People need to think about them in historical terms," he says, "and they're making very portentous choices." ■

Legacy of the Eight-Year Study

Marjory Collins/Library of Congress

Boxes of tarnished trophies and other long-forgotten memorabilia symbolizing East High School's earliest sports triumphs lie in storage, replaced in school display cases by the honors bestowed on more recent generations. Even fewer traces of the Denver school's academic legacy endure.

No plaques identify it as one of some 30 schools or districts initially selected for the historic experiment in high school curriculum that came to be known as the Eight-Year Study. And today's administrators, teachers, and students are virtually unaware of the national reputation for innovation that their school earned some six decades ago.

By Kathleen Kennedy Manzo

But there is some evidence, however scant, that the study begun in 1932, and ending in 1940, has had a lasting impact on East and other high schools throughout the country. The project allowed participating schools and districts to depart from the college-preparatory curriculum that dominated secondary education and to design courses and programs that better related to the lives of individual students.

The 1,600-student school still maintains a "school-within-a-school," with a special program for at-risk students, a concept that took root there in the 1930s when a portion of the student body participated in the study. Cooperative learning and curricula that are more relevant to students' lives are also mainstays.

But when the Commission on the Relation of School and College released its five-volume report on the study in 1942, its title hailed the experiment as an "Adventure in American Education."

The details of the study reveal what a daring endeavor it was.

Appointed by the Progressive Education Association, the commission set out to prove that the conventional high school curriculum, and the fear that diverging from it would limit students' options for higher education, squelched innovation in most secondary schools.

The 26-member commission believed that the curriculum no longer served the needs of the nation's high school population, which had exploded from 1 million to 10 million in the first three decades of the 20th century. The high school, the commission concluded, could provide more relevant schooling for the five out of six students who did not go on to college, while giving the one student who did a stronger foundation on which to build.

And so, after two years of planning, and with a guarantee from hundreds of colleges that students could gain admission without the requisite coursework, the schools and districts selected for the study "set out upon their eight-year journey of exploration and trailblazing," Wilford M. Aikin, who directed the project, wrote in Volume 1 of the report, *The Story of the Eight-Year Study*.

FRIGHTENED BY FREEDOM

Even with the newfound freedom, a bold departure from tradition was difficult for many of the schools. As one participating principal put it: "My teachers and I do not know what to do with this freedom. It challenges and frightens us. I fear that we have come to love our chains."

One school—Pelham Manor in New York City—dropped out of the experiment because of its commitment to another major study. Some schools opted for only subtle changes in the content of courses.

Others, though, took greater advantage of the flexibility their involvement in the study allowed and pushed at all the boundaries that had defined education for decades.

At Bronxville High School, in New York's Westchester County, students abandoned traditional subjects to explore broad themes, as some schools do today. Instead of the conventional chemistry course, students studied "the physical environment and some aspects of the nature of matter, of the changes in matter, chemical and physical, and of the nature of the various energies."

Students at the private Lincoln School at Teachers College, Columbia University, applied the problems of Greek civilization to modern American life when they "spent eight to 10 weeks being Greeks."

"The students lived, worked, and thought as Spartans, Athenians, Corinthians, Syracusans, Thebans, and Milesians," the report says. An early example of a multidisciplinary program, the course combined language and literature, art, music, civics, history, economics, mathematics, and science.

Seniors at Radnor High School in Wayne, Pa.—for whom employment, not college, was the next likely step—tested the job market, spending two weeks at a time working in various businesses and industries.

In school, they studied labor unions, collective bargaining, Social Security, housing, uses of leisure time, and becoming an informed consumer.

And in all of Denver's five public high schools, the study gave momentum to the curriculum reforms there

Barry Allen

that had begun in the late 1920s. As part of the Progressive Education Association study, some boys and girls would spend only two hours a day with their teachers discussing various units of study encompassed in the districtwide core curriculum.

The remainder of the time was for independent exploration, with the overall goal being "a continuous attack upon the problems which are persistent in the lives of adolescents as members of a democratic society."

Nationally, the schools in the study were both public and private, rural and urban, and served the children of the working class as well as the well-to-do. The directions they took were equally varied, but they had in common some of the progressive ideals that began influencing schools earlier in the century.

Most schools broke away from the strictures of the traditional classroom and school day. Teachers changed the way they taught, relying less on lectures and textbooks and more on informal exchanges with and among students.

Students who had been used to sitting straight and still in their desks, eyes focused on the teacher, were now free to roam the classroom, to sit in groups, or to work by themselves. They were encouraged to move beyond the memorization of material to develop reflective thinking and skill in problem-solving.

By most accounts, the initiative was a success. An independent evaluation of the 1,475 students who participated in the program showed that they performed slightly better in college than a comparison group of students who had been exposed to a tra-

Above: David Peters teaches an Advanced Placement class in European history at Denver's East High School. Few at the school are aware of its role in a pioneering curriculum study in the 1930s.

Left: The Lincoln School at Teachers College, Columbia University, was one of some 30 schools or districts that were allowed to diverge from the traditional curriculum as part of the Eight-Year Study. Once in college, participating students, such as these 6th graders shown in 1942, were found to perform slightly better than a comparison group of more conventionally educated peers.

ditional high school curriculum.

The study was evidence, in the eyes of the progressives, that a lockstep sequence of courses was not the only way to prepare young adults for college or life.

Those skeptical of the results claimed the experiment was skewed because the youths selected to participate were primarily high-achieving students.

'NEVER FULLY APPRECIATED'

The Eight-Year Study has been called both the most influential curriculum study in American history and the most forgotten. The first volume of the commission's report was released in the spring of 1942, just months after the United States entered World War II. The war turned schools' attention away from innovation.

"We went to war, and that was the end of that story because no one cared about public education when there was a war going on," says Jon Snyder, the director of teacher education at the University of California, Santa Barbara, and a senior researcher for the National Commission on Teaching & America's Future.

But the study was not a total loss. Al-most a decade later, representatives of half the participating schools and districts gathered for a post-mortem. While they lamented problems they had encountered implementing and maintaining changes, most agreed the effort had been worthwhile.

"In many ways, it's a study that has never been fully appreciated, and it doesn't get the scholarly attention it deserves," says Frank B. Murray, a professor of education at the University of Delaware. "Yet, it is a gold mine of anecdotes and details of how these 30 high schools reformed themselves."

While the details of the curricular overhaul had faded years later—many of the schools reported they had returned to a traditional curriculum within a few years of the study's end—they left an impression on many of the schools. That was especially true of private institutions, such as the John Burroughs School in St. Louis, that had always been committed to a progressive approach.

PRIDE IN PARTICIPATING

In Denver, East High School's reputation for innovation carried at least into the 1970s, recalls Robert L. Colwell, who was the principal from 1960 until he retired in 1974.

"I remember the pride of having been a part of the Eight-Year Study and recognized as one of the big progressive schools in the country," Colwell says.

Aiming to maintain that reputation, Colwell started a Senior Seminar program for 100 students selected to reflect the makeup of the East High enrollment. Some spent the length of the six-week course living in a hogan with local Navajo families to study American Indian culture. Other students were paired with state legislators to learn about politics.

Modern-day reform efforts are also steeped in the ideals that fueled the Eight-Year Study, some scholars say, but they are linked only indirectly.

"In education, things have a tendency to come back around again," says Victor L. Dupuis, a professor emeritus of education at Pennsylvania State University. "Things like independent study, guided education, the effective-schools movement are all the old ideas coming back, but the people who are doing them are not likely to know about the Eight-Year Study." ∎

Vocational Education

I n *The New Republic,* a pundit argues that "vocational education is, irreducibly and without unnecessary mystification, education for the pursuit of an occupation." Not so, counters another. Vocational education should have "as its supreme regard the development of such intelligent initiative, ingenuity, and executive capacity as shall make workers, as far as may be, the masters of their own industrial fate."

Such a debate would be timely in political journals today. These words, though, date back to 1915.

By Mary Ann Zehr

The first writer was David Snedden, the education commissioner of Massachusetts. He believed in "social efficiency"—the notion that education could prepare youths for the niches they were destined to fill as adults. To that end, he argued, some students should receive vocational education, and others a general education.

His critic, the philosopher and educa-tor John Dewey, attacked this policy as "social predestination." Instead of focusing on specialized skills with machines, he argued, schools should give all students a broad understanding of the world of work.

Snedden, it turned out, won the argument, and his views consequently set the course for American schools' vocational curriculum for most of the 20th century. Whether that was the wisest course is now a matter of debate.

At the time of World War I, most students who wanted to pursue a particular industrial or agricultural career attended trade schools, usually privately run by manufacturers, mechanics' institutes, and similar groups. A few public "manual training" schools taught skills such as woodworking and metalworking for the purpose of complementing boys' intellectual pursuits. Some regular high schools embraced that philosophy by teaching selected manual-training courses.

But for the most part, vocational education was not a regular feature of the public school curriculum.

This changed as concerns about the feverish pace of industrialization began to preoccupy the nation. Businesses needed workers, and society looked to the public schools to produce them.

Charles Prosser, one of Snedden's former colleagues in graduate school at Teachers College, Columbia University, was one of the leaders of this movement. Perhaps best known for championing the much-derided "life-adjustment movement" in schools in the 1940s and '50s, Prosser wrote key provisions of the first federal legislation for secondary-level vocational education.

The resulting law—the Smith-Hughes Act of 1917—provided money for agricultural, trade, industrial, and home economics education for students over 14 "who are preparing for a trade or industrial pursuit." It set up the funding in such a way that vocational education began to be administered and taught on a mass scale separately from general education, either in its own wing of a regular high school or in its own building.

In the 1920s and 1930s, vocational education students typically took a set of skills-based courses to prepare them to work in a specific occupation. In some states, students took those courses for only half a day; they studied academics along with general education students for the rest of the day. Elsewhere, students stayed all day in a vocational education track.

Over time, states broadened their definitions of vocational education. By the 1940s, many states offered a "building trades" track, which taught carpentry, plumbing, and roofing all in one.

But those who helped carry out that model of vocational education disagree about whether it served the country well.

Herbert M. Kliebard, a former vocational education teacher and now a professor emeritus of curriculum and instruction and educational policy studies at the University of Wisconsin-Madison, says separate training for narrowly defined jobs was never a good idea at the high school level.

"This greatly exaggerated emphasis on education not simply as getting ready generally but as direct and explicit preparation for what lies ahead is perhaps the cruelest of the legacies of vocationalism," he writes in *Schooled to Work*, a book released recently by Teachers College Press.

But others maintain that vocational education, as envisioned by Snedden and Prosser, was successful—for a while.

"Smith-Hughes served a wonderful purpose when America was in that basic orientation to specific jobs and mechanical types of applications," says Hobart H. Conover of Delmar, N.Y., who taught clerical skills to high school students from 1935 to 1949.

In the 1940s, secondary and postsecondary vocational education schools trained 7.5 million people for jobs in defense and war production for World War II, according to the Association for Career and Technical Education.

The quality of vocational education programs began to decline in the 1960s and 1970s, says Gene Bottoms, who, as the senior vice president of the Southern Regional Education Board, directs the High Schools That Work program. That program extends to vocational students the same challenging academic courses provided to college-bound students.

Bottoms argues that federal legislation passed during those decades, such as the Vocational Education Act of 1963, placed too much emphasis on at-risk students. "Access became paramount, but what that got translated into was lowering standards for vocational studies," he says.

Anthony P. Carnevale, a labor economist and the vice president for public leadership for the Educational Testing Service,

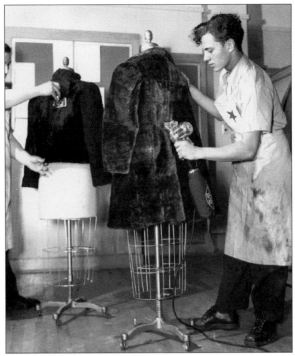

Corbis-Bettmann

adds that the value of a narrowly defined vocational education decreased with the reduction of manufacturing jobs in the early 1970s. Now, he says, "people need more general education and more general skills."

Most educators today agree that the course vocational education has taken for most of the century must be redirected.

"We have to face the reality that vocational education conjures up in people's minds an image of something that is not as rigorous, that's preparing people for the jobs of the past, not the future," says Patricia W. McNeil, the assistant secretary for the U.S. Department of Education's office of vocational and adult education.

Most reforms call for blending vocational education with challenging academics. The Carl D. Perkins Vocational and Applied Technology Education Act of 1990, for example, encourages the integration of academic and vocational education. The School-to-Work Opportunities Act of 1994 aims to expose students of all academic levels to experiences in the workplace.

Reform programs also include "tech prep"—which links high school students' vocational education with two years of study at the postsecondary level—and "career academies," schools structured around an occupational theme.

The philosophy driving this "new vocationalism" is reminiscent of John Dewey, according to W. Norton Grubb, an economist in the school of education at the University of California, Berkeley.

"You use occupations as a lens back into other subjects, such as English and math," he says. "That's the real Deweyan application of vocational education." ∎

High school students in New York City could study a variety of retail-related trades at the Central High School of Needle Trades in the heart of the city's garment district.

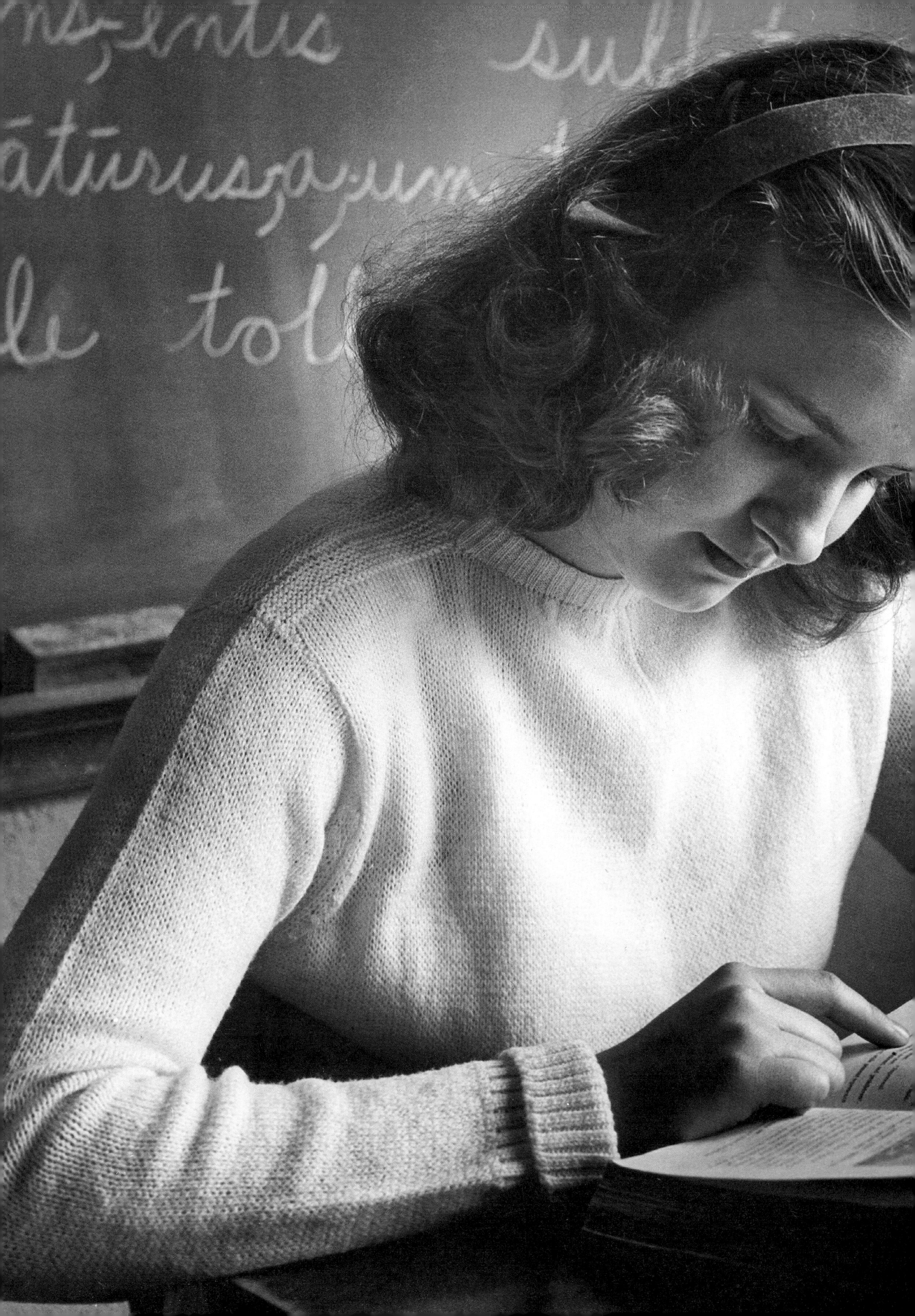

Book Smarts

From their early years as vehicles of adventure to what some say are updated yet lifeless versions of their former selves, textbooks have remained key in the battle over what children should learn.

By Kathleen Kennedy Manzo

For the young pupil who daydreamed of exotic places and heroic deeds early in this century, a schoolbook could quench the imagination. Back then, history textbooks were plump with lively narratives about the glorious conquests of brave explorers and the noble struggles of the nation's founders to create a new republic.

One 1910 text likened Christopher Columbus' discovery of America to a providential mission. "Columbus believed that God had chosen him to go out as a missionary to these far-off lands. He kept that belief to the end. It gave a certain dignity to his work and made his life noble in many ways," began one story in *Leading Facts of American History*, published by Ginn & Co.

Other history books and school readers were filled with similar tales. They, too, led children on exciting expeditions through uncharted territory and to chance meetings with Indians in the vast wilderness. They exposed them to the great orations of Roman statesmen, the wonders of scientific discoveries and modern inventions, and the patriotic fervor that bound great men together to form a government of, by, and for the people.

Through more than a century of criticism, protests, and censorship, textbooks have held their place in the hands of the nation's schoolchildren.

At night, before you go to sleep, think whether you have done anything that was wrong during the day, and pray to God to forgive you. --The McGuffey Reader

It would be hard to find such passion in modern textbooks. Today, scholars, teachers, and parents decry books that they say are dull and lifeless, devoid of context, and prisoners of "adoption" processes that value political correctness over quality.

But school texts—the de facto national curriculum—have rarely enjoyed wholesale acceptance. More often than not, textbooks—especially those in subjects that now make up social studies and language arts—have been at the center of an ages-old tug of war over what becomes the "official knowledge" transmitted through them, and who gets to define it, says Michael W. Apple, a professor of curriculum and instruction and educational policy studies at the University of Wisconsin-Madison.

"Current issues surrounding texts—their ideology, their very status as central definers of what we should teach, even their very effectiveness and their design—echo from [the past]," Apple and his colleague, Linda K. Christian-Smith, write in their 1991 book *The Politics of the Textbook*.

Throughout history, textbooks have been the target of scathing criticism, violent protests, and censorship.

Long before the 20th century, schoolbooks had their detractors. Thomas Jefferson and James Madison were among the first to lash out at "Northern textbooks," which generally portrayed the people of Virginia, the Carolinas, and Georgia as culturally inferior to New Englanders. In 1789, they aimed their objections at the geography book written by Jedidiah Morse, known as the "father of American geography." The popular text pronounced that the young men of Virginia, with the exception of a few affluent landowners and wise statesmen, "generally speaking are gamblers, cockfighters, and horse-jockies," among other unflattering stereotypes. The early opposition to Northern textbooks was a prelude to efforts a century later to keep books contrary to Southern ideals out of the schools, noted a 1947 article in the *Journal of Southern History*.

In what may have been the first full-scale textbook war in America, Irish Catholics fired shots in 1839. As the number of Irish immigrants swelled and they gained political clout, they fought back against textbooks with a distinctly Protestant bias, which prevailed in public and private schools alike and often portrayed

the newcomers as dirty drunkards. Some texts described a rapidly changing New York City as "the sewer of Ireland," and warned that Roman Catholics were opposed to democracy and, therefore, should be prevented from serving in public office.

As the 20th century opened, Catholics—who by then had made a strong commitment to operating their own schools—represented a large enough market to force publishers to write versions of schoolbooks that were sensitive to their beliefs. The famous "Dick and Jane" readers were adapted to include such stories as "God in Our Home" and "Our Friends and God." Illustrations in other stories showed churches and religious symbols. Even the mainstream texts began recognizing Irish-American political leaders and the laborers from Ireland who had toiled to build the nation's infrastructure.

While the Irish Catholics in the North were battling publishers over their derogatory portrayals, the South took another tack to force publishers' hands. Southern states began to remove control of textbook purchases from local school boards, partly to ensure that ideas they deemed threatening to Southern culture and their own view of history did not seep into schools, according to Apple. Thus began the practice of state adoption that still guides textbook purchases in 22 states.

The competition to get on state-approved adoption lists, and the potential to dominate a large market, gave publishers a powerful incentive to give those states what they wanted. Well into the middle of the 20th century, some texts still taught students below the Mason-Dixon line not about the Civil War, but the War of Northern Aggression. Some claimed slaves had been generally happy and well cared for, and glorified the agricultural life upon which the South's economy depended.

Subsequent social and political issues played out in later campaigns to reform textbooks. Beginning in the late 1930s, a social studies series elicited the almighty wrath of American industry for its critical view of capitalism and its recommendations for a national economic plan. Once the best-selling books, written by Harold

Rugg of Teachers College, Columbia University, were pegged as communist propaganda by the National Association of Manufacturers and the American Legion, their brisk sales faded to a trickle.

"Textbooks have always reflected the values of the people in power," and incited the indignation of those who are not, says Joan DelFattore, a professor of English at the University of Delaware.

Once the Catholics' and Southerners' concerns were appeased, textbooks changed very little throughout the remainder of the first half of the century.

"From the 1890s on, what the texts said about American history would appear to children to be the truth," writes the Pulitzer Prize-winning author Frances FitzGerald in her 1979 critique of American history texts, *America Revised*.

Despite their enduring and romanticized image, the books had serious flaws.

"In the 'Dick and Jane' readers I read in school, you couldn't find a child with black hair and brown eyes like me," recalls DelFattore, the author of *What Johnny Shouldn't Read: Textbook Censorship in America*. "In the history books prior to 1970, the United States was always right, heroes were heroes, and George Washington did not own slaves."

In some cases, however, publishers were only complying with the law. Several states had enacted laws during the 1920s prohibiting the use of textbooks that did not present the nation's history in a positive light. Wisconsin forbade any schoolbook that "falsifies the facts regarding the war of independence, or the war of 1812, or which defames our nation's founders, or misrepresents the ideals and causes for which they struggled and sacrificed." Mississippi demanded textbooks be fair and impartial in their representation of the Civil War.

Oregon censored any textbook "which speaks slightingly of the founders of the republic, or of the men who preserved the union," wrote J.K. Flanders in the 1927 yearbook of the National Society for the Study of Education, the predecessor to the Association for Supervision and Curriculum Development. Flanders concluded

The Charleston Gazette

A dispute over social studies textbooks erupted in Charleston, W.Va., in 1974.

that "it is hardly probable that a book which satisfies Oregon as giving sufficient credit to the 'men who preserved the union' will at the same time be regarded by Mississippi as 'fair and impartial,' or that a book which meets the requirements of Texas will at the same time be acceptable to Wisconsin."

Texts of that era perpetuated harmful racial and ethnic stereotypes, or failed to discuss whole segments of American society altogether.

In *Muzzey's American History*, first published in 1911 by Ginn, David Saville Muzzey's view that some races were inferior to others was evident. He described American Indians as a "treacherous, cruel people," and "Negroes" were "lazy." It wasn't until a half-century later, in the 1961 edition of the text, that author Muzzey, who died in 1965, suggested that blacks be included among the numbers of "Southern people," according to FitzGerald.

Such portrayals made textbooks a prime target during the civil rights movement and the subsequent fight for women's rights. Large-scale protests from minority groups started to wear down publishers.

In 1962, civil rights organizations were successful in forcing school boards in Detroit and Newark, N.J., to withdraw racially biased texts and set new policies for reviewing all materials used in the school system. Other districts followed suit.

Like the Irish-Americans and Southerners of earlier eras, the latest advocates realized the power of school texts in advancing their causes. Soon followed, in FitzGerald's words, "the most dra-

matic rewriting of history ever to take place in American schoolbooks."

Later on, Hispanics, homosexuals, and other groups tired of being absent from or maligned in texts rallied for their own fair representation.

"There are crusades for women's rights and crusades against communism. There are crusades for conservative causes and for liberal causes. There are crusades for a better environment. There are crusades for and against sex education. There are crusades by various ethnic groups for recognition of their cultures," publishing executive John H. Williamson wrote in "The Textbook in American Society," an overview of a 1979 conference that brought together scholars and publishers to discuss the problems of the textbook.

"Those who develop learning materials for the schools," he continued, "know that all of these groups have one thing in common—the conviction that textbooks and related materials are a major vehicle for furthering their crusades. Aware of the sensibilities of various groups, publishers go to great lengths to avoid offending. But they cannot escape."

To a great extent, critics of today's textbooks blame publishers precisely for their attempts to satisfy all groups. "Texts are so badly overstuffed and so diced that they are in places unintelligible," argues Gilbert T. Sewall, the president of the American Textbook Council.

At a news conference with National Education Association officials in 1974, Gloria Steinem announces a plan to remove sexist portrayals of individuals from U.S. textbooks.

That group was established more than a decade ago to monitor and lobby for improving the quality of history, social studies, and humanities textbooks.

The revisions and compromises made along the way are evident in current best sellers. In *United States*, a 1997 5th grade book from Macmillan/McGraw-Hill's best-selling "Adventures in Time and Space" series, Columbus no longer takes center stage. Long a prominent introductory figure in history books—in 1867 he was even featured in the title of one text, *A History of the United States of America: From the Discovery of the Continent by Christopher Columbus to the Present Time*—he is relegated in the 1997 text to the sixth chapter, after dozens of pages outlining Native American civilizations. And in the few pages devoted to his explorations, Columbus shares the spotlight with the Taino, the native people who greeted him when he landed at San Salvador.

Science and mathematics texts, while undergoing alterations to reflect discoveries or innovations in those fields, were long considered largely immune from philosophical battles. In science, discussion of the theory of evolution has been the most persistent point of contention.

Most arguments over science and math books have emerged in more recent decades. Not until the late 1950s and early 1960s, after the National Science Foundation was enlisted by Congress to rewrite curricula in those subjects, did those texts undergo significant restructuring to conform with what was being called the "New Math" and the "New Science."

The academic-standards movement that began in the late 1980s spawned further dramatic changes in math and science textbooks. With few exceptions, publishers rewrote their books to incorporate the new standards, which tended to emphasize both theory and hands-on experimentation.

Eventually, the movement awakened those academics, policymakers, and parents who favor traditional approaches that emphasize teaching specific content over exploratory learning.

In recent years, the debate over math and science instruction has been especially heated.

To satisfy both points of view, publishers today must produce books that find a balance between imparting skills and developing conceptual understanding.

However intense the debates over math and science books, the humanities remain the focus of sharpest contention.

The changes in history and social studies schoolbooks have never rested quietly with critics who argue that attempts at rectifying past omissions have gone too far.

For example, in Chicago after World War I, the Hearst newspapers and the mayor objected to what they perceived as pro-British bias in some books. The Sons of the American Revolution filed a complaint with the California school board in 1947 over "unpatriotic" themes in the *Building America* textbook series.

In 1974, parents and other residents in Kanawha County, W.Va., shut down the schools to prevent their children from being exposed to social studies textbooks they deemed "godless" and "dirty." In particular, they protested the texts' treatment of evolution and the lack of clear moral lessons.

More than 12,000 people attended anti-textbook rallies that ended after one protester was shot and several schools were bombed.

In 1980, Mel and Norma Gabler of Texas, who became nationally known critics of what they see as left-wing bias in textbooks, objected to publishers' failure to portray women in domestic roles despite statistics showing that half of mothers still worked only inside the home at that time.

The backlash has also been aimed at literature and language arts texts, which have been accused of undermining the classics to make room for a more diverse group of modern authors.

Critics have also voiced their objections to what they see as a slackening of academic standards and the texts' submission to "faddish" instructional methods, such as whole language.

But publishers have long defended the changes in textbooks as meeting market demands.

"As the standard, scriptural authority, the textbook is forever inviting the attacks of the revolutionary who has now learned more than what is in the textbook," Williamson, the publishing executive, wrote two decades ago.

Industry officials continue to echo Williamson's view that they cannot escape the almost impossibly complex pressures placed on them.

They are bound to the strict policies of nearly half the states, which, early in the century, enacted adoption policies requiring local districts to spend state money only on texts that meet the state's strict criteria.

Those criteria can range from dictating the number of authors from various minority groups to subjecting the books to readability formulas that strive to keep the

It is estimated that over twenty-five percent of the deaths that occur yearly in this country could be averted if all people lived in a hygienic manner. —A Civic Biology

writing at an appropriate level of difficulty.

Such strictures, combined with the need to recoup the millions of dollars companies invest in creating texts, rule what the publishers do.

"Few teachers and few publishers or authors consciously call for textbooks that are too easy for learners, that involve little writing, that are overly illustrated," James Squire, the vice president of Ginn, wrote in "The Textbook in American Society" in 1979. "But given the high-risk investment decisions … few publishers will or can consciously risk exclusion from adoption procedures by ignoring widespread customer preferences, however they might wish to do so."

The industry's critics counter that the companies are too quick to compromise rigorous academic principles to raise profit margins. The single voice of authority, even if strongly opinionated, that gave previous generations of texts credibility, they say, has been replaced by heavily edited, committee-written texts that may display the names of several prominent scholars but little of their original work.

Writing in the foreword to *A Conspiracy of Good Intentions: America's Textbook Fiasco*, a 1988 analysis by Harriet Tyson-Bernstein, A. Graham Down, then the executive director of the Council for Basic Education, observed: "The public regards textbooks as authoritative, accurate, and necessary. And teachers rely on them to organize lessons and structure subject matter. But the current system of textbook adoption has filled our schools with Trojan horses—glossily covered blocks of paper whose words emerge to deaden the minds of our nation's youth, and make them enemies of learning."

At the same time, a consolidation of the industry in recent years may be further limiting schools' options. The field has been whittled down since 1979, when some 400 companies, 49 of them considered major players, were writing textbooks.

Now, fewer than half a dozen publishers dominate the $3 billion-a-year market. That worries those who have studied the impact that the structure of the industry has had on the choices available to schools.

Concentration in the industry is nothing new, however. For much of the first half of the century, the American Book

Co. was the only major publishing house catering to the school market. Created by the merger of three companies in the late 19th century, American Book had a lock on three-fourths of the market.

The new company continued to publish the venerable McGuffey Readers. Those readers and the other texts published by the company essentially became the national curriculum, some historians say.

By the 1940s, that book trust had dissolved, and concern over public education was resulting in more money for educational materials. The next two decades proved to be a boon for the industry, which allowed hundreds of smaller publishers to flourish.

The demands placed on publishers

Corbis-Bettmann

continue to grow. With the current focus on standards and assessments, states are shopping for instructional materials that meet more specific criteria for content. While the needs of the largest adoption states—California, Texas, and Florida—wield the most influence on publishing companies, textbooks must also be marketable to thousands of other schools and districts throughout the country.

To some observers, the market is ripe for new approaches. Not far in the future, DelFattore predicts, publishers will have to diversify and find a way to meet the varied demands—through "niche" publishing, by producing more supplemental materials for teachers, or by changing the nature of textbooks themselves.

In the next century, technology is expected to transform the development and use of instructional materials. Some states, such as Texas, already have adopted computer software that can be used instead of traditional textbooks. And the Internet has made it easier for teachers to supplement books with a virtually unlimited array of other resources, such as historical documents and news accounts.

As technology continues to advance and makes production even faster and less expensive, schools may be able to customize their own books, DelFattore says. Through "modular" publishing, educators could select from a menu of chapters or sections to satisfy their particular appetites for topics, instructional approaches, even ideologies. Colleges have already begun to tap into such technology.

"Publishers might have three possible chapters on slavery or Vietnam," says the University of Delaware professor. "Like modular furniture, districts could mix and match, and choose which version of which chapters suits their tastes."

Such a future might solve some of the problems of creating books that are as acceptable to adoption committees in California and Texas as they are to local school boards in Boise, Idaho; Bloomington, Ind.; or New York City. But it is not likely to ease the concerns of those who fear that, without a common history or national identity, the very essence of the United States and its credo, *e pluribus unum*—out of many, one—will be lost. ∎

The Chronic Failure of Curriculum Reform

The system has a genius for incorporating curriculum change without fundamental reorganization.

A perspective by David F. Labaree

One thing we have learned from examining the history of curriculum in the 20th century is that curriculum reform has had remarkably little effect on the character of teaching and learning in American classrooms. As the century draws to a close, it seems like a good time to think about why this has been the case.

The failure of curriculum reform was certainly not the result of a lack of effort. At various times during the last 100 years, reformers have: issued high-visibility reports proposing dramatic changes in the curriculum (*Cardinal Principles of Secondary Education* in 1918, *A Nation at Risk* in 1983); created whole new subject areas (social studies, vocational education, special education); sought to reorganize the curriculum around a variety of new principles (ability grouping, the project method, life adjustment, back to basics, inclusion, critical thinking); and launched movements to reinvent particular subjects ("New Math," National Council of Teachers of Mathematics math, phonics, whole language).

In spite of all these reform efforts, the basic character of the curriculum that is practiced in American classrooms is strikingly similar to the form that predominated in the early part of the century. As before, the curriculum continues to revolve around traditional academic subjects—which we cut off from practical everyday knowledge, teach in relative isolation from one another, differentiate by ability, sequence by age, ground in textbooks, and deliver in a teacher-centered classroom. So much effort and so little result.

How can we understand this problem? For starters, we can recognize that curriculum means different things at different levels in the educational system, and that curriculum reform has had the greatest impact at the level most remote from teaching and learning in the classroom. Starting at the top of the system and moving toward the bottom, there is the *rhetorical curriculum* (ideas put forward by educational leaders, policymakers, and professors about what curriculum should be, as embodied in reports, speeches, and college texts), the *formal curriculum* (written curriculum policies put in place by school districts and embodied in curriculum guides and textbooks), the *curriculum-in-use* (the content that teachers actually teach in individual classrooms), and the *received curriculum* (the content that students actually learn in these classrooms).

Each wave of reform dramatically transforms the rhetorical curriculum, by changing the way educational leaders talk about the subject. This gives the feeling that something is really happening, but most often it's not. Sometimes the reform moves beyond this stage and begins to shape the formal curriculum, getting translated into district-level curriculum frameworks and the textbooks approved for classroom use. Yet this degree of penetration does not guarantee that reform ideas will have an observable effect on the curriculum-in-use. More often than not, teachers respond to reform rhetoric and local curriculum mandates by making only marginal changes in the way they teach subjects. They may come to talk about their practice using the new reform language, but only rarely do they make dramatic changes in their own curriculum practice. And even the rare cases when teachers bring their teaching in line with curriculum reform do not necessarily produce a substantial change in the received curriculum. What students learn is frequently quite different from what the reformers intended. For as curriculum-reform initiatives trickle down from the top to the bottom of the educational system, their power and coherence dissipate, with the result that student learning is likely to show few signs of the outcomes promoted by the original reform rhetoric. As David B. Tyack and Larry Cuban show in their book *Tinkering Toward Utopia*, the dominant pattern is one of recurring waves of reform rhetoric combined with glacial change in educational practice.

Why has this pattern persisted for so long? Consider a few enduring characteristics of American education that have undermined the impact of curriculum reform on teaching and learning.

Conflicting Goals: One factor is conflict over the goals of education itself. Different curriculum reforms embody different goals. Some promote democratic equality, by seeking to provide all children with the skills and knowledge they will need to function as competent citizens. Others promote social efficiency, by seeking to provide different groups of children with the specific skills they need in order to be productive in the different kinds of jobs required in a complex economy. Still others promote social mobility, by providing individual students with educational advantages in the competition for the best social positions. One result is that reform efforts over time produce a pendulum swing between alternative conceptions of what children need to learn, leading to a sense that reform is both chronic ("steady work," as Richard Elmore and Milbrey McLaughlin put it) and cyclical (the here-we-go-again phenomenon). Another result is the compromise structure of the curriculum itself, which embodies contradictory purposes and therefore is unable to accomplish any one of these purposes with any degree of effectiveness (the familiar sense of schools as trying to do too much while accomplishing too little).

Credentialing Over Learning: From the perspective of the social-mobility goal, the point of education is not to learn the curriculum but to accumulate the grades, credits, and degrees that provide an edge in competing for jobs. So when this goal begins to play an increasingly dominant role in shaping education—which has been the case during the 20th century in the United States—curriculum reforms come to focus more on sorting and selecting students and less on enhancing learning, more on form than substance. This turns curriculum into a set of labels for differentiating students rather than a body of knowledge that all children should be expected to master, and it erects a significant barrier to any curriculum reforms that take learning seriously.

A Curriculum That Works: Another factor that undermines efforts to reform the curriculum is the comfortable sense among influential people that the current course of study in schools works reasonably well. Middle- and upper-middle-class families have little reason to complain. After graduation, their children for the most part go on to find attractive jobs and live comfortable lives. Judging from these results, schools must be providing these students with an adequate fund of knowledge and skills, so they have little reason to push for curriculum reform as a top priority. In fact, such changes may pose a threat to the social success of these children by changing the rules of the game—introducing learning criteria that they may not be able to meet (such as through performance testing), or eliminating curriculum options that provide special advantage (such as the gifted program). Meanwhile, families at the lower end of the social-class system, who have less reason to be happy about the social consequences of schooling, are not in a powerful position to push for reform.

Preserving the Curriculum of a Real School: Curriculum reform can spur significant opposition from people at all levels of society if it appears to change one of the fundamental characteristics of what Mary Metz calls "real school." Since all of us have extensive experience as students in school, we all have a strong sense of what makes up a school curriculum. To a significant extent, this curriculum is made up of the elements I mentioned earlier: academic subjects, which are cut off from practical everyday knowledge, taught in relative isolation from one another, stratified by ability, sequenced by age, grounded in textbooks, and delivered in a teacher-centered classroom. If this is our sense of what curriculum is like in a real school, then we are likely to object to any reforms that make substantial changes in any of these defining elements. This shared cultural understanding of the school curriculum exerts a profoundly conservative influence, by blocking program innovations even if they enhance learning and by providing legitimacy for programs that fit the traditional model even if they deter learning.

Preserving Real Teaching: This conservative view of the curriculum is also frequently shared by teachers. Prospective teachers spend an extended "apprenticeship of observation" (in Dan Lortie's phrase) as students in the K-12 classroom, during which they observe teaching from the little seats and become imprinted with a detailed picture of what the teacher's curriculum-in-use looks like. They can't see the reasons that motivate the teacher's curriculum choices. All they can see is the process, the routines, the forms. So it is not surprising that they bring to their own teaching a sense of curriculum that is defined by textbooks, disconnected categories of knowledge, and academic exercises. Teacher-preparation programs often try to offset the legacy of this apprenticeship by promoting the latest in curriculum-reform perspectives, but they are up against a massive accumulation of experience and sense impression that works to preserve the traditional curriculum.

Organizational Convenience: The traditional curriculum also persists in the face of curriculum-reform efforts because this curriculum is organizationally convenient for both teachers and administrators. It is convenient to focus on academic subjects, which are aligned with university

disciplines, thus simplifying teacher preparation. It is convenient to have a curriculum that is differentiated, which allows teachers to specialize. It is convenient to stratify studies by ability and age, which facilitates classroom management by allowing teachers to teach to the whole class at one level rather than adapt the curriculum to the individual needs of learners. It is convenient to ground teaching in textbooks, which reduce the demands on teacher expertise while also reducing the time commitment required for a teacher to develop her own curriculum materials. And it is convenient to run a teacher-centered classroom, which reinforces the teacher's control and which also simplifies curriculum planning and

student monitoring. Curriculum-reform efforts are hard to sell and even more difficult to sustain if they can only succeed if teachers have special capacities, such as: extraordinary subject-matter expertise; the time, will, and skill required to develop their own curriculum materials; the ability to teach widely divergent students effectively; and the ability to maintain control over these students while allowing them freedom to learn on their own.

Loose Coupling of School Systems: Another factor that undercuts the effectiveness of curriculum reform is the loosely coupled nature of American school systems. School administrators exert a lot of control over such matters as personnel, budgets, schedules, and supplies, but they have remarkably little control over the actual process of

instruction. In part, this is because teaching takes place behind closed doors, which means that only individual teachers really know the exact nature of the curriculum-in-use in their own classrooms. But in part, this is because administrators have little power to make teachers toe the line instructionally. Most managers can influence employee performance on the job by manipulating traditional mechanisms of fear and greed: Cross me and you're fired; do the job the way I want, and I'll offer you a promotion and a pay increase. School administrators can fire teachers only with the greatest difficulty, and pay levels are based on years of service and graduate credits, not job performance. The result is that teachers have considerably more autonomy in the way they perform their fundamental functions than do most employees. And this autonomy makes it hard for administrators to ensure that the formal curriculum becomes the curriculum-in-use in district classrooms.

Adaptability of the School System: Curriculum reform is also difficult to bring about because of another organizational characteristic of the American educational system: its adaptability. As Philip Cusick has shown, the system has a genius for incorporating curriculum change without fundamental reorganization. This happens in two related ways—formalism and segmentation. One is the way that teachers adopt the language and the feel of a reform effort without altering the basic way they do things. The system is flexible about adopting curriculum forms as long as this doesn't challenge the basic structure of curriculum practice. The other way is inherent in the segmented structure of the school curriculum. The differentiation of subjects frees schools to adopt new programs and courses by the simple process of addition. They can always tack on another segment in the already fragmented curriculum, because these additions require no fundamental restructuring of programs. For this reason, schools are quite tolerant of programs and courses that have contradictory goals. Live and let live is the motto. By abandoning any commitment to coherence of curriculum and compatibility of purpose, schools are able to incorporate new initiatives without forcing collateral changes. The result is that schools appear open to reform while effectively resisting real change.

Weak Link Between Teaching and Learning: Finally, let me return to the problem that faces any curriculum-reform effort in the last analysis, and that is trying to line up the received curriculum with the curriculum-in-use. The problem we confront here is the irreducible weakness of the link between teaching and learning. Even if teachers, against considerable odds, were to transform the curriculum they use in their classrooms to bring it in line with a reform effort, there is little to reassure us that the students in these classes would learn what the reform curriculum was supposed to convey. Students, after all, are willful actors who learn only what they choose to learn. Teachers can't make learning happen; they can only create circumstances that are conducive to learning. Students may indeed choose to learn what is taught, they may also choose to learn something quite different, or they may decide to resist learning altogether. And their willingness to cooperate in the learning process is complicated further by the fact that they are present in the classroom under duress. The law says they have to attend school until they are 16 years old; the job market pressures them to stay in school even longer than that. But these forces guarantee only attendance, not engagement in the learning process. So this last crucial step in the chain of curriculum reform may be the most difficult one to accomplish in a reliable and predictable manner, since curriculum reform means nothing unless learning undergoes reform as well.

For all the reasons spelled out here, curriculum-reform movements over the course of the 20th century have produced a lot of activity but not very much real change in the curriculum that teachers use in classrooms or in the learning that students accomplish in these classrooms. But isn't there reason to think that the situation I have described is now undergoing fundamental change? That real curriculum reform may now be on the horizon?

We currently have a substantial movement to set firm curriculum standards, one that is coming at us from all sides. Presidents Bush and Clinton have pushed in this direction; state departments of education are establishing curriculum frameworks for all the districts under their jurisdiction; and individual subject-matter groups have been working out their own sets of standards. This is something new in American educational history. And combined with the standards movement is a movement for systematic testing of what students know—particularly at the state level, but also at the local and federal levels. If in fact we are moving in the direction of a system in which high-stakes tests determine whether students have learned the material required by curriculum standards, this could bring about a more profound level of curriculum reform than we have ever before experienced. Isn't that right?

Not necessarily. The move toward standards and testing would affect only one or two elements in the long list of factors that impede curriculum reform. If this movement is successful—which is a big if—it would indeed help tighten the links in a system of education that has long been loosely coupled. It might also have an impact on the problem of student motivation, by convincing at least some students (those who see the potential occupational benefit of education) that they need to study the curriculum in order to graduate and get a good job. But this movement has already run into substantial resistance from religious conservatives and supporters of school choice, and it goes against the grain of the deep-seated American tradition of local control of education. In addition, I don't see how it would have a serious impact on any of the other factors that have for so long deflected efforts to reform the curriculum. Conflicting goals, the power of credentialing over learning, keeping a system that works, preserving the curriculum of the real school, organizational convenience, and system adaptability—all of these elements would be largely unaffected by the current initiatives for standards and testing.

The history of reform during the 20th century thus leaves us with a sobering conclusion: The American educational system seems likely to continue resisting efforts to transform the curriculum. ■

David F. Labaree, a professor of teacher education at Michigan State University in East Lansing, is the author of How To Succeed in School Without Really Learning *and* The Making of an American High School, *both published by Yale University Press.*

Reform efforts over time produce a pendulum swing between alternative conceptions of what children need to learn, leading to a sense that reform is both chronic and cyclical.

assessment culture

G auging the knowledge students acquired was an endeavor of educators long before the 20th century dawned, but it has become a national obsession as the century ends.

In the 19th century, teachers relied on recitations and, later, written examinations, but shortly into the 20th century, testing experts devised new breeds of assessments—designed to calculate intelligence and to measure achievement in a standardized fashion.

The objectivity and speed with which the new tests could be scored made them a popular commodity. Soon, multiple-choice and true-false questions displaced the written examination. But critics contended that the results inaccurately reflected student ability, particularly for girls and members of racial and ethnic minorities.

Over the decades, administrators often used *IQ* tests to track students by ability and standardized achievement tests to evaluate students' mastery of the curriculum. By the 1970s, state and federal officials began wielding standardized assessments as tools to judge how well schools did their jobs.

Today, students are finding the stakes attached to tests are rising for them as well.

Photo by Corbis/Genevieve Naylor

Tests such as the SAT, being administered here in 1953 to students in Lincoln, Neb., have become part of the fabric of school life.

Corbis/Genevieve Naylor

Made to Measure

Standardized testing has moved far beyond its modest beginnings in urban districts, becoming a tool used nationwide to judge what is taught and how.

Come every spring, Texas students from the 3rd to the 10th grades take the Texas Assessment of Academic Skills.

They toil at least two full days filling in the bubbles for multiple-choice and true-false questions on mathematics and reading. Eighth graders spend another two days on social studies and science tests. To graduate, high school students must pass such tests in reading, writing, and math.

Also at stake are bragging rights for their schools, the reputations of their teachers, and even the values of the homes they live in.

By David J. Hoff

Testing programs like the one in Texas are becoming standard among states as the century nears its end. Forty-eight states have testing systems, and most rely on the results to determine a wide range of life-changing events, including whether teachers will receive bonuses or the school will wear a badge of honor—or shame—for its scores. Texas and 18 others also require students to pass an exam to qualify for a diploma.

This current generation of exams is the culmination of a century in which tests and other assessments—ranging from IQ tests to SATs to statewide proficiency exams—have played an increasingly pervasive part in the lives of students and the operation of the schools they attend.

At the start of the 20th century, standardized testing was the province of urban districts, and it was employed mostly to measure how well students were learning. The test scores usually remained under wraps to all but a select number of administrators.

A hundred years later, tests are the tools of the state and federal governments, directing or influencing what is taught and how it is taught.

The deeply held belief in the value of such testing is rooted in the political ideals that shaped this country, argues Eva L. Baker, a co-director of the Center on Research on Standards and Student Testing, a federally financed research project, and a professor at the University of California, Los Angeles.

Frenchman Alexis de Tocqueville, the astute early-19th-century observer of the United States, noted that Americans believed in the "perfectability of man," Baker says, and the American obsession with testing in the 20th century reflects that creed. Educators continue to search for the perfect instrument to help them provide the best possible educational program for their students.

But the use of tests also raises a host of issues about another cherished American value: equal opportunity.

Since the civil rights and women's rights movements of the 1960s and '70s, schools and colleges have been bombarded with complaints and lawsuits contending that standardized tests aren't fair to minority students and girls. Tests' biases produce scores that track students into special education and less challenging courses and away from competitive colleges, the critics claim.

School leaders, meanwhile, have complained that tests are unfair barometers of how well they are educating children and should not be the sole criterion used to make decisions on students' futures, such as whether a 10th grader in Brownsville, Texas, or Newton, Mass., graduates from high school.

THE PRINTED EXAM

As early as 1845, schools began testing their students in a uniform way. At the time, oral examinations were state-of-the-art assessments.

That year, Boston became the first American district to print short-answer tests that would be used throughout its system, according to *How Research Has Changed American Schools* by Robert M.W. Travers.

Students were tested in geography, grammar, history, rhetoric, and philosophy. The city's school committee proposed to test every student in its schools, but only about 20 or 30 students in each school took the tests. About 500 students took each subject test out of the city's 7,000 students.

In a reaction that will sound familiar to present-day educators, Boston school leaders were shocked by the poor performance. The students tested failed to answer 40 percent of the questions correctly in any subject, Travers writes in his 1983 book.

The results, concluded a contemporary report on the exams, "show beyond all doubt, that a large proportion of the scholars in our first classes, boys and girls of 14 or 15 years of age, when called upon to write simple sentences, to express their thoughts on common subjects, without the aid of a dictionary or a master, cannot write, without such errors in grammar, in spelling, and in punctuation."

The tests were given again in 1846, but by 1850, Boston had abandoned its strategy, reverting to nonstandardized exams that were mostly based on oral presentations, Travers writes.

In 1874, Portland, Maine, experimented with standardized testing for the first time, according to *The One Best System: A History of American Urban Education*, by David B. Tyack.

Samuel King, the Portland superintendent, created uniform curriculum for the city's schools and wrote a test to measure whether students successfully learned it.

"System, order, dispatch, and promptness have characterized the examinations and exerted a helpful influence over the pupils by stimulating them to be thoroughly prepared to meet their appointments and engagements," the superintendent wrote about his exam, according to documents cited in Tyack's 1974 book.

King published each student's score in the newspaper, raising the ire and opposition of teachers and parents that led to his resignation in 1877. His successor never published scores, but he continued the tests, even if he did make them easier so more students would pass than they did under King.

RISE OF THE IQ

The experiences of Boston and Portland were common in city districts until the turn of the century. But in the first two decades of the 20th century, education researchers such as Edward L. Thorndike started to create standardized tests to measure students on uniform scales in arithmetic, handwriting, and other subjects.

Standardized tests held great appeal because they removed the subjectivity of individual teachers' grading methods. With an objective test, the experts said, a student's score could be confidently compared with those of his classmate in the next seat and his counterparts in a city across the country.

All those tests had a single goal: to measure how well students performed against a prescribed curriculum. But in the early years of the century, psychologists started to draft a new form of test: one designed to measure innate ability and predict future performance, instead of evaluating whether students had mastered the material in a curriculum.

In 1904, the Paris school system hired Alfred Binet to design a test to identify students who would be unable to benefit from instruction. He devised a scale that predicted how well a child would learn and estimated his or her "mental age." The American psychologists Henry Goddard, Lewis M. Terman, and others adapted Binet's work in 1912 to create the Intelligence Quotient, or IQ—calculated by dividing a person's "mental age" by his chronological age.

Terman, a Stanford University professor, unveiled what is called the Stanford-Binet scale in 1916 in his book *The Measurement of Intelligence*. In it, he outlined how the Binet test was to be administered and explained how its results would yield data revealing a student's innate intelligence.

In a crucial development, Terman's newest version could be administered to students using pencil and paper, making it much easier and cheaper for schools to administer than earlier versions requiring the services of a specially trained psychologist.

When Terman published the third volume of the test, he claimed that a student's score would be constant over time. By 1922, Terman said that 250,000 students had taken the test.

IQ tests "are now being used to classify schoolchildren of all degrees of intelligence and are being developed as important aids in vocational guidance," Harlan C. Hines, a professor at the University of Washington wrote in the April

A student in Indiana takes the ISTEP, or Indiana Statewide Testing for Educational Progress, in 1988, the first year the statewide assessment was administered. The legislature approved the test the year before as part of an education reform plan.

Rich Miller/Indianapolis News

Testing Across Time

Over the century, students have been faced with various forms of assessments. What follows is a sampling of questions; wording and punctuation are as they appeared to test-takers.

■ 1904 *College Entrance Examination Board test*

Test-takers were assigned to write a two-page essay on one of the four statements listed below. The test did not identify the works of literature.

1. Describe the character of Mr. Burchell, and compare or contrast him with Dr. Primrose. How far does he influence the course of events in the story?

2. Locksley shoots for the prize.

3. The elements of greatness in Shylock's character.

4. Describe, from the point at which the Albatross "begins to be avenged", the events that precede the Mariner's being left "alone, on the wide, wide sea".

■ 1922 *8th grade civics, language, and grammar exam given in the territory of Alaska*

1. Is a boy or girl who has finished the eighth grade any better prepared to be a good citizen than one who has dropped out of school before he or she reaches the eighth grade? Why?

2. Write a letter to Gibson and Company, 2301 Michigan Avenue, Chicago, ordering a book that you know they publish but the exact title of which you cannot recall. Describe the book so accurately that the publishers will know at once what you refer to and will send it without delay.

■ 1921-23 *geography, hygiene, and elementary science section of the Stanford Achievement Test*

1. A sweet-smelling flower is the

    daisy   poppy   rose

2. Soap is made from

    fats   lemons   sugars

3. Bacon comes from the

    cow   hog   sheep

4. Planes are used chiefly by

    barbers   blacksmiths   carpenters

1922 edition of *The American School Board Journal*.

In at least one state, which Hines did not name, "high school pupils are being classified on the basis of intelligence tests alone," he added.

TRACKING BY TEST

Even though that was a blatant misuse of the test, it was common practice, say Robert Glaser and Edward Silver, two University of Pittsburgh researchers.

In the early part of the century, enrollment in the nation's schools swelled, thanks to a flood of immigrants and compulsory-attendance laws. Administrators wanted a way to sort students by ability because they believed it was the best way to provide individualized instruction.

Intelligence tests provided the scientific data needed to assign students to separate tracks, Glaser and Silver write in *Review of Research in Education, 20th Edition*.

Testing was a "convenient and powerful instrument of social control" then, they write, and has remained so throughout the century.

The widespread adoption of tracking reflected the consensus of social scientists at the time that intelligence was a hereditary trait. By using a scientific instrument to group students, went the thinking in those days, school officials could find the right place to serve students according to their innate abilities.

By the middle of the century, the Scholastic Aptitude Test became an annual rite for college applicants, and by the 1970s, students were classified for special education and remedial education in federal programs based on test scores.

Whether those tests should be used for such purposes was a question as early as the 1920s, and it is one that persists. Based on results from the earliest versions of the tests, recent immigrants from Southern Europe were said to be less intelligent than others. The findings were used to set quotas to restrict immigration from Italy, Greece, and other Mediterranean countries. Later, a disproportionate number of black students ended up in special education programs, where they failed to catch up with their peers, because they scored poorly on such tests.

Those uses, according to Glaser, Silver, and other testing experts, are part of a pattern of inappropriate and unfair use of such exams. The University of Washington's Hines recognized the potential for problems early on.

"The writer has come to feel that a test

loses its value and becomes a dangerous weapon in the hands of the untrained," Hines concluded in his 1922 article.

The following year, Terman crafted an assessment very different from his intelligence tests. His product was similar to Boston's and Portland's standardized tests of the 19th century, as well as others that started to hit national markets in the first two decades of this century.

In his Stanford Achievement Test, Terman set out to measure student achievement in specific subjects across several grades. With it, a school could measure how well students in grades 2 through 8 performed.

More important, the Stanford results could be compared with those from a national sample of 350,000 students, according to *Lewis M. Terman: Pioneer in Psychological Testing*, a 1988 biography by Henry L. Minton. The sample was far bigger than any from similar tests available at the time.

The form and substance of the Stanford exam "foreshadowed the future," according to Glaser and Silver. Throughout the rest of the century, standardized tests would be modeled after Terman's work.

MEASURING CONTENT MASTERY

One such battery was the Iowa Tests of Basic Skills, one of the three most routinely administered standardized tests in schools today.

The testing program started as a scholarship competition run by the University of Iowa in 1929. In the first year, the tests had sections dedicated to grammar, English and American literature, world history, American history, algebra, geometry, science, physics, typing, and stenography, according to *The Iowa Testing Programs*, a history of the program written by Julia J. Peterson.

Like many tests of the era, the Iowa exams were based on textbooks commonly used throughout the state. To speed scoring, the authors relied on multiple-choice, true-false, matching, and fill-in-the-blank questions; the only free-response questions were on the math exam. The tests could be graded so quickly that students knew their scores and whether they advanced to the next round of competition before leaving the auditorium.

By 1935, the scholarship program had been replaced by a battery of tests, also called the Iowa Tests of Basic Skills. Like the Stanford Achievement Test, the ITBS covered all grade levels and spanned the basic curriculum: reading, language, study skills, and arithmetic.

■ 1937 *Progressive Achievement Tests, elementary battery for 4th, 5th, and 6th graders*

Bob paid $2.25 for a new tire, 75 cents for a seat, and 50 cents for paint. He had $4.00 to repair his bicycle. How much did he have left?

■ 1979 *Iowa Tests of Basic Skills, 7th grade science*

To what does a hypothesis most closely compare?

1. A statement of a problem

2. A procedure for solving a problem

3. A statement of a known fact

4. A possible explanation of something

■ 1989 *Comprehensive Test of Basic Skills, 4th Edition, 1st and 2nd grades*

Find the picture of someone who most probably comes from another country.

○ ○ ○

■ 1994 *Maryland School Performance Assessment Program, 5th grade science*

Test-takers were instructed to create a saline solution and asked to perform several experiments with it. Then, they were told to form groups of four students and do the following.

Step A Working with your group, pour one half of your fresh-water sample into an empty cup and an equal amount of your salt-water sample into an empty cup. Mix the two water samples together in a third cup and test the mixture with your hydrometer. Record your observations and measurements below.

Step B Did your investigation cause you to accept or reject the prediction you made? Explain why, using evidence from your investigation.

Trends in SAT Scores: 1962-63 to 1986-87

Bruce Katz

U.S. Secretary of Education William J. Bennett, at a 1988 news conference, points to declining SAT scores as proof that the nation's schools are inadequate.

Each district received a confidential report ranking its students against the mean of a statewide sample, as well as the number of correct answers. The designer of the Iowa exam, E.F. Lindquist, intended that it be "diagnostic in character" and able to evaluate whether a district's curriculum was working well, Peterson writes in her 1983 book.

Within four years of the program's start, 30,000 Iowa students had taken the basic-skills tests. The tests began their spread across the country, with Kansas City, Mo., and South Carolina purchasing them for use in their classrooms.

The market for the tests continued to grow. In 1940, the University of Iowa testing bureau contracted with the Houghton Mifflin Co. in Boston to distribute the ITBS nationally. The first four versions brought the university $330,000 in royalties.

The Iowa and Stanford tests were not the only such achievement tests of the era. Throughout the '30s, competitors such as the California Test Bureau also grew at rapid rates.

"Publishers had come to recognize that testing provided a new and lucrative market which developed rapidly during the 1930s, not just in the three R's but in the knowledge areas of the curriculum," Travers writes in his history of educational research.

A VALIDATION

The 1940s saw the increased use of another standardized test: the Scholastic Aptitude Test. Like IQ tests, the SAT's objective then and now is to predict performance. Instead of being a device to sort students within schools, the SAT's purpose was to divide them among colleges and universities.

The standardized version of the SAT was born in the 1920s when Harvard University decided to offer scholarships to underprivileged students and others who hadn't attended New England's elite preparatory schools.

Harvard contracted with the College Entrance Examination Board to create a new test to select the recipients. Since 1900, the board—now known simply as the College Board—had given essay exams in fields such as rhetoric, Greek, and other elements of the traditional prep-school curriculum.

Though the College Board continued to offer the essay tests for 10 years after the first SAT was given in 1926, the new exam soon became the standard hoop college applicants needed to jump through.

When servicemen returned from the Second World War and began flocking to colleges under the GI Bill, the importance of the SAT grew along with enrollments.

"It was truly the return of the GIs after World War II that spurred the growth in college enrollment and, therefore, admissions testing," says Brian P. O'Reilly, the College Board's executive director of guidance and admissions-testing programs.

When the SAT established its 800-point scale for each of its two sections in 1941, 10,000 students took the test, O'Reilly says. Seven years later, the number had doubled. In 1964, more than a million took it; that number had jumped to 2 million by 1967.

The SAT became the preferred method of evaluating college applicants because its maker, the Educational Testing Service, working with the International Business Machines Corp., used machines to scan answer sheets quickly. Contestants in the Iowa scholarship program could know their scores in a few hours in the days before computer scanners. But the numbers of students applying to that program paled in comparison with the flood of postwar college applicants.

The importance of the SAT, Baker writes, along with her UCLA colleague Regie Stites, in a 1991 essay on testing trends, is that it "legitimated" multiple-choice tests, especially among the highly educated class of people who grew up to be policymakers.

"Our best and brightest, and their influential parents, accepted the validity of such tests for college admissions," they write. "Thus, the experience of being tested successfully themselves bred not contempt but reaffirmation of the accuracy of the measure for the use by others."

But critics have long charged the SAT is not a fair measure for the rest of society.

"The data are clear" that the SAT discriminates against minorities and sometimes girls, says Monty Neill, the executive director of the Center for Fair & Open Testing, known as FairTest. "It hasn't changed substantially [since the beginning]." FairTest was founded in the 1980s by civil rights and consumer advocates to monitor testing practices and campaign against those its leaders deemed unfair.

Photopress

The biggest problem the bias creates may not be in the admissions process, Neill suggests, but in students' decisions about where to apply. A student who scores a combined 1000 on the test will shy away from applying to schools that publish an average SAT score of 1100, he says. "It reinforces the existing hierarchies of race and class," he asserts.

The College Board maintains that the SAT is the second-best predictor of how well a student will perform in college.

"We're very comfortable in knowing high school grades are the [best predictor], but only by a tiny little bit over test scores," O'Reilly says. "Nothing else contributes very much."

High school grades, of course, are derived in large part from the tests prepared by teachers—the tests that "count" in students' eyes. Little research is available to show how these assessments have changed.

What SAT scores are not a good barometer of, he adds, is school quality.

Since the 1970s, real estate agents, newspaper editors, and U.S. secretaries of education have cited SAT data in an attempt to judge the quality of schools. As scores started to decline in the 1960s, critics pointed to SAT scores as a sign that the quality of education was declining. In the 1980s, the U.S. Department of Education annually compared states' SAT scores in gauging their relative educational performance.

But such comparisons are meaningless,

O'Reilly and other researchers say. They say the comparisons ignore the fact that SAT-taking is the product of a self-selected group rather than a consistent sample that represents the population as a whole.

"Trying to compare schools just on SAT scores ... ignores a whole lot of other things that are going on in the schools," O'Reilly says.

THE FEDERAL PLUNGE

The SAT set the stage for the next step in the use of testing. While the SAT, IQ tests, and other selection tests held high stakes for individual students throughout the century, until the 1960s there were no assessments that held consequences for the people who ran schools.

Testing programs such as the Iowa and Stanford ones had been around since at least the 1920s, but their results were intended to inform teachers on how to instruct students, not to rate how well they themselves did their jobs.

"We used to have standardized achievement tests [in the 1950s], but they were never used to judge the quality of schooling," says W. James Popham, a former science teacher who went on to become a leading testing expert as a professor at the University of California, Los Angeles.

Before the 1970s, test scores were considered "for internal use only" and rarely were reported to state or federal officials, or the public, Joy A. Frechtling, then the

In January 1990, a coalition of education and civil rights groups urged President George Bush and state governors to back away from an emphasis on multiple-choice tests. Appearing at a news conference are, from left, Barbara A. Willer of the National Association for the Education of Young Children, Cinthia Schuman of FairTest, A. Graham Down of the Council for Basic Education, and Monty Neill of FairTest, the group that organized the signing of the "Statement on Genuine Accountability."

director of educational accountability for the Montgomery County, Md., schools, writes in a 1989 text on educational measurement.

All that changed when the federal government started to play an increasingly important role in subsidizing schools and wanted to see returns on its investment.

In 1965, the U.S. Office of Education contracted with the sociologist James S. Coleman to study whether American schools offered equal opportunity to white and black students.

The report remains one of the biggest and most significant studies of educational achievement ever. Coleman and his team surveyed 570,000 students and 60,000 teachers throughout the country. They found that students' family backgrounds and the socioeconomic makeup of their schools were more meaningful factors in student achievement than the quality of their schools.

Those findings have been debated ever since, but the study served as a prototype for conducting education research that put test scores at center stage.

"The Coleman report formally reduced the question of how well schools serve low-income and minority students to a single criterion, student performance on multiple-choice tests of basic skills," Baker and Stites write.

That assumption began to drive how the federal government ran its growing investment in precollegiate education. After President Lyndon B. Johnson signed the Elementary and Secondary Education Act in 1965, its program to help schools with high concentrations of poor children soon began to reflect a test-driven definition of success.

To qualify for Title I money, the federal government said, school districts had to show results. The government created the Title I Evaluation and Reporting System—also called TIERS. It required schools to evaluate their federal programs by using norm-referenced tests—which compare students against a national sample—and it contributed to the "substantial expansion" in the use of them throughout the decade, according to a 1998 paper by Robert L. Linn. He is a co-director of the Center on Research on Standards and Student Testing, or CRESST, at UCLA and a professor of education at the University of Colorado at Boulder.

TIERS encouraged schools to test Title I students twice a year, Linn writes, because the best way to prove academic growth was to compare a student's scores in the fall against those in the spring. Studies showed that schools following

Pencil Leaves Its Mark

By Adrienne D. Coles

Over the 20th century, the tests designed to measure what students know have changed like the seasons, but one thing has remained a constant: the tool necessary to record such measurement—the lead pencil.

That was not the case during the 19th century, when, in succession, one writing implement replaced another.

Still, the development of written tests was hampered by the crude and impractical materials available to record and correct answers.

But by the beginning of the 1900s, the pencil had found its way into the classroom, and eventually led to a different and far simpler way of assessing students.

In earlier days, students used slates or slateboards as writing tablets in conjunction with slate pencils. Made of layered rock, the slate pencils produced scratchy writing, and, as Robert M.W. Travers notes in his book *How Research Has Changed American Schools*, the friction from the slate pencil on the slate surface made writing slow and clumsy.

"It was nothing like writing with a pen or [lead] pencil. It was more like scratching and not very smooth," according to Richard Casey, an instructional designer at the Blackwell History of Education Research Museum, housed at Northern Illinois University.

While chalk was available, that kind of marker was even more cumbersome and messy to use, Casey says.

Using slates for test-taking wasn't feasible either. Teachers could hardly store the relatively heavy tablets for later grading. Nor could students go without the slates that they used on a daily basis, Travers writes in his 1983 book.

Consequently, the preferred method of assessing students was oral examination.

With the invention and spread of the steel pen, however, the written exam gained in popularity in schools in the waning years of the 19th century. Students could write at length with the devices without having to refill the pens, but, of course, there was little room for error.

The lead pencil had been around long before, but its expense—some sold for as much as 75 cents a dozen—had kept it out of schools.

It wasn't until 1866, when Joseph Dixon was granted a patent for his wood-planing machine at his Jersey

that pattern exhibited more student improvement than those that tested once a school year.

Nine years after the inception of Title I, the federal government ordered a different kind of testing in a new special education law.

The 1975 Education for All Handicapped Children Act required schools to test slow learners to determine whether they would qualify for individualized services under the program.

The law even mandated that schools assess every potentially disabled child twice, Linn writes in the 1989 edition of *Educational Measurement*. That provision was included to ensure accuracy, but, like TIERS, it doubled the time dedicated to testing.

It also reinforced the role of IQ tests and other psychological instruments designed to test innate ability.

A NATIONAL SNAPSHOT

Meanwhile, support had been growing among federal leaders in the 1960s for a new assessment designed to provide a snapshot of national student achievement.

U.S. Commissioner of Education Francis Keppel formed a panel of experts in 1963 to explore ways of crafting such an assessment system.

"The nation could find out about school buildings or discover how many years children stay in school; it had no satisfactory way of assessing whether the time spent in school was effective," Keppel wrote in 1966, a year after leav-

City, N.J., company, that the mass production of pencils—132 per minute—began.

With the advent of mass production, the price of the pencil dropped, with some selling for as little as a penny apiece.

Demand for pencils became fairly steady, says Henry Petroski, the author of *The Pencil: A History of Design and Circumstance* and a civil engineering and history professor at Duke University.

By the 1870s, it was estimated that more than 20 million pencils were being sold in the United States each year.

A 1903 circular advertised the penny pencil—one with an eraser built into the end. It was popular, but not with educators. Teachers didn't like the idea of erasers on pencils, Petroski says, because they thought that feature would encourage students to be careless.

But the no-frills penny pencil—which was made with bare wood and lacked the typical yellow paint and varnish—had the great virtue of affordability.

"The pencil revolutionized the ability to grade tests automatically," Petroski says.

An electronic-scoring machine went on the market in the late '30s.

Hand-scoring gave way to optical readers that could detect the graphite content the pencil left. The popularity of answer sheets soared in the late 1950s, however, with the invention of a far speedier model that came out of the University of Iowa.

"This technology gave birth to the standardized test," says Larry Ganzell, the vice president of sales administration at the Scantron Corp., a manufacturer of electronic-answer forms.

"The number-two pencil was dark enough for teachers to read but light enough for students to erase," Ganzell says.

And the answer sheets allowed a high volume of tests to be given and graded in a timely manner.

Thus was born an inexpensive way to measure the performance of thousands of students, something that could not have been done without the pencil. ■

FUSING NEW AND OLD

In 1929, researchers at the University of Iowa began to develop the Iowa Tests of Basic Skills. By the next decade, researchers fused a new technology—the electronic answer-sheet scanner—with an old technology, the pencil.

ing his federal post.

To lead the committee, Keppel named Ralph W. Tyler, who had led the evaluation of the landmark Eight-Year Study of progressive education at the secondary school level 30 years earlier.

The Tyler committee recommended a regular sampling of students in basic subjects for the program that became known as the National Assessment of Educational Progress. Because local school administrators objected to reporting a breakdown of scores by state, Tyler's panel proposed that the scores be reported by four regions.

While the compromise was necessary to assuage worries that the federal test would drive state and local curriculum decisions, it also meant NAEP results would be useless for evaluating the effec-

tiveness of schools, according to Maris A. Vinovskis, a University of Michigan historian who wrote a history of the program in 1998.

The lack of comparable state data forced federal officials to rely on other data, such as SAT scores, in their "Wall Chart" in the 1980s designed to grade states.

Consequently, the job of evaluating school districts fell to states.

Starting in the early '70s, states set out to define the minimum students should know before they graduated. To measure whether individuals met those basic standards, states created so-called minimum-competency tests.

The standards were "the most minimum imaginable," according to Popham, the UCLA professor emeritus.

From 1973 to 1983, the number of states with minimum-competency tests grew from two to 34, Linn writes in a 1998 essay published by CRESST about the growth of testing during the past 50 years.

A 1977 North Carolina law, for example, called for a testing system to fulfill three purposes: ensure that high school graduates "possess minimum skills," identify their strengths and weaknesses, and hold schools accountable for what they teach students.

Like the IQ tests and SATs before them, the minimum-competency tests raised questions of racial fairness.

In 1977—the first year of Florida's test—75 percent of white students passed on the first try, Linn notes, compared with 60 percent of Hispanics and fewer than 25 percent of their African-American counterparts.

Twenty years later, minority students had narrowed the gap but not closed it, according to data cited by Linn. In 1984, 70 percent of black students passed on the first try, but by then, almost 90 percent of white test-takers were doing so. Since then, the African-American passing rate has declined gradually, while white students have continued to score at about the same level.

Once states committed to attaching what are now called "high stakes" to student testing, they didn't turn back. If anything, they have upped the ante over the past 16 years.

In 1983, a federal panel released the influential report *A Nation at Risk*. It declared the nation's schools woefully inadequate and called for ways of measuring whether students had mastered a rigorous curriculum.

The call set off activity not only to append significant consequences to, but to increase the difficulty of, statewide tests.

Most states—just as they have whenever the number of students being tested rises dramatically—relied on standardized tests, setting off a debate over whether norm-referenced tests should be used to decide school sanctions or rewards and whether students would be promoted or graduated.

"A good norm-referenced test will give you in great detail, skill by skill, a child's strengths and weaknessess," says Maureen DiMarco, the vice president for educational and governmental affairs for Riverside Publishing Co., the division of Houghton Mifflin that distributes the Iowa tests.

On an aggregate level, such a test can play a role in accountability decisions "if it's part of a system, not the sole charac-

teristic," adds DiMarco, who was a high-profile education adviser to former California Gov. Pete Wilson. "It can be the predominant one. It's going to be your strongest and most objective measure."

In the late 1980s and early 1990s, some states experimented with "authentic assessments" based on portfolios of student work and questions that required them to write essays on exams—even in such subjects as science and math that traditionally eschewed them.

California abandoned its program after conservatives, DiMarco among them, charged that the test questions pried into students' personal beliefs, and traditionalists complained that a student could score well on a math problem by writing a high-quality essay but failing to comprehend the mathematical principles behind it.

In 1996, Vermont added a standardized test to supplement its portfolio-based assessments after scoring was found to be unreliable for individual results. Kentucky is also adding standardized tests to its assessment package.

Maryland, meanwhile, continues to rely on its performance-oriented system.

The dependence on standardized tests hasn't changed much in the '90s, testing experts say, even though states declare that their tests are aligned with curriculum standards they have adopted.

So general are many of the standards, however, that test writers need to do little more than revise off-the-shelf products to satisfy the needs of states, says Popham, who occasionally competes for contracts as an independent testing consultant.

"The present watchword of alignment is mostly a farce," says Eva Baker, the director of the federal testing center at UCLA.

"More often than not, they look like warmed-over versions" of standardized tests, Popham says of the state tests. "The mentality [test publishers] bring when they create a test is what they know, and they don't know [anything] about instruction."

The Texas test, Popham points out, is written by Harcourt Educational Measurement, one of the three leading test publishers. Harcourt's Stanford Achievement Test-9th Edition is used in several other states. CTB/McGraw-Hill is the contractor for Kentucky's testing program.

Even those who support the concept of aligning content standards and tests say the match isn't always perfect.

"It's still an open question: What does an aligned system look like?" says Matthew Gandal, the director of standards and assessments for Achieve Inc.,

a group of corporate and state leaders pushing for increased student achievement. "Rhetorically, everybody is there. But in reality, what does it look like?"

HIGH-STAKES TESTING

While states were raising the difficulty level on their own tests, the federal government raised the stakes on NAEP. Starting in 1990, the national assessment began producing scores on a state-by-state basis.

For many states, NAEP results carry significant weight—in substantive as well as public relations terms. California's poor showing on the 1994 NAEP reading test, for instance, armed critics of the state's whole-language philosophy. They succeeded in forcing the state to shift toward phonics instruction. This year, Kentucky has had to defend its increases, deemed statistically significant, from critics who say the gains occurred because the state excluded a higher percentage of students in 1998 than in 1994.

And if President Clinton's proposal for new voluntary national tests becomes a reality, the NAEP tests might have consequences for individual 4th and 8th graders. The plan is currently being studied by the board that oversees NAEP, but it is unlikely to overcome deep-seated opposition by both Republicans and Democrats in Congress.

Nothing like the recent occurrences in Kentucky and California would have happened at the beginning of the century—for the simple reason that test scores were not made public.

In 1925, for example, Texas undertook what probably was "at the time one of the most extensive investigations of the operations of a state's schools and department of education ever made," according to a history of the states' role in education compiled by the Council of Chief State School Officers.

The Texas study reported on student access and bureaucratic structure, but it didn't mention test scores. Indeed, the 1969 book detailing the history of the state's role in education doesn't mention the testing system at the time.

But by 1980, Texas started relying on test scores in making significant decisions. That year, it began requiring minimum-competency tests in reading, mathematics, and writing.

In 1990, the state introduced the Texas Assessment of Academic Skills. Unlike the scores from its predecessors, TAAS results mete out consequences for everyone in schools: students, teach-

AP/Wide World

ers, administrators, and board members.

Still, testing experts question whether programs such as TAAS should be the primary criteria for defining successful schools.

"They have items in there that do a terrible job at measuring school quality," Popham says. "What is being measured is what kids come to school with, not what they learn there."

And most academic experts warn against relying on a single test to make critical decisions, such as whether a student will move to the next grade or graduate from high school.

"A test score, like other sources of information, is not exact," a National Academy of Sciences panel writes in a 1998 report. "It is an estimate of the student's understanding or mastery at a particular time. Therefore, high-stakes educational decisions should not be made solely or automatically on the basis of a single test score, but should also take other relevant information into account."

Testing advocates agree that test scores should not be the sole factor in accountability decisions. But they do look to tests to play a leading role.

"They have to be at the center of accountability policies," Gandal says. "They are one of the only reliable indicators of what students are learning. It doesn't mean they can't be supplemented very well by what teachers and schools bring to the equation."

But calls for moderation are unlikely to sway policymakers and the public. Policymakers are hungry for data to prove that their schools are succeeding, and they are relying on test results for a variety of report cards, teacher bonuses, and penalties for school officials whose students score poorly.

The public—from newspaper reporters to real estate agents—use test data as "a vicious tool for self-interest," contends Sherman Dorn, an assistant professor of educational history at the University of South Florida.

Now, school administrators are the ones on the hot seat.

"History has played a cruel joke on school administrators," Dorn says. "They used those tests to track students, sometimes in vicious ways ... and now they're used against them." ∎

Texas began using the TAAS in 1990, and the test has consequences for students, teachers, administrators, and school board members. Above, a student's paper at a Houston elementary school in 1996 shows how important the Texas Assessment of Academic Skills is to schools and students.

Pioneers of Modern Testing

(1874-1949)

Edward L. Thorndike

Without the work of Edward L. Thorndike, the children living in the fictional town of Lake Wobegon would not know that they are all above average. A leading psychologist based at Teachers College, Columbia University, for the first half of the century, Thorndike was the originator of a scale of achievement covering a wide variety of subjects. Educators could then compare their students' performance against the average achievement—commonly called the norm—of a representative sample of children.

The work of Thorndike and his graduate students from 1908 to 1916 established norms for arithmetic, reading, handwriting, and other subjects, according to a history of educational testing published by the National Academy of Sciences in 1982. Thorndike's work focused mostly on handwriting because he believed that its style, beauty, and uniformity revealed as much about test-takers' intelligence and character as did content knowledge in other subjects. The norms established by Thorndike gave school administrators their first chance to compare the knowledge and abilities of their students against an average.

Today, all major national tests—from standardized tests available at all grade levels to the

Milbank Library/Teachers College, Columbia University

SAT college-entrance exam—compare individual test-takers and groups of students against such norms. Thorndike went on to work with Robert M. Yerkes, Lewis M. Terman, and other leading psychologists in developing the famed Alpha-Beta tests for the U.S. Army during World War I. After the war, the three of them were part of the group that created the National Intelligence Tests. Within a few years of its introduction, school officials relied on that test's results when assigning students to academic tracks.

(1877-1956)

Lewis M. Terman

A pioneer in the development of intelligence and achievement tests, Lewis M. Terman also was one of the first to use the instruments for longitudinal research. The Stanford University professor tracked the test scores and a variety of other data—such as physical measurements and medical records—of 1,470 gifted schoolchildren in the early 1920s. Terman and his research team collected more than 100 pages of data on each subject, whose IQs ranged from 135 to 200. The researchers concluded that gifted children performed two to three grade levels higher than their peers and that they scored about the same

distance ahead on tests designed to measure character traits.

Perhaps the most important finding dispelled the belief that smart children were "one-sided and neurotic," Henry L. Minton writes in *Lewis M. Terman: Pioneer in Psychological Testing.* "It suggested that gifted children had the kinds of well-rounded personalities and skills that ... could be harnessed for leadership roles in Terman's meritocratic society," Minton notes in his 1988 book.

Terman pursued the subjects of his original study of gifted children, surveying them again in 1936, 1940, 1945, and 1952. In those follow-ups, he found that the gifted students continued to excel in school and throughout their careers, with the students who scored higher than 170 on the IQ test achieving the most success, Minton writes. In the final volume of the research, published in 1959, the subjects—by then in their 40s—continued to be successful in their careers and were as healthy emotionally as their peers who scored lower on IQ tests.

Terman used IQ tests to investigate the link between intelligence and heredity. In 1929, one of his Stanford students completed a dissertation suggesting that children's intelligence was not influenced by their environment. Even though it was disputed by simultaneous research conducted at the University of Chicago, Terman continued to believe there was a genetic link to intelligence, Minton notes. Until 1935, Terman was active in the racially charged eugenics movement, which advocated the propagation of individuals who were deemed to be genetically superior.

Stanford University

(1876-1956)

Robert M. Yerkes

Since the start of intelligence testing, scores have often been used to support existing stereotypes. Perhaps no research has been cited as doing so more than Robert M. Yerkes' analysis of tests given to World War I soldiers.

The Johns Hopkins University psychologist led a team of his peers on the Committee on the Psychological Examining of Recruits. The team created the Alpha-Beta tests to gauge the intelligence of young men. (The Alpha assessed the literate recruits; the Beta tested the illiterate.)

In 1921, Yerkes edited a volume analyzing the results. The data suggested that black men as well as Southern and Eastern Europeans scored the worst. Even though the report called for a cautious interpretation of the results, policymakers in the United States cited them in 1921 and 1924 as reason for restricting immigration from such countries as Russia, Italy, and Poland. Educators also pointed to the scores as justification for the belief that African-Americans were intellectually inferior because of their ancestry. "The seeds of prejudice were deeply embedded in American culture ... and the new science of testing seemed to provide them a medium within which they could grow," Robert M.W. Travers writes in his 1983

Yale University

history of the impact of research on schools.

It wasn't until the 1930s that other research disputed the findings in Yerkes' 1921 book, according to Travers. Few of the immigrants knew English when they took the test, and the average African-American in the South attended schools only about half the amount of time that white students did. Such disadvantages, the later research said, were bound to lower their scores.

From the commercial tests first
published before World War I,
the testing business has
profoundly affected schools.

By Mark Walsh

Monterey, Calif.

Willis W. Clark was a quiet,
scholarly man who liked
almost nothing better than
tinkering with his theories
about measuring the abilities and achievement
of students.

His wife, Ethel M. Clark, on the other hand,
found the subject of testing rather boring. But
when educators outside Los Angeles started
expressing interest in one of the tests created
by her husband, the assistant director of
research for the Los Angeles public schools,
Mrs. Clark's imagination soared.

The district wasn't in the business of
marketing tests, she knew, so why not set up a
commercial concern and become the
middleman, or the middlewoman?

Mrs. Clark worked up the courage in 1926 to
approach her husband's boss, the district
superintendent, to ask for the rights to the Los
Angeles Diagnostic Tests in the Fundamentals of
Arithmetic. Permission granted, she worked out
a royalty arrangement with the district and then
proceeded to do market research that has become
legendary. Mrs. Clark sent out penny postcards—
that's all they cost back then—to 25 large
districts, promoting the availability of the test.

Quiz Biz

*Willis W. Clark, fourth from right, his wife, Ethel, and
daughter, June Duran, pose with California Test Bureau
staff at a Monterey, Calif., retreat in the late 1950s.*

Photo courtesy of June Duran

The Iowa Testing Program relied on teams of sharp-eyed scorers, shown here circa 1950, before program director E.F. Lindquist perfected automated machinery for the task by the middle of the decade.

And then she waited. And waited.

Nearly a year went by, according to the Clarks' daughter, June Duran. "She had practically forgotten about them," Duran recalls.

Ethel Clark would probably have moved on to her next money-making scheme, of which she had several. But then an order came in.

The Kansas City, Mo., district wanted 20,000 copies of the test. The California Test Bureau was in business. From these humble beginnings, the Clarks helped shift the field of student testing from the province of academe into the commercial marketplace.

To educators across the country, the little company that was capitalized, in a sense, on a 25-cent investment in postcards, is now known as CTB/McGraw-Hill, the testing division of a publishing giant, the McGraw-Hill Companies Inc.

Known for its California Achievement Test and the Comprehensive Test of Basic Skills, CTB/McGraw-Hill is one of the big three purveyors of K-12 tests, along with Harcourt Educational Measurement, the San Antonio-based publisher of the Stanford Achievement Test and the Metropolitan Achievement Tests, and the Riverside Publishing Co. of Itasca, Ill., which publishes the Iowa Tests of Basic Skills. These companies have prospered for decades by offering off-the-shelf standardized tests.

"It is a relatively small segment of educational publishing," George F. Madaus, the director of the Center for the Study of Testing, Evaluation, and Educational Policy at Boston College, says of the market for precollegiate tests. "But it's lucrative. It must be, or else they wouldn't be in business."

But the landscape has changed in the past decade, as more states have adopted high-stakes accountability programs with their own academic standards and assessments. To be sure, the major school test publishers have stepped forward to bid on developing and processing these customized tests. But such specially crafted state tests are more expensive than the off-the-shelf variety.

Commercial publication of tests began before the First World War. In 1916, Houghton Mifflin Co., a leading textbook publisher at the time, began publishing the Stanford-Binet intelligence scale, an individual-intelligence test created by the psychologist Lewis M. Terman of Stanford University. The test quickly took hold in schools.

In addition to intelligence tests, the schools had dozens of achievement tests and "scales" written by university professors or school district research directors. Many of them were published for sale around the country.

At first, sales were handled by the test developers themselves, or by university research bureaus. In 1918, the yearbook of the National Society for the Study of Education included a report about educational tests.

It listed dozens with such distinctive names as Courtis' Standard Research Tests in Arithmetic, Ayres' Handwriting Scale, Woody's Arithmetic Scales, Murdoch's Scale for Measuring Certain Elements in Hand Sewing, and Brown's Connected-Latin Test.

The education society noted in its yearbook that "in only a few cases are the tests published on a commercial basis, and for this reason, one may be reasonably certain that the tests may be obtained at approximately the cost of printing."

In 1922, a writer in *The American School Board Journal* observed: "Within the past five years, so many tests have been produced that the teacher who wishes to secure a measure of her instruction frequently is at a loss to know which of a great number of tests to select. For general circulation, there are now 31 tests in reading, 30 in language, 26 in arithmetic, 24 in handwriting, and 17 in spelling."

Although Houghton Mifflin published the Stanford-Binet individual-intelligence test—and still does—the company passed up the chance to publish the first group-intelligence tests, which, unlike the Stanford-Binet, could be administered to many students at once.

When the company declined, Terman and his associates turned to another textbook publisher with which he had dealings, the World Book Co. of Yonkers, N.Y.

World Book was founded in 1905 by Caspar W. Hodgson, a Stanford University graduate who became a school principal in Indiana and California. A former textbook salesman for D.C. Heath and Co., he started his own publishing company at the urging of the schools superintendent for the Philippines, who had complained about the unsuitability of the textbooks available for his system.

The World Book Co., which was not affiliated with the famous encyclopedia, built its niche with elementary school texts—and with tests.

"Hodgson really saw the potential of group tests," says Henry L. Minton, a professor of psychology at the University of Windsor in Ontario and a biographer

University of Iowa News Service

of Terman.

Before World War I, World Book published an intelligence scale designed by Arthur S. Otis, a student of Terman's at Stanford. After the war, the company published the National Intelligence Tests, a creation of the same group of psychologists that developed the famed Army Alpha tests.

World Book also published Terman's own group-intelligence tests, which the Stanford professor had formulated in 1919 for grades 7-12.

Terman had become a sort of scholarly adviser to World Book by the early '20s. Hodgson even asked him to take a leave of absence from Stanford to become the company's test expert.

"If we could have such a man as you for about one year to get us headed right

as an expert in tests and measurements and to some extent as a psychological editor of textbooks in general, we would feel that we might get a younger man started with you before you get through to carry on the work," Hodgson wrote Terman in June 1921. The letter is one of many in Terman's papers archived at Stanford that help shed light on the commercial origins of testing.

Terman declined the offer, telling Hodgson he was too busy and couldn't possibly take a leave. But he did agree to become the general editor of the *Measurement and Adjustment Series*, a set of books and monographs that was meant to advance the testing movement among classroom teachers and school administrators.

In 1921, Terman wrote to World Book to propose "an all-round achievement test covering in three- to eight-page test booklets all the school subjects from grade three to grade eight."

"The average superintendent is rather

lost among the great numbers of tests for every sort of purpose," Terman added. "It costs a good deal of money and more time to test out all the different subjects of the curriculum at the present time because there is no one satisfactory battery of tests covering the whole ground. I am convinced the time has come for such a battery of tests."

Thus began the Stanford Achievement Test, one of the most frequently administered school tests today.

Of course, Terman explained, such a battery would be more complicated to write than his previous tests. He and his co-authors at Stanford demanded more than the standard 5 percent royalty on tests. They ended up getting 9 percent, just shy of the 10 percent World Book paid textbook writers.

As Terman and his colleagues were refining the tests, he and the publisher began to bandy names around. Hodgson suggested the Terman

Annual sales of the Stanford Achievement Test exploded from 115,000 in 1923, its first year, to 1.5 million by 1925.

Achievement Test.

"The only objection to using the name Stanford is that it might prejudice its sale a little in California among the University of California people who predominate in the schools," a market-conscious Hodgson wrote to Terman.

Terman replied, without elaboration, that he preferred the Stanford name.

Annual sales of the Stanford Achievement Test exploded from 115,000 in 1923, its first year, to 1.5 million by 1925.

That a textbook company would also publish and sell intelligence and achievement tests might be called synergistic today. But in the field's infancy, it appears that educators paused to consider whether such an arrangement was appropriate.

According to a letter in Terman's papers, the brand-new American Educational Research Association debated the commercial publication of tests sometime in 1918 or 1919. In a 1952 exchange of letters, a longtime World Book employee, O.S. Reimbold, tried to get Terman to help him remember the details.

"[Arthur] Otis and other authors who had contracted with World Book Company for the publication of their tests

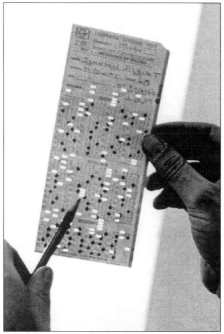

CTB/McGraw-Hill

were given a vote of censure," Reimbold recalled in his letter. But a year later, after World Book had published its first tests, "the same AERA voted not only approval, but an expression of satisfaction with the product," Reimbold wrote.

Besides displaying the tests at the

major education conventions of the day, World Book and other publishers used their network of textbook salesmen to push tests throughout the market.

They also employed advertisements. A 1923 ad in the *School Board Journal* touted the Otis Classification Test. A classroom set of 25 exam booklets and the scoring key cost $1.30. A manual was available for an additional 25 cents.

By that time, Willis Clark was hard at work in Los Angeles on one of those many single-subject tests that Terman was trying to replace.

When the order came in from Kansas City for 20,000 copies of the arithmetic test, Ethel Clark went on a frantic mission to find a printer to fill it. "The first thing they asked me was how I was going to pay for it," she says in a company history compiled by her daughter. "Well, that was something I hadn't thought about, so a second mortgage on our house paid for the 20,000 tests."

Mrs. Clark and her mother, Jeanette King, stored the printed tests in the family garage. When the tests were ready to ship, the two put them in a big piano box. The package was so heavy, the bottom fell out. Repacked in smaller boxes, the tests eventually arrived in Kansas City.

With training from a secretarial school, Mrs. Clark had long helped supplement her husband's income by typing master's theses and doctoral dissertations. Because of that experience and the expense of printing out-of-house, Mrs. Clark decided her fledgling company could print the tests itself. So she bought a printing press, a purchase that came in handy when the company found itself doing more business printing business cards and stationery than tests, says Duran, the Clarks' daughter.

Early in the life of the California Test Bureau, Mrs. Clark came up with another idea for making money from schools. State textbooks were distributed from a depository in San Francisco, even though the bulk of student enrollment was in Southern California districts, which paid an extra 5 percent in shipping

CTB/McGraw-Hill

fees. Upon learning this, Mrs. Clark opened the Southern California Book Depository in 1930.

"She was off on another venture," her daughter says. At times, the testing business became "sort of a stepchild," Duran says.

Willis Clark continued working for the Los Angeles schools and continued writing tests. In 1933, he and Ernest W. Tiegs of the University of Southern California developed a test battery known as the Progressive Achievement Tests, which was later renamed the California Achievement Test.

"The name really wasn't tied in to the progressive movement" in education, Duran says. The tests were well-received in schools, and Ethel Clark retrained her focus on test publishing.

About the same time, another invention helped advance the testing business. With the advent of the multiple-choice test around 1915, students circled their answers on a test form or booklet. Scoring was tedious, even with stencils that were laid over the answer sheets to speed up the process.

Around 1936, the International Business Machines Corp. created an electronic test-scoring machine that made grading multiple-choice tests more efficient.

Duran remembers the machine because, as a youngster who worked after school in her mother's business, "I was the scoring department," she says.

"The machine was as big as a desk, and the procedure was to take an answer sheet and drop it in the slot, one at a time," Duran says. "The graphite [from pencil marks] that came through produced a little electrical charge, which was indicated on a volt meter on the desk. You had to drop every one of those damn tests in the slot, but it was an improvement."

As Duran recalls, her parents were not getting rich from the business. When schools didn't pay their bills right away, the couple took second and third mortgages or used the accounts payable as collateral for loans.

World War II proved especially challenging. The U.S. Army decided it needed

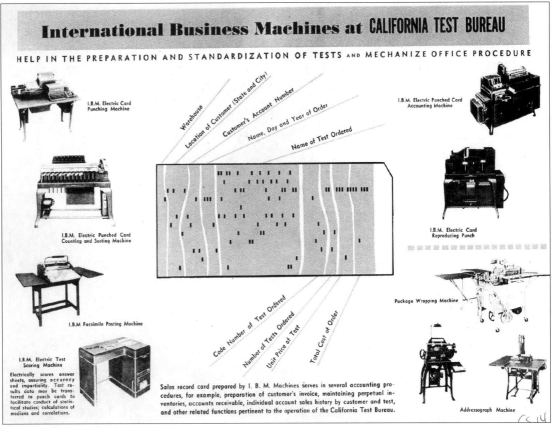

International Business Machines at CALIFORNIA TEST BUREAU

HELP IN THE PREPARATION AND STANDARDIZATION OF TESTS AND MECHANIZE OFFICE PROCEDURE

I.B.M. Electric Card Punching Machine

I.B.M. Electric Punched Card Counting and Sorting Machine

I.B.M. Facsimile Posting Machine

I.B.M. Electric Test Scoring Machine

Electrically scores answer sheets, assuring accuracy and impartiality. Test results data may be transferred to punch cards to facilitate conduct of statistical studies; calculations of medians and correlations.

Warehouse
Location of Customer (State and City)
Customer's Account Number
Name, Day and Year of Order
Name of Test Ordered

Code Number of Test Ordered
Number of Tests Ordered
Unit Price of Test
Total Cost of Order

I.B.M. Electric Punched Card Accounting Machine

I.B.M. Electric Card Reproducing Punch

Package Wrapping Machine

Addressograph Machine

Sales record card prepared by I. B. M. Machines serves in several accounting procedures, for example, preparation of customer's invoice, maintaining perpetual inventories, accounts receivable, individual account sales history by customer and test, and other related functions pertinent to the operation of the California Test Bureau.

CTB/McGraw-Hill

CTB's Los Angeles facility and ordered the company to vacate the premises within 30 days. The company had a huge book inventory, as well as printing presses, linotype machines, and other equipment.

Mrs. Clark sold off the book-depository inventory, and the family was left with its test business and a staff depleted by the war. CTB moved to smaller quarters on Hollywood Boulevard.

Other challenges had also emerged for test publishers.

In the late 1930s, a Rutgers University professor, Oscar K. Buros, began publishing the *Mental Measurements Yearbook*, a sort of *Consumer Reports* for the users of standardized tests.

He asked reviewers to examine the popular tests of the 1930s and published their comments in the 1938 yearbook, causing a stir in publishing circles. *Time* magazine reported that test publishers appealed to Buros "in the name of common decency" to stop the presses. "A distraught publisher: 'Now, Oscar! Is this sporting?' "

The *Mental Measurements Yearbook* is still published by the Buros Institute of Mental Measurements at the University of Nebraska at Lincoln.

In a lecture shortly before his death in 1978, Buros lamented what he viewed as a lack of substantial progress in educational tests since the 1930s. "Today's tests are more attractively printed and

Above: A 1947 pamphlet from the California Test Bureau shows the various IBM machines in use at the company to process standardized tests. Punch cards made it easy to read, copy, store, and interpret data.

Left: CTB used a test-scoring machine developed by IBM that electronically scored tests by reading the graphite pencil marks on the answer sheets. An operator inserted the sheets into the machine one at a time.

Today, answer sheets containing essays and other written responses are scanned into high-speed computers. Below, a CTB employee scores a student's work based on specific guidelines.

are generally machine scorable, but otherwise, they show relatively little improvement," he said.

Buros did, however, single out for praise work at the University of Iowa.

The Iowa testing program started out in 1928 as a state academic contest open to all high school students. An education professor at the university, E.F. Lindquist, became the director of the program, and the tests became known as the Iowa Every-Pupil Tests. Later, Lindquist and his colleagues created the Iowa Tests of Basic Skills and the Iowa Tests of Educational Development.

The Iowa tests were gaining popularity in neighboring states, so in 1940, Lindquist reached an agreement with Houghton Mifflin to distribute them. The company that published the most popular individual-intelligence test but had spurned group ones in the early part of the century was now a player in the growing achievement-test market. The University of Iowa was, and remains, the recipient of royalties for the Iowa tests.

Lindquist also assisted with test-scoring. Although IBM had come out with an optical-scoring reader in 1936, which speeded up the process, it was a rela-

tively slow machine. Lindquist liked to tinker at night, and he devised a plan for an optical-scoring machine that would read specially printed score sheets at a rate of hundreds per hour.

Over at the World Book Co., times got a bit tough during the Great Depression, especially for book sales. It didn't help that company President Caspar Hodgson was diverting profits to his own use, which included paying off a blackmail threat involving his mistress, according to Minton, the biographer of Lewis Terman.

Terman and other test authors were concerned about their royalty payments, but the publisher eventually got its house back in order. In 1934, World Book sent Terman an advertising circular extolling the fact that 24 million Stanford Achievement Tests had been sold. World Book considered the test "one of our mainstays, and [we] believe it will be profitable for authors and publishers for years to come," it wrote Terman.

Later that year, Terman wrote to World Book and evidently expressed some concern about a new test the company had begun publishing, the Metropolitan Achievement Tests. The MAT was written for use in the New York City schools, and World Book was making it available as a competitive offering even with its own Stanford tests.

A World Book executive tried to allay Terman's concerns. "In view of our experience, we felt that we should have a new achievement test to satisfy that class of school people who are always on the lookout for something new," the executive wrote. Had World Book not published the Metropolitan, "it is very likely that either the New York City board or some other publisher would have done it," he added.

The Stanford Achievement Tests "seem to be as much in demand as ever," the letter said.

As things would turn out, the Stanford and Metropolitan achievement tests would outlast the World Book Co. By 1960, the clubby world of book publishing was undergoing a transformation from small, privately held firms into public ownership and mergers.

World Book could no

Rick Pharoh

The Iowa testing program started out in 1928 as a state academic contest open to all high school students.

longer survive on its own. In 1960, it merged with the venerable publisher Harcourt, Brace & Co. to form Harcourt, Brace & World Inc. The merger was a good fit. Harcourt was a leader in high school- and college-textbook publishing, while World Book still had many elementary texts along with the Stanford, the Metropolitan, and other tests.

By the 1950s and '60s, change was buffeting the California Test Bureau as well. Although the company had survived World War II and the loss of its book-depository business, it faced a new threat in the early 1950s. June Duran says that her mother always paid union wages to her print and bindery workers, even though she insisted on maintaining an open shop.

Nonetheless, the International Typographers Union attempted to organize workers in 1951 and demanded that Ethel Clark sign a union contract.

"There was no way in hell my mother was going to let anyone organize the company," Duran says.

Mrs. Clark and others at CTB packed up tests and other inventory and shipped them off to branch offices in Madison, Wis.; Dallas; and New Cumberland, Pa. The union began 11 months of picketing CTB's headquarters in Los Angeles , but Mrs. Clark organized caravans to bring her workers across the lines.

The union, says Duran, alerted fire marshals about the piles of paper scraps that were typical of any printing operation. So Mrs. Clark had her workers pack up the paper trimmings and take them home at night.

The labor battle subsided, but CTB was changed, Duran says. Printing was moved permanently to the Midwest, with more shipping and scoring services performed by the branch offices as well.

By the late '50s, CTB was outgrowing its offices on Hollywood Boulevard. The Clarks were considering other properties in the area when it came time for their annual retreat to their summer home on the Monterey peninsula. CTB had held its annual sales conferences at the Del Monte Lodge in Monterey. Why not move the whole operation to such a beautiful area, the Clarks thought.

After finding a suitable site in a new research park, Ethel Clark returned to Los Angeles to tell her workers about the move. She gave them two weeks' paid vacation to check out Monterey.

"She couldn't imagine anyone not wanting to move there," Duran says.

In September 1960, trucks carried some 300 tons of tests, files, desks, and 24 IBM scoring machines to a new, $375,000 headquarters overlooking Monterey Bay. But of some 60 to 70 CTB employees who were expected to move, fewer than 30 actually did.

CTB struggled through scoring season that fall. Finding employees was harder on the less populous peninsula. Duran recalls that many military wives from nearby bases were hired temporarily.

The company faced other hurdles. Early in the 1960s, it received a line of credit from a local bank so work could proceed on the updated standardization of its tests. But the bank changed hands, and the line of credit was withdrawn. Finances were again tight.

Willis Clark's health began to deteriorate, and some employees became apprehensive about the future of the company, Duran says. They tried to buy out the Clarks, but couldn't raise enough money. Longtime loyalties within the close-knit company were being split.

John Stewart, who joined CTB in 1963 as an "evaluation consultant," the firm's term for sales representative, remembers that the company was struggling. "It was on pretty shaky ground," says Stewart, who had worked for the Illinois education department before taking over a huge Midwestern sales territory for CTB.

Willis Clark died of a cerebral hemorrhage in 1964 at the age of 69. Ethel Clark, then 66, worried that she would not be able to continue running the company. Though CTB had received inquiries previously, Mrs. Clark had not been interested in selling. In her behalf, friends began making overtures to purchasers, including McGraw-Hill.

In June 1965, McGraw-Hill acquired Ethel Clark's 81 percent interest in CTB for $200 a share. The overall selling price wasn't disclosed. With roots in business and technical books and maga-

zines, such as *Business Week*, McGraw-Hill was a newcomer to educational publishing in the 1960s.

When McGraw-Hill took control of CTB, Duran was offered a management position in the new division. "I couldn't believe they wanted me," she says. "It was the highlight of my life."

She worked as the managing editor of tests, then oversaw intellectual-property issues and author contracts. She became active in the test committee of the Association of American Publishers.

Ethel Clark, for reasons June Duran does not fully understand, did not approve of her daughter's staying on. Mrs. Clark died of cancer in 1969.

McGraw-Hill's purchase of the California Test Bureau came at a propitious time. In 1965, Congress enacted the Elementary and Secondary Education Act, which included Title I. The compensatory education program funneled federal dollars into education on a grand scale and called for "program evaluation." That meant a significant increase in norm-referenced tests—those that compare student against student.

"I remember that when Title I went into effect in 1966, schools called up CTB and bought the catalog," says Ross Green, now a senior research manager there.

"The accountability push led to a lot of developments," he adds.

For one, CTB rolled out its first major new test in many years soon after being acquired by McGraw-Hill. The Comprehensive Test of Basic Skills became as well-known and as widely used as the company's longtime flagship, the California Achievement Test. Today, the CTBS is the core assessment in the company's 2-year-old TerraNova program.

By 1968, CTB/McGraw-Hill, as it was called by then, had annual revenues of $2.8 million.

Other mergers were occurring. In 1970, Harcourt purchased the Psychological Corp., which had been formed in 1921 by eminent psychologists, such as Edward L. Thorndike of Columbia University and Lewis Terman, to make tests

24,OOO,OOO
Stanford Achievement Tests
have been used

Pieced together they would form a ribbon 45,OOO miles long

With these twenty-four millions of
STANFORD ACHIEVEMENT TESTS
schools have been able to —

I grade and classify twenty-four million pupils—place them in the groups where learning and teaching are most efficient.

2 analyze the achievement of twenty-four million pupils, determining their difficulties as a basis for effective remedial programs

3 evaluate the instruction of thousands of teachers as a basis for improving both supervision and teaching methods

4 make valid economies in thousands of schools by greatly increasing the efficiency of administration and instruction

The eminent qualifications of the Stanford Achievement Test (including also the New Stanford) for accomplishing these purposes account for this extensive use. Its popularity has been won by its fundamental soundness. School people know that back of every test detail is the infinite labor and expert judgment of leaders in the testing field. Their long established confidence in the test is due to the continued satisfaction its results afford.

(over)

A 1934 brochure from the World Book Co. extols the widespread popularity of the test created by the psychologist Lewis M. Terman of Stanford University.

for practicing psychologists. By the time Harcourt bought it, Psychological Corp. had annual revenues of $5 million.

Harcourt, of course, already had a testing division from its merger with World Book, and it already owned major school tests, such as the Stanford and Metropolitan achievement tests. Psychological Corp. added a whole catalog of tests such as the Wechsler Intelligence Scale for Children, probably the most widely used intelligence test after the Stanford-Binet.

Today, Harcourt Educational Measurement, based in San Antonio, is the educational testing division of Psychological Corp., which in turn is part of the publishing and media conglomerate Harcourt General Inc.

Meanwhile, Houghton Mifflin renamed its test subsidiary Riverside Publishing Co. in 1979. The company wanted a separate name for its testing business, "to avoid the perception in the marketplace that a school needed to use Houghton Mifflin instructional materials in order to use Riverside Publishing's tests," according to a company history.

The distinction is one that McGraw-Hill and Harcourt have never copied, given the close links between those companies' testing divisions and their parent companies. At times, they have faced questions about the perceived alignment of the tests and their parents' curriculum materials.

For example, Harcourt came under fire in Texas this year because of a brochure advertising its math texts and other educational materials as "the only program to have tests written by the same company that helps to write the [Texas Assessment of Academic Skills] test." Harcourt is a subcontractor for the state's basic-skills test.

A decade ago, similar questions were raised about a test-practice kit sold by McGraw-Hill, which contained the same or similar questions as those on CTB's California Achievement Test.

That and other criticisms of the commercial test publishers have done little over the years to lessen schools' reliance on the leading standardized tests. In fact, as the accountability movement took hold in the late 1980s and 1990s, the role of the three major test publishers grew, even though they have had to retool their products to meet states' changing demands.

A number of states had long prescribed the use of the publishers' off-the-shelf tests as their de facto state achievement tests. CTB had a state-contracts department as long as two decades ago. Back then, creating a state achievement test was no more difficult than "taking a shelf product and putting a custom cover on it," says Linn Williams, a CTB national accounts manager.

But as states wrote their own academic standards, many wanted their tests to better reflect those expectations. They wanted customized tests.

Some states tried producing their own. But the costs, as well as concerns about reliability and validity, dampened their enthusiasm. Meanwhile, the commercial publishers responded quickly and began marketing their ability to produce customized assessments.

Today, CTB/McGraw-Hill is the publisher of state assessments in 22 states, including New York, Colorado, and Indiana.

The competitiveness of the market these days can be seen by examining

As the accountability movement took hold in the late 1980s and 1990s, the role of the three major test publishers grew.

CTB's native California.

In 1997, the state solicited bids for a standardized-testing program after its pioneering performance-based version was felled by political conflicts. CTB, Harcourt, and Riverside Publishing bid on the contract.

The state had authorized spending as much as $35 million for the first year of the program, or $8 per student. Riverside bid $8; CTB, $4.85; and Harcourt, $2.89.

After getting the advice of dozen of educators, state Superintendent of Public Instruction Delaine Eastin recommended CTB's Comprehensive Test of Basic Skills for a one-year contract, although she was unenthusiastic. All three submissions, she said at the time, "were seriously flawed, with the level of test content falling years below grade-level expectations."

In its proposal, CTB had emphasized its California roots, as well as the use of its tests in 70 percent of the state's districts. It had reserved 4 million pounds of paper and space at five printing plants for the booklets and answer sheets that would be used to test California's 4.3 million pupils.

When the state board of education met that November, CTB was in for disappointment. The board voted 9-2, to award a five-year contract to Harcourt. Beginning in 1998, the state's students would all be required to take the Stanford Achievement Test, not the Terra-Nova.

In 1998, CTB bounced back from its defeat by winning a four-year, $30.5 million contract to produce Kentucky's tests. CTB is heading up a consortium that includes three smaller companies.

The Kentucky contract highlights the fact that CTB, Harcourt, and Riverside may dominate the off-the-shelf-testing business, but other players are elbowing their way into the growing market for customized state tests.

The most prominent is Minneapolis-based National Computer Systems Inc. A leading test-scoring company, it has won the testing contract in Arizona, with CTB as a subcontractor, to create the test.

"There are a number of smaller companies that will bid on these state con-

tracts," says Madaus of Boston College. "I don't think they will get to the size of the big three, but they are real players."

Just how big the big three are today is not easy to measure, given the way in which their parent companies break down finances. But Simba Information Inc., a Stamford, Conn., business-research firm, estimates that CTB/McGraw-Hill, Harcourt, and Riverside Publishing would have combined 1999 sales of $221 million.

In a 1997 report, Simba estimated that CTB had K-12 test sales of $80 million in 1996, Harcourt had $50 million, and Riverside had $48.7 million, for a total of $178.7 million.

A CTB newsletter for employees says that in 1998, the company "achieved a revenue milestone—exceeding $100 million in sales."

"Right now, there is a great demand out there for assessment," David Taggart, the president of CTB/McGraw-Hill, says. "The challenge for remaining profitable is figuring out how to remain competitive as we go from shelf business to custom business. This business has become driven by the states."

CTB has come a long way from the 25 penny postcards that Ethel Clark mailed in 1926.

A few years ago, it moved into new headquarters in Monterey, a huge building on a hilltop that overlooks the bay. The facility is home to its test-development and -research operations. It also handles a small portion of CTB's scoring and reporting tasks.

CTB sold 10 million tests last year and scored twice that many, says Michael H. Kean, the company's vice president for public and governmental affairs.

June Duran still lives in the Monterey area and sometimes finds herself visiting the headquarters of the company her mother founded when June was only 6.

She thinks back to when her father became interested in testing. As a sociologist at the Whittier State School for Boys, Willis Clark got hooked on the idea of writing "case histories" of each

child in an effort to discover the cause of delinquency.

He became convinced that his theories about curtailing improper behavior could be applied to the vast numbers of students in the public schools through the use of diagnostic and achievement tests.

Today's high-tech score reports, with their detailed information about a child's strengths and weaknesses, remind Duran of her father's original goals.

She also thinks about her family's business struggles and how CTB probably would not have survived without the McGraw-Hill purchase.

"McGraw-Hill really pumped the money in, and the personnel, and everything it needed to be a success today," she says. "When I go by the building today, I just feel very proud." ■

Making America Smarter

A perspective by Lauren B. Resnick

Standards, tests, and accountability programs are today's favored tools for raising overall academic achievement. Testing policies are also meant to increase equity, to give poor and minority students a fairer chance by making expectations clear and providing instruction geared to them. In practice, though, it is proving hard to meet the twin goals of equity and higher achievement. This is because our schools are trapped in a set of beliefs about the nature of ability and aptitude that makes it hard to evoke effective academic effort from students and educators.

What we learn is a function of both our aptitudes for particular kinds of learning and the effort we put forth. Americans mostly assume that aptitude largely determines what people can learn in school, although they allow that hard work can compensate for lower doses of innate intelligence. Our schools are largely organized around this belief. IQ tests or their surrogates are used to determine who has access to enriched programs. As a result, some students never get the chance to study a high-demand, high-expectation curriculum.

Traditional achievement tests are normed to compare students against one another rather than against a standard of excellence. This approach makes it difficult to see the results of learning and thereby discourages effort. (If one is going to stay at about the same relative percentile rank no matter how much one has learned, what is the point of trying hard?) Similarly, college entrance depends heavily on aptitude-like tests that have little to do with the curriculum studied. Like IQ tests, they are designed to spread the student population out on a statistical scale rather than to define what any particular individual has learned.

These commonplace features of the American educational landscape are institutionalized expressions of a persistent belief in the importance of inherited aptitude. The system they are part of is self-sustaining. Assumptions about aptitude are continually reinforced by the results of practices based on those assumptions. Students who are held to low expectations do not try to break through that barrier, because they accept the judgment that inborn aptitude matters most and that they have not inherited enough of that capacity. Not surprisingly, their performance remains low. Children who have not been taught a demanding, challenging, thinking curriculum do poorly on tests of reasoning or problem-solving, confirming many people's original suspicions that they lack the talent for high-level thinking.

Two converging lines of research—one from cognitive science, one from social psychology—now give us reason to believe that we don't have to continue in this way. We don't need to pit excellence against equity. We can harness effort to create ability and build a smarter America.

Intelligence-in-Practice:
Habits of Mind

For more than 20 years, psychologists and other students of the human mind have been experimenting with ways of teaching the cognitive skills associated with intelligence. These include techniques as varied as generating analogies, making logical deductions, creating and using memory aids, and monitoring one's own state of knowledge (*metacognition*).

Early experiments on teaching specific, isolated components of intelligence yielded a common pattern of results: Most of the training was successful in producing immediate gains in performance, but people typically ceased using the cognitive techniques they had been taught as soon as the specific conditions of training were removed. In other words, they became *capable* of performing whatever skill was taught, but they acquired no general *habit* of using it or capacity to judge for themselves when it was useful.

As a result of these findings, cognitive researchers began to shift their attention to educational strategies that immerse students in demanding, long-term intellectual environments. Now, positive results are coming in. In experimental programs and in practical school reforms, we are seeing that students who, over an extended period of time are treated *as if* they are intelligent, actually become so. If they are taught demanding content, and are expected to explain and find connections as well as memorize and repeat, they learn more and learn more quickly. They think of themselves as learners. They are able to bounce back in the face of short-term failures.

This experience is giving rise to a new conceptualization of intelligence-in-practice: Intelligence is the habit of persistently trying to understand things and make them function better. Intelligence is working to figure things out, varying strategies until a workable solution is found. Intelligence is knowing what one does (and doesn't) know, seeking information and organizing that information so that it makes sense and can be remembered. In short, one's intelligence is the sum of one's *habits of mind*.

Being Smart and Getting Smart: Two Popular Beliefs About Intelligence

Here is where the research by social psychologists comes in. Two decades of studies have shown that what people believe about the nature of talent and intelligence—about what accounts for success and failure—is closely related to the amount and kind of effort they put forth in situations of learning or problem-solving.

Some people believe that intelligence and other forms of talent are fixed and unchangeable. Intelligence is a thing, an entity that is displayed in one's performance. Doing well means that one has ability; doing poorly means that one doesn't. According to this belief, people who are very talented perform easily; they don't need to work hard to do well. Hence, if you want to appear to *be smart*, you should not appear to be working very hard. Any educator working with adolescents knows how this belief can drive some students away from schoolwork.

Other people believe that intelligence is something that develops and grows. These people view ability as a repertoire of skills that is continuously expandable through one's efforts.

Intelligence is incremental. People can *get smart*. When people think this way, they tend to invest energy to learn something new or to increase their understanding and mastery.

But it is not just brute effort that distinguishes these learners from people who think of intelligence as an entity. Incremental thinkers are particularly likely to apply self-regulatory, metacognitive skills when they encounter task difficulties, to focus on analyzing the task and generating alternative strategies. Most important, they seek out opportunities to hone their skills and knowledge, treating task difficulty (and thus occasional setbacks) as part of the learning challenge rather than as evidence that they lack intelligence. They get on an upward spiral in which their intelligence is actually increasing. Meanwhile, their peers who think of intelligence as fixed try to avoid difficult tasks for fear of displaying their lack of intelligence. They enter a downward spiral by avoiding the very occasions in which they could learn smarter ways of behaving.

Effort-Based Education and Learnable Intelligence: Principles for Teaching and Learning

The good news is that people's beliefs about intelligence aren't immutable. They respond to the situations in which people find themselves. This means that it is possible to help students develop learning-oriented goals and an incremental view of intelligence and thus set them on the upward spiral by which they can become smarter and deliver the kinds of high-level academic achievement everyone is hoping for. To do this, we need to create effort-based schools in which academic rigor and a thinking curriculum permeate the school day for every student.

For several years, the Institute for Learning at the University of Pittsburgh has been working with school systems across the country to set students—and whole school faculties—on the upward, getting-smarter spiral. A core set of principles guides this work, principles that educators have found both inspiring and practical. These principles, which can be

illustrated in multiple examples of specific school and classroom practice, are based on cognitive research and research on learning organizations. Here they are in a nutshell:

• *Organize for Effort.* An effort-based school replaces the assumption that aptitude determines what and how much students learn with the assumption that sustained and directed effort can yield high achievement for all students. Everything is organized to evoke and support this effort. High minimum standards are set, and all students' curriculum is geared to these

standards. Some students will need extra time and expert instruction to meet these expectations. Providing that time and expertise helps send the message that effort is expected and that tough problems yield to sustained work.

• *Clear Expectations.* If we expect all students to learn at high levels, then we need to define what we expect students to learn. These expectations need to be clear—to school professionals, to parents, to the community, and, above all, to students themselves. With visible accomplishment targets to aim toward at each stage of learning, students can participate in evaluating their own

work and setting goals for their own effort.

• *Recognition of Accomplishment.* Clear recognition of authentic accomplishment is a hallmark of an effort-based school. This recognition can take the form of celebrations of work that meets standards or intermediate expectations. It can also be tied to opportunity to participate in events that matter to students and their families. Progress points should be articulated so that, regardless of their entering abilities, all students meet real accomplishment criteria often enough to be recognized frequently.

• *Fair and Credible Evaluations.* Long-term effort by students calls for assessment practices that students find fair. Most importantly, tests, exams, and classroom assessments must be aligned to the standards and the curriculum being studied. Fair assessment also means using tests and exams that are graded against absolute standards rather than on a curve, so students can clearly see the results of their learning efforts.

• *Academic Rigor in a Thinking Curriculum.* Thinking and problem-solving will be the "new basics" of the 21st century, but the common idea that we can teach thinking without a solid foundation of knowledge must be abandoned. So must the idea that we can teach knowledge without engaging students in thinking. Knowledge and thinking must be intimately joined. This implies a curriculum organized around major concepts in each discipline that students are expected to know deeply. Teaching must engage students in active reasoning about these concepts. In every subject, at every grade level, the curriculum must include commitment to a knowledge core, high thinking demand, and active use of knowledge.

• *Accountable Talk.* Talking with others about ideas and work is fundamental to learning. But not all talk sustains learning or creates intelligence. For classroom talk to promote learning, it must have certain characteristics that make it *accountable*. Accountable talk seriously responds to and further develops what others in the group have said. It puts forth and demands knowledge that is accurate and relevant to the issue under discussion. Accountable talk uses evidence in ways appropriate to the discipline (for example, proofs in mathematics, data from investigations in science, textual details in literature, documentary sources in history). Finally, it follows established norms of good reasoning. Accountable talk sharpens students' thinking by reinforcing their ability to use knowledge appropriately. As such, it helps develop the skills and the habits of mind that constitute intelligence-in-practice. Teachers can intentionally create the norms and skills of accountable talk in their classrooms.

• *Socializing Intelligence.* Intelligent habits of mind are learned through the daily expectations placed on the learner. By calling on students to use the skills of intelligent thinking and accountable talk, and by holding them responsible for doing so, educators can "teach" intelligence. This is what teachers normally do with students they expect much from; it should be standard practice with all students.

• *Learning as Apprenticeship.* For many centuries, most people learned by working alongside an expert who modeled skilled practice and guided novices as they created authentic products or performances. This kind of apprenticeship learning allowed learners to acquire the complex interdisciplinary knowledge, practical abilities, and appropriate forms of social behavior that went with high levels of skilled performance. Learners were motivated to do the hard work that was involved by the value placed on their products by people who bought objects, attended performances, or requested that important community work be done. Much of the power of apprenticeship learning can be brought into schooling through appropriate use of extended projects and presentations, and by organizing learning environments so that complex thinking and production are modeled and analyzed.

differential aptitude for learning that have been eclipsed by new discoveries. Yet changing them has been slow because the nature of educational reform in this country is largely one of tinkering with institutional arrangements. Rarely has reform penetrated the "educational core."

But now that is happening. With the movement for standards-based education, America has begun to explore the potential of designing policy structures explicitly to link testing, curriculum, textbooks, teacher training, and accountability with clearly articulated ideas about what should be taught and what students should be expected to learn. Our hopes for breaking this century's pattern of disappointing cycles of reform—and of enabling our children to function effectively in a complex new century—rest with this vision of creating effort-based systems grounded in knowledge-based constructivism—systems that allow all students to reach high standards of achievement. ∎

Lauren B. Resnick is the director of the Learning Research and Development Center at the University of Pittsburgh.

Two converging lines of research—one from cognitive science, one from social psychology—now give us reason to believe that we don't need to pit excellence against equity.

A s we approach a new century, it is increasingly evident that the educational methods we have been using for the past 70 years no longer suffice. They are based on scientific assumptions about the nature of knowledge, the learning process, and

the course of teaching

T he men and women charged with educating the nation's young people occupy a special place in American society. Teaching has long been considered more than just a job—even a calling.

Yet, even though teachers are at the heart of the educational enterprise, they've had to struggle to gain competitive salaries, decent working conditions, and manageable class sizes.

They've also waged a broader, cyclical battle throughout the century for the respect and autonomy commanded by other professions. Collective action in the form of unionism has yielded clear benefits, but it also has cost educators dearly. Much of the public was dismayed by the rise of a more militant brand of teacher.

Outside pressure on what takes place inside the classroom also has been a perennial issue. Often, teachers have balked at being told what to teach—a debate that persists with today's standards movement.

Teachers have come a long way from the days of this one-room schoolhouse in Grundy County, Iowa. But they are still struggling to build a true profession.

Photo by Arthur Rothstein/Library of Congress

Arthur Rothstein/Library of Congress

'The Not-Quite Profession'

Throughout the 20th century, teachers struggled for respect and recognition.
They've made progress but still have a long way to go.

By
Ann
Bradley

The 20th century was young when the activist Margaret Haley dared to speak from the floor of the National Education Association's convention in Detroit, challenging the assertions made by its president. As William T. Harris cited statistics showing public education to be flourishing under capitalism in 1901, Haley begged to differ. Teachers, she complained, were grossly underpaid.

"Pay no attention to what the teacher down there has said," Harris told the assembly, "for I take it she is a grade teacher, just out of her schoolroom at the end of school year, worn out, tired, and hysterical." Haley, who was an organizer for the Chicago Teachers Federation, was undeterred. Three years later, in St. Louis, she delivered a powerful speech at the NEA meeting arguing that teachers should join the union movement. Salaries, she said, were "wholly inadequate"; teachers had insecure tenures and no provisions for their old age; and they faced "overwork in overcrowded schoolrooms."

In addition to those concerns, Ha touched on a broader theme. The tende toward "factoryizing education," warned, made teachers automat "whose duty it is to carry out mechanic and unquestioningly the ideas and orders of those clothed with the authority of position."

Over the next nine decades, teachers would continue to struggle with the issues so forcefully delineated by Haley, the first woman ever to speak from the floor of an NEA convention.

As teaching moved from a short-term occupation—primarily for young, unmarried women—to a career, activists won pension benefits and job protections. Class sizes have become dramatically smaller than the typical 50- to 60-pupil classrooms common in the 1940s and 1950s. Teachers now earn middle-class incomes, although less than many similarly educated workers, and are among the most heavily unionized of all employees.

But teachers have not won the autonomy and control over their own work that Margaret Haley, John Dewey, and other reformers sought in the name of making schools democratic institutions equipped to prepare students to live in a democracy.

For her efforts, in fact, Haley was blasted as "a fiend in petticoats," write David B. Tyack and Elisabeth Hansot, who describe Haley's lively exchange with the NEA president in *Managers of Virtue: Public School Leadership in America, 1820-1980*, published in 1982.

Teaching both in Haley's day and now,

very interesting quote! ⟹

practitioners (more than 3 million), custodial aspects of the job, and the widespread perception that "no agonistic

struggle" is involved in becoming a teacher, the scholars Gerald Grant and Christine E. Murray write in their book published in 1999, *Teaching in America: The Slow Revolution*.

That teaching is also a predominantly female occupation, historians and sociologists agree, has colored virtually every aspect of the field.

"The perceptions that teachers were 'mothering,' or that women teachers were only marking time until marriage, had unfortunate effects for the image of professionalism," Geraldine Jonçich Clifford writes in a chapter of *American Teachers: Histories of a Profession at Work*, published in 1989.

While members of other professions gained control by laying claim to specific bodies of knowledge, the idea of "professionalism" in teaching evolved much differently. What characterized a professional teacher, Grant and Murray write, was altruistic service, natural ability, and virtuous womanhood.

Americans' reluctance to tax themselves to pay teachers more and their attitudes about both working with children and intellectualism further complicate teachers' status.

"Teaching is too intellectual to be worthy of respect in a society that has an anti-intellectual cast to it and is suspicious of impractical work," says David F. Labaree, a professor of education at Michigan State University. "Teachers also are way too familiar and too visible, and what they know seems to be all too common."

Still, over the 20th century, teaching has

gained some of the trappings of a profession: standards for licensing, a national accreditation organization, and a system for advanced certification of outstanding teachers. In the process, the requirements for the initial academic preparation of teachers and their continuing professional development have mushroomed.

But today, it remains what the noted teacher-educator John I. Goodlad has called "the not-quite profession."

The 'Woman Peril'

By 1900—as immigration, urbanization, and westward expansion produced rapidly growing student populations—nearly three-fourths of the nation's teachers were women. Thirty years earlier, when reliable state and national statistics on teachers' gender first became available, two-thirds of teachers were women.

What scholars call the "feminization" of teaching represented a turnabout from earlier times. In Colonial America, teachers were overwhelmingly men, tutoring or teaching in private homes or schools operated for a fee. Most were young and didn't teach for long, moving on to higher-status professions such as the ministry or law.

But the growth of America's system of free public education, and particularly the rise of city school systems, attracted young women to teaching. It was a respectable choice for modestly educated women hoping to marry who could earn modest sums in exchange for their labors.

As states began to assert greater control over teacher education and licensing, a process that began in the mid-19th century, more and more regulations made teaching unattractive to men. In most cities, they could earn far more with their backs, in steel mills or factories, than in a job that required increasing amounts of formal preparation.

"While a stint of teaching might buy a woman a trousseau," Clifford writes, "the same experience could not provide most young men with the means to marry and establish a household."

At the same time, she notes, male administrators and college professors debated the "woman peril" in teaching, fearful that women would drive out men altogether and make inroads into their own ranks.

Along with the feminization of teaching came paternalistic rules governing teachers' lives. Job contracts were highly specific and forbade all sorts of personal behavior, including socializing with men, going out alone in the evening, and marrying. Some teachers were told how to dress and wear their hair.

"Teachers were surrounded by prohibitions, some by contract, others by custom—no drinking, no dancing or card-playing where the community attitude was against it, no 'gallivantin' around,' no slang. … [W]e wore ruffled thing-a-mabobs to conceal our maidenly forms," wrote Rosa Schreurs Jennings, who taught in Iowa late in the 19th century.

Jennings began teaching in the 1890s after completing 16 weeks at the Iowa State Normal School, founded in 1876. Like other country teachers, she boarded with families as she taught in one-room schoolhouses, writes Mary Hurlbut Cordier in her 1992 book, *Schoolwomen of the Prairies and Plains*. The tradition came to be known as "boarding 'round."

The additional requirements Jennings faced for keeping her license—fulfilled by attending normal courses or summer teachers' institutes—were typical of state efforts to upgrade their teaching forces.

By 1910, however, only 5 percent of the nation's teachers had more than a high school education. Teachers with the

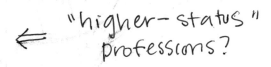

'Triumph of Credentials'

Unprecedented teacher shortages after the First World War prodded states and

In rural areas, teachers often worked in rundown schools with limited resources. Conditions tended to be worse for black teachers, who were paid one-third to one-half of what white teachers earned. Below, a teacher in the Mississippi Delta looks over her students' lessons in 1939.

Marion Post Wolcott

districts to act to improve the conditions of teaching and raise professional requirements to enter the classroom.

Until the mid-1800s, states did not exercise significant authority over who taught. Instead, licensure was in the hands of local authorities or teacher-certification agencies, which gave permission to teach on the basis of examinations. But the growth of state education departments gave rise to centralized standards for teaching.

By 1911, 15 states issued teacher certificates; another 18 set regulations and generated questions for examinations, though they were corrected by county authorities, who issued certificates.

Nevertheless, when faced with the need to hire teachers, states and districts lowered their standards and granted permits to people otherwise unqualified to teach, a course some continue to take today.

At the end of the war, complaints about the qualifications and shortage of teachers were rampant. Low salaries, lack of status, and the military buildup that drew male teachers into the armed forces had combined to force a crisis.

In 1920, Harry W. Rockwell, the president of the Buffalo Normal School in New York, complained bitterly about the plight of teachers in his state. His address, printed in the May issue of *The American School Board Journal* under the headline "Normal Schools and the Teacher Shortage," was billed as an accurate picture of conditions typical across the country.

The state's 10 normal schools, he wrote, had fewer than half the students they had in 1916. With poor salaries, few people wanted to teach. Rockwell was outraged that a popular, recently deceased Buffalo high school principal had earned $1,000 a year less than a locomotive engineer for the Pennsylvania Railroad.

"It is evident that it is more profitable to 'mind a train' than to 'train a mind,'" he wrote.

Of the 600,000 teaching positions in the United States, Rockwell reported, 60,000 were either vacant or held by "teachers of very inferior qualifications." Only one-fifth of teachers had graduated from high school and a normal school or college.

In response to such alarms, policymakers raised salaries, instituted tenure provisions, relaxed barriers to married women teachers, and adopted uniform-salary schedules to reduce what Michael W. Sedlak, a professor of the history of education at Michigan State University, calls "whimsical" reward systems.

And education leaders argued successfully for states to raise certification standards for elementary teachers as a way to improve the professional status of teaching.

Only 10 states required four years of higher education for secondary teachers in 1920, and none required elementary teachers to possess more than a normal-school education.

"Providing instructors for the ever-expanding population of students had made it difficult to improve the educational qualifications of teachers much beyond the pace of the population in general," Sedlak writes in *American Teachers*.

States' efforts paid off, and standards marched steadily upward, even during a

saw that at camp too ←

In fact, the basic model for licensing—or what Sedlak calls "the triumph of credentials"—was firmly fixed in place for the next half-century.

"Historically," he says, "standards have been raised most aggressively during times of relative shortage."

EARLY ACTIVISM

Teachers' low status and poor pay during the early part of the 20th century captured the attention of activists such as Margaret Haley. She also campaigned vigorously against the trend toward "scientific management" that was standardizing all aspects of schooling.

To gain a voice, Haley joined the labor movement. The Chicago Teachers

← *great quote!*
← *holy shit really?!*

Association was explicitly a professional association. And when it came to teachers' issues, the NEA was asleep at the switch. Dominated by male professors and administrators, the NEA had some 30 departments concerned with administration, curriculum, teacher education, and even audio-visual instruction.

The NEA's department of classroom teachers was not formed until 1913—late for an association founded in 1857, according to *NEA: The First Hundred Years, The Building of the Teaching*

Profession, by Edgar B. Wesley, who was commissioned to write the organization's history in 1957.

Unlike other branches of the association, the department had no membership rolls and no income. But every NEA member who was a classroom teacher below the college level automatically belonged.

The explanation for the association's delay in embracing teachers' issues, Wesley wrote, had to do with the second-class status of women. Since women weren't guaranteed the right to vote until the ratification of the 19th Amendment in 1920, the political leverage of the majority of the teaching force was limited.

While the NEA passed various resolutions calling for higher salaries, "for more than half a century it did little to ire them," according to Wesley.

The educational leaders assumed that building of a profession took cedence over problems of the personal lfare of teachers; that once the profession was established, teachers would naturally achieve status, security, and dignity," Wesley explained. By "profession," Wesley meant the entire enterprise of public education, with its trained administrators and their theories of curriculum, pedagogy, and supervision.

But teachers weren't content to wait. Classroom teachers' organizations had begun to emerge in states around 1910, according to *Education in the States: Development Since 1900*, a 1969 report by the Council of Chief State School Officers. The "classroom-teacher movement" caused state associations to start paying more attention to teachers' welfare.

Haley, who was also a member of the NEA, helped draft what Wesley called "vigorous" NEA resolutions denouncing teacher-rating scales and calling for the establishment of advisory councils of hers to give expert advice to erintendents and school boards.

Chicago, Haley successfully took ity companies to court for failure to their school taxes. She and Ella Flagg Young, who was serving as Chicago's superintendent of schools in 1909, argued for the creation of teacher councils to counter the increasing weight of the administrative hierarchies that relegated teachers to the bottom of the heap.

"Haley is really central in trying to define teaching as work, but also work that has a professional aspect," says Kate Rousmaniere, an associate professor of educational leadership at Miami University of Ohio.

Chicago's teacher councils faded when Young's historic superintendency—she

Teachers Across Time

1906

National Education Association (founded in 1857) chartered by Congress as a nonprofit, charitable, tax-exempt organization.

1910

Ella Flagg Young, superintendent of Chicago public schools, elected first woman president of NEA.

1916

American Federation of Teachers founded.

Chicago Historical Society

1920

NEA forms Legislative Commission, which presses for federal aid to schools and a U.S. Department of Education with a secretary in president's Cabinet.

1926

Teachers College, Columbia University, abandons undergraduate programs in education in favor of advanced professional training of educational leaders.

1932

Willard Waller, a professor of sociology at the University of Nebraska, publishes the classic *The Sociology of Teaching*, describing teachers as hired hands who must do the community's bidding to keep their jobs.

1933

First advisory council on teacher education and certification created in Kentucky.

1940

First National Teacher Examination licensing test administered.

1946

Teachers in Connecticut, Minnesota, and New York go on strike.

1948

American Association of Colleges for Teacher Education formed.

1954

National Council for Accreditation of Teacher Education established.

1955

Tenure laws protecting teachers are in place in 32 states.

1966

NEA merges with American Teachers' Association, whose members are African-American.

1972

NEA-PAC, National Education Association's political action committee, endorses first candidates for seats in U.S. House and Senate.

1974

Merger talks between National Education Association and American Federation of Teachers break off.

1975

Dan C. Lortie publishes *Schoolteacher: A Sociological Study*, finding that teaching occupies "a special but shadowed social standing" in America.

1976

NEA endorses first presidential candidate—Democrat Jimmy Carter, who pledges to create an Education Department.

AP/Wide World

1984

In wake of critical 1983 federal report on education, *A Nation at Risk*, dozens of states begin implementing teacher-testing programs.

1990

Teach for America launched to recruit young liberal-arts graduates to teach for two years. Advocates of formal preparation charge program doesn't offer enough training.

1996

National Commission on Teaching & America's Future releases influential report, "What Matters Most," arguing for policy changes to ensure a caring, competent, and qualified teacher in every classroom.

1998

Delegates to NEA's annual Representative Assembly resoundingly reject guidelines for merging with American Federation of Teachers.

Teachers in St. Paul, Minn., picket in 1946. The strike by the American Federation of Teachers local shocked the nation. Teachers' unions in Norwalk, Conn., and Buffalo, N.Y., also staged walkouts that year.

Surprise, surprise... →

building administrators were more concerned with using the councils to head off teachers' attempts to unionize, scholars agree, than they were in giving them a legitimate vehicle to make their concerns known.

While the NEA remained a conservative organization, it hired a woman, Charl Williams, a former Tennessee teacher and administrator, to travel the country to recruit new members, Rousmaniere notes. The NEA's research department, established in 1922, also tackled issues of vital interest to classroom teachers, including working conditions, salaries, and school finance.

NEW SALARY SCHEDULES

On the local level, teachers' associations joined with school administrators to ask state legislators for relief from property-tax limitations that thwarted their efforts to raise salaries, according to *Education in the States*. They also began to fight for what they called "equal pay for equal work."

Salary schedules typically paid teachers based on their years of experience, gender, race, and grade level. Whites earned more than blacks, while secondary school teachers—who typically were men and better educated—were paid more than female elementary teachers.

In 1921, Denver and Des Moines, Iowa, became the first cities to introduce single-salary schedules that paid all teachers according to years of experience and academic preparation, eliminating discriminatory practices. By 1950, according to Allan Odden, an expert on teacher compensation at the University of Wisconsin-Madison, nearly all urban districts had shifted to similar salary schedules. Such schedules—objective, measurable, and not subject to administrative whim—remain the prevailing practice nearly 50 years later.

State teachers' associations also began helping their members on another front: They increasingly began to provide legal defense and to advocate for tenure protection. By 1945, 38 states had tenure laws, which offer teachers procedural guarantees against arbitrary dismissal.

Despite such activism, the NEA leadership promoted membership in the association as "a demonstration of professional behavior," while it considered membership in militant, union-style organizations unprofessional, Grant and Murray write in their book.

Such attitudes prevailed. By 1925, the NEA had 150,100 members, while the AFT claimed only 11,000. The AFT's early organizing activities were stifled by the prevailing anti-labor sentiment, Rousmaniere says, and then by the Great Depression.

During the 1930s and 1940s, moreover, the AFT's leaders were caught up in a struggle with Communists within their ranks for control of the union. The bitter internal battles—which eventually resulted in the 1941 expulsions of the New York City and Philadelphia affiliates—"almost totally diverted the attention of the union from the everyday problems of teachers that were deepening as the Depression wore on," Wayne J. Urban, a professor of history and educational policy studies at Georgia State University, writes in *American Teachers*.

BLACK TEACHERS' PLIGHT

The surplus of teachers caused by widespread unemployment during the Depression allowed states to continue raising standards for entrance into the classroom.

G.H. Walker/Life Magazine

The Depression also brought about "a phenomenal change" in the composition of the teaching force, according to *Education in the States*.

While a declining birthrate caused a drop in elementary school attendance, youth unemployment contributed to a rapid growth in secondary school enrollment. The proportion of high school instructors in the teaching force grew from 25 percent in 1930 to 35 percent by 1945, and the number of men in teaching climbed with those increases at the secondary level.

Some of that growth in the ranks of male teachers may have been due to the firing of married women teachers, a policy that many districts followed during the Depression to make room for men who were seen as their families' chief breadwinners.

Hard times also underscored the abysmal conditions facing black teachers in the South, described by Linda M. Perkins in *American Teachers* as "abbreviated school years, starvation salaries, inadequate curricula, and inferior buildings and equipment."

Compounding the problems, rural black teachers themselves tended to be poorly educated. A 1930 study found that 39 percent of all black teachers in the South had not earned a high school diploma, while 58 percent had studied less than two years beyond high school—the usual minimum for teaching elementary school at the time—and only 12 percent were college graduates, Perkins writes.

The average annual salary for black teachers in the United States was just $360—or about one-third to one-half of what white teachers earned.

In contrast to the South, major Northern cities with black high schools attracted black educators with outstanding credentials. Regardless of their educational levels, black men and women could find work as teachers in segregated schools when few other jobs were open to them. In the black community, in fact, "teaching and preaching" were the two primary occupations open to educated people.

The National Association for the Advancement of Colored People began a campaign in 1936 to eradicate salary differences between black and white teachers in 15 Southern states. By the end of 1941, it had won half the suits it had filed on behalf of black teachers, Perkins writes.

Advocates could not turn to the local teachers' associations for help. Local and state chapters of the National Education Association barred blacks as members in the South, although the national organization never had racial restrictions on membership. In 11 Southern states, black teachers formed their own organizations, which made up the American Teachers' Association.

The two organizations formed a joint committee in 1940 to try to improve the status of black educators in the national association, according to the *NEA Handbook*. Among other measures, the committee drafted policies by which black teachers who were members of the ATA could serve as delegates to the NEA's Representative Assembly. It also worked with publishers to identify textbook authors, editors, and consultants who were free of racial bias, and it studied the health problems of black children.

In 1966, the NEA and the ATA merged— an event commemorated annually at the NEA's Human and Civil Rights Awards Dinner.

World War II. To crusade for improvements, association leaders created the loftily named National Commission for the Defense of Democracy Through Education.

Donald DuShane, the president of the association, described the conditions of the time: "classes overcrowded … criticism rampant … when charges are made, there is no method to meet them … there is no one to speak for the profession … it is just as important to defend democracy thru [sic] the schools as it is to defend democracy thru [sic] the army or armament."

The commission campaigned for higher salaries, academic freedom, and tenure protection, and "investigated individuals and organizations who were critical of public schools," wrote Wesley, the NEA historian.

For example, in 1944, the commission publicly rebuked Mayor Fiorello H. La Guardia of New York for illegally interfering with the city's board of education. It also expelled the superintendent of the Chicago public schools from the NEA, Wesley wrote, after declaring the city's schools "to be the worst educational situation in the United States."

In 1942, the NEA established the Kate Frank Fund, named for a teacher in Muskogee, Okla., who was discharged by the school board, apparently for her role in exposing financial irregularities in the district. Frank was reinstated after a vigorous defense by the association.

"Teachers all over the nation became aware of the growing power and influence of the NEA," Wesley concluded. Its membership skyrocketed from 271,847 in 1944 to 659,190 in 1956.

At the local level, teachers began to take to the streets with their grievances. Teachers in Norwalk, Conn.; Buffalo, N.Y.; and St. Paul, Minn., went on strike in 1946. They were protesting the effects of the rampant inflation that accompanied the end of wartime price controls, Georgia State University's Urban notes. The walkouts shocked the public and many teachers themselves, but were a harbinger of more to come.

Indeed, 1946 was a nadir of sorts for the profession. The war had drained the schools of teachers, creating another severe shortage.

A *Reader's Digest* article proclaimed, "America's classroom crisis is no joke." With the average annual salary for principals and teachers less than $2,000, classrooms were losing talent as teachers fled to take better-paying jobs as waitresses, taxi drivers, and auto-plant workers.

Salaries had sunk so low, the article posited, that teachers were losing the time-honored community respect that had always taken the sting out of relatively poor pay.

As a result of the shortages, it said, more than 2 million children between the ages of 6 and 15 didn't attend school in 1945. And while the NEA advised that classes should never be larger than 35 pupils, they sometimes exceeded 50 or 60 children.

Besides half starving teachers, the *Reader's Digest* article said, "we also like to bully them. No group of women outside religious orders is asked to live as prim a life as the teacher in an American small town."

ATTACKS ON QUALIFICATIONS

In contrast to the 1940s, which saw rumblings of teacher unrest, the 1950s proved a relatively quiet decade in labor relations, despite the strains of the postwar baby boom. Schools were consumed with just finding room for the children arriving at their doors. It was an era of crowded classrooms, split shifts, and feverish construction.

At the same time, the composition of the teaching force changed markedly, Clifford observes in *American Teachers*. Remaining prohibitions against married teachers were dropped; there were simply too many students needing instruction to send married women home.

Still, the proportion of men in teaching grew from one in five in 1940 to one in three by 1968, Clifford writes. The new crop of young male teachers also elevated the general educational level of the profession, according to *Education in the States*, as the men were more likely to pursue graduate work.

Those young men, that Council of Chief State School Officers history says, were "activist in outlook," comfortable with collective bargaining in private employment, and impatient with the "public relations approach" to teacher-related issues.

Americans, who had flocked to the cities in the early 1900s, began to flee them. As the suburbs grew, they attracted a well-educated, well-to-do class that owed its success to education. Those same people, however, were quick to bite the hand that had fed them. Public discontent with the quality of schools became a common theme in the 1950s—and teachers a prime target, as they remain today.

A number of stinging commentaries about teachers and teacher education during the 1950s raised or underscored affluent parents' concerns about teachers' qualifications. Books such as *Quackery in the Public Schools* by Albert Lynd, a former school board member, drew wide attention.

Many such critics were inflamed by the lack of rigor of the so-called life-adjustment courses of the late 1940s and early 1950s, which stressed everyday skills and social relationships at the expense of academics.

"The parents saw teachers as having less education in total, and certainly the ~~academic rigor of teachers' education was~~

big jump! ⟹

RISE OF UNIONISM

The next decade proved to be a watershed for the nation's teaching force.

Teachers' discontent with their salaries and lack of respect boiled over in the 1960s in a wave of militancy that forever changed the image of the profession. Collective bargaining did not come to teachers without a struggle and a great deal of internal controversy.

In 1952, the historian Marjorie Murphy writes in her 1990 book *Blackboard Unions: The AFT and the NEA, 1900-1980*, the American Federation of Teachers reaffirmed its no-strike policy. But by

1958, spurred by the efforts of President Carl Megel to educate members about the process, the AFT urged the repeal of no-strike legislation and edged closer to collective bargaining.

The National Education Association remained steadfastly against strikes by teachers.

From 1952 until the landmark New York City teachers' strike of 1962, Murphy writes, the move toward collective bargaining for teachers was "a slow, often discouraging, and sometimes extraordinarily frustrating battle of wits between young, dedicated, idealistic organizers and a stubbornly ensconced bureaucracy that was bent on ignoring them."

In New York City, organizers led by Dave Selden and Albert Shanker of the AFT began planning for a strike to earn collective-bargaining rights. The one-day strike in November 1960 won the union an election, held the following spring.

About the same time, the idea of collective bargaining was spreading. Wisconsin passed a law in 1959 allowing public employees to bargain, and President John F. Kennedy signed legislation in 1962 permitting federal employees to organize and bargain collectively.

Although New York City teachers had won the right to bargain, they had to strike to have their demands met. On April 12, 1962, 20,000 teachers, about half the city's teaching force, went out on strike.

It was "not just a local affair," Murphy says of the strike. "Hundreds of thousands of other teachers and public employees in other parts of the country looked to the New York strike as an important precedent."

By 1966, 30 teacher strikes had taken place; in 1967, the number had jumped to 105.

The teacher militancy made the NEA leaders distinctly uncomfortable. In 1964, Murphy notes, William Carr, the executive director of the association, warned against the AFL-CIO—the giant umbrella organization for organized labor—and characterized unionization as "an assault on professional independence."

Instead, Urban points out, the NEA continued to lobby for what had been its primary focus since the 1920s: securing a federal education bill that would funnel general aid to schools.

Over time, the NEA's reluctance to embrace collective bargaining waned as it began to compete head to head with the AFT. Between 1961 and 1965, the two unions competed in 40 different elections

to determine who would represent teachers, Murphy writes. Although the NEA won the majority, the AFT took the larger districts and thus gained more new members.

The unions also began to talk about using the bargaining process to achieve what they considered to be "professional" compensation, hours, and working conditions, a new twist on the word.

By the early 1970s, the national principals' and administrators' groups that had been affiliates parted ways with the NEA over the issue of collective bargaining. In some cases, they were forced to move out of the association's Washington headquarters into their own office space.

Union activism spread from New York, Chicago, and other major cities to smaller ones such as Cincinnati in the 1970s. Tom Mooney, the president of the Cincinnati Federation of Teachers, started his career in 1975 and recalls his own frustration and that of his friends. They were, he says, "getting out of college, starting a career, making no money, facing double-digit inflation, and districts were unable to pay decent salaries and didn't care much."

The 1960s and 1970s also challenged teachers as a wave of federal programs and continued social change, including desegregation, put strains on schools. Indeed, the scholars Grant and Murray write, teachers taught through nothing less than "overlapping social revolutions," struggling to find ways to reach students with social backgrounds and expectations dramatically different from their own.

But while it has improved teachers' financial circumstances and given them a measure of collective control over the conditions of their work, unionism also has had negative effects on the profession.

Many Americans were uncomfortable with militant, striking teachers, and remain so today, eroding public sympathy for teachers. Southern affiliates of the NEA still take pains to disassociate themselves from the union label; some teachers instead belong to "professional educator" groups that specifically renounce bargaining and striking and are not affiliated with the national labor unions.

In 1975, when collective bargaining was still relatively young, the noted sociologist Dan C. Lortie presciently warned that teachers could find a "trap" in attempting to correct what he called "status deficiencies" through collective bargaining.

By using restrictive rules, he wrote in his landmark book *Schoolteacher: A Sociological Study*, "they may appear uncaring and uncommitted; various publics may conclude that the work rules are intended to reduce total effort rather than to enhance teaching effectiveness.

"If teachers' actions are construed as little more than attempts to get greater benefits for less effort," Lortie concluded, "they will lose the advantages of reputation which have made teaching something more than simply a job."

STANDARDS-BASED TEACHING

The early 1980s saw a resurgence of criticism of public education, marked by a number of influential reports calling for radical changes in the structure of teaching.

A Nation at Risk, the 1983 report of the National Commission on Excellence in Education, warned that too many teachers were being drawn from the bottom quarter of graduating high school and college students and that their preparation programs were loaded with methods courses rather than subject-matter work.

But the report also was sympathetic to teachers, arguing that their professional work life was "on the whole unacceptable." Teachers were poorly paid, required to supplement their salaries with summer and part-time jobs, and had little influence over critical professional decisions such as textbook selection.

In 1986, the Carnegie Task Force on Teaching as a Profession took those themes further. In *A Nation Prepared: Teachers for the 21st Century*, the panel argued for building a teaching profession based on high standards, a professional environment that freed teachers to decide how to meet state and local goals for student learning, and a restructured teaching force with "lead teachers" to provide leadership in such schools.

A year later, the Carnegie Corporation of New York helped launch the National Board for Professional Teaching Standards, which over the past decade has built a voluntary system for certifying outstanding teachers. The board evaluates teachers through a series of performance assessments based on teachers' work in classrooms.

States and districts across the country have offered financial rewards and other incentives for teachers to seek board certification. Education schools also have begun to retool their coursework around the national teaching standards.

Michael Viola/Philadelphia Inquirer

over their work.

But the concurrent movement to set high standards for students—accompanied by the press for so-called high-stakes testing to increase the accountability of schools and educators—also threatens to undermine teacher professionalism, many observers believe.

"When you hold teachers accountable for a fixed curriculum with behavioral objectives and monitor it through test after test after test, the old-fashioned autonomy that my mother used to enjoy as a 1st grade teacher really gets restricted," says Joseph W. Newman, a professor of educational leadership and foundations at the University of South Alabama and the author of a widely used textbook about American teachers.

This tension between teacher judgment and externally imposed curricula, tests, and accountability measures brings teachers full circle at the close of the 20th century.

"The more and more that policymakers get into specifying school practice, the more they are interfering with the development of a profession," says Goodlad, the noted teacher-educator and author of numerous books on teacher education.

Echoing Margaret Haley nearly 100 years ago, he asks: "Who wants to get well-prepared to teach, and then discover that what you have to do is being dictated?" ∎

With rising salaries have come rising expectations. Parents and policymakers have begun to hold teachers to higher standards. In Philadelphia, parents demonstrate outside the school board's offices in 1986.

So unfair ⇒

The Paradoxical Teacher

In a world that likes to pigeonhole people, Albert Shanker was a paradox. He was one of the fathers of collective bargaining for teachers but also one of the strongest voices for teacher professionalism. He was a fierce defender of public education but at the same time, one of its most clear-eyed critics. He was a lifetime crusader for civil rights but led a bitter strike in New York City that provoked charges of racism.

He was the president of the American Federation of Teachers but quick to admit that some teachers couldn't measure up.

By Ann Bradley

He represented a solidly Democratic organization but had the ear of business leaders and policymakers of all political stripes. He was worldly, but also shy and ill at ease with small talk.

Yet, one trait remained constant: Shanker was always a teacher.

His weekly "Where We Stand" column, which ran as a paid advertisement in *The New York Times* (and later *Education Week*), covered an array of topics. Shanker wrote about affirmative action, Andrei Sakharov, vouchers and tax credits, discipline, and the need for higher standards for schools. In each column—and in his numerous, and famously lengthy, speeches—Shanker used a common-sensical, explanatory tone. The same approach was evident in his participation in crafting the influential 1986 report *A Nation Prepared: Teachers for the 21st Century*.

The report argued for creating a National Board for Professional Teaching Standards, for restructuring schools to allow teachers to make more instructional decisions, and for creating "lead teachers" to help their colleagues uphold high standards, among other changes.

But the notion of differentiating among teachers didn't sit well with Mary Hatwood Futrell, then the president of the larger National Education Association and a member, along with Shanker, of the task force that issued the report. In a footnote, she argued that such an arrangement would send the message that "some teachers are more equal than others."

In rebuttal, Shanker wrote a brief statement supporting the recommendations. In characteristic teacherly fashion, he pointed out that not everyone gets his way.

"When teachers criticize part of a contract I have helped negotiate," Shanker wrote, "I tell them that I could have written a better one myself. But that's not what negotiations or task force reports are about." The exchange illustrated the national unions' opposing views on issues of teacher professionalism, a gap that would narrow to a sliver by the end of the 1990s.

HUMBLE BEGINNINGS

Albert Shanker, born on the Lower East Side of Manhattan in 1928, was the son of working-class, Russian-immigrant Jews. He attended Stuyvesant High School and the University of Illinois at Urbana-Champaign before going on to do doctoral work in philosophy at Columbia University. Out of money to finish his disserta-

Benjamin Tice Smith

Though he first came to national prominence as the leader of a bitter strike in New York City, Albert Shanker later emerged as a widely respected spokesman for high-quality public education.

tion, Shanker began teaching mathematics in the New York City schools in 1952. He joined the Teachers Guild, one of more than 100 associations in the city speaking for teachers.

Shanker worked with other young trade unionists to build the guild, arguing that unionism and professionalism could go hand in hand. The organization staged a strike in 1960. A year later, under its president, Charles Cogan, the guild won bargaining rights as the United Federation of Teachers, speaking for all the city's 45,000 teachers.

In 1968, as the union's second president, Shanker led a series of strikes over a decision by the governing board of the Ocean Hill-Brownsville district in Brooklyn to fire 13 white teachers and six administrators. The largely African-American district was experimenting with "community control," seen by black activists and the sponsoring Ford Foundation as a way to improve urban schools.

As a unionist, Shanker demanded that the teachers be given due process instead of being fired. He was jailed for 15 days for defying a court order to end the strike—and was branded a racist in the protest.

In a 1980 interview, Shanker explained that he would not be cowed by prevailing liberal sentiment. "It was just as wrong for a group of black extremists to fire white teachers without due process," he said, "as it was for white extremists to fire black teachers without due process."

Throughout his career, Shanker adhered to the same principles. In 1974, he became the president of the New York union's national parent, the American Federation of Teachers. He built the AFT's membership to nearly 1 million, partly by organizing paraprofessionals and workers in noneducational fields such as city government and health care.

When the 1983 publication of *A Nation at Risk* ushered in the current era of education reform, Shanker embraced the conclusions of the national commission that found American schools in severe trouble. Until his death of cancer on Feb. 22, 1997, he worked to help improve public education, vigorously throwing the AFT's weight behind national standards and testing.

Shanker told his members why he had done so at the union's 1983 convention. Organizations mired in petty interests, he warned, would be "swept away" in times of great turmoil. But those willing to participate, compromise, and talk would not be.

"They will shape the direction of all the reforms and changes that are about to be made," Shanker said. "That is what we in the AFT intend to do." ■

Educating the Educators

I n 1857, the year the National Education Association was founded, teacher and lecturer William Russell made a bold proposal: Give teachers control over entry into their profession.

"Let a teachers' association receive a charter from the state and proceed, without further authorization, to examine and pass upon applicants for membership," wrote Russell, who made his home in Massachusetts. "The state and public will quickly, gladly, and appreciatively accept such an assumption of responsibility by the teaching profession."

By Ann Bradley

But the system suggested by Russell, followed in fields such as law and medicine, was not to be. Instead, the 20th century has been marked by criticism and controversy over the quality and rigor of licensure standards and teacher education—subjects that continue to stir strong passions.

By the early 1900s, states had begun to assert significant control over teaching. The local practices of the 19th century— in which school districts issued teaching permits on the basis of examinations— gave way to a system that closely entwined licensure and teacher education.

Along the way, the normal schools that the 19th-century education reformer Horace Mann so optimistically called "a new instrumentality in the advancement of the race" were left by the wayside. Such schools provided their students, who were mostly young women, with academic courses beyond the elementary education most had received, along with pedagogical training.

But over the 20th century, those institutions underwent what the teacher-educator John I. Goodlad calls "a rite of passage"—from normal school to teachers' college to state college to regional state university.

The transformation, he writes in his 1990 book *Teachers for Our Nation's Schools*, was accompanied by "a severe loss of identity for teacher education."

'QUANTITY OVER QUALITY'

Teachers themselves were required to gain increasing amounts of formal education. In the past 35 years alone, according to the NEA, teachers' qualifications have increased dramatically. In 1961, 14.6 percent of teachers had less than a bachelor's de-

gree, and 23.5 percent had earned advanced degrees. By 1996, just 0.3 percent of teachers lacked college degrees, and 56.2 percent held advanced degrees.

"The horizon has lifted almost with each generation," says Donald Warren, the dean of the education school at Indiana University. "But more formal preparation has not necessarily meant better."

Though normal schools were established to train teachers for the nation's burgeoning common schools, from the start they attracted people who had no intention of going into teaching. Instead, those students simply sought a convenient and inexpensive education beyond high school.

Normal schools also were under pressure to produce teachers quickly and cheaply, observes David F. Labaree, a professor of education at Michigan State University, or districts would hire teachers without any formal training at all.

"So normal schools adapted by stressing quantity over quality," he writes in a 1999 article in *Academe* magazine, "establishing a disturbing but durable pattern of weak professional preparation and low academic standards."

Eastern normal schools tended to attract modestly educated women and offered a course of study to bring them up to a 7th or 8th grade level, Goodlad notes, while those in the Midwest were geared to the secondary level. The Midwestern schools also began to prepare young men to enter school administration.

In large cities, high schools offered courses to prepare people to teach. "City normals" were established in Boston, Chicago, New Orleans, New York City, St. Louis, and other major urban areas.

Cities also continued to perform their own gatekeeping functions until well into the century; the New York City board of examiners, which administered its own licensing tests for prospective teachers, remained in place until 1990. The cumbersome system meant that applicants had to take examinations to earn both state and city licenses. Rural teachers, in contrast, typically entered the classroom with little formal education and received coursework at summer "teacher institutes."

After all, Edgar B. Wesley observed in the 1957 history *NEA: The First Hundred Years*, *Building of the Teaching Profession*, people with the ability and ambition to succeed in normal schools weren't likely to take poorly paid, short-term jobs teaching in one-room schoolhouses.

LICENSE TO TEACH

By the late 1960s, nearly all states had made college degrees a prerequisite for initial certification. The rapid increase in requirements reflected the drive for the centralization of teacher standards overseen by state education departments.

Year	Elementary teachers	Secondary teachers
1900	0	2
1910	0	3
1920	0	10
1930	2	23
1940	11	40
1950	21	42
1960	39	51
1967	47	52

NOTE: Numbers include the District of Columbia and Puerto Rico.

SOURCE: *Education in the States: Development Since 1990*, Council of Chief State School Officers, 1969.

As teacher-training programs were established, states began to license teachers on the basis of normal-school diplomas or some type of prescribed college curricula. By 1900, according to *Education in the States: Development Since 1900*, a 1969 report by the Council of Chief State School Officers, 41 states accepted such evidence in lieu of examinations.

Critics would come to deride such requirements as evidence of the education establishment's focus on "inputs" rather than results, but the rules represented an improvement over the previous examination system. The exams weren't always rigorous, and were open to patronage abuses because they were administered locally.

The professionally trained administrators who ran the state education departments, in fact, took great pride in the body of professional knowledge represented by the coursework.

Library of Congress

LOW PRIORITY

In the 1930s, according to *Education in the States*, states formed advisory councils on teacher education and certification to involve members of the profession in setting standards and requirements. (Later, in the 1970s, the NEA pushed for the creation of teacher-majority "professional-standards boards" to regulate entry into the field.)

States also began to administer the National Teacher Examination in 1940, a time of a relative teacher surplus. But the shortages created by World War II put a damper on enthusiasm for teacher testing.

By the end of the war, normal schools had virtually vanished in favor of four-year teachers' colleges, which soon became state colleges that awarded degrees in a variety of fields. In the process, teacher training slipped further down higher education's agenda, in favor of preparing administrators, conducting research, and offering continued professional education to practitioners.

Consistent with that focus, most debates about teacher licensing and education were conducted by administrators, faculty members, and state education department employees.

But in 1946, the NEA formed its National Commission on Teacher Education and Professional Standards, known as TEPS. The establishment of the commission, strongly supported by the association's department of classroom teachers, marked the first attempt by teachers to gain a voice in professional training.

Participants at TEPS' many regional conferences agreed that licensure was intended to protect the public from incompetent teachers, according to David L. Angus, a late professor at the University of Michigan. But it was also meant to protect the members of the profession from unfair competition from untrained people.

At the time, Angus writes in a paper to be published posthumously by the Thomas B. Fordham Foundation, that concern was sensible: Approximately 109,000 people were teaching on emergency licenses following the war.

TEPS councils in the states pushed for more formal education for elementary teachers, the elimination of examinations, and five-year programs for high school teachers. They also sought to have classroom teachers represented on states' teacher education advisory councils.

During the 1950s, states moved to the "approved-programs approach" for licensing teachers. Instead of specifying courses and hours for teachers, a state approved teacher education programs and left the details to faculties to determine.

UNDER ATTACK

Various professional associations, including the American Association of Colleges for Teacher Education, joined together in 1954 to form the first national accrediting organization for education schools.

The National Council for Accreditation of Teacher Education was not met with enthusiasm by the colleges and universities whose programs it would scrutinize, however.

The debut of the accrediting body also failed to stave off public criticism of teacher education as an intellectually weak effort. Particularly after the 1957 launch of the Soviet satellite Sputnik I, Angus points out, professional educators came under attack.

"The notion that the hegemony of professional educators over virtually all aspects of the American educational system had led to a loss of seriousness of purpose became far more plausible," he writes.

James B. Conant, a former president of Harvard University, criticized the academic and professional training offered to teachers in *The Education of American Teachers*, published in 1963.

Even harsher was James D. Koerner in *The Miseducation of American Teachers*, brought out the same year. He summed up "educationists" as a "sincere, humanitarian, well-intentioned, hard-working, poorly informed, badly educated, and ineffectual group of men and women."

Neither critic proposed any particular model for teacher education. Conant threw his support behind a lengthy period of practice-teaching, dismissing professional coursework and enraging educators in the process.

Conant's teacher education report did not mention the quality of schools, Good-

ate Teachers College

lad observes, and Conant's previous tome on high schools had failed to mention teachers.

It wasn't until the early 1980s, Goodlad says, that school reformers began to make the connection between good schools and well-prepared teachers. At that time, political leaders and the public became worried about the relatively low scores of prospective teachers on the SAT, and a perceived lack of rigor in their training drew renewed concern.

States had begun administering tests to prospective teachers in the mid-1960s. Still, only a handful of states, mostly in the South, tested teachers until the 1980s. Today, 44 states do so.

The 1980s saw the release of "Tomorrow's Teachers," a report of the Holmes Group, made up of education deans at leading research universities, who castigated themselves and their institutions for their relative neglect of teacher education.

The 1986 report was followed by two more calling for reforms, including the establishment of professional-development schools.

Often likened to teaching hospitals, those schools proliferated during the late 1980s and early 1990s, raising nagging questions among educators about their quality.

Meanwhile, NCATE, during the past decade, has overhauled its standards and gained more credibility. The accrediting organization has forged closer working relationships with the states, most of which now use the national accrediting body's standards for teacher preparation in evaluating programs.

The organization also has written standards for professional-development schools as a benchmark for districts and universities involved in such partnerships.

As it has increased its authority, however, NCATE has attracted some competition. The Teacher Education Accreditation Council, launched in 1998 with the support of college presidents upset about NCATE's requirements, is trying to create an alternative system—evidence that the teaching profession remains divided.

A multistate consortium is cooperating on new ways to license teachers, with a focus not just on subject-matter and professional knowledge, but also demonstrated skill in the classroom.

Together with the nascent efforts of the National Board for Professional Teaching Standards to identify and certify outstanding teachers, the profession has gained the "three-legged stool" of quality assurance—licensing, accreditation, and advanced certification—that characterizes more-mature professions.

Nonetheless, teacher education finds itself often on the defensive.

New accountability provisions in federal law, for instance, will require institutions to show how many of their students pass state basic-skills tests—evidence that the public still doesn't think much of the quality of professional preparation for teachers. ∎

The responsibility of educating teachers has shifted from the normal school to the teachers' college to the full-fledged college or university over the course of the 20th century. More than 3,000 students were enrolled in summer school at the North Texas State Teachers College in Denton in 1928.

A Teaching Gem

By Robert C. Johnston

Ostrander, Ohio

Opal McAlister was young, ambitious, and grateful when she took her first teaching job in 1923. Not only did the $810 annual salary seem like a fortune, she also welcomed the adventure of moving to a new town 18 miles from her central Ohio home. But soon, she found drawbacks to her new profession. When she bobbed her hair during Christmas break that first year, her father warned that she'd be fired for the rebellious, midneck cut.

"When I was interviewed at the school, I was told I couldn't smoke or date during the week," recalls McAlister. "Yes, I think they would have fired me" for the haircut. Rather than take that risk, she spent the rest of the school year covering her missing brown locks with a hairpiece.

It was in this confining but opportunity-rich world of early-20th-century teaching that Opal McAlister found her calling.

For the next 52 years, she was a dedicated teacher and pioneer who would add her unique stitch work to the vast and diverse fabric of public education. Yet many of her experiences parallel the twists and turns of teaching across the century. McAlister was the first woman in her area to coach a boys' varsity basketball team, and the first female principal in one local school. She also taught baking and military law during World War II and championed teachers' rights as a union official.

But, at the end of each day, she was foremost a teacher, whose unwavering passion was helping students learn.

"A good too many teachers look at retirement instead of the pupils in front of them," McAlister says. As for herself, she declares, "I wouldn't have taught 52 years if I felt that way, now would I?"

McAlister lives alone in a neatly kept, modest farmhouse here ringed by pine trees, six miles from where she first taught. A brisk walker and tireless storyteller, she exercises daily, reads romance novels, and takes no pills. She directs a bridge club at the YMCA in nearby Marysville every Monday and speaks at local schools.

She thanks teaching for contributing greatly to her long and abundant life.

"I have a museum of gifts I could show you from wall to wall, and a great number of students who are my friends," she says. "But the biggest thing that I got from my students was the zest, impetus, and urge to live."

Just 18 and one year out of high school, McAlister was a fairly typical first-year teacher in her day. Enrollments were growing, and because women were forced to quit when they married, turnover was high.

After completing a one-year teacher-preparation program at Union County Normal School and passing a general-knowledge test, she was hired to teach 38 5th and 6th graders at Watkins Public School in Watkins, a tiny town about 40 miles north of Columbus. She took the test annually until earning her lifetime-teaching certificate in 1928.

Teaching wasn't a bad life for a young woman during the 1920s. For the first time,

> "I had one student who went to work with IBM.
> He wrote and asked me if he should marry Mary Kay Jones.
> I told him, 'Look, I'll advise you on all things except for marriage.'"

she had no trouble coming up with 50 cents to see a Zane Grey western movie. And a middy, pullover blouse with a pleated skirt together sold for $10 from Sears, Roebuck and Co.

Watkins was 18 miles from her family's home, so McAlister paid $3 a week for a room and meals with a local family. Her father made the 36-mile round trip twice a week by car to drop her off and pick her up.

Housed in a sturdy two-story, red-brick building, the school's 200 students in grades 1-12 were mostly from poor farming families. The one black family in the community sent its children there.

A rookie teacher with little supervision, McAlister was expected to get through textbooks in arithmetic, reading, history, geography, and agriculture. Otherwise, her oversight came Friday afternoons, when the superintendent reviewed the next week's lesson plan. "If you got through the books, that was fine," says McAlister. She favored taking her students on nature hikes and assigning them what are now called "hands on" activities over digesting textbooks.

Her first classrooms were vastly different from the ones she would later know. Students sat at oak desks bolted in rows to hardwood floors. They bought their books and wrote with pens fed by inkwells on their desks.

McAlister's main visual aids consisted of a slate board and chalk. Former students say her most valuable teaching aid, however, was a creative personality.

"Before her, we didn't do too many activities," recalls 83-year-old Eleanor Conklin Heirdorn, who was in McAlister's 5th grade class in 1926 and lives nearby. "Then Opal came along. She was a lot younger [than other teachers] and dressed nice. She didn't let us sit around much. We went outside getting leaves. Other teachers never even brought that up with us."

While McAlister was a strict disciplinarian, she also appreciated a good prank. One favorite local story is about the time some boys put a skunk in the window well outside her classroom. The punishment she meted out? It stayed there all day. "Boy, did it smell," she cracks mischievously.

As McAlister talks, her hazel eyes sparkle with interest from behind pink-framed glasses. Her gesturing hands and arms are an extension of her carefully ar-

ticulated message. Today, her short, curly white hair has replaced the old rebellious style of her youth. A natty dresser, she prefers bright dresses and colorful brooches. Tall and trim, McAlister also walks with the determined gait of someone who knows where she is going. Given her demeanor, it is no surprise when she talks about being at odds with administrators early in her career.

When her superiors chastised her for wasting time with low-performing students by tutoring them at home for free, she grew more determined to help.

"I defended them because, having been born into a family without too many resources, I know what it's like to be poor," says McAlister. Her father, who immigrated to the United States from Switzerland as a child, worked as a laborer and then turned to farming to support his three children. Her mother, born in a Conestoga wagon, was a homemaker. "But I never knew what it was to be neglected."

There was a point halfway in her first year, however, when she was not so tolerant of struggling students and was prepared to quit. After her father reminded her that she had to fulfill her one-year contract, McAlister had an epiphany that shaped her teaching from then on. "I realized that you need to start where the students are," she explains. "Teaching became fun. A whole new world opened up to me."

And it was a world that held many surprises, starting that winter when her superintendent asked McAlister to take his place as the boys' varsity-basketball coach.

"The superintendent couldn't get along with the boys," says the self-described former tomboy, who grew up sandwiched in age between two brothers. "He wasn't a basketball man, so he asked me if I would do it."

Such an arrangement was unheard of in 1924—and remains rare today. Still, she accepted the challenge, and the boys welcomed their new female coach. At one point, a male coach whose team was trounced by McAlister's cagers complained to the county superintendent that boys shouldn't be coached by women. Unswayed, the administrator backed her.

McAlister coached three years before

Watkins School '25-'26

St. Louis Ordnance Depot '45

moving to a school in Flint, Ohio, which is now part of Columbus. There, she started a junior high basketball program. One of her players was Frank Truitt, who went on to help coach Ohio State University to a national basketball championship in 1960.

"She got me started," says Truitt, who also coached at Kent State from 1966 to 1974 and now owns a real estate firm in Columbus. "She taught us that basketball was a team sport. She also had command over a classroom better than anyone I've ever seen, including me."

McAlister's keen memory vividly details the sweeping changes in education dating back to the days when horses pulled the "school buses." While they may seem trivial today, she says some of the most dramatic innovations came early in her career.

Before mimeographs and laser printers, there was the "gelatin board" in the early 1920s. The gadget was used to make copies by tracing an image onto a piece of purple carbon paper, which was pressed against a board covered with gelatin and then transferred to paper for student use. "That was a marvelous innovation," says McAlister, who traveled 40 miles to Columbus to buy the board herself for $2. ("Teachers still pay for the extras," she remarks.)

McAlister also remembers the joy of getting world maps—one large map for each continent—and a pointer for the teacher. "That was a real improvement," she says. "Before that, you had a globe, if you were lucky."

Seemingly ahead of her time during much of her career, McAlister found herself at the front of a cultural shift in how marriage was viewed. Matrimony and teaching did not go hand in hand for young women at the beginning of the century. As a result, many female teachers spent their lives as spinsters.

But it never occurred to McAlister that she would not marry. And in 1930, at the age of 26, she wed Dan McAlister, a radio salesman from Columbus whom she met as he installed a new radio at a friend's house. By allowing her new husband to slip a wedding band on her finger, she assumed she was losing more than her

Left: Opal McAlister, who provided scrapbook photos to illustrate this story, appears front-row center with her students.

Above: McAlister is on the right.

maiden name of Dunn. Her teaching days were over as well, or so she figured.

She was wrong. Instead, her male superintendent asked her to stay.

"I was never so shocked in all my life as when he said, 'We need you out there,'" says McAlister, who still seems surprised by the decision.

"After that," she says, "they just stopped firing people when they got married."

By 1942, the war sweeping across Europe and the Pacific had drawn in the United States and, with it, the dutiful educator from rural Ohio.

"One day I was holding a history book, talking about the news, current events, war, and patriotism," McAlister recounts. "I thought to myself, 'Why am I standing up here? Why don't I do something about it?'"

In December of that year, with her husband in the Civil Air Patrol, and one year after the Japanese attack on Pearl Harbor, she reported to the Women's Auxiliary Army Corps in Des Moines, Iowa.

By February 1943, detailed to a mechanics' group at Fort Oglethorpe in the northwest corner of Georgia, a chagrined McAlister reminded her superiors that she was a teacher. Soon, she was the head of a training division where she taught baking, military law, current events, and other subjects.

"You name it, I taught it," she says. "I had to learn new subjects very fast."

Among her keepsakes is a graduation speech she delivered June 6, 1943, to a graduating WAAC class. The neatly penned, five-page speech implores the young cooking school graduates to dedicate themselves to their mission.

"Your first step of improvement is to keep growing because only as long as we are green do we grow. We must continue to be creative and imaginative," she wrote. "When our foods become scarce, and they will, our troops must still be fed."

With each successive class, McAlister hoped that she was closer to a trip to Europe. But her commanders valued a good teacher too much to let her go. "They kept telling me, 'Just one more class.' But I never did [get sent overseas]. I definitely wanted to go."

As the Second World War wound down, she was put in charge of property and a restaurant at the St. Louis Ordnance Depot. Even there, she couldn't repress her instinct to teach. She taught two Italian prisoners of war under her charge to read and write English. They rewarded her with a small replica of their former battleship, which she has today.

"I could have been court-martialed for that," she says of her fraternization with the Italian prisoners. "But they were such young fellows. They felt just like your family."

By 1946, the war over, Americans were turning back to domestic concerns. For the McAlisters, that meant settling into their new home and 65-acre farm about 40 miles northwest of Columbus.

But, as Opal McAlister was chopping wood in her front yard on a chilly morning shortly after they moved in, the school bell rang. Two administrators visited to offer her a teaching job at Ostrander School, which served grades 1-12. McAlister, then 42, demurred, but only briefly. She offered to teach a self-contained 7th and 8th grade classroom at the school, which was just one mile away from her home.

The administrators didn't immediately bite. McAlister's idea didn't mesh with Ostrander's organization of specialized 45-minute periods. The next day, though, the school officials were back to grant her request, as long as she'd teach home economics, too.

"The best thing that ever happened to me was when they said, 'We need you.' Look what I would have missed if I hadn't gone back," she says, waving to a stack of student photos and notes spread across her dining room table. "And I would have been here milking the cows."

From that day on, and through three retirements, there was little time, indeed,

1967—My Retirement Party—by our P.T.A

"When I was in school, there would be an oil lamp and my ma and pa. They would learn what we were learning in school. … Parents today just don't know what students are learning in school, then something argumentative comes up, and they want to void a book from the library."

to milk cows. And, as the McAlisters never had children of their own, students became their family.

Upon her return to the classroom, McAlister discovered another innovation: movable desks. In one of her first experiments with unsecured seats, she let students work in groups on plays for a statewide Ohio-history contest. "There was one group, and oh, were they arguing. It got louder and louder, and I remember thinking, 'Can I just hold my own and not say anything for a bit?'" Finally, the students quieted down.

When the boisterous group won the competition, she learned a lesson: "If I had interrupted, the kids would have pouted, and we wouldn't have won. You don't hold down debate or an argument till it gets to fisticuffs, because out of an argument comes a good idea."

An even bigger change, however, had taken place in the teacher herself. Having seen new places and prepared servicewomen to be sent to foreign lands, McAlister now wanted her students to see beyond their own parochial worlds. She took students on field trips and taught girls in her home economics courses how to order in nice restaurants. She urged all her students to put off marriage and think about careers.

"[The war] made me more conscious of the fact that we have to have people prepared to take their places in the communities," observes McAlister, who has always been active in her community.

She helped lead a drive to build a library in Ostrander in 1991 and sold tickets in 96-degree heat at the town's July Fourth picnic in 1999.

Within two years of her return to teaching, she was given the duties of vice principal—a role she held for 20 years without additional pay. She also kept score for basketball teams, advised cheerleading squads, and became the president of the local teachers' union. And when children needed extra help, she tutored them before and after school, or during summer vacation.

Even today, she regularly shares her ear, thoughts, and lemonade with the boys who mow her lawn—a chore she did herself

until two years ago. Waving her finger the way she does when she has a point to make, she adds, "You help a child when they need the help and are asking for it."

As the postwar economy boomed and a segment of the population became fascinated with a gyrating Tennessean named Elvis, the efficiency of small school districts became a major issue in education.

Ostrander went through two consolidations between 1950 and 1962. Enrollment grew from about 400 to about 1,000 in that time, and the district's size expanded from 25 square miles to 200 square miles, making it Ohio's second-largest district geographically. Nationwide, the number of districts fell from 83,718 in 1950 to 40,520 in 1960.

"Our classes became so large that instead of contained classrooms for each grade, we needed four rooms for the 7th and 8th grades and were forced to departmentalize," McAlister laments. "How can you teach your subject and understand each student as well when you are with them just 45 minutes a day?"

As student populations changed, so did teacher-parent relations. Parents were now split between two and three schools, which meant they had to limit PTA participation. "They couldn't be as involved as when their children were at the same school," McAlister says.

McAlister disputes popular images of the 1950s and '60s, which hold that nearly all mothers stayed home to care for their children after school. After World War II, more mothers took jobs, she says, thus beginning an early backslide of parent involvement in education. "When children came home, mothers weren't there waiting for them with milk and cookies."

Attitudes toward teachers also changed. "At the time I taught, teachers were on a pedestal," McAlister says. "What the teacher said, the parent supported. If a child was paddled at school, they probably got paddled again at home." (She reckons

she herself paddled fewer than a dozen students in her long career.)

As teachers became more vulnerable to complaining parents or the whims of school board members, McAlister got more involved in the Delaware County chapter of the Ohio Teachers Association.

A member of the National Education Association state affiliate since 1923, McAlister was elected president of the county chapter in 1963. She keeps a faded salary schedule that shows starting teachers earned $4,650 that year, compared with $6,000 for accountants and $6,800 for engineers. "They were all above teachers," she says.

Despite her union advocacy, she has no patience for poor teaching. Her take on teacher tenure must make some union officials bristle. "Tenure is the poorest thing that ever happened," she argues, "simply because it means that a poor teacher can hold on to her position."

And she's not afraid to point the finger on occasion at teachers for students' lack of motivation. "Teachers say kids are bored, disinterested, and don't obey. This can be the teacher's fault," she says. "I think the teacher has lost respect for the child. When teachers lose respect for the child, they lose respect for you."

McAlister saw new encroachments in schools by state and district officials in the 1960s. For example, there were repeated mandates for school counselors, but no money to pay for them.

She remains most chagrined over the state's elimination of funding for the Ohio-history competition, which she had participated in regularly. "I'll never forgive this one," she declares. "I think the state forgot to talk to the grassroots when it wanted to mandate changes."

Today's teachers, she acknowledges, feel even more outside influences in the classroom—from state standards and exams. "When I first started, you had certain subjects, but how you taught was never questioned," she says. "Now, there are such restrictions and requirements that come without money, it limits what they can give the student."

By all accounts, McAlister remained a

"Kids never intimidated me. If I can't be ahead of a kid,
I had no business being a teacher."

strong and respected teacher late in her career. "We got a lot more done in her class than we did in the other classes. She demanded more and didn't waste much time," says Bill Conklin, a 7th grade math student of hers in 1964. Adds Conklin, who taught for 17 years himself: "A lot of teachers are superstrict but don't have any relationship with students. She could do both. She never had any outcasts."

Later in 1964, at the age of 60, McAlister became the first female principal of what was then Ostrander Elementary School.

At the time, the civil rights movement was roiling national politics. McAlister says the almost exclusively white, rural community followed the events, but by and large felt little direct impact. "Our only opinion was sorrow," she recalls of student reaction to the plight of African-Americans seeking equal educational and employment opportunities. "They asked, 'Why does this have to happen?' Even though we are mostly white, they have empathy for an underdog."

Across the country, the tide of the youthful counterculture also was rising, and questions were growing over the escalating conflict in Vietnam.

Local unrest, though, was mild. One day, a young teacher sent McAlister a pair of rebellious boys clad in bright lavender and pink pants. McAlister asked them what she ought to do. The youths said they expected her to send them home to change, which is what she did.

"Later, they told me they just wanted to see my reaction."

Despite enjoying her leadership role, even with the school's chronic funding woes, she retired in 1967 to be with her ailing husband, who had emphysema. Her retirement party attracted 250 people, according to newspaper accounts. It also drew an emotional letter from John Gusler, whose daughter had studied under McAlister.

Gusler's typewritten letter was sent from Port Royal, Jamaica, where he was the captain of a sailboat for tourists. "No matter what may present itself in years to come, the kindness and real understanding you have given so unselfishly to this very special child will be her strength, and be reflected through her to posterity. This is immortality."

But McAlister was not through teaching yet. After her husband's death two years later, alone and restless, she returned to Ostrander School in 1970 to teach math. She had always enjoyed that subject, and of all the curricular ideas she's seen in her day, the move to what was known as the "new math" was the worst, she insists. "No matter what, two plus two still equals four, and students must be taught that," she says. There is nothing wrong with teaching basic addition and multiplication skills through repetition, she adds.

In 1972, McAlister traded her math post for a long-term substitute position in order to free up a teaching spot. "There were a lot of unemployed teachers then," she says.

While McAlister has seen innumerable changes in education during her career, one element, she says, has remained relatively constant: the behavior of students.

"At the time, and when I substitute-taught for 100 days, and even now, I don't see a difference," she says. "As a teacher, I guess my reputation went before me, and I never had difficulty." Almost apologizing for her benign view of youthful behavior, she adds, "I just cannot find bad kids."

In July 1975, she came down with pneumonia and was hospitalized for three weeks. Her doctor said she could return to school the next January. But McAlister says, "I got so busy, I just never thought to go back."

McAlister has kept active in her latest retirement, but is always ready to talk in local classrooms about her wartime experiences or local history. Far from marveling at computers, crowded halls, and body-piercing in today's schools, McAlister says her visits reaffirm a truth about herself, and about children.

A talk to high school students about World War II on Veterans Day 1999 triggered a twinge of nostalgia. "When I saw those senior kids, they were so thoughtful. They didn't push to get out of the room, but they stopped to thank me," she says. "I'll never forget those kids. That's when I think, if I were just in that classroom." ■

Teaching in 2020: The Triumph Of 'the Slow Revolution'?

A perspective by Gerald Grant

My wife Judith is a 4th grade teacher, and I teach graduate seminars. At the dinner table, conversation often turns to the problems and challenges of teaching. We talk as equals, teacher and professor, about the common challenges we face in the classroom, as if we were members of the same profession. Our experience has taught us that the fundamental acts of teaching and the central questions all teachers confront are essentially the same. But professors and precollege teachers are not seen as members of the same profession. Why should that be?

The work is essentially the same, but the conditions, status, and pay of one profession are vastly different from those of the other. The work is institutionalized in different ways. Yes, professors have more training and do more research. The fact that professors are still mostly men and schoolteachers are mostly women is also a large part of the answer.

Male patriarchs dominated both professions at the end of the 19th century before the massive expansion of the educational system in the United States took place. Both were top-down systems. College presidents hired and fired the faculty and dictated the curriculum, as did most school superintendents. The power of the presidents was absolute.

My wife's great-grandfather, Melancthon Woolsey Stryker, was the president of Hamilton College in upstate New York in the 1890s. Like most college presidents then, he personally interviewed the faculty, told them what courses they would teach, and did not hesitate to tell them what color trim they could paint their houses on College Hill. Similarly, school superintendents wrote the manuals for teachers to follow and specified the appropriate length of a teacher's hair.

There were some important differences, however. While the college presidents wielded enormous power as institutional leaders (as long as they maintained the confidence of their boards of trustees), they were not seen as more expert than the faculty. Most of the private college presidents were ordained ministers. As the great centralization of public schools took place early in the 20th century, however, the school superintendents succeeded in establishing themselves as the true educational experts. They got doctorates in educational administration at Columbia or Wisconsin and wrapped themselves in the mantle of scientific management. They conducted expensive surveys of emerging urban school systems that convinced the public that educational effectiveness and efficiency could be achieved only through the application of their expertise and their understanding of the principles of scientific management. Teachers with low levels of formal education could be had cheaply because they could be trained on the job in schools that sorted pupils by age and aptitude. All the teacher had to do was to follow the curriculum guidelines written by the new experts. They could turn out literate students just as workers for the Ford Motor Co. could turn out Model T's.

Although superintendents preferred normal-school graduates, certification of teacher expertise carried little weight with the public. But as major research universities began to multiply in the 1920s and 1930s, the Ph.D. degree imported from the German universities became the badge of expertise for the highest ranks of the professoriate. Professors with doctorates in chemistry or philosophy were highly sought after by universities and colleges eager to achieve research eminence. The professors were no longer willing to submit to the autocratic rule of a largely clerical college presidency.

Out of these tensions came the first academic revolution. Professors stripped college presidents of their powers to determine the curriculum and fire the faculty at will. They took charge of their teaching and research by forming the American Association of University Professors, which established the rights of tenure and academic freedom that gave the faculty essential control of the educational process at the college level. Schoolteachers, however, remained locked in a mostly hierarchical system in which they were treated as hirelings whose work was mandated by a male administrative elite. They followed detailed curriculum outlines and adjusted the teaching day to change subject matter when administrators rang the bells. Although teachers often complied only symbolically once the classroom door was closed, since the supervisors couldn't watch everybody all the time, they were treated as functionaries, not as professionals capable of independent judgment.

In *Teaching in America*, Christine Murray and I use the term "slow revolution" to describe the gradual accretion of efforts by teachers to take charge of their practice in ways analogous to the professoriate's. As a result of our classroom observations and interviews with more than 500 teachers in new roles as mentors, lead teachers, and policymakers over the last decade, we believe this slow revolution has approached its final stage. The outcome is far from certain, however. It may be that instead of a completion of the second or "slow revolution" of teachers by 2020, there will be a repeal of the first academic revolution achieved by the professoriate. There would be no downward spread to schoolteachers of the kind of empowerment professors won in that revolution. On the contrary, there would be—and to some extent already is—an upward spread of more tightly engineered and centralized higher education systems with most faculty working on contracts without tenure. Professors would look more like schoolteachers than the reverse.

The recent chairman of the Massachusetts board of higher education, James F. Carlin, a multimillionaire who previously ran insurance and real estate companies, personifies this trend. He put faculty on notice that a counterrevolution had begun and that if he had his way, colleges and universities would be run more like General Motors. Boston newspaper editorialists cheered when he ridiculed the idea that faculty should run the academic side of institutions and announced that he wouldn't accept the faculty rights written into current contracts. Mr. Carlin viewed tenure as "an absolute scam" that had turned faculty jobs into sinecures and made tuition excessive. In a 1997 poll, 56 percent of New York voters said they were opposed to giving teachers tenure.

A more optimistic scenario foresees the hastening of the slow revolution. Some "leveling" of professions in America will occur. More of the work of the traditional high-status professions, particularly medicine, will occur in bureaucratic or large organizational settings under the watchful eye of managers, whether these be administrators of health-maintenance organizations, in the case of doctors, or bureaucrats who supervise the work of lawyers employed in government agencies. While doctors are accepting more and more regulation, the schoolteachers and nurses will slowly break out of long-established bureaucratic hierarchies and share more of the autonomy previously enjoyed by members of the high-status professions. The increasing political strength of the women's movements will create upward pressure to elevate the status and pay of the traditionally female "helping professions" of teaching, nursing, and social work. The gender gaps in professional work will also close as more men enter traditionally female fields and more women are employed as lawyers, doctors, and architects. By the late 1990s, nearly half the students at leading law and medical schools were women; at Harvard, slightly more than half the first-year medical class was female by 1997.

The eventual triumph of the slow revolution for teachers depends on four developments, which are well advanced in some districts while lagging in others:

• Creating a Professional Culture. Teachers must assume responsibility for developing and assessing the competence of those who enter the profession. This means moving beyond orientation programs for new hires to thoughtful and sustained mentoring. Assessment also requires the courage to weed out the incompetent at all levels. Continuing development of professional skills for all teachers necessitates restructuring the school day so that teachers have more time for interaction, curriculum planning, and mentoring, as well as development of stronger links with professional-school faculty members. Success of the slow revolution would enable teachers to take charge of their practice and strengthen the essential acts of teaching—knowing their subjects and their students, engaging them in learning, acting as models of a good life, assessing students' moral and intellectual growth, and reflecting on the arts of teaching that enable that growth. Reforms should be judged by that standard. If they do not contribute to strengthening the essential acts of teaching, they are of little worth.

• Accepting Role Differentiation. Teachers and their unions must end the pretense that all 4th grade teachers are equal except for years on the job. Not all have the competence to be thoughtful and effective mentors of new recruits. Differential rewards should be provided to teachers who have the knowledge and skill to fill such roles. The teaching profession should not assume a highly stratified structure in the manner of the military. But some hierarchical distinctions would be made, as between interns, teachers, and lead teachers or mentors. Roles would be differentiated at the upper levels according to teachers' preferences. For example, some lead teachers might be engaged in curriculum design, others in mentoring or development of new uses of computers in the classroom. No other profession can do its work and exercise its responsibilities to the public without such role differentiation, and teaching will never be a profession as long as it is an exception.

• Fair and Rigorous Selection for Leading Roles. The Rochester, N.Y., school district moved toward the pattern suggested here, with some teachers assuming these roles with major pay increments and reduced teaching hours so they could have time for observing and mentoring young teachers. Our research shows Rochester achieved some success, but its plan was compromised because of suspicions that teachers selected (by a committee nominated partly by the union and partly by high-level administrators) were sometimes chosen for their loyalties to the union or the superintendent, rather than for their talents. Those who are selected for such roles become the trustees of the profession. Both the public and other teachers must see them as those most qualified for assuming such responsibilities. This requires a selection process that is viewed as rigorous by the public and as fair by the teachers. One of the most significant advancements for teaching in the latter 20th century has been the development of the National Board for Professional Teaching Standards. For more than a decade, the national board—composed of expert teachers, scholars, and policymakers—set the goal of developing assessments of teaching that would be as rigorous as tests taken by lawyers, doctors, or architects.

Like medical boards, the tests are taken in specific areas in which teachers seek advanced certification. The assessment takes several days to complete; it involves written tests as well as demonstration of the candidate's ability to assess and diagnose complex matters of teaching practice. Surveys of those who have taken the board test show that both those who failed and those who passed felt it was not only fair but also the first test they had taken that captured the complexities of teaching.

• Achieving Results for Children.
Before World War I, the American university ranked low in world status. Americans only rarely won a Nobel Prize for scientific achievement. The first academic revolution by the professoriate would not have occurred had the professors not achieved significant and highly visible breakthroughs. While our analysis of international comparisons of school achievement is more positive than many reports that fail to take account of the series of dramatic social transformations American schools and teachers also underwent, we see the need for major improvements in outcomes for pupils, particularly poor minorities in urban school systems. There will be no triumph of the slow revolution without achieving significant results for children.

Will it happen? Large systems seldom change unless there is no other alternative. The public education system now in place was an incredible achievement of the late 19th century, and it came about because doing nothing was not an option as millions of poor immigrants came to America and cried out for more educational opportunity.

Two political battles that will have a large impact on the completion of the slow revolution will be settled within the next five years. One will take place in the major teachers' unions: Will they not only accept but encourage role differentiation and take responsibility for rooting out incompetence in their own ranks? The second will be decided in governors' offices, state legislatures, and among school boards: Will they attach major incentives to national-board certification? To date, incentives have been adopted in some form in 23 states and 61 school districts. But few have yet gone as far as North Carolina in granting an automatic 12 percent pay increase to any teacher who becomes board-certified. While only a few thousand teachers are now certified nationally, the board predicts more than 100,000 will be by 2005. If the board assessment retains its rigor, that would begin to change public perceptions about the teaching profession.

Two significant differences with the first academic revolution also bear on the outcome. The professors' was a revolt of sons against their fathers. The triumph of the slow revolution would be the first time a predominantly female profession forced an entrenched patriarchy to share its authority, an authority more embedded in law than was the case with college presidents. Most difficult is the goal of achieving results for children.

The revolution by the professoriate was congruent with the dominant societal values of individualism and an emphasis on opportunity to learn that presumed radical inequality of outcomes based on individual effort and talent. The tracking system established then for sorting talent in higher education is still largely in place and mostly unchallenged. It sorts students by SAT scores and faculty by research prestige. The push that accompanies the second academic revolution is to do just the opposite: to untrack the schools and to educate all students to higher levels in more inclusive settings. No one argues for equality of outcomes across the board, but an enormous change in values and beliefs is required to make the distribution of test scores in America look more like that of the Japanese, who are rightly said to have the strongest "bottom quarter" in the world. It won't be easy. ■

Gerald Grant is the Hannah Hammond professor of education and sociology at Syracuse University in Syracuse, N.Y., and the co-author with Christine E. Murray of Teaching in America: The Slow Revolution, *published by Harvard University Press. His previous books include* The World We Created at Hamilton High *and* The Perpetual Dream: Reform and Experiment in the American College.

PROVIDENCE
OF
GOD SCHOOL
GRADE 2
SR M MARIO
FEB 19 1957

a private choice

T he term "private school" had only recently entered the lexicon of American education at the end of the 19th century. Earlier in the nation's history, few distinctions were made between institutions based on how they were financed and governed. But when the "common school" arrived on the scene, any school that did not fit that mold suddenly seemed different.

Many parents still chose to send their children to private schools, even after states began guaranteeing a free education to all. Private education promised something many families believed a public school could not: the preservation of their religious and cultural identities. Even parents who could afford to send their children to the country's prominent prep schools did so as much to instill enduring virtues as to give them a leg up in life.

For a country perpetually caught between the ideals of pluralism and the melting pot, such motivations have made the history of private education an often tumultuous one. Under those circumstances, what's remarkable is just how much the public schools have learned from private ones.

Parents have long looked to Catholic and other private schools to give their children values along with academic fare.

Photo courtesy of Archdiocese of Chicago

Photo courtesy of Archdiocese of Chicago

Uncommon Values

Throughout the 20th century, parents have provided their children with a private education to preserve the values they feared would be lost in public schools.

I n November 1884, America's Roman Catholic bishops assembled in Baltimore for a series of meetings. They debated topics ranging from the appointment of church leaders to the burial of members of their flocks in non-Catholic cemeteries.

But none of the questions raised at what was called the Third Plenary Council seemed more urgent than how best to educate the next generation.

Public education, the bishops feared, was becoming increasingly secular. Once public school primers had begun lessons on the alphabet with "in Adam's fall, we sinned all."

By Jeff Archer But in the church leaders' judgment, it appeared that many educators saw intellectual and religious development as separate matters. "If ever in any age, then surely in this, our age," the prelates warned, "the church of God and the spirit of the world are in a certain wondrous and bitter conflict over the education of youth."

Thus the bishops decreed that every parish in the country that didn't have its own parochial school would establish one within two years. Catholic parents were not just exhorted, but commanded, to seek out a Catholic school education for their children.

In fact, the ideal of having every Catholic student in a parochial school would never be met. Even at its peak around 1960, the proportion of Catholic children in parochial schools stood at

about 50 percent. But the plenary council's decrees were important for the angst they expressed.

The apprehension was not over academics, which the clergy believed the public schools could readily provide. Above all else, the bishops wanted Catholic children in Catholic schools to instill in them Catholic beliefs and values.

Whether Catholic, Jewish, evangelical Christian, or Muslim, it has largely been such concerns that have led parents to help establish and send their children to private schools. Even where a school doesn't profess a specific faith, it usually holds fast to an explicit worldview.

"Education is inevitably a value-laden enterprise," says James C. Carper, an education professor at the University of South Carolina. "It deals with questions of the nature of the cosmos, of the moral foundation of right and wrong, and of the appropriate roles of men and women. People of goodwill differ radically in their answers to those questions, and so it's extremely difficult for a government institution to package a particular set of beliefs and values to suit everyone."

Not surprisingly then, religion has been one of the few constants in private education—by its very nature, a world of diversity within diversity. In 1999, as in 1900, the vast majority of U.S. students in private education attend religiously oriented schools. And the overall proportion of American children in private schools has remained fairly steady as well, never rising above 15 percent nor dipping below 7 percent.

COMMON CONCERNS

In the nation's early years, privately organized and operated schools represented not an alternative, but the prevalent form of education. The modern sense of the words "public" and "private," in fact, had yet to be formed. The thousands of fee-charging academies that had flourished briefly before the advent of the tax-supported high school were often called "public" because they were seen as serving the public good.

"What counted as public was much less rigidly defined than it is today," says Thomas C. Hunt, an education professor at the University of Dayton. "Instead of public control and support, a public purpose seemed to be what was most important."

That view changed with the rise of the "common school," which not only indelibly affixed the label of "private" to all alternatives, but also gave new impetus for religious minorities to establish their own schools.

Horace Mann, the 19th-century father of state-supported universal education, saw moral instruction as an essential element of the common school. The school system Mann envisioned was one based on a kind of nondenominational Christianity that he believed all Americans could accept.

But not everyone did. Despite the increasing popularity of public education, the 19th century saw the founding of new schools by Calvinists, Presbyterians, and Seventh-day Adventists, to name a few. For some of those faiths, the watered-down religion of the public schools represented too great a compromise. Others recognized an opportunity for their churches to evangelize and serve the broader community through their schools.

No religious minority, however, was more concerned about the tenor of the new common school than Roman Catholics. Though Mann believed the common school espoused a broadly inclusive form of Christianity, in practice it was a distinctly Protestant institution. When students read from the Bible, it was from the King James version.

A generation before the Third Plenary Council, Catholics weren't concerned that the public schools were too secular; they worried they were too Protestant. This clash of values had occasionally boiled over. Riots erupted in Philadelphia in 1844 during a dispute over which translation of the Bible Catholic children could read in the public schools.

The push to set up a separate school system gained steam.

From the very beginning, these new religious schools were met with suspicion. If the common schools promoted unity and patriotism, many public education supporters reasoned, then any other form of schooling was divisive and un-American.

As with the fears raised by earlier in-fluxes of Irish, Germans, and other groups, the turn-of-the-century tidal wave of immigration posed deeply emotional questions about the changing character of American society. Largely because of the newcomers, the U.S. Catholic population grew from about 6 million around 1880 to more than 14 million by 1910. While many political and opinion leaders viewed public education as a way to assimilate the foreign-born into American society, some Catholics saw it as the tool that could destroy their faith and culture.

By then, many Catholics had become more concerned that public education no longer seemed to be stressing religion—Protestant or otherwise. Several legal challenges to mandatory Bible reading in schools had been initiated in state courts, and theology apparently played no role in the nascent progressive education movement.

The turn of the century also marked the founding of many private schools that appealed less to parents' religious values than to their concerns over conditions in the public schools, especially in the cities.

Those in the nation's growing number of upper-income families became increasingly interested in boarding schools. Even more popular among this group were the somewhat less expensive day schools that began flourishing in the first decades of

In 1922, the Ku Klux Klan was part of a coalition that backed an Oregon law requiring all children to attend public school through the 8th grade. The campaign to eradicate private schools in the state was later dashed by the U.S. Supreme Court.

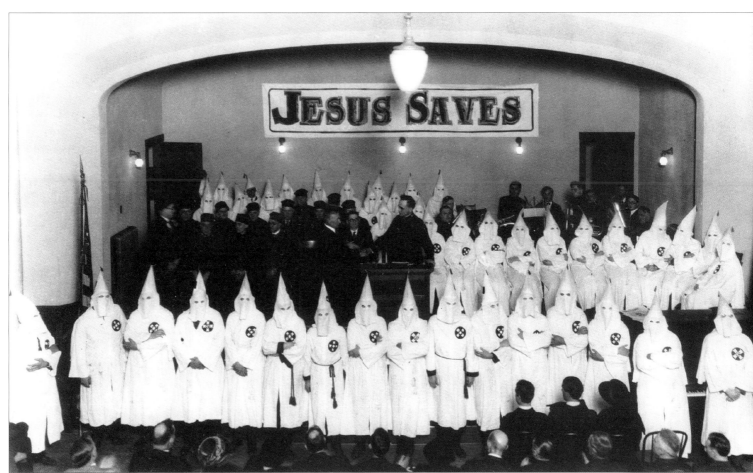

Oregon Historical Society

Corbis-Bettmann

Public school students in San Antonio pray at the beginning of the school day in 1962. Prohibitions against prayer and other religious displays provoked many parents to choose private schools for their children.

the 20th century. Governed independently of any church, many nonetheless did have some religious orientation, such as Quaker or Episcopalian.

While many of the most famous New England residential high schools were established during this time, a handful of older academies—including Andover and Exeter—were transforming themselves from comparatively informal philanthropic ventures into some of the nation's most prominent boarding schools.

LEGAL VICTORIES

Among Protestants, the Germans who founded the Lutheran Church-Missouri Synod were especially adamant about wanting their children's faith and education interwoven. Its founding constitution mandated that member churches operate a school if they wanted to join the synod.

"The Missouri Synod had a great deference for doctrine," says R. Allan Zimmer, a former dean of the college of education at Concordia University in River Forest, Ill. "And in order to teach doctrine, you needed a systematic manner and approach, and a great deal of time."

As important, the synod's schools also provided German instruction. At a time when

most of the group's religious services were held in their native language, it was essential that their children become fluent.

"Culture and religion and language were all interconnected," says the Rev. Jon Diefenthaler, the pastor of Our Savior Lutheran Church in Laurel, Md., who has written on the history of Lutheran schools. "People felt that if their children started speaking English or if they ventured out into the wider world of American culture, critical elements of their faith would be diminished in some fashion."

Many Lutherans never saw the need for separate schools. Still, interest was intense enough that enrollment in Missouri Synod schools rose from about 30,000 in 1872 to roughly 75,000 by 1900.

As fears of foreign influence were kindled by immigration and brought to a roaring blaze by the First World War, those schools found themselves the targets of nativist fervor.

"If you tended to hold on to old-world customs like religion and language, your patriotism could be questioned," says Hunt of the University of Dayton.

The prejudice against foreign cultures seeped into state laws. Around 1890, Indiana and Wisconsin mandated that core subjects be taught only in English in all schools. Both measures were repealed within a few years following intense lobbying by Lutherans and Catholics. Some Catholic schools taught classes in students' native languages, too.

Such victories were quickly forgotten, however, as the Great War brought back the campaign against old-world customs with a vengeance. Nineteen states enacted foreign-language restrictions the year after World War I ended, according to William G. Ross, the author of the 1994 book *Forging New Freedoms: Nativism, Education, and the Constitution, 1917-1927*.

Nebraska passed the so-called Siman Act, which forbade the teaching of any foreign language before the 9th grade.

Some Lutheran schools dodged the measure by teaching German only during extended "recesses." But a teacher named Robert T. Meyer refused to resort to such a subterfuge, and, when a county prosecutor walked in on his class, the educator continued teaching in German. He was convicted and fined $25, about the equivalent of his monthly salary.

At the time, Ross says, rumors abounded of Lutheran students saluting the German flag and singing the German national anthem. In truth, by World War I, many of those schools had largely dropped the use of German.

Meyer lost the fight against the Siman Act in his state's highest court, but his fortunes changed in 1923 when the U.S. Supreme Court ruled that the law violated the 14th Amendment. The justices said it interfered with "the calling of modern-language teachers, with the opportunities of pupils to acquire knowledge, and with the power of parents to control the education of their own."

By suggesting that the U.S. Constitution protected numerous rights not explicitly spelled out in the document, the high court in *Meyer* v. *Nebraska* also set the groundwork for many later civil rights battles. And it laid the foundation on which private schools would win their greatest legal victory.

Throughout the early 1920s, nativist sentiment prompted attempts not just to control the content of private education, but to wipe it out. An unsuccessful campaign to force all parents in Michigan to send their children to public schools took the slogan "One Language, One Flag, One School."

A similar measure narrowly passed as a ballot measure in Oregon in 1922, with heavy backing from the Ku Klux Klan and a coalition of organizations called the Oregon Federation of Patriotic Societies. Throwing his own support behind the measure, Democratic gubernatorial candidate Walter M. Pierce said, "We would have a better generation of Americans, free from snobbery and bigotry, if all children ... were educated in free public schools."

The law required that every child between the ages of 8 and 16 who had not completed the 8th grade attend public school. But far from ridding the state of private education, it brought together religious and secular private schools in a unified opposition. An order of nuns, the Society of Sisters of the Holy Names of Jesus and Mary, joined with a nonreligious military school in mounting the legal challenge.

In arguing *Pierce* v. *Society of Sisters* before the U.S. Supreme Court, lawyers for the state often invoked the prevailing alarm about left-wing revolutionaries. If the law were struck down, they warned, "Bolshevists, syndicalists, and Communists would form schools."

Relying heavily on *Meyer*, the high court ruled that no such fears could justify so great an intrusion by government into family matters. "A fundamental theory of liberty," the justices wrote, "excludes any general power of the state to standardize its children by forcing them to accept instruction from public teachers only." In the ruling's most famous words, the majority declared: "The child is not the mere creature of the state."

CATHOLIC BOOM TIMES

Whether as a result of the Great Depression or the greater disuse of German in classrooms and worship services, enrollment in the Missouri Synod's schools fell to 67,650 by 1942.

In contrast, Catholic education between 1900 and 1960 enjoyed an almost uninterrupted period of growth, during which enrollment exploded from about 855,000 to more than 5 million.

To raise quality, the Catholic hierarchy in the United States decided that some standardization and centralization were necessary in the largely parish-based system. By 1930, nearly two-thirds of the U.S. bishops had set up school boards and superintendencies to oversee their education programs, according to Timothy Walch, the author of the 1996 book *Parish School: American Catholic Parochial Education From Colonial Times to the Present*. The formation in 1904 of the Catholic Educational Association—which added "National" to its name in 1928—further unified parochial schools across the country.

"There was a more concerted effort on the part of Catholic school educators to become observant of what was going on in public education," Walch says. "And as public education professionalized, so did the parochial schools."

Catholic schools generally maintained an academic curriculum for all children, rather than allow some to pursue different tracks as was typical in public high schools by the early 20th century.

"Many immigrant families did not want their children to have vocational education because they saw it as not opening up opportunities, but placing limits on their kids," says Peter B. Holland, a co-author of the 1993 book *Catholic Schools and the Common Good*.

When it came to teaching methods, the schools were short on innovation, though there were a few exceptions, as Walch points out. In the first two decades of the century, Thomas Edward Shields, a professor at Catholic University of America, promoted the John Deweyesque idea that schools should nurture students' comprehension rather than just drill them will facts. But at most Catholic schools, educators remained skeptical, relying more on memorization and drill, at least through 1950.

They also continued to teach from *The Baltimore Catechism*, which came into use as a result of the Third Plenary Council in 1884. Organized as a series of questions with prescribed answers, the book served as the primary tool for teaching children the central tenets of the faith into the 1960s.

The numerous Catholic high schools founded by religious orders were among the most resolute about maintaining a college-preparatory curriculum. Many, such as the Jesuits, saw their secondary schools in part as feeders for their own colleges and universities. Often run without financial backing from the local diocese, almost all were single-sex schools and charged tuition when most parochial schools were financed by donations and parishioner "taxes."

Underlying the rapid expansion of parochial school education—and its accessibility to the children of poor and working-class Catholics—was its cheap source of labor. The tens of thousands of nuns who made up the vast majority of the teaching force in parochial schools received only modest stipends. At the same time, Walch says, the great demand for sister-teachers often made it difficult for schools to release them to get formal training in education. Many younger nuns simply learned the ropes from the veterans at their schools.

Some state governments brought pressure to bear in the 1920s and 1930s when they began applying new teacher-certification rules to public and private schools. Catholic organizations generally supported those measures, seeing them as an opportunity to leverage improvement while also demonstrating to parents that their schools were the equals of those run by the government.

While religious communities responded by establishing "normal schools" for teacher training, and a few dioceses even founded their own programs for preparing teachers, many nuns had to earn their credentials through summer courses.

Space became a precious commodity for Catholics, too, as the country entered the era of the post-World War II baby boom. The U.S. Catholic population jumped from 24 million in 1940 to 42 million in 1960, prompting the construction of hundreds of new parochial schools. The New York archdiocese alone built some 200 schools in the 1950s, according to Walch. Even with the new buildings, the typical class size soared to 50 or more.

Around that time, many Catholics started questioning the rationale behind parochial education. In her 1964 book, *Are Catholic Schools the Answer?*, Mary Perkins Ryan argued that parochial schools had served immigrant families well early in the century, but that by the 1960s, Catholics were clearly part of the American mainstream. By then, the country had put a Catholic in the White House. In short, she argued, the old justifications for a separate school system were gone.

Bolstering that perspective were the results of the Second Vatican Council, a series of meetings of the world's Catholic bishops between 1962 and 1965. The many changes adopted there had the effect of greatly liberalizing the church. For example, local languages largely replaced Latin in the celebration of the Mass, and many orders of nuns modified or discarded their habits. Moreover, Catholics also sought to forge closer ties with other faiths.

"Catholics' consciousness of themselves before that was much more that they were a breed apart," Holland says. "There had been a whole sense of identity and of marking yourself as different. A big part of Vatican II was saying that that's not the most important thing to consider."

At the school level, the Vatican II reforms translated into a new commitment to educate non-Catholics, especially those who are poor, and to experiment with different forms of schooling and methods of instruction, as spelled out in an influential statement, "To Teach as Jesus Did," issued by the U.S. bishops in 1972.

Regardless of this new sense of purpose, Catholic school enrollment began a long and sharp decline, hitting bottom in 1991, when it stood at about 2.4 million. By that point, Catholic schools accounted for only half the private school enrollment in the United States—down from 90 percent in the late '50s. Urban flight played a role, as more Catholic families moved to suburbs where fewer parochial schools existed. So, too, did the rising cost of Catholic schooling, as a growing dependence on lay teachers made the schools more expensive to run.

But the biggest factor may simply have been that Catholic parents no longer saw the public schools as robbing the next generation of its religious identity—or, in the spirit of a more secular age, were less worried by that prospect.

A FUNDAMENTAL SHIFT

Almost as soon as Catholics acknowledged their place in the American mainstream, a growing number of evangelical Christians began seeking alternatives to public education.

The conversion was swift. According to the Association of Christian Schools International, fewer than 350 of its 3,300 member schools were established between 1956 and 1970. More than 1,600 were founded between 1971 and 1985. Enrollment in the group's schools now tops 564,000.

In their 1976 book, *The Schools That Fear Built*, David Nevin and Robert E. Bills portray much of the interest in Christian schools as a reaction to racial integration. Most of the early growth, they point out, occurred in the South just as the public schools were undergoing court-ordered desegregation.

Some of those schools were unabashedly segregationist, most notably those in Mississippi started with the support of the Citizens Council, a grassroots group firmly opposed to integration.

A 1975-76 enrollment application for the council's schools stated that "forced congregation of persons in social situations solely because they are of different races is a moral wrong," according to Nevin and Bills. (In contrast, many of the nation's largest Catholic dioceses publicly declared their opposition to school segregation as early as the 1950s.)

But integration wasn't the only revolution under way. The role of women was changing, and homosexuals were beginning to demand legal protections and social acceptance. Many conservative Christians were especially troubled by the relaxation of sexual mores and the proliferation of drug use.

"It's not just desegregation," says Carper of the University of South Carolina, "but the perceived decline of public education and the turmoil of the 1960s all led many Christian parents to see the world as coming unglued."

To many Christian families, the 1960s also marked the final expulsion of religion from the public schools. Until then, public education still retained enough religious elements to give such parents a "comfort zone," says ACSI's president, Kendall Smitherman, who worked as a public school administrator from 1963 to 1970.

"During the years when I was working in the public schools, as a Christian, there was never the least bit of discomfort in addressing things from out of my own belief system," he says. "Christmas was celebrated with a religious Christmas program. Our parent-teacher organization started their meetings with a prayer. Those things were significant."

But in a pair of opinions handed down in 1962 and 1963, the Supreme Court ruled that prayer sessions and Bible readings sponsored by the public schools were unconstitutional. "The cumulative effect of those two cases was to tell evangelical Christians that school was no longer God-centered," Hunt says.

Having seen the "word of God" squeezed out of public education, evangelical Christians were uncompromising in their treatment of religion in their own schools. Christianity wasn't relegated to one period of Bible study a day, but rather infused throughout every academic and extracurricular program.

"We want something more than simply story problems that insert religion," Smitherman says of math instruction. "Two plus three is still five, but what we try to do is lay out the broader idea that the whole world of mathematics is one more reflection of God as the creator of order."

But throughout the late '70s, many Christian schools felt dogged by the perception that they were segregationist. In 1978, a change in federal tax policy forced many to prove that they didn't discriminate on the basis of race or risk losing their tax exemptions, a move some took as an assault on their independence.

A number of states also stepped up their regulation of private schools, occasionally leading to outright hostility, as when Nebraska in the early '80s padlocked a Christian school and jailed its founder and students' parents in a long-

Rich Janda/Omaha World-Herald

standing dispute over enforcement of teacher-certification rules.

Such actions appear only to have added to the resolve of Christian school supporters. By some estimates, the number of students in evangelical Christian schools grew by nearly 800 percent between 1965 and 1989.

PLURALISM'S NEW AGE

American Jews also have been embracing private education in increasing numbers since midcentury.

Orthodox Jews established their first schools in the United States in the late 19th century. But the movement expanded substantially as Jews fled to North America in the 1930s to escape persecution by Nazi Germany. The schools allowed them to educate their children in a climate that accommodated their strict codes of conduct.

As a result, the number of students enrolled in Jewish day schools in the United States and Canada climbed from 7,700 to 55,800 between 1940 and 1960, according to Alvin Schiff's *The Jewish Day School in America*, published in 1966.

Full-time religious education has more recently begun to spark increased interest among other branches of Judaism.

In 1957, leaders of the Jewish Conservative movement passed a resolution promot-

ing Jewish day schools as a way to ensure "a reservoir of intensely educated and deeply dedicated men and women."

Leaders of Judaism's most liberal branch similarly proclaimed, three decades later, that while they still supported public education, Jewish day schools with a Reform orientation should be established to provide parents with more options.

"This is much more of a coming to, rather than a running away from something," says Rabbi Joshua Elkin, the director of the Partnership for Excellence in Jewish Education, which provides seed money and technical assistance to Jewish day schools. "It comes down to needing adequate exposure to a language, to traditional texts, a system of worship, and a grounding in ethics and appropriate behavior. You just can't give that in two or even six hours a week."

Though the vast majority of Jewish parents in the United States still send their children to public schools, current estimates peg enrollment at about 185,000, some 80 percent of whom are in Orthodox schools.

Some observers say the recent rise in popularity among liberal Jews, however, shows that dissatisfaction with the public schools has risen to a new level. Throughout most of the 20th century, mainline American Jews have been among the strongest supporters of public education,

Students return to the Faith Christian School in Louisville, Neb. Authorities had padlocked the private school in the early 1980s and jailed its founder and students' parents for refusing to follow the state's teacher-certification rules.

Corbis-Bettmann

Even though advocates say home schooling was never actually illegal, some states restricted parents who wanted their children taught at home. Above, a Pennsylvania youngster lobbies lawmakers at the Capitol in Harrisburg in 1985 to gain recognition for the practice.

which they have seen as key to their upward mobility.

Even more recently, the rapid growth of the United States' Muslim population—thanks to immigration and to religious conversion among African-Americans—has spurred the creation of private schools with an Islamic orientation. To many of the families they serve, such schools are not only places that accommodate their children's religious practices, but also havens from what they see as elements of decadence in American society. The number of Muslim schools in the United States has grown from roughly 50 to 180 in the past decade.

AN 'UNDERGROUND RAILROAD'

No other form of nonpublic education, though, has grown as rapidly in recent years as home schooling. Recent estimates of the number of home-schooled children range from 1 million to 1.8 million—up from roughly 100,000 in the early 1980s.

Although most closely identified with conservative Christians, the home schooling movement of recent decades gained impetus from the progressive "alternative" schools of the 1960s and 1970s. One of its most ardent early supporters was free-school advocate John Holt, who had taught in private school. Throughout the 1960s, Holt complained that schools were overly structured and stifled student initiative.

At first, he hoped that open-minded public school educators would embrace his vision of a learning environment in which children's own interests largely directed their work. But he eventually grew skeptical that even alternative schools could go far enough. "He saw that these schools were still just soft jails instead of hard jails," says Patrick Farenga, the president of Holt Associates, the home schooling publisher and information clearinghouse Holt set up before his death in 1985.

In 1976, Holt published *Instead of Education: Ways to Help People Do Things Better*, in which he proposed "a new Underground Railroad to help children escape" from school. A year later, he launched a home education magazine, *Growing Without Schooling*.

Shortly thereafter, evangelical Christians started holding home schooling conferences, and the primary motivation for home education began to shift from the pedagogical to the religious. Some families found justification in what they viewed as the Bible's pronouncements that parents bear ultimate responsibility for educating their children. Others who might have sent their children to a Christian school discovered that none existed in their communities or were unaffordable.

Between the early 1980s and the early 1990s, many states officially recognized the rights of parents to teach their children at home—a practice that some believed had previously been illegal.

Legal skirmishes, nevertheless, continue—though home school advocates say the battleground has shifted. Parents today are rarely told they have no right to home school. Instead, challenges tend to center on whether states are being heavy-handed in their regulation of home schooling. Some parents, for example, have refused to submit curriculum plans to education officials, as required in some states.

Although Christians make up the bulk of home schoolers today, the movement is diversifying.

"It doesn't matter whether the parent is an atheist, or Bahai, or Christian, adults usually think they know what is best to pass on to their children," says Brian D. Ray, the president of the National Home Education Research Institute.

IN THEIR OWN RIGHT

Confident in their ability to instill values, many private schools have seemed defensive about the quality of their academic programs—at least until recently. As public schools added new facilities and course offerings during the first half of the 20th century, for instance, Roman Catholic schools often struggled against the view that their bare-bones curriculum didn't measure up.

But by the 1980s, public education seemed to be losing its edge.

In 1982, sociologist James S. Coleman published the study "High School Achievement: Public, Catholic, and Private Schools Compared." The findings suggested that Catholic schools did more than public schools to narrow the performance gap between rich and poor students. Similar conclusions were offered that same year in research carried out by Catholic priest and noted sociologist the Rev. Andrew Greeley of the National Opinion Research Center.

"What Coleman and Greeley found in their research was that Catholic schools weren't inferior," says the Rev. Richard Jacobs, a Villanova University professor. "At the time, it was astounding. It counteracted the conventional wisdom."

Not everyone was convinced. Some argued that the differences had more to do with the fact that private schools could choose their students. Regardless, those studies and others increasingly opened up the possibility that Catholic schools might actually be better than public ones, particularly in inner cities.

Non-Catholics began seeking out parochial schools for academic, safety, and discipline reasons—in far greater numbers than ever before. Between 1970 and 1988, the proportion of non-Catholics in Catholic schools grew from less than 3 percent to more than 11 percent. Many of the new students were African-American children who partially filled the void created as white Catholic families moved out of the cities. By 1984, more than half the Catholic school students in Detroit, Los Angeles, and New York were members of minority groups.

While the Catholic schools were finding a new source of students, their traditional pool of teachers was shrinking. The number of men and women entering religious life plummeted after the 1960s. Within a few decades, the schools went from faculties that were 90 percent religious to 90 percent lay.

Even though Catholic school enrollments began to rise again after the start of the 1990s, the shortage of nuns has brought new challenges. Lay teachers require more competitive salaries—thus pushing up the cost of running schools. And the rise of all-lay schools is posing a once unthinkable question: How can these schools be sure of maintaining their religious identity?

"The problem now," says Jacobs, "is how are they going to be anything other than just good private schools."

Indeed, the demand for "good private schools," regardless of church affiliation, appears to be on the rise.

The number of day students in schools belonging to the National Association of Independent Schools alone has jumped from fewer than 315,000 to more than 425,000 during the 1990s.

"The independent schools, which used to be particularly immune to societal changes, began to feel some external pressure in my tenure," says John Esty, who led the organization from 1978 to 1991.

"By the end of the 1970s, they were dramatically changing their student bodies to be less white and less affluent. Partly it was because of changes in NAIS policy, but those were also the first inklings of parents' perceiving the decline in the academic performance of the public schools."

For some, those inklings found confirmation in the 1983 report *A Nation at Risk*. While its damning assessment of America's public schools helped prompt a wave of changes in education, it also added to the list of reasons why parents seek alternatives.

For their part, public schools seem more willing to learn from their private counterparts. The arrival of charter schools, magnet schools, and interdistrict-transfer programs within the public system has had the effect of casting private education not as something at the fringe, but as part of a continuum of options.

"In the early 1800s, the line between public and private was very blurred, and then it became very distinct," says Carper, the South Carolina scholar. "Now, I wonder if we are not coming back to a point where we think of the education of the public as being through a variety of means." ■

Public vs. Private

Corbis/National Archives

Many Catholics had high hopes for gaining federal aid when John F. Kennedy ran for the presidency. But early in his campaign, the Democrat declared that no federal money would go to support private schools. Above, photographer Don Phelan and his family watch one of the historic debates between Kennedy and Republican candidate Richard M. Nixon.

As ferocious as today's debate is over private school vouchers, it may be surprising that early in the history of the republic, American religious schools periodically received generous public funding.

By the mid-19th century, however, the great "Schools Question" was tearing at the national social fabric. And decades later, the nation continues to struggle with the essence of that question: To what extent may, or should, the government provide aid to religious schools or their students?

By Mark Walsh

In the early years of the United States, direct government subsidies for private schools, which were virtually all religious in character, were not uncommon. St. Peter's Roman Catholic Parish in New York City began receiving money from the state school fund in 1806, according to *Between Church and State:* *Religion and Education in a Multicultural America*, a 1999 book by historian James W. Fraser. But funding for denominational schools was cut off by the 1820s as the Protestant-dominated Public School Society gained control over the city's public schools.

By the 1870s, though, as their church's influence grew, Catholics were successful in removing Bible reading—usually from the King James version—from the public schools in some cities.

Moreover, the New York Archdiocese was receiving public funds again— $700,000 in 1871, according to Steven K. Green, the legal director of Americans United for Separation of Church and State.

'NOT ONE DOLLAR'

Protestant determination strengthened. In 1875, in what was largely an appeal for the Protestant Republican vote as he eyed a bid for a third term, President Ulysses S. Grant gave a famous speech in which he resolved that "not one dollar ... shall be appropriated to the support of any sectarian schools."

Another Republican who planned to seek the 1876 presidential nomination, Rep. James G. Blaine of Maine, proposed a constitutional amendment that would prohibit the states from allowing public money to "ever be under the control of any religious sect." The Blaine Amendment fell short in Congress in 1876.

"The movement it propelled, however, would prove to be largely successful," says Joseph P. Viteritti, a professor at New York University who has written frequently about public aid to religious schools.

While Congress didn't muster enough support to amend the U.S. Constitution, it insisted for the next several decades that states entering the Union prohibit public aid to religious schools. Several older states also adopted such provisions, and, by 1917, 29 states had Blaine-like language in their constitutions.

"It is one of the great ironies of American constitutional history that the Blaine Amendment, which erupted out of a spirit of religious bigotry and a politics that sought to promote Protestantism in public schools, eventually became an emblem of religious freedom in some states," Viteritti writes.

For example, the federal enabling act that made Arizona a state required a Blaine-like provision in its constitution, and the state's 1910 constitutional convention obliged. In 1999, members of the Arizona Supreme Court vigorously debated the reach of the state constitution's prohibition against public support of religious schools. The court voted 3-2 to uphold a state tax credit for donations to private school scholarship funds that offer tuition aid for religious schools. The U.S. Supreme Court in fall 1999 declined to hear an appeal of that decision.

The great question of public funding for religious schools was quelled somewhat after the defeat of the federal Blaine Amendment. One liberal Catholic prelate, Archbishop John Ireland of St. Paul, Minn., promoted a plan that would have moved Catholic schools and public schools closer together.

Under the so-called Poughkeepsie plan, public school authorities would rent Catholic schools and pay staff salaries for teaching only secular subjects during the regular school day. Religious instruction would be pushed to after-school hours. The archbishop's proposal engendered considerable opposition from conservative Catholics, who, by that time, wanted little to do with the public schools. And only a handful of public school boards, dominated by Protestants, in such cities as Poughkeepsie, N.Y., and Florissant, Mo., were willing to go along with it.

CHILD-BENEFIT THEORY

In the 1920s, the Supreme Court—in *Meyer* v. *Nebraska* and *Pierce* v. *Society of Sisters*—struck down state laws that were anathema to religious schools, whether by restricting language instruction or seeking to force all children into the public system.

A few years later, in 1930, the high court first enunciated the "child benefit" theory of public aid for religious schools in the somewhat obscure case of *Cochran* v. *Board of Education*. In *Cochran*, the court rejected a challenge to a Louisiana law that made textbooks available to children in both public and parochial schools.

The true recipients of the aid were the children, the court reasoned, and it was students and the state that benefited from the appropriation.

States and school districts where Catholics exercised considerable political influence soon began to experiment with new forms of indirect aid. In New Jersey, a state law that allowed districts to pay the transportation costs of all pupils, including those in religious schools, led to the 1947 Supreme Court decision in *Everson* v. *Board of Education*.

The court upheld the law, but its 5-4 decision came in a series of complex opinions. "The court's signal to the nation was less than clear" about what forms of aid to religious schools might be permissible under the Constitution, historian Fraser says.

Many Catholics had high hopes that with the election of John F. Kennedy as president in 1960, the federal government might get involved in aiding parochial schools. But early in his quest for the presidency, the Catholic candidate had to dispel fears that he would promote a religious agenda if he became the first of his faith to win the White House.

"There can be no question of federal funds being used for support of parochial or private schools," Kennedy told *Look* magazine in 1959.

When Kennedy proposed a package of federal education legislation, private schools were left out. It was his successor, Lyndon B. Johnson, who deftly brought together public school groups and religious school leaders in support of the Elementary and Secondary Education Act of 1965, which guaranteed remedial aid for poor children regardless of the school they attended.

Beginning in the late 1960s and continuing into the '70s, a wave of cases dealing with various state plans for aiding religious schools came before the Supreme Court.

The loan of textbooks was—again—upheld. But salary supplements for parochial school teachers, state aid for repairing religious school facilities, tuition reimbursement for private school parents, and the provision of nontextbook instructional materials were among the forms of aid struck down.

In 1985, the court also barred public school teachers from providing federally funded remedial classes on the premises of religious schools. That decision would be reversed a dozen years later by a more conservative court.

TAX CREDITS AND VOUCHERS

Beginning in 1983 with the Supreme Court's decision upholding a tuition tax credit for all parents, including those who sent their children to religious schools, the tide began to shift.

The idea of private-school-tuition vouchers as a market force that might improve public education began with the economist Milton Friedman in the '50s. But in many towns in Maine and Vermont, an early, small-scale version of vouchers called "tuitioning" had been in use for more than a century.

Vermont's tuitioning program, in which towns without high schools paid the private school tuition of their residents, even covered religious schools until 1961, when the state supreme court limited it to secular private schools.

Much larger voucher experiments in Cleveland, Milwaukee, and, most recently, Florida have sparked the latest strife over aid to religious schools. Proponents argue that vouchers that give parents the freedom to choose where to send their children do not have a primary purpose of aiding religious schools. Opponents contend that the money still ends up in the religious school coffers—thus violating the First Amendment ban on a government establishment of religion—and that vouchers will undermine the public school system.

Though the U.S. Supreme Court let stand a ruling that upheld the Milwaukee voucher plan, the justices have yet to weigh in definitively on such programs. Most observers believe the court will take up the issue within the next few years.

Meanwhile, the court in its 1999-2000 term was considering a major case from Louisiana concerning a federal program that provides computers and other technological forms of aid to religious schools. The court has been swamped with briefs, including some that mention the 19th-century war over school aid in New York City, the Blaine Amendment, and the high court's long history of cases addressing different forms of aid.

The nation has not yet resolved the great Schools Question. ∎

A League of Its Own

By Jeff Archer

Andover, Mass.

The crowd had plenty to celebrate as it filed into the gymnasium for the Phillips Academy's 1908 alumni dinner.

The school, better known as Andover after the Massachusetts town in which it is located, had held its 130th commencement earlier that June day under what the local newspaper described as "perfect skies." Diplomas had been handed out to 81 young men, about half of whom were going on to Yale, while most of the rest were headed to Harvard and a smattering of other private colleges. The event capped a year in which Andover beat archrival Exeter in baseball after a sixth-inning comeback.

But when the meal was over, Alumni Association President Henry L. Stimson made a solemn proclamation. Andover, he observed in the annual alumni address, was at "one of those turning points of life in which the entire future of institutions, as of men, lies in the balance."

Schools like Andover, he said, sat between two trends. On one side, the rapid rise of the public high school meant more young men could prepare for college tuition-free without leaving home. On the other, the growth of the nation's universities meant they were no longer cozy places that fostered moral development, but had become purely academic institutions in which students pursued their own interests.

Given that, he asserted, the residential high school remained the one place where young men could learn not just subject matter, but also the values of modesty, democracy, and faith. If "our boys

Andover has undergone dramatic changes in the past 100 years, but the quintessential boarding school has remained true to its mission of building character while preparing students for college.

Far left: The Andover campus today has few equals in physical appearance, academic and extracurricular offerings, and other amenities.

Courtesy of Phillips Academy

Left: Andover has long stressed athletics along with academics. The school's polo program, formed in 1929, was dropped in the 1940s. Today, it offers 30 different sports.

Opening photo by Benjamin Tice Smith

are not to lose this invaluable social training," said Stimson, who would later become the U.S. secretary of state and of war, "it is our schools or at least to some of them, that we must look for its perpetuation."

Although Stimson's speech was ultimately a pitch for donations, the school was indeed at a watershed. Over the next 25 years, the academy constructed a new campus that still easily outshines those of many of the country's most prominent colleges.

At the same time, it built an already outstanding academic program into one that few other schools in the country could match. In doing so, it became what many people now view as the quintessential American boarding school.

Today, Andover remains an institution with few peers. Its 450-acre campus includes art and archaeology museums, an arboretum, and a radio station. The vast majority of faculty members hold graduate degrees in their academic specialties, and its 1,080 students in grades 9-12 enjoy an average class size of 14. But all that comes at a price. In 1999, tuition and board ran $24,500 a year—steeper than what many colleges charge—though 40 percent of students here benefit from one of the largest financial-aid budgets in private education.

Andover enjoys so many advantages that it's easy to judge the school as insular, even irrelevant. To be sure, within the membership of the National Association of Independent Schools, boarding students make up only about 10 percent of total enrollment.

As with higher education's Ivy League, however, the role played by such schools has been a disproportionately large one. Not only have they produced more than their share of influential Americans, they have helped pioneer some of the 20th century's most important educational innovations.

But the boarding school's most distinctive feature is the way it fulfills the twofold mission to which Stimson alluded: building character while preparing students for college. To an exceptional degree for a precollegiate institution, it selects who will attend and sets the boundaries for students' lives 24 hours a day. As a result, a board-

ing school is able to create a total learning environment in a way that no other type of school can.

Certainly the past 100 years have seen dramatic changes in what that environment looks like. The once all-boys and nearly all-white Andover is now half female and 30 percent minority.

But the basic modus operandi remains the same. Says Andover history teacher Anthony Rotundo: "What we have is the

Richard Graber/Courtesy of Phillips Academy

power to create an intentional community, to create a faculty and a student body that in many ways mirror the world as it is, or the world as we would like it to be."

Before 1900, Andover was a much humbler place than it is today. Until then, the school looked and operated much like the thousands of other American academies established in the 18th and early 19th centuries to provide a broader secondary education than did the Latin grammar schools of the Colonial era. Theodore R. Sizer, who later became one of Andover's best-known headmasters, wrote in the 1964 book *The Age of the Academies* that they served "the material hope of getting ahead and the political hope of improving the republic."

The Revolutionary War was still under way when Samuel Phillips Jr. founded Andover in 1778 near the mill he owned about 25 miles north of Boston. An uncle founded the Phillips Exeter Academy in New Hampshire three years later.

Adhering to the democratic ideals of the age, Samuel Phillips believed the new nation's survival depended on the cultivation of knowledge and virtue in its youths. As such, his school stressed both utilitarian-

ism and morals, which in his day had an intensely Calvinist bent. Pledging to serve "youth of requisite qualifications from every quarter," Andover's constitution promises to "learn them the great end and real business of living." Its oldest motto is *non sibi*, a Latin phrase meaning "not for one's self."

With the advent of the publicly supported high school in the late 19th century, however, such academies faced the threat of extinction. A handful, including Andover and Exeter, transformed themselves into modern boarding schools, places with unrivaled educational advantages.

The high school had long been something of a stepchild to the Andover Theological Seminary, which the academy's leaders set up in 1808 to prepare Calvinist ministers. But by the time Henry Stimson gave his prophetic address, the then-struggling seminary had decided to move to Harvard University and sell its land and buildings to the high school. The sale gave Andover the freedom to reinvent itself.

More than half its students—who were generally older than today's—lived in nearby rooming houses. The school's small cluster of buildings, though stately, bore little resemblance to the campus's current expanse.

But the academy quickly underwent a physical metamorphosis. Trustee Thomas Cochran, an 1890 graduate and a partner in J.P. Morgan & Co., donated millions of dollars to the academy and helped shape the vision of a new campus of wide lawns and elm-covered walks that more resembled a liberal-arts college than a high school.

Between 1910 and 1930, the academy completed more than a dozen major construction projects, even pulling some of its older buildings from their foundations and moving them. The completion of new dormitories meant that by 1929, all boarding students could live on campus. The school continued to serve a small number of day students from the town and surrounding communities, as it does still.

Many of the new structures were named for prominent Americans who had some connection to the academy: George Washington, who had sent his nephews there; Paul Revere, who first cut the school's seal; and the writer Oliver Wendell Holmes, who graduated from Andover in 1825. When the makeover was complete, legend has it that a teacher from Exeter, after taking in the new school, exclaimed: "We're beaten! Exeter can never catch up."

But Exeter did quickly catch up as a result of a windfall of donations that allowed it to rebuild its own campus.

Back then, Andover had plenty of competition. The United States between 1880 and 1910 saw the birth of many of today's most prominent New England boarding schools—Groton, Choate, and Hotchkiss among them.

In large measure, those schools owed their prosperity to the impact of industrialization on American society, according to the 1970 book *American Boarding Schools: A Historical Study*, by James McLachlan. The industrial boom of the late 19th century created a new circle of wealthy Americans, and many of them became increasingly concerned about what they saw as the growing squalor of urban America, with its vast immigrant population.

Boarding schools offered those parents a chance to remove their children to more tranquil environs. But such an education also, many hoped, promised to secure their children's place in America's leadership class, much as they believed the prominent English "public schools" like Eton were capable of doing. In the 1930s, one out of every 35 living Andover graduates was in *Who's Who in America*.

At Andover, the growing affluence was somewhat tempered by the academy's long tradition of financial aid. Around 1900, when the school enrolled about 430 students, Andover gave out some 40 scholarships a year.

One of the most successful efforts the school used to recruit needy students was a program that scoured the ranks of the nation's newspaper-delivery boys for qualified applicants.

Still, most students paid full fare, which then amounted to about $310 for tuition and board—no small change at a time when most American families earned less than $1,000 a year.

While the school in the first decades of the century was ethnically more diverse than many other boarding schools, it was still a creature of its time. A few black students were admitted to Andover as early as the 1850s, but some academy officials doubted they could fully benefit from an Andover education. And in the 1920s, the headmaster wrote that "except in very rare instances colored boys ought not to be encouraged to come," according to the 1979 book *Youth from Every Quarter: A Bicentennial History of Phillips Academy, Andover*, by Frederick S. Allis Jr., then a history teacher here.

Jews were admitted in greater numbers than blacks, but they, too, occasionally faced discrimination.

The student-run secret societies, which Andover abolished in the 1950s, rarely accepted Jews, and, as late as the 1930s, administrators said it was important to keep their numbers on campus from growing too large. "Did we totally accept them? No," recalls Osborne Day, a 1939 graduate. "It's a horrible thought, but they weren't invited into the fraternities, even though we liked those guys."

Critics around the turn of the century began accusing boarding schools of being "hotbeds of snobbishness." But those charges belied the mission that schools such as Andover saw themselves as fulfilling, according to McLachlan's book. While the school undeniably served large numbers of boys who were privileged by birth, its goal was to turn them into men who merited their positions on ability.

Indeed, social class received no mention when Andover Headmaster Claude Moore Fuess answered his own question in his 1939 book *Creed of a Schoolmaster*: "What should be our function? I believe it to be the development of character among our students—and character shown, not by the mere avoidance of vice and misdemeanors, but by service to the state."

Andover began acting much like a

Left: "Schools that say they're a sanctuary from the world don't interest me," says Theodore R. Sizer, a former headmaster, who made it his goal to expose Andover's students to life beyond the campus.

Below: Before students ever arrive, "they hear that the whole point is not just about coming here and finding yourself, but about learning to live a useful life, including serving the community," says Barbara Landis Chase, Andover's first female head of school.

Benjamin Tice Smith

Benjamin Tice Smith

Above: Andover went coeducational in 1973, when it merged with nearby Abbot Academy, a pre-eminent boarding school for girls. Girls now make up half the enrollment at Andover, but their numbers are underrepresented in student leadership positions.

Right: The completion of additional dormitories in 1929 meant that young men no longer had to live in rooming houses off campus.

modern college years before its outward appearance resembled one. It was during Cecil Bancroft's tenure as principal from 1873 to 1901 that the school's classics-laden curriculum was expanded to include a greater emphasis on science, English, and modern foreign languages.

Bancroft also oversaw the institutionalization of many extracurricular activities, including baseball and the student newspaper. And he democratized the operations of the academy by parceling out authority to numerous faculty committees.

Its new curriculum in place, the academy set off to build the caliber of its instructors. Alfred E. Stearns, who was appointed principal in 1903, helped raise $1 million from alumni to increase teacher salaries. (The school changed the title of its top administrator from "principal" to "headmaster" while Stearns held the position.)

The educators Andover sought were experts in their fields, not the graduates of mere normal schools. Many were accomplished scholars, having had their own work published in books and academic journals. The academy considered it a significant victory, for instance, when it lured Dudley Fitts away from Choate. Fitts was a renowned poet and a translator of many important works from Greek, Latin, and Spanish.

Faculty members were uncompromising in the academic standards to which they held their students. If it took a mark of 60 to pass, many didn't hesitate to give out a

59. And the school was willing to expel students not just for bad behavior, but for persistently poor performance, as it did in 1918 when it dismissed Humphrey Bogart, the son of an Andover alumnus.

"They were pretty darn tough on you," Day says. "But you knew many were being tough to help you. I think all of us had the feeling they weren't out to try to get you or humiliate you."

As a boarding school where teachers and students interacted round-the-clock, Andover expected its teachers to possess great intellect and be good role models. To this day, many faculty members and their families spend years living with students in the dorms, and all teachers are expected to supervise students outside the classroom in some capacity.

Some teachers seized on any opportunity to emphasize the importance of good character. Day recalls an English teacher who began a discussion about a comedy that dealt with adultery with this reproachful aside: "As if there were anything funny about adultery."

"The teachers kept talking about what's right and what's wrong, and about ethics all the time," Day says. "And there was a sense that even if you didn't believe [in] them, you knew what they were."

Many of the activities outside the classroom also were geared toward reinforcing values.

Attendance at the school's nondenominational chapel services was mandatory. Athletics served the dual purpose of building character and burning up excess adolescent energy.

By filling students' days—morning till night—with chapel, classwork, homework, and sports, Andover sought to instill self-discipline. The intense regimen was seen as doing more to keep the boys out of trouble than the rules spelled out in the school's code of behavior. "These were tough schools, and not just in the academic sense," says Hart Leavitt, an Exeter graduate who taught English at Andover from 1936 to 1975. "They were demanding in many ways."

In 1944, *Fortune* published a seven-page spread on the academy headlined "Andover: A Study in Independence." Lauding the school's top-notch faculty, rigorous standards, and tradition of financial aid, the article posited that "Andover is not particularly a rich boy's school, but it is a rich school and has all the opportunities that institutional opulence has thrust upon it."

In one area, though, the academy appeared lacking, the *Fortune* writer argued. For all its freedom and wealth of resources, the school had contributed little in the way of educational innovations. "Andover's blessings," he wrote, "have induced singularly little pioneering work in either curriculum or pedagogy."

By contrast, Exeter in the 1930s had instituted fundamental changes in its teaching methods by reorganizing classes into seminars.

Soon after the publication of the *Fortune* article, Andover began to show greater willingness to experiment.

One of the school's first innovators was James H. Grew, the chairman of the French department. He believed that high school students could benefit from the same kind of intensive foreign-language instruction that the military had started using. Grew, around World War II, began teaching all his courses entirely in French.

The approach flew in the face of the idea that students should first learn a language's grammar before striving for fluency. While some instructors at first resisted the method, it proved so successful that, within a few years, it was the universal approach toward language instruction at the school.

The academy also helped pioneer a new style of physical education. In the 1950s, Andover teacher Joshua Miner was dispatched to Europe to observe schools modeled on Outward Bound, which used survival skills to foster the traits of resourcefulness and cooperation. After he returned, the sight of Andover students rappelling down the side of the school's 170-foot bell tower became a regular occurrence. Miner went on to promote Outward Bound throughout the United States.

Midcentury also witnessed the birth of what became perhaps the academy's greatest contribution to American education. While the school had always prided itself on providing the best possible preparation for college, by then some Andover graduates felt so well-prepared that the first year of college seemed boring. As recounted by Allis in *Youth from Every Quarter*, John M. Kemper, who became headmaster in 1948, complained

Courtesy of Phillips Academy

that "boys from the best independent schools often find that their early courses in college are repetitious and dull."

A graduate of West Point, Kemper began discussing the problem with the heads of other boarding schools and college officials. Before long, Andover embarked on a study of the transition from high school to college financed by the Ford Foundation. Other participants were Exeter and the Lawrenceville School, along with Harvard, Princeton, and Yale.

The group concluded its work by recommending the development of new tests for determining whether high school graduates could skip lower-level classes at college. In 1954, the first Advanced Placement exams were administered by the College Board, the sponsor of the country's most widely used college-entrance exam.

Since then, the incentive offered by the system has spurred tens of thousands of high schools, both public and private, to establish senior-level courses geared toward the exams.

However influential, the changes Andover underwent until the early 1960s would seem like mere tinkering compared with what followed.

In 1965, Kemper appointed a committee of eight faculty members to undertake a yearlong study of the school and its place in the modern world. The recommendations in the panel's report covered topics from the recruitment of teachers to the updating of facilities. But student life was the aspect of the school receiving the greatest attention.

Re-emphasizing the responsibilities of instructors as role models, the report called for greater interaction between adults and students. The recommendation resulted in a "cluster system," in which the students were divided into groups of roughly 200, each with its own dean and core of faculty members for support.

To render the disciplinary system more humane, the school also shifted its process from one of automatic demerits and reviews by schoolwide panels to one left more to the discretion of each cluster and individual house master. In a symbolic move, the title "house master" was changed to "house counselor."

More significantly, the steering committee recognized that Andover needed to reflect better the world outside.

The academy had a long, albeit sometimes grudging, tradition of accepting African-American youths. But they had not been actively recruited. That passivity changed dramatically in the early 1960s with A Better Chance. The program, created by Andover and 22 other prominent prep schools, identifies promising students from minority and disadvantaged backgrounds and helps them apply to member schools. By 1970, Andover had about 50 black students, up from the

Benjamin Tice Smith

Dean of Studies Vincent Avery, far right, hands out awards to Andover students in the Cochran Chapel, named for one of the school's most generous benefactors.

dozen or fewer accepted 20 years earlier.

About that time, the school also endowed a new need-based scholarship program for foreign students. Ever since, about 10 percent of the enrollment has come from overseas.

Meanwhile, a number of campus traditions were scrapped in an effort to create an environment that welcomed all students as equals. Dining-hall duty and other chores were no longer the sole responsibility of students receiving financial aid; all students were expected to perform them.

Overall, the academy sought to be a less insular place. The school's summer session, which began during World War II to give extra instruction to Andover students about to enter the armed forces, evolved into a much larger program that mostly served public school students.

Starting in the 1960s, students from across the country began to spend several weeks at Andover in intensive study of writing, foreign languages, math, and science.

The academy's course offerings were greatly expanded, and students were permitted to take many more electives than in the past.

New interdisciplinary programs were also created, including an innovative "Man and Society" course, in which students spent a term living and working in either inner-city Boston or rural Mexico.

Theodore Sizer, appointed headmaster in 1972 after serving as the dean of Harvard's graduate school of education, made it his mission to break the academy out of its cloister as much as possible. "Schools that say they're a sanctuary from the world don't interest me," says Sizer, who later wrote the popular *Horace* trilogy on school improvement and founded the Coalition of Essential Schools, a network of public and private schools. "They shouldn't be sanctuaries; they should be institutions which use their extraordinary strengths to stand for things worth standing for, on behalf of everybody, not just themselves."

In 1964, Andover admitted girls to its summer programs for the first time. Despite the policy's success, the move to bring coeducation to the year-round program took nearly a decade.

Many faculty members believed that if they were preparing their students to attend colleges that had gone coed—and to

While pointing out where Andover leaves room for improvement, Dalton adds that she knows of no other boarding school that is working so consciously to find ways to resolve issues of equity between boys and girls. In 1996, for instance, the academy created the Brace Center for Gender Studies, which sponsors research on the role of gender in education.

As fast as Andover was changing in the late 1960s and early 1970s, the pace was not rapid enough for many students. The same unrest that led college students to take over administration buildings and make bonfires with their draft cards ushered in a brief period of turmoil at many boarding schools.

While much of the anger was directed at the Vietnam War and racial inequality, boarding school students more generally showed a willingness to question all convention. Administrators were forced to justify or amend numerous policies regulating student life, and the enforcement of long-standing rules often resulted in brazen violations.

At Andover, the affronts to authority occasionally turned frightening. A crude bomb was discovered, improperly armed, in the school's bell tower in 1971, and an attempt to steal disciplinary records prompted a security guard to fire a shot over a student's head, according to Allis' book. That same year, the administration was presented with a petition declaring a "lack of confidence" in the faculty and staff—signed by two-thirds of the students.

Along with the new danger of illegal drug use on campus, such episodes made it an unnerving time for running a boarding school, says John Richards, a retired history teacher who also served as the dean of students during the unrest. "We were confronted on an almost daily basis with demonstrations and pranks," he says. "I think one of the things that bothered the students the most was the fact that they had no say in school policy, and the faculty wasn't about to give them a say—they still don't."

While Andover refused to hand the keys over to its students, it did respond to their complaints. As headmaster, Sizer didn't favor rules for their own sake. When students broke the prohibition against walking on the school's neatly kept lawns, Sizer said it was OK so long as they altered their paths so as not to wear down the grass.

By the mid-1970s, the demonstrations and other forms of rebellion had sub-

live and work in a coed world—then Andover should be educating both sexes. But the question was how.

One option was simply to start admitting young women, as Exeter had done in 1970. Another was to remain essentially an all-boys school, but to coordinate some programs and classes with the neighboring Abbot Academy, an all-girls residential school that opened in Andover in 1829. About one-third the size of Andover, Abbot had long been recognized as one of the nation's pre-eminent girls' schools.

The route Andover wound up taking in 1973—to merge fully with Abbot—didn't immediately win the unanimous support of either school's faculty. Some Andover teachers voiced concerns that Abbot's academic expectations were not on a par with its neighbor's. And the fact that the unified school would be called Andover was not lost on Abbot's teachers and alumnae.

"Here were two schools, each of which was perfectly comfortable in their own traditions and success," says Jean St. Pierre, an Abbot English teacher who now works at Andover. "But the world was changing, and coeducation was the wave of the future."

The climate of the merged school felt different to many teachers as the hard-nosed competitiveness of Andover melded with the nurturing atmosphere Abbot stressed. "Andover became a more progressive, humane place for kids after that," says Andover history teacher Kathleen M. Dalton, who has written a book about the school's experience with coeducation.

Coeducation also pushed Andover's enrollment past 1,200, making it one of the largest boarding schools in the country. Because the campuses sat side by side, students could walk between them in five minutes. No one was more pleased with the transformation than parents. Between 1973 and 1980, the number of applications from boys increased 50 percent, while those from girls more than doubled.

Though young women now make up half of Andover's enrollment, Dalton says the legacy of the school's all-male past lives on. Girls rarely hold, for example, leadership positions in student government and on the student newspaper.

In 1994, the academy appointed its first female head of school, Barbara Landis Chase, a public high school graduate who had served as the head of an all-girls school in Baltimore. Women now make up half the faculty, but men still chair two-

sided. Also by that time, the school had given up two of its oldest traditions: the dress code and mandatory attendance at religious services. Though virtually all boarding schools felt compelled to adapt to the social currents of the time, Andover was reputed to have gone further than most. Exeter, for instance, still maintains a formal dress code.

The Andover of today no longer conforms—if it ever truly did—to the stereotype of the snobbish blue-blooded boarding school as portrayed in books like *The Catcher in the Rye*. Its immaculate campus of neo-Georgian and Federal brick buildings conjures up images of a buttoned-down past, but the academy's students look much like students anywhere. A few wear ties or other formal clothes by choice, but most prefer the casual wear that predominates on modern college campuses.

When it comes to their work, however, the academy's students are all business. Acting up in class is almost unheard of, and homework typically keeps students up well past midnight.

The school often encourages students in their nonconformity. When the academy held its annual fall art show in 1998, it showcased a fourth-year student's painting of Jesus kissing St. Sebastian on the mouth. Though the work generated controversy, the faculty agreed that the rendition showed tremendous talent and saw no reason to reject it.

"A lot of adults think of boarding schools as being like prisons, and that's just so far from the truth," says Laura Mistretta, a member of the class of 2000. "There are rules here, and you have to abide by them, but one of the major things about this place is the trust they give you. They trust that if you say you're going to be some place, that you will be."

In most respects, the academy has never been more heterogeneous. Eight percent of students are black; 3 percent, Hispanic; and 18 percent, Asian. The school also has set up support programs for gay, lesbian, and bisexual students. One in 10 students is on a full scholarship, and, for many of those, the aid even includes air travel between school and home three times a year. About half of Andover's students attended public elementary schools. By intention, the diversity of the student body has become one of the school's most important teaching tools.

"For me, it hasn't just been about the work or the classes," says Aimionoizomo Akade, another senior who attended a public middle school in Brooklyn before coming to Andover. "It's also been about learning about different people and coming into contact with people who didn't grow up like you. You don't have people from Hong Kong living in Brooklyn."

Yet more than half its families still pay full tuition and board. And even with a $7.5 million financial-aid budget, the school's admissions process is not completely need-blind. Each year, a handful of qualified students are denied entrance for no other reason than their inability to pay.

While serving "youth from every quarter," Andover doesn't yet mirror American society as a whole.

But perhaps the most significant privilege enjoyed by Andover's students is the variety of its academic and extracurricular offerings. The academy boasts 30 different sports—from tai chi to Nordic skiing—as well as an observatory, a symphony orchestra, and a state-of-the-art electronic film-editing studio. Its course listings include four-year programs in nine foreign languages and seminars on topics ranging from Victorian England to nuclear-weapons proliferation. Classroom instruction often is augmented by lectures from visiting heads of state, Pulitzer Prize winners, and Nobel laureates.

This feast of opportunity is largely what continues to attract families, despite a base tuition more than three times what it was in 1981, when it stood at $7,200 a year. (Since the 1980s, hikes have been closer to the inflation rate.) The increasing competitiveness of college admissions has meant that the academy can no longer promise that nearly all its graduates will go on to the Ivy League. But it can guarantee that virtually any interest will find fertile soil here.

While the new deference to students' individual preferences may attract parents, some have worried that this trend among boarding schools may go too far. In a 1996 essay, "The Strange Fate of the American Boarding School," David Hicks, a former rector of St. Paul's School in Concord, N.H., complained that such institutions were becoming "deconstructed." While their tough regimen once was aimed at producing idealistic future leaders, the essay argued, modern boarding schools seem more concerned with letting young people find themselves.

As Hicks wrote, enrollment patterns did suggest something was amiss in the boarding school world. The number of

boarding students in America had fallen by nearly 10 percent over the previous decade, even as enrollments in independent day schools had risen dramatically. The decline would have been even greater were it not for a sudden increase in the number of foreign students. All that led Hicks to warn that the boarding school was "an endangered species of the independent school genus."

Andover officials say the academy does not fit the unflattering portrait painted in Hicks' essay. Unlike some other boarding schools, Andover hasn't had to increase its percentage of foreign students or day students to maintain enrollment. And admissions at Andover remain as competitive as ever. The average scores of its students who take the Secondary School Admissions Test—an entrance exam used by many private schools—rank at about the 90th percentile.

"I don't think it's any harder to say we believe in honesty, in justice, and in compassion—those things are human values," says Chase, the head of school. "From before the first moment they arrive, they hear that the whole point is not just about coming here and finding yourself, but about learning to live a useful life, including serving the community."

Undeniably, though, the academy has recently entered a period of readjustment. The dorms were remodeled to increase the number of adults living with students. Rules on residential life were tightened somewhat. Students were promised more intensive advising. And in its most radical move, the academy committed to becoming smaller, reducing enrollment from about 1,225 in 1992 to about 1,030 by the 2000-01 school year.

"I think the school had grown very complicated, in its diversity and in its many offerings," says Jane Foley Fried, Andover's dean of admission. "We still want to be able to offer double-dutch rope jumping for some kids, but when you do all that, you need to find ways that kids can make sense of it all."

The recent changes appear to have pleased parents. Since 1992, the school's so-called yield rate—the proportion of accepted students that actually enrolls—has climbed from 60 percent to nearly 70 percent, akin to a gold standard in today's competitive market.

By all appearances, then, Andover's future is as bright as ever. The school in 1999 launched a $200 million capital campaign, an amount double the size of its current endowment and ranking as the largest fund-raising drive in private school history. The money will shore up financial aid and teacher salaries, while also paying for facilities improvements, including the construction of an Olympic-sized hockey rink.

Most think the school, which is older than the U.S. Constitution, will be here 100 years from now. If they're right, one thing is almost certain, especially if the past century offers any lesson. To keep fulfilling its promise of building character while providing superior academic training, Andover will have to keep responding to shifting circumstances, deciding which parts of the outside world to let in and which to keep out.

"The real thing," says Chase, "is deciding what it is that you're never going to change, but also what you *are* going to change to keep meeting your mission." ■

Famous Andover Alumni Of the 20th Century

Philip K. Wrigley, class of 1915, chewing gum magnate and Chicago Cubs owner

Courtesy of Phillips Academy

Benjamin Spock (center), class of 1921, child-rearing expert

Walker Evans, class of 1922, Depression-era photographer

Lyman Spitzer, class of 1931, astronomer who designed the first telescope-bearing satellite

Ring Lardner Jr., class of 1932, Hollywood writer

Harlan Cleveland, class of 1934, U.S. ambassador

Robert W. Sarnoff, class of 1935, president of NBC

Robert C. Macauley, class of 1941, founder of relief agency AmeriCares

Courtesy of Phillips Academy

George Herbert Walker Bush, class of 1942, 41st president

Jack Lemmon, class of 1943, Academy Award-winning actor

Otis Chandler, class of 1946, *Los Angeles Times* publisher

Alexander B. Trowbridge, class of 1947, U.S. secretary of commerce

Frank Stella, class of 1954, abstract artist

A. Bartlett Giamatti, class of 1956, president of Yale; baseball commissioner

Tracy Kidder, class of 1963, Pulitzer Prize-winning author

Courtesy of Phillips Academy

George W. Bush, class of 1964, governor of Texas

Jeffrey K. MacNelly, class of 1965, Pulitzer Prize-winning editorial cartoonist

James Shannon, class of 1969, U.S. congressman

John Ellis "Jeb" Bush, class of 1971, governor of Florida

H.G. "Buzz" Bissinger, class of 1972, Pulitzer Prize-winning journalist and author

Dana Delany, class of 1974, television actress

Courtesy of Phillips Academy

John F. Kennedy Jr., class of 1979, *George* magazine publisher

Reflections on a Century Of Independent Schools

A perspective by Arthur G. Powell

During the 1930s and '40s, astute leaders of influential nonpublic preparatory schools campaigned with some success to change the popular designation of their institutions from "private" to "independent." In Depression-era America, the word private had negative connotations. High-tuition, high-Protestant schools emphasizing college preparation were classic examples. The word independent emphasized the safer virtue of freedom. It focused on the autonomous boards of trustees by which prep schools were typically governed, and thus on the schools' independence from bureaucratic external control. The new label proved appealing to most leaders of these schools even though, confusingly, many public school districts were also called "independent."

But a vocal minority of private school leaders actively opposed the word independent. They were proud of being private. More to the point, they believed the independent designation was highly misleading. Just because schools were governed by boards of trustees didn't make them truly independent. They were dependent on their boards' preferences and money, on parent wishes, on college-entrance requirements, and on the wisdom of state governments to avoid crippling regulation of curriculum and teacher licensing. Although many schools celebrated their isolation from the wider society—they were walled gardens, in one headmaster's memorable phrase—these dissenters knew independent schools were creations of a powerful segment of American society, and not immune from influences of the larger culture.

In the second half of the century, the boundaries between independent schools and American society became far more permeable. In important respects the schools became even less independent than they had been. State intrusiveness increased, federal regulation grew beyond the wildest imagination of any pre-World War II school head, and vulnerability to lawsuits became a permanent source of anxiety. Above all, the students changed. Not just in the sense of increased racial and economic diversity, although this was substantial, but perhaps more important in the sense of values and expectations.

Unimagined affluence in the hands of youth, the liberating power of numerous modern psychologies of development and growth, and the tremendous educative influence of the youth-culture industry delivered by the new mass media all forced schools to take greater account of student preferences. Schools lost authority as students and their parents became familiar with the roles and rights of consumers. These consumers became the "market" with which schools had to communicate and which they had to understand, and—in the end—please. By century's end, it was possible to discern in independent school literature a pragmatic conception of accountability based mainly on the idea of the satisfied customer.

So independent schools today operate very much in the real world, exposed to many of the main currents of American life. Most no longer are exotic places, as most surely were as late as the early '60s. Still flourishing then were single-sex schools, formal relations between teachers and students, strict dress codes, required religious observances, overwhelmingly white student enrollments, girls' finishing schools, and the image of boarding school as the quintessential independent school experience. Today most of these signature features have been downgraded or abandoned, because the schools and their market sought to eliminate the social exclusivity they implied. In many respects, the prep schools now resemble affluent public schools without vocational education.

Shorn of their most exotic features, what remains most distinctive about independent schools? The answer is other traditional characteristics, which have proven to be perfectly in tune with

Prep schools became more mainstream and respected not only because of what they abandoned, but also because of what they retained.

the needs of public school reform in the century's last two decades. The prep schools became more mainstream and respected not only because of what they abandoned, but also because of what they retained. (The softening of religiosity in Roman Catholic schools had the same general effect. The discovery that Catholic school characteristics might help advance public school reform could occur precisely because formerly contentious religious features of those schools withered away.)

At the heart of the realization that independent and other private schools have a constructive message about school improvement is a national end-of-century consensus about the central problems reform should address. One problem is weak academic standards—for all students during the years when it seemed the Japanese and Germans would "defeat" us economically, and for poor and minority students in more recent times when the first position is less tenable. A second problem is how to reduce the isolation of young people from healthy adult interaction and supervision.

The independent school story in these two areas can be quickly sketched. To combat poor student performance, they urge higher expectations, more requirements, and more focused institutional missions. To combat impersonalism and student anonymity, they urge smaller schools, smaller classes, and greater personalization. To combat apathy or resistance and to encourage commitment, they urge various versions of school choice. To combat youth's increasing disconnection from adults, they urge strengthening schools as communities and extending their reach to students' out-of-class lives. To combat teachers' and principals' feelings of professional impotence, they urge school-site management and greater within-school decentralization of decisionmaking.

By and large, this story is powerful and instructive. School reform today embraces most of its elements, from highly visible successes like Central Park East Secondary School in New York City to the explosive charter school movement. Even reformers suspicious of excessive decentralization, who prefer standards to be set outside individual schools, find the independent school story applicable. Throughout this century, independent schools have relied heavily on standards set outside themselves—the prewar College Boards, the postwar SATs, and especially Advanced Placement. External examinations of the right sort can legitimize and make accountable schools' work with critical constituencies such as knowledgeable parents and college-admission officers.

But to tell only this one story would miss the larger point that independent schools can inform thinking about school improvement in less well-known ways. Perhaps their least-told important story—because it is not sufficiently problematic to enough Americans—concerns the distinction between the independent schools' heavy emphasis on *academic achievement* and their much weaker emphasis on cultivating *enduring interests of mind*. The latter aim celebrates reflective intellectual life, which lies at the heart of all school encounters with the liberal arts. Interests of mind suggests *activity* broadly concerned with ideas voluntarily engaged in mainly for the pleasure and satisfaction of the activity itself. Activity includes doing things where the doing or its result is readily visible to others—making a watercolor, writing a letter to the editor, leading a family discussion about some public issue. Activity also includes the less visible, more private inner lives of people—what they think about, talk about, read, watch, and listen to. Activity can mean goal-directed projects, such as solving a problem or puzzle. But it may equally mean activity with no tangible end product except the enjoyment of the activity.

All too often, in observing independent schools over two decades, I came upon evidence that this sort of educational objective was weakly valued and nurtured. Here's but one example. A small group of juniors loudly argued in their school cafeteria about the causes of the Civil War. Some other juniors wandered by, observed the raging debate, and proclaimed their puzzlement. "Why are you talking about this *here*?" they asked their classmates. "We're not in class anymore."

If these advantaged schools are not unusually welcoming toward the life of the mind, it is hard to imagine schools less advantaged and independent from mass culture being so.

The onlookers were perfectly willing to discuss the causes of any war in class or through homework essays. They cared about good academic performance just as much as did the cafeteria conversationalists. After all, this was an independent prep school. Doing academic work was part of the school's ethic. What perplexed the observers was that a few peers cared enough to continue the conversation beyond the classroom—when they didn't have to and when they weren't being watched or assessed. It never occurred to them that an academic obligation could become voluntary, pleasurable, and enduring.

I have long believed that independent schools should nurture lifelong intellectual curiosity and passion as a primary mission. They should be, as David Riesman once argued, a countervailing force against prevailing cultural mores hostile to the life of the mind. If they are ever to be aggressively independent in any one area, it should be in this one, where they can capitalize on their unique advantages of economic privilege, academic orientation, and historic association with the liberal-arts tradition in higher education. Some do this, but most do not. It is worth exploring why this is so. If these advantaged schools are not unusually welcoming toward the life of the mind, it is hard to imagine schools less advantaged and independent from mass culture being so.

Their attitude is not a recent one. Independent schools have not fallen from a former golden age of intellectual enthusiasm. Academic achievement has always trumped intellectual engagement, because the results of academic performance have important short-term consequences on college admission. The long-term results of intellectual engagement are notoriously vague and hard to measure. No incentives exist to assess long-range school effects, especially in such areas as mental habits and activity. Further, academic studies have often been justified to independent school parents on grounds of their practical utility, rather than by their capacity to deepen understanding of the world and the human condition. It's not the *substance* of these subjects but the general *skills* derived from them that educators usually celebrate—problem-solving, critical thinking, and the like. Even the recent enthusiasm for "understanding"

as an educational aim tends to define understanding primarily in the narrow, pragmatic, and scientific sense of being able to "apply" ideas to new situations. The capacity and interest to dig deeper into an idea gets short shrift.

Moreover, the central goal parents have had for independent schools throughout the century is neither academic nor intellectual, but what is usually called character development. That the meaning of character development has changed considerably, along with the means of bringing it about, is less important than the tenacious resilience of the general idea. The dream of transforming a student in the sense of values (especially values distant from the life of the mind) and behavior toward others is what created most independent schools and sustains them still.

Especially in the first half of the century, religion, team sports, and even academics were considered character-building mainstays (the latter because they taught discipline and perseverance in the face of difficult and often unpleasant tasks). Later on, the idea of character development became more specialized, professionalized, and programmatic. Psychological and therapeutic approaches supplemented and often supplanted religious ones. Decent character became defined almost as much by what it sought to prevent (low self-esteem, substance and other abuses, intolerance) than by what it stood affirmatively for (kindness, honesty, altruism). It is easy to understand why schools invest large sums on workshops addressing chemical dependency and nothing for weeklong immersions on the future of Russia. Our absorption with mental health and happiness is an understandable fact of modern life, and will expand in all schools according to available funding. But given limited resources, it is another obstacle to emphasizing interests of mind.

One more long-term independent school circumstance must be considered. Over the century such schools have had to figure out how best to serve a student population of very diverse academic capabilities, but where most students are college bound, all parents are paying the same high price, and all deeply believe their children to be special in one way or another. To put it mildly, an emphasis on intellectual culture has not proven effective in dealing with this fundamental pedagogical problem. Independent schools know how to

Independent schools know how to increase the academic performance of average students through a combination of personal attention and strong work expectations. But they have no comparable success in instilling a love of learning in students who are not especially talented academically.

So they try another tack. They commit themselves to providing opportunities where virtually any worthwhile interest can be discovered. Intellectual pursuits become only one of many school offerings. Schools assume that every student has the potential to do something well. The job of the school is to help students find that something.

Despite their small size, independent schools are under great pressure to mount additional programs and expand facilities—the arts and sports are current examples. It is no accident that they have been heavily influenced by Howard Gardner's ideas about multiple intelligences. Instead of seeing his ideas as diminishing intellectual values, they regard them as liberation from narrow educational ambitions. They validate a broader curriculum and teaching style in which every student can find success. If privileged parents insist that prep schools help all their children discover something they are good at, it is not hard to imagine the same impulse soon present in all parents. The effort to maximize human potential thus places the topic of enduring intellectual interests further back on the burner.

independent schools into American society has also exacted a price. It has increased, I believe, the barriers that prevent them from becoming more ambitious educationally. In particular, they overemphasize short-term academic achievement for short-term ends.

In so doing, I admit, they usually satisfy their immediate constituencies. Yet I wish they were less afraid of being called "elitist," a wonderful word

Arthur G. Powell's latest book is Lessons From Privilege: The American Prep School Tradition *(Harvard University Press, 1996). While director of the Commission on Educational Issues of the National Association of Independent Schools between 1978 and 1990, he was the senior author of* The Shopping Mall High School *(Houghton Mifflin, 1985).*

Over the century, but especially since the 1960s, independent schools have become much less independent from political and cultural influences. They have lost most of their exoticism, and are less exclusive, snobbish, elitist, and *different* than they once were. Most are proud of these changes. And one undeniable advantage is that their central remaining traditions stand out. These are of constructive use to the ongoing public school reform debate. That is good for all schools and for independent schools.

But the mainstreaming of

that to them now suggests, unfortunately and incorrectly, the taint of social superiority rather than the constant aspiration for intellectual excellence.

Genuinely elite schools do not just ape conventional high-end school reform (technology and multiculturalism are current enthusiasms). They relentlessly pursue the cultivation of enduring interests of mind. This ambitious goal, even if undertaken against the odds, best justifies their oft-stated ambition to be private schools with public purposes. They should rediscover the proud and democratic dimensions of elitism. ∎

SCYLLA OR CHARIBDIS?

who's in charge?

A merican education grew up from the community outward. From Colonial times onward, local citizens built the schools, raised the money, hired the teachers, and chose which books to use. They also elected local leaders to oversee the job.

The process was often fractious, and more players have entered the fray in the 20th century. The voices of elected board members and their constituents have been joined by a discordant chorus: a new breed of education professionals, the courts, the federal and state governments, teachers' unions, and advocates for a host of other competing groups and interests.

Meanwhile, new legislation and rules have spawned bureaucracies and moved decisions further from local communities. The result is what the historian David B. Tyack calls "fragmented centralization."

Today, that system is under challenge from market-based approaches as Americans once again ask questions about who controls their schools and how they are run.

As this 1915 American School Board Journal *cartoon shows, school boards have long struggled to balance many conflicting interests.*

Illustration reprinted from The American School Board Journal, January 1915

Reprinted from The American School Board Journal, January 1915

Pulling in Many Directions

Governing America's schools involves a hodgepodge of competing local interests and—increasingly—intervention from the states and Washington.

By Lynn Olson

Before the 20th century, education was a decidedly local affair. The young American democracy, which had grown up in opposition to the hierarchies of Europe, operated on the simple premise of keeping government limited and close to home. Local citizens decided whether to have schools, raised the money, hired the teachers, and chose which books to use. They also elected lay leaders, in the form of local school trustees, to oversee the job.

That made eminent sense for a widely dispersed, overwhelmingly rural population, in which education lasted eight years at best, schools had to be within walking distance, and raising funds for even a single one-room schoolhouse was a struggle.

But since then, the voices of school trustees have been joined by a cacophony of players on the education scene: the courts, the federal and state governments, teachers' unions, and groups representing racial and ethnic minorities, women, the disabled, and others.

Policymakers have responded with a raft of laws and regulations that have spawned new bureaucracies and removed decisions further from local communities.

The result, according to Stanford University professor Michael W. Kirst, is a "political system with everybody and nobody in charge."

It's messy, untidy democracy writ large. And while it's a system that makes no one very happy, there is no unified view of the alternative.

"We're in a big muddle, as we always are," says Paul T. Hill, a professor of political science at the University of Washington. Indeed, school governance seems to be pushing and pulling in contradictory directions simultaneously.

THE RISE OF THE EXPERT

On one hand, education governance has never been so centralized: From the state capital come academic standards, tests for every student, and accountability systems that reach down into individual schools. At the same time, states are experimenting with such decentralized, market-driven approaches as charter schools, vouchers, and tuition tax credits.

"I believe that governance is the cutting edge of school reform in America today," says Donald R. McAdams, a member of the Houston school board. "It is not a silver bullet, but without it, it's very difficult to do anything else right."

Writing about the history of American education in 1919, Stanford professor Ellwood P. Cubberley reflected on "how completely local the evolution of schools has been with us."

"Everywhere," he observed, "development has been from the community outward and upward, and not from the state downward."

Some states had as many as 45,000

local school trustees. In many rural counties, noted one writer, there were more than 100 districts, some not more than two miles apart.

Rapid industrialization and a swelling populace, however, soon put a strain on this organically grown system of school governance. As high schools became a permanent fixture of public education, small, rural districts struggled to pay for them. In cities, the large number of local school trustees invited graft and other corruption.

Reformers contended that board members elected by wards advanced their own, parochial interests at the expense of the larger school system. In some cities, an excessive number of subcommittees made it difficult to get things done. In 1905, Philadelphia had 43 elected district school boards with a total of 559 members. The Cincinnati school board had 74 subcommittees.

Many of those elected, lay leaders were immigrants, small-business owners, and other members of the lower-middle and working classes. In contrast, those seeking to change the governance structure typically represented the business and social elites and a new cadre of university-trained education professionals.

"Our American school systems are thoroughly 'of the people, for the people, and by the people,'" Cubberley wrote. "This is both their strength and their weakness. They are thoroughly democratic in spirit and thoroughly representative of the best in our American development, but they also represent largely average opinion as to what ought to be accomplished and how things ought to be done."

'ABOVE' POLITICS?

The solution, he and others asserted, was to operate schools more like industry. Inefficient, one-room districts would be eliminated or "consolidated" into larger jurisdictions. ~~In the cities~~ smaller school boards ~~com~~ ~~ment~~ citizens, would ~~~el~~ ., to whom the b~ · d deleg~ ~e amounts of auth~

B~ ~. ~decentr~ ~control, and elin ~ ~ ~ ~~ yısm and patronag~ ~ ~~pant, such a system would p~ education "above politics" and leave its guidance to experts.

The historian David B. Tyack dubbed this model the "one best system." And it would dominate education for the first half of the 20th century.

"If you see the way the reformers talk about democracy," he says, "they talk about the schools being an instrument of democracy run by apolitical experts, with authority in the hands of those who really represent the interests of the children of the United States." But, he adds, in reality it has been impossible to divorce education from politics: "The question isn't whether politics, but whose politics."

A 1927 study showed that the newly centralized boards in urban districts were composed heavily of upper-class professionals and businesspeople. In St. Louis, after reforms were adopted in 1897, the proportion of professionals on the board jumped from 4.8 percent to 58.3 percent, and representatives drawn from big business rose from 9 percent to 25 percent. In contrast, small-business men dropped from 47.6 percent to 16.7 percent, and wage earners from 28.6 percent to none.

It was a model, notes Jerome T. Murphy, the dean of Harvard University's graduate school of education, that served the growing class of education administrators well. "If they could argue that they were 'above politics,' then it gave them much more influence to do the kinds of things that they thought needed to be done," he says. "I'm not making the argument that this was any sort of diabolical plot. But they just subsumed under their authority lots of things that no longer are assumed to be technical questions of expertise."

DISTRICT CONSOLIDATION

By 1930, the reorganization of urban school governance was largely complete.

Between 1890 and 1920, Tyack points out, the average size of school boards in large cities declined from 21 to seven members. Sometimes, a small contingent of reformers secured statutes or charters from state legislatures that reorganized urban systems without any popular vote.

In contrast, the consolidation of thousands of rural districts was a much slower, more painful process—one that, in many ways, continues today. The people, after all, liked their schools. Although the push to consolidate one-room districts began in 1900, it didn't gain much momentum until the Great Depression, and didn't really accelerate until after World War II.

In 1897, a committee on rural education of the National Education Association recommended a thorough reorganization of school districts. Between then and 1905, some 20 states enacted legislation authorizing and encouraging districts to consolidate. Even so, by 1917, the United States had an estimated 195,400 school districts, compared with fewer than 15,000 today.

In those days, state education departments were typically small, sometimes only two or three people. Their work was primarily confined to gathering statistics, preparing reports, rallying public support for education, and distributing what little state aid there was. In 1890, California's entire education department consisted of the superintendent, a deputy, a statistical clerk, a textbook editor, a textbook clerk, and a porter.

The rise in state power and the shift toward consolidation picked up steam with the Depression. By 1933, local financing—which accounted for about 80 percent of school support—was in a sham-

Below: As U.S. commissioner of education, Harold Howe II was put in charge of implementing many of the new federal education programs passed in the 1960s, including the Elementary and Secondary Education Act of 1965.

Corbis/Bettmann-UPI

Corbis/Bettmann-UPI

In September 1968, members of the United Federation of Teachers in New York City voted to strike on the first day of the school year to demand reinstatement of teachers transferred from the Ocean Hill-Brownsville district.

"Without question, American school reform is being led at the state level."

William J. Moloney
Colorado Commissioner
of Education

bles in many districts.

States stepped in to pick up the pieces. Between 1930 and 1940, state support for public education increased from 17.3 percent of the total to 29.2 percent. By 1950, it was 39.8 percent. Today, state funding for K-12 education makes up, on average, the single largest component of local school budgets.

MANDATES FROM ON HIGH

With state support came state oversight. In 1915, only five states had adopted a minimum teacher salary, for example. By 1930, 15 had, and by 1955 the number had risen to 34 states. Even so, local decision-making retained its pre-eminence until midcentury, when several events would propel both the states and numerous other players more prominently onto the education stage.

After the 1950s, local control of education would remain sacrosanct in theory, but was significantly curtailed in practice. The U.S. Supreme Court's 1954 decision in *Brown* v. *Board of Education of Topeka* led to the desegregation of previously segregated school systems. The decision immediately made the court a powerful player on the education scene. It also threw the established practices of local school boards and administrators into doubt.

Then, in 1957, the Soviet Union launched Sputnik I. Americans worried that the nation was slipping behind internationally, in part, because of shortcomings in the schools. The following year, Congress passed the National Defense Education Act, which provided federal money to promote better math, science, and foreign-language instruction in the schools.

In the 1960s, the civil rights movement and the Great Society-era anti-poverty campaign led to a torrent of education-related legislation in Congress, including the Vocational Education Act of 1963, the Civil Rights Act of 1964, and the Elementary and Secondary Education Act of 1965.

"The legislative branch for the first time in our history has assumed in the 1960s a major voice in American educational policy," wrote James D. Koerner in his 1968 book *Who Controls American Education? A Guide for Laymen*. Since the Soviet launch of the tiny satellite, he observed, the U.S. Office of Education had nearly tripled in size. "No longer an obscure bureau that cab drivers can't find," he quipped, "the Office of Education now has plenty of 'visibility.'"

In 1930, the federal government provided only 0.3 percent of public school revenues. By 1960, the federal share of school spending had increased to about 4 percent. And by 1965-66, to about 8 percent.

Harold Howe II remembers stepping in as the U.S. commissioner of education in December 1965, during those first, heady days of federal largess. "I picked up at the point when the [ESEA] legislation had been passed but nothing had been done," he recalls. Writing the regulations and distributing the money according to them, he says, was a complicated undertaking. "It really meant building a whole new bureaucracy in Washington and in the districts of the country. But we pulled it off, and we got it going."

While state officials fretted that federal activism would usurp state authority in education, the new initiatives contributed to the growth in state government. Before the 1960s, state education departments often were viewed as weak links in the education system, lacking the manpower or the expertise to play a dominant role. As Koerner noted, the states were "better in pushing from the rear than in marching boldly out in front."

The ESEA would change all that. As part of the good-government reforms of the 1960s, the act encouraged better-managed and -staffed state departments of education. It required state agencies to approve local projects that requested federal aid. And it set aside 1 percent of federal funding specifically to strengthen state education agencies.

With the influx of cash and federal mandates, the state agencies swelled. The number of people employed in them doubled between 1965 and 1970, to 22,000, according to the Education Commission of the States. In states such as California, the expansion was financed almost wholly with federal money.

Moreover, the proliferation of federal programs was mirrored at the state level. By the early 1980s, 20 states administered their own bilingual education programs, and 16 had programs for compensatory education for poor students. States also spent six times as much as the federal government on educating students with disabilities.

At the local level, parallel bureaucracies to administer the new programs flourished. In large urban districts, the bureaucratic staff increased faster than the teaching force. In the mid-1950s, there was an average of one professional administrator for every 18 teachers in the big urban systems. By the late 1970s, the ratio had shrunk to one for every 12.

OTHER VOICES, OTHER DEMANDS

At the same time, the social militancy of the '60s swept through the schools. Suddenly, everyone was fighting for a voice and for an equal opportunity to succeed in America. In the schools, such activism took the form of separate advocacy organizations for racial and ethnic minorities, children with handicaps, and other interests. Teachers were becoming more militant as well. In the 1950s, teachers began to employ such tactics as labor strikes and work stoppages to improve their salaries and working conditions.

In 1960, the United Federation of Teachers led a one-day strike to demand a collective bargaining election for New York City's 43,500 teachers and then went on to win the election in December 1961.

The ensuing publicity led to huge increases in the national membership of the American Federation of Teachers, of which the UFT was the largest local affiliate. Soon after, the rival National Education Association embraced collective bargaining and more forceful labor tactics. The number of strikes nationwide escalated, reaching 131 in 1969-70. Where school boards could not meet the demands for higher salaries, they bargained over work rules, from class size to the use of classroom aides.

In New York City and other urban centers, minority groups—frustrated with the slow pace of integration and the failure of urban schools to improve—demanded community control. If they could not create a common school for all, they would create separate schools that were more responsive to their needs.

One of the most infamous—and influential—fights occurred in New York City. In May 1967, the Ford Foundation announced that it would provide the financial backing for three experimental school districts, in the Bronx, Brooklyn, and the Lower East Side of Manhattan, to be carved out of the regular school system. The idea was to give parents and other community leaders in those pilot districts a greater say over principal selection, school programs, and other education policies.

From the outset, the historian Diane Ravitch points out in her 1974 book *The Great School Wars*, the authority granted to the pilot districts was unclear. In early 1968, their governing boards drew up a position paper that demanded, among other authority, total control of all money, the power to hire and fire all school personnel, and the authority to contract for the building and rehabilitation of schools. In some cases, the New York City board of education had never promised such power, Ravitch writes. In other cases, the shift in authority would require a change in state laws.

By April 1968, state legislators in Albany were on the verge of approving a decentralization plan. But it fell far short of the pilot districts' demands.

An unsuccessful attempt in one of the three districts, Ocean Hill-Brownsville in Brooklyn, to oust teachers who were deemed unsupportive of the project— and the ensuing fight over decentralization—provoked a bitter struggle with the United Federation of Teachers that culminated in a series of citywide strikes in the fall of 1968. Race, and allegations of racism, were never far from the surface. The union was overwhelmingly white; the governing board in Ocean Hill-Brownsville was overwhelmingly black.

"I think it really set back the schools terribly because you ended up with, first of all, wariness and conflict among people who really needed to be cooperating and collaborating to improve the schools," says Sandra Feldman, who is now the president of the AFT. Feldman, then a UFT field representative, was involved in efforts to set up the pilot districts, and later helped negotiate a decentralization law in the state legislature.

"You had schisms and anxiety between parents and teachers," she recalls, "between principals and teachers, between superintendents and school boards. And then, we lost any sense of a citywide curriculum, which we had before. That was totally dismantled."

Finally, in April 1969, the legislature passed a decentralization bill. Some 30 community school boards, which until then had been purely advisory, were given much more power, including the ability to select principals and superintendents. The pilot districts were dissolved, and the fight for community control dissipated.

Based on her research, Marilyn Gittell, a professor of political science at the City University of New York, who had served as a consultant to the Ford Foundation, argues that parents in the pilot districts felt more empowered and positive about the schools as a result of community control. "I think it had a profound influence on the country as a whole," she says. "I don't think people remember how schools excluded parents, and I think Ocean Hill-Brownsville blew that open."

But she admits that, with the exception of Chicago, community control has remained more rhetoric than reality. In 1988, the Illinois legislature's Chicago School Reform Act gave parent-dominated councils at every school in the city the power to hire and fire the principal, approve a school-improvement plan, and allocate anti-poverty funds.

Feldman is less positive about the legacy of community control in New York. "I think it imploded because it was really divorced from substantive school improvement efforts," she says. "It was purely a fight over power and governance. It had nothing to do with what it takes to improve schools."

EROSION OF LOCAL CONTROL

By the late '70s and early '80s, some observers were cautioning that the large number of pressure groups in education and the increasing tendency of the courts and the state governments to step in were seriously undermining local control.

In a 1979 book, *Legislated Learning*, Arthur E. Wise warned about the rise in centralized, bureaucratic authority. Collective bargaining by teachers, the demands of special-interest groups, and increased litigation on matters from school finance to desegregation, he wrote, were shifting the locus of control over schools and colleges to the state. The result, he cautioned, would be an "incremental bureaucratic centralization" that was neither flexible nor desirable.

Wise predicted that the winners in that struggle would be elected and appointed officials associated with general government, such as mayors, state legislators, and governors. The losers would be local school boards, teachers, and ordinary citizens.

In 1982, Thomas W. Payzant became the superintendent of the San Diego Unified School District, the second-largest in California. He remembers his surprise at

AP/Wide World

Above: In the 1980s and '90s, states began assuming a greater role in local education issues. In Kansas, citizens packed a January 1993 hearing of a state Senate committee to protest a new accreditation system that they believed strayed too far from basic academics and usurped local control.

Right: In 1988, the Illinois legislature passed a law creating local school councils for each Chicago school as part of an effort to shift decisionmaking away from the central office. In November 1989, council members were sworn in during a ceremony at the University of Illinois at Chicago.

learning that the system had one full-time and one part-time employee representing the district year round in Sacramento.

"That was new to me," he says. "And then, I very quickly learned that in terms of governance ... that's where most of the decisions get made. Local school districts really had to have a major presence in Sacramento and be very much a part of the legislative debate in order to make the case for schools."

Moreover, the most aggressive policy-making on the part of states was yet to come. In the early 1980s, concerns that the United States was falling behind economically spurred a renewed bout of educational policymaking. At the same time, court rulings overturned the school finance systems in 18 states and set the stage for more aggressive state control of education.

Once again, business leaders pushed for improvement, as they had early in the century. But this time, they were allied more with governors and state legislators than with education professionals.

Between 1982 and 1984, more than 200 state-level commissions on education were formed as part of efforts to improve the schools.

And soon, state after state passed omnibus reform packages that addressed everything from the number of course credits required to graduate to the pay and qualifications of teachers. In 1984, Kirst, a former president of the California state school board, complained that the state education code's five volumes were so thick they would "sprain the back of almost any adult who tried to lift them."

Many of the new state initiatives were aimed at the core of instructional policy: what should be taught, how, and who would teach it.

That trend has become even more pronounced in the 1990s, as states have set standards for what students should know and be able to do, devised tests to measure their progress, and begun to hold schools, students, and educators accountable for results.

"From a local school district's standpoint, this development on the standards front should be viewed as good rather than bad news," argues Gary K. Hart, who served in the California legislature for 20 years and is now the state secretary of education. "If a state has a system of standards-based education that is clear and precise, people know what the rules are, and the system has credibility, I think there will be growing pressure for the state to get out of the rules-based business."

A COUNTER-MOVEMENT

Today, Americans are closer to a centralized system of governance in education than their forefathers could likely have imagined. The president of the United States has promoted federally supported national achievement tests (albeit voluntary) in reading and mathematics. Even such strong local-control states as Colorado now test students in the core academic subjects and threaten to penalize districts that are not up to par.

"Without question, American school reform is being led at the state level," says William J. Moloney, the Colorado commissioner of education. "It is being led not by educators, but by elected officials, by governors, by legislators."

"Although much of the public expresses support for the concept of local control," adds Ron Cowell, who served in the Pennsylvania legislature for 24 years, "it's that same public that goes to state capitals and demands that state officials 'do something' to fix the education system."

But while centralization has squeezed the system pretty hard in the past 20 years, it has also generated a counter-movement. The same states that are threatening to take over local districts are also reducing and consolidating their education codes, promoting the creation of charter schools, and permitting families greater freedom to choose public schools. Such policies are meant to increase flexibility and choice in education and to create competition that will spur schools and districts to improve.

They're also based on the recognition that individual schools can't be held accountable for results unless they have real control over day-to-day decisions such as staffing and budget allocations.

Eighteen states now have open-enrollment policies that allow parents to send their children to any public school in the state.

Thirty-six states permit the creation of charter schools. And states such as Arizona and Iowa provide tuition tax credits to help parents cover the costs of K-12 education, whether their children attend a public or a private institution.

A few states also are experimenting with vouchers to increase the educational options available for poor children, in particular. In Cleveland and Milwaukee, low-income parents can receive state-financed tuition vouchers to send children to the private or parochial schools of their choice, with the money following the child. In 1999, the Florida legislature agreed to provide vouchers to students in academically failing public schools.

In several cities—notably Chicago, Cleveland, and Detroit—mayors have been given more direct control of the public schools, rebuffing the traditional notion that education is, or should be, "above politics."

"I think the choice movement has put a lot of pressure on the existing system to change," says Terry Moe, a professor of political science at Stanford University and an advocate of the use of market forces in education. "We're getting more magnet schools, more open enrollment, more charter schools. In another 10 or 20 years, things will look very different because the power structure is being nibbled to death."

CHALLENGE ON ALL SIDES

Some worry, though, that in the rush toward market or quasi-market forces,

public education will lose its concern with the common good and focus too much on individual ends. They also worry that inequality in educational opportunities will increase and that permitting each school to do its own thing will result in a lack of standards.

What both the accountability movement and the parental-choice movement have in common is a focus on individual schools as the locus for change and improvement in education. Chester E. Finn Jr., the president of the Thomas B. Fordham Foundation, argues that standards-based improvement efforts and competition-based innovations are mutually reinforcing.

Competition and choice put additional pressure on the existing system to improve, he says, and provide for the creation of new and different schools when existing ones cannot meet the standards.

On the other hand, virtually all advocates of school choice agree that well-informed consumers and comparable data are necessary for the marketplace to thrive. Most also acknowledge that schools must make their standards and results public. "Thus," Finn writes, "we shouldn't be surprised to see a hybrid strategy appearing in many places."

In 1999, for example, the National Commission on Governing America's Schools, appointed by the Education Commission of the States, recommended two alternative approaches to school governance.

The first approach would build on the existing framework, but clarify the roles and responsibilities of those within the system. States and districts, for example, would focus on establishing clearly defined goals for schools and districts, and

providing them with the resources, tools, and supports they needed to succeed.

Most schools would still be directly operated by local districts, but they would have more autonomy and flexibility— such as writing their own budgets and allocating resources as they saw fit—in exchange for greater accountability.

Under the second model, districts would no longer directly run schools. Instead, districts and "chartering boards" would contract with independent entities—such as nonprofit and for-profit organizations, sole proprietorships, and cooperatives—to run schools, in much the same way they now do with charter schools.

Districts would reward schools that fulfilled the requirements of their contracts and withdraw funding from those that did not, but the central administration would essentially be reduced to a contracting agency.

"With the current governance system, good schools are going to remain the exception," argues Adam Urbanski, a member of the commission and the president of the Rochester (N.Y.) Teachers Association, an affiliate of the AFT. "We're looking for a governance system that would make good schools the norm."

In some ways, the tumult in school governance that's occurring now resembles that of the 19th century, when a wide mix of public and private schools competed to provide educational services.

"What you're seeing is a monolithic education system being challenged from every angle," Murphy of Harvard says. "And I think that kind of turbulence that's being created in the short run feels as if it's a bad thing, but in the long run, it's a good thing." ∎

Bill Stamets/Catalyst

Financial Burden Shifts

In 1900, when the town of Stow in eastern Massachusetts was paying Josephine Newhall the less-than-princely sum of $323 to teach three grades for one semester, the townspeople more than likely picked up the tab.

At the time, schooling was largely considered a community responsibility, and Stow and towns and cities like it all across the United States shouldered nearly 80 percent of the costs of educating their young citizens. Massachusetts, chipping in a meager 15 percent on average, was no different from most states.

How times have changed.

By
Debra
Viadero

Over the decades to follow, states began to bear a larger proportion of schooling costs. The shift has been so complete that, by 1978, state and local governments shared equal portions of the costs of education. Each side now picks up roughly 45 percent of the tab. The federal government, a newcomer in the school funding mix, pays about 7 percent of K-12 education costs.

It's a trend that is here to stay. With concerns on the rise about making school spending fairer and more equitable for all children, state and federal governments will likely be asked to assume even greater shares of costs in the next century.

In Stow, as in most Massachusetts communities, citizens had assumed financial responsibility for their schools since the 1600s, according to Madelyn Holmes and Beverly J. Weiss, who document the town's educational history in their 1995 book *Lives of Women Public Schoolteachers.* And, as late as the 1870s, when Miss Newhall was just beginning her career, teachers boarded with townspeople and taught in one-room schoolhouses built with the sweat and the pooled resources of local families.

But education changed dramatically as the 20th century dawned. Compulsory education laws in most states were drawing more students to schools. Families were moving from farms to cities, making it easier for children to attend school regularly. Established school systems were building high schools for the first time. And immigrant children were showing up at schoolhouse doors in record numbers.

GLARING INEQUITIES

To meet the demand, state aid to schools increased 1½ times from 1900 to 1915, according to a 1960 school finance textbook. But local support outran it, more than doubling over the same period. And the story was much the same over the next 15 years.

It quickly became apparent, however, that rapid, uneven growth was leading to some striking inequities in school spending. Wealthier, more populated communities, able to generate more property-tax dollars, could afford to spend more to get better schools. Rural communities often just scraped by.

In Arkansas, for example, the highest-spending school districts were devoting 20 times more to education than the lowest-spending communities in 1940, according to one midcentury text. Such spending variances led many states to establish "minimum foundation programs," beginning in the early 1920s. Those were formulas that set basic funding levels for schools, resulting in some substantial increases in education spending.

But state governments did not decisively enter the funding picture until the 1960s and 1970s, when a string of lawsuits forced them to do so. The lawsuits argued that minimum school funding was not enough, and that to give every student an equal shot at schooling, districts had to spend equal amounts of money.

The precedent for those suits came in *Serrano* v. *Priest*, decided by the California Supreme Court in 1971. The decision, based on the equal-protection clauses in the federal and state constitutions, opened up new legal channels for equity advocates in many states.

THE STATES STEP IN

A major side effect of that burgeoning equalization movement was a significant increase in state spending on schools. "The only way you could really start equalizing across districts with different levels of property wealth was to use states' larger revenue-raising capacity," says James W. Guthrie, a professor of education and public policy at Vanderbilt University.

At the same time, state governments, buoyed in part by new infusions of federal money, were just beginning to come of age, says Allan R. Odden, a professor of educational administration at the University of Wisconsin-Madison.

"The machinery of state government, which hadn't been able to handle the tough issues before, began tackling education, welfare reform, and health," he says. "The whole scope of government action expanded, and education was a frontal piece for a lot of that attention."

The federal role in that expansion was also crucial. Long a bystander in most education matters, the federal government in the mid-1960s, as part of President Lyndon B. Johnson's War on Poverty, enacted a wide range of programs requiring or pushing states to do more to serve their neediest, most challenging students.

Title I programs for poor children sprang up along with Head Start services for disadvantaged preschoolers. A new federal special education law passed in 1975 required schools to provide a "free, appropriate education" to children with disabilities.

While growing, federal dollars still subsidized only a small fraction of education costs. But federal mandates and financial incentives began to drive more and more state spending.

A new wave of finance lawsuits in the 1990s has forced yet another re-examination of school funding practices. "We're not satisfied with equal dollars now," says Guthrie. "The whole challenge now is to make them adequate." States are being forced to figure out how good is good enough when it comes to academic performance—and how to pay for it.

Each of these waves of equalization litigation has, in the end, resulted in progress. School finance experts say funding gaps within states have narrowed considerably since the turn of the century.

But while there has been improvement within states, "we haven't addressed the main problem, which is the vast disparities that are interstate," says Richard Rothstein, a research associate at the Economic Policy Institute, a Washington think tank.

In a forthcoming report prepared for the Century Foundation, a New York City-based philanthropic group, Rothstein points out that even after adjustments are made for regional cost differences, the richest district in the poorest state spends less than the poorest district in the richest state.

Some experts say that evening out those differences may, in the end, mean a greater role for the federal government. But the fierce tradition in the United States of local control of schools likely means that any greater federal control over school spending won't happen without strong opposition. ∎

A New Breed of Professional

By Bess Keller

When a former student and colleague sought an affectionate nickname for Ellwood P. Cubberley, the Stanford University professor who would become one of the century's most influential educators, the young man chose "Dad." The name stuck, and from about 1903 to his retirement in 1933, "Dad" was how Cubberley was known to his students.

The teacher and scholar had no children of his own, but he fostered the careers of two generations of school administrators. In fact, Cubberley helped create the profession. In large part as a result of his work, administration parted ways with teaching, growing into a separate field.

Cubberley, the founding father of a profession, was paternal in other senses, too.

Though hardly remarked on in his day, his views were riddled with assumptions about the natural superiority of men like himself—white, Anglo-Saxon, native-born—and the American society they had shaped. In practical terms, the reforms he and his circle spurred helped ensure that women would largely remain the workers in a system managed by men.

Born just after the Civil War in the tiny town of Andrews, Ind., the future leader attended the local public schools and helped out at his father's drugstore. Because his high school lacked a year of the required four for admission to college, Cubberley completed a college-preparatory program at Purdue University.

He was cool to his father's plan that he attend the pharmacy school there, but it was not until he heard David Starr Jordan, the president of Indiana University, lecture on "The Value of Higher Education" that he set his own course. Cubberley entered Indiana University with Jordan as his adviser. During his senior year, Cubberley ran the stereopticon lantern that often enlivened Jordan's public lectures. Handsome, friendly, and hard-working, the physics major made a good impression.

After a year's interruption to teach at a one-room school near his hometown, he earned his degree in 1891. Jordan successfully recommended him for a science teaching position at a small Baptist college and a little later for a similar position at Vincennes University, also in Indiana.

After two years as a professor there, at the age of 25, Cubberley was named president of the institution.

In 1896, once again thanks to his mentor Jordan, the young college president moved up to become the superintendent of the San Diego public schools. Probably without knowing it at the time and still thinking of himself as a scientist with a particular interest in geology, Cubberley not only changed jobs, he also changed the focus of his professional life from then on.

BUSINESS AS A MODEL

His two-year tenure in the California district was not smooth, and it left the former college president with a strong sentiment against "politicized" school boards and elected school officials.

Already an enthusiastic student of biological evolution, Cubberley concluded that a similar process was at work socially. The existing social order was therefore the product of an objective process that weeded out maladaptive arrangements. Further, in the face of massive immigration and labor unrest, the urgent mission of the schools was to win the day for solidarity and the American way of life while preparing individuals for their differing destinies by class.

Reflecting the temper of the times, Cubberley was also enamored of "business efficiency." He believed that the best way to achieve efficiency in education, as in business, was by building a multilayered organization headed by experts.

"Cubberley had an intensely hierarchical view of leadership," with little room for decisionmaking by teachers, write David B. Tyack and Elisabeth Hansot in their comprehensive 1982 account of public school leadership, *Managers of Virtue.*

Craving a wider scope for his talents, Cubberley in 1898 accepted an appointment to Stanford University, which was then headed by his old mentor, Jordan. Though he had never taken an education class and had no advanced degree, Cubberley became the second professor in the new education department, with orders to make the field respectable or face closing up shop.

The energetic and organized Cubberley not only saved the department, he also remade himself into a fit head for it, earning master's and doctoral degrees at Teachers College, Columbia University, during leaves from Stanford. At the same time, he began to formulate a program for the "scientific" study of school administration and met other educators who were to form his intellectual circle.

WIDESPREAD INFLUENCE

Entrenched school bureaucracies and the "tracking" of students in high schools have their roots in the successes of Cubberley and others in the informal network of academics, foundation leaders, and urban school superintendents that held the greatest sway in American education from about 1910 to 1930. Like Cubberley, many of them attended graduate school at Teachers College early in the century.

In time, Cubberley became a renowned author and consultant, carrying his message of social improvement to the nation. In the midst of public lectures, teaching, and scholarship, he found the time to propose and edit the first widely used series of education textbooks—106 of them, 10 written by Cubberley. And he published in 1919 what for many years was the standard history of American education, *Public Education in the United States.*

In California, Cubberley's influence was widespread. Eventually stepping up to dean of the education school at Stanford, he advised on professional and policy matters, and he helped dozens of graduates find jobs through personal connections—a power one observer likened to that of New York City's Tammany Hall politicians.

Much of that activity was profitable, and Cubberley invested well. He enjoyed a comfortable life with his wife, Helen, provided for her after his death in 1941, and gave more than $360,000 to his beloved Stanford University for a new building to house the school of education.

The leadership ideal that Cubberley held and embodied was, in Tyack and Hansot's term, "an educational Teddy Roosevelt"—charging up the San Juan Hill of ignorance one minute, gracious to women, children, and subordinates in the next.

The image, however, cannot comfortably stretch to cover non-European men, or lay people, or women, and the dean led the way in disparaging the very electoral processes that were most likely to bring outsiders to the decisionmaking table.

Cubberley's influence was profound for a half-century, but by the 1970s, his outlook and many of his ideals seemed hopelessly outdated and undemocratic. What education historian Lawrence A. Cremin called the "wonderful world" of Ellwood P. Cubberley had dimmed at last. ■

The Evolving Federal Role

I t was a moment steeped in symbolism. President Lyndon B. Johnson stood before the one-room schoolhouse in Stonewall, Texas, that he once attended. Flanked by his former teacher at the school, he signed into law the Elementary and Secondary Education Act.

That action, on April 11, 1965, was a watershed in the evolution of the federal role in American schooling, a turning point both in sheer dollars—by some estimates, federal K-12 spending tripled between 1964 and 1966—and influence on districts nationwide.

By Erik W. Robelen

"I will never do anything in my entire life, now or in the future, that excites me more, or benefits the nation I serve more ... than what we have done with this education bill," the president proclaimed two days later in a White House ceremony.

Historians credit Johnson, himself a former teacher, and his administration with a masterful performance in navigating the legislation through Congress. "In an astonishing piece of political artistry, the Congress had passed a billion-dollar law, deeply affecting a fundamental institution of the nation, in a breathtaking 87 days," wrote the historian and former Johnson aide Eric F. Goldman in 1968. "The House had approved it with no amendments that mattered; the Senate had voted it through literally without a comma changed."

Today, the federal government's involvement in precollegiate education is complex and still evolving. While many agencies run programs that assist schools and children, the U.S. Department of Education is the flagship, largely because of its stewardship of the ESEA. Even so, as much as Washington's role has grown and spending has climbed, the federal share of funding remains small in comparison to that of states and school districts. Currently, only about 7 percent of education expenditures for schools come from federal coffers.

In securing passage of the ESEA, Johnson had capitalized on the momentum that followed his landslide victory in the 1964 election, which brought with it larger Democratic majorities in both the House and the Senate—including a big increase in the number of liberals in Congress. He made federal education aid a top priority for his Great Society legislative agenda in 1965.

Many obstacles had long stood in the way of broad-based federal aid to precollegiate education: Southern lawmakers who feared it would compel them to end segregation, Roman Catholic school advocates who opposed any aid that excluded private schools, teachers' unions that insisted that federal dollars go only to public schools, and conservatives who believed that more federal money would inevitably mean policy intrusions into what was essentially a state and local concern.

The first of those obstacles had largely been surmounted a year earlier with the passage of the Civil Rights Act of 1964, which, among other provisions, outlawed racial discrimination in schools and other institutions that received federal aid. As for the other roadblocks, the Johnson administration wove a delicate tapestry

Curbis/Bettmann-UPI

On April 11, 1965, outside the school he once attended in Stonewall, Texas, President Lyndon B. Johnson signs the Elementary and Secondary Education Act into law. Seated next to him is his first teacher, Katherine Deadrich Loney. The ESEA dramatically expanded federal aid for K-12 education.

that brought unions and Catholic representatives together around an education proposal that was essentially an anti-poverty program, a critical component of the president's War on Poverty.

While earlier proposals typically involved general aid or plans to support school construction and teacher salaries, Johnson's solution was to abandon that

approach in favor of a "categorical"—or targeted—program for Title I of the ESEA, the law's centerpiece. Funding was aimed at concentrations of disadvantaged children, regardless of whether they attended public or private schools.

The ESEA represented "the first really direct reach into [all] school districts in the United States," says the man charged with implementing the new law, Harold Howe II, the U.S. commissioner of education from 1965 to 1968.

The law committed the federal government to a bold new role in promoting educational equity—helping the most needy in society—that remains a central focus of federal involvement in education.

THE ROAD TO 1965

Even in the 1960s, the debate over federal support for schools was hardly a new one. From 1870 to 1890, Congress considered a variety of bills on providing general aid to schools, but none of them became law. Similar attempts to provide general federal aid continued for much of the 20th century.

That is not to say the federal government had no involvement in schools prior to 1965. In fact, the roots of the federal role predate the U.S. Constitution. The Land Ordinance of 1785 specified that proceeds from the sale of a portion of land in every township established in the Northwest Territories be set aside for public schools.

After the Civil War, the federal government required that new states admitted into the Union provide free, nonsectarian public schools. The first federal "department of education"—which was later renamed the Bureau of Education and then the U.S. Office of Education before assuming its current status—was created in 1867, just two years after the war between the states ended. By the turn of the century, the office was still largely occupied with gathering and disseminating national statistics on education.

The first significant step toward a new federal role in schooling came with passage in 1917 of the Smith-Hughes Act. The law provided the first categorical federal aid to schools; in this case, it was grants to support vocational education programs. Though historians view the law's passage as something of a turning point, they note that it would be decades before Congress approved anything else like it.

President Franklin D. Roosevelt

pushed through a few emergency measures during the Great Depression that delivered some aid to schools, most of it to be used for school construction and teacher salaries. The New Deal's Civilian Conservation Corps and its National Youth Administration provided some money for educational purposes.

Several aid programs for areas affected by federal activities were enacted during and after World War II, beginning in 1941 with the Lanham Act, which provided federal payments in lieu of taxes to local school districts affected by the military mobilization. In 1950, two other laws were passed that provided school construction and operating-cost grants, or "impact aid," for schools in areas where federal acquisition of property decreased local tax revenues and increased school enrollments. In fiscal 2000, impact aid funding totaled $910 million.

Separately, in 1944, Congress had enacted the GI Bill of Rights, which dramatically expanded access to higher education by helping millions of World War II veterans attend college.

In 1946, the federal school lunch program was launched, followed by the school milk program in 1954. The two initiatives, operated by the U.S. Department of Agriculture, continue to subsidize meals for millions of schoolchildren nationwide.

SERVING THE NATIONAL INTEREST

It was the Cold War that provided the impetus for one of the most significant steps toward more active federal involvement in schools.

In October 1957, the Soviet Union stunned the United States when it successfully launched the first man-made satellite, Sputnik I, into orbit around the Earth. The National Defense Education Act, passed the next year, was a response to widespread concern that America had fallen behind its Communist rival in the contest for scientific, technical, and military superiority. The law provided specialized aid to improve mathematics, science, and foreign-language instruction in schools and colleges.

The act "demonstrated that, under certain circumstances, Congress could enact a major aid-to-education bill," wrote the congressionally established Advisory Commission on Intergovernmental Relations in a 1981 report. The law proclaimed: "The national interest requires ... that the federal government give assistance to education for programs which are important to our national defense."

In their 1968 book *ESEA: The Office of Education Administers a Law*, Stephen K. Bailey and Edith K. Mosher call the NDEA an "important harbinger of the kinds of federal support for American education that blossomed in the mid-1960s." Even so, they observed that the law was fairly narrow in scope. "And even within its own limited domain, the act tended to strengthen superior and wealthier secondary schools. ... Poorer schools in the countryside and in the urban ghettos were left largely untouched."

It was really not until President Johnson stood before his former Texas schoolhouse that federal education aid and involvement, though fixed in a targeted program, were set in place for K-12 schools on a scale comparable to today's.

Of course, the ESEA was only the beginning. John F. Jennings, the director of the Center on Education Policy and a former longtime aide to congressional Democrats, argues that the 1965 law was "the landmark ... that paved the way" for an increasingly large federal presence in education policy. Laws were created over the next decade to assist various special-needs groups through the Bilingual Education Act, the Native American Education Act, the Education for All Handicapped Children Act (later renamed the Individuals with Disabilities Education Act), and other new programs. Separately, in 1965, the Head Start program for early-childhood education was created, and the Higher Education Act was enacted.

Even so, deep philosophical differences have persisted over whether federal activism in education is wise or proper. In fact, a domestic priority for President Ronald Reagan when he took office in 1981 was to curtail sharply the federal role in education and to abolish the fledgling Department of Education. The Office of Education had been split off from the Department of Health, Education, and Welfare and promoted to Cabinet-level status two years earlier, during the Carter administration.

Reagan's plan, however, never won enough support—even in the Republican-controlled Senate—to succeed. The department saw more attacks when Republicans took control of both chambers of Congress in 1995, but those efforts also failed.

President Reagan also sought to reduce federal education spending—which had climbed steadily during most of the 1960s and 1970s—and to lump large portions of aid into block grants to states.

Ultimately, funding did drop somewhat in inflation-adjusted dollars in the early 1980s, but the trend has been reversed in recent years. Although some consolidation of programs occurred in 1981, the underpinnings of the ESEA and other major K-12 programs enacted since 1965 remained intact.

It was during the Reagan years, some observers say, that the federal government's "bully pulpit" role in encouraging educational improvements came into its own. The signal event was the 1983 release of *A Nation at Risk*, the report of a commission created by Secretary of Education Terrel H. Bell, which helped drive a movement to improve schools and spurred a national dialogue on education standards.

Many observers also point to the 1989 "education summit" in Charlottesville, Va., as a pivotal moment. President George Bush and the nation's governors—including one of the most influential participants, Gov. Bill Clinton of Arkansas—agreed to set national education goals. In 1994, with Clinton now in the White House, Congress passed his Goals 2000: Educate America Act, which provided federal aid to help states devise their own academic standards, define achievement, and create aligned assessments to measure progress toward their academic goals. The same year, Congress embedded the standards-based reforms into the reauthorization of the ESEA.

Questions about the ESEA's effectiveness also fueled a new emphasis on results and educational progress.

According to Marshall S. Smith, who was acting deputy secretary of education in 1999, the federal government has become increasingly aware of the need to help lead the way to better schools. "It's a clear change in the way people thought about the use of federal finances," he says. "It was there to leverage, to stimulate change, to support state reforms ... and still with a big focus on the poorest kids in the country."

But Education Department programs continue to draw critics. Many Republicans, in particular, propose handing states and school districts far more flexibility in spending federal dollars as long as they demonstrate achievement gains among all students.

"[I]t is time to rethink the federal role in education," Rep. Bill Goodling, R-Pa., the chairman of the House Education and the Workforce Committee, said in fall 1999 as his committee prepared to approve such a plan. "Federal money should be focused on helping children and their schools, not on maintaining separate categorical federal programs."

The debate serves as a gentle reminder that the federal role is not fixed. As Carl F. Kaestle, a professor of education and history at Brown University says, the federal role has grown substantially over time, "but it's had a fairly bumpy ride and is fairly fragile." ∎

No Easy Answers

Swinging back and forth between local control and central authority, Detroit's schools have reflected both the history of the city and trends in governing urban schools throughout the century.

By Caroline Hendrie

Detroit

Shortly after slipping into the driver's seat of the Motor City's schools, Detroit's newly created school board came close to getting run off the road. Convened for their first public meeting, the board's seven members at first found it impossible to proceed amid the shouts of protesters opposed to the takeover law that had led to their appointment just weeks earlier. It was only after Chairman Freman Hendrix ordered police to "have the hecklers removed—now," that things quieted down and the board was able to get on with its business.

In the months that followed, the meetings grew calmer. Yet the anger expressed during that tumultuous first gathering in spring 1999 did not disappear. At its root were questions that have divided Detroit—and communities across the nation—throughout the course of this century: Who should be in charge of the public schools, and how should they be run?

In the 1920s, students in Detroit enjoyed what were then considered some of the finest public schools in the United States.

The answers the city has settled on during the past 100 years have often mirrored broader trends in how Americans, especially those who live in cities, have chosen to organize and govern their schools.

These have ranged from Progressive-era innovations in the early part of the century to experiments with decentralization, desegregation, and school restructuring during the past 30 years. "Detroit participated in (and in some cases led) virtually every important reform effort involving urban schools," the education historian Jeffrey E. Mirel writes in a recent paper published by the Brookings Institution.

Yet in other respects, the story of Detroit's schools is inseparable from the history of the city itself. As interest groups and individuals have competed to forge new frameworks for governing public education, they have often been guided as much by the circumstances of their time and place as by forces at work in the nation at large.

These economic, social, and political conditions have exerted powerful influence over how schools function and how students learn.

Motown's schools rose with their city in the early decades of the century to become one of the finest education systems in the country, only to slip into severe decline in later years as the city itself descended into urban decay and racial unrest.

In the midst of these challenges, the school system repeatedly resorted to dramatic shakeups in the way the schools were governed. Yet a century of experimentation in Detroit and elsewhere has shown that shifts in governance often disappoint those hoping for tidy solutions.

"We're looking for structural panaceas and political quick fixes to very complex issues," says Michael D. Usdan, the president of the Washington-based Institute for Educational Leadership. "Tinkering with the structure might be useful, but that in itself is not going to bring about the changes that people want."

At the turn of this century, as automotive pioneers were giving birth to an industry that would transform the nation, an elite corps of school reformers here was plotting changes of its own.

Since the official establishment of Detroit's public schools in 1842, they had been run almost as a collection of village schools. Each of the city's political subdivisions, known as wards, maintained substantial control over its own schools. For most of the 19th century, those wards sent "inspectors" to sit on a central school board, which expanded as the city added wards.

That method of governance was typical of urban schools until about the 1890s, notes David B. Tyack, a professor of education and history at Stanford University. But around then, groups of reformers, typically drawn from their communities' social and business elites, began pressing for change.

"Defenders of the ward system argued that grassroots interest in the schools and widespread participation in school politics was healthy, indeed necessary, in large cities," Tyack writes in his 1974 book *The One Best System: A History of American Urban Education*. But, he adds, "centralizers saw in decentralization only corruption, parochialism, and vestiges of an outmoded village mentality."

In Detroit, a cadre of upper-crust reformers, many of them women, launched a campaign in 1902 aimed at overhauling the governance structure and ousting the incumbent superintendent.

As in many other cities, a central goal was to replace the sprawling, ward-based school board with a smaller one elected by voters citywide. The reformers focused heavily on the alleged character flaws of the ward-based politicians—including the ties some of them had to liquor interests.

"The conflict in Detroit centered almost entirely on who should rule, not on specific policies or practices," Mirel writes in *The Rise and Fall of an Urban School System: Detroit, 1907-81*, published in 1993.

In 1911, the reformers won a narrow majority on the ward-based board, only to lose it two years later. But in that same year, 1913, they persuaded the Michigan legislature to pass a bill creating a seven-member, nonpartisan board elected to staggered, six-year terms. In 1916, Detroit voters overwhelmingly ratified the change in a citywide referendum.

One of the new board's first moves was to consolidate power in the superintendent. It also got rid of the committees through which the old, 21-member board had regularly circumvented the schools chief.

Such steps reflected a national trend from 1900 to 1930 to transfer control of the public schools from community-based lay people to university-trained education professionals. In Detroit, the shift was viewed as critical to enabling the schools to keep pace with changes in the fast-growing city.

In the first three decades of the century, as Detroit established itself as the axis of America's automobile industry, the city's population mushroomed from 285,000 to nearly 1.6 million people. Finding enough teachers and space for the children of the new arrivals, many of them from Eastern and Southern Europe, was a formidable challenge. From fewer than 30,000 youngsters in 1900, K-12 enrollment swelled to 235,000 by 1930, although many students had to attend only part time for lack of space.

From the advent of the small school board until the onset of the Great Depression, the city saw relatively little political dissension over the basic priorities

Walter P. Reuther Library/Wayne State University

Corbis/Bettmann-UPI

of expanding and adapting the system to accommodate the enrollment boom, Mirel says. Superintendent Frank Cody, named to the position in 1919, served as the district's chief for what today seems an extraordinary 23 years. If the Detroit schools ever enjoyed a golden age, Mirel suggests, that was it.

"Every major interest group in the city strongly supported efforts to provide a high-quality, 'modern' public education to the children of the city," he says. "This support gave Detroit school leaders the unprecedented opportunity to create one of the great urban school systems of the 20th century."

But the consensus crumbled under the economic burdens of the Depression. As unemployment soared and relief lines lengthened, the city schools faced a staggering fiscal crisis.

Business leaders soon broke ranks with school officials, chastising them for moving too slowly to bring spending in line with the blighted economy.

Despite their reluctance, district officials retrenched in the early 1930s, cutting the budget by constricting teacher pay, halting construction, increasing the size of classes, and eliminating programs that critics decried as superfluous.

During those lean times, the nascent Detroit Federation of Teachers, at first operating underground, began trying to in-

fluence school board elections, with limited success. That activity on the part of the fledgling American Federation of Teachers affiliate aroused fierce criticism in the business community.

After the country entered World War II, Detroit emerged as an arms-producing powerhouse. That enhanced the clout of business and labor alike, which continued to clash over school funding and curricular issues.

As its ranks swelled during the 1940s, the DFT increasingly tried to influence the outcome of school board elections and decisions, with limited success.

Yet in 1947, the union came out on top in a struggle over salaries, which the union insisted must take precedence over building projects aimed at catching up with years of neglect. The district capitulated after teachers threatened to walk out.

Mary Ellen Riordan, the president of the union from 1960 through 1981, views the near-strike as a major step in the DFT's eventual emergence as the most powerful interest group in Detroit school politics. "That was the first big watershed," she says.

Business-backed groups reacted with outrage to the labor action and the resulting pay hikes, and in 1948, state lawmakers passed legislation outlawing strikes by public employees.

Above: In the summer of 1967, long-simmering racial tensions spilled into open violence as devastating riots in Detroit left 43 dead.

Left: As a state senator, Coleman A. Young sponsored legislation that revamped the Detroit school board. In 1974, he became the city's first African-American mayor.

AP/Wide World

In January 1976, as a court-ordered busing plan takes effect for the Detroit schools, African-American students arrive at a school on the city's east side.

Another effect of the showdown with the teachers was a growing sense that the district needed fiscal autonomy to set funding priorities as it saw fit.

"[T]he power of the mayor and City Council over the activities of the school district effectively made the public school system a department of the city," the Citizens Research Council of Michigan noted in a 1990 report.

After vigorous lobbying by school officials and municipal leaders, the legislature granted the district financial independence in 1949. That governance milestone freed the school board from relying on the city to approve both its budgets and borrowing requests. And it made the capacity to deliver votes, rather than wield influence behind the scenes, of greater value in the political equation.

The shift served to bolster the political fortunes of various interest groups in the city, including labor unions and the city's growing population of African-Americans.

Drawn from the South by plentiful wartime jobs, blacks climbed from just 9 percent of Detroit's population in 1940 to more than 16 percent in 1950. At the same time, many Southern whites were migrating to the city, fueling tensions that burst into outright conflict during a devastating race riot in 1943.

Racial strains sometimes ignited in the schools throughout the 1940s. After the 1943 riot, groups representing African-

Americans stepped up their pressure on school officials to address their grievances, which included a dearth of black school employees, a pattern of unofficial segregation, and the rundown condition of schools in black neighborhoods.

On some of those issues, notably that of facilities, black leaders were sometimes at odds with the DFT, whose overriding concern was teacher pay. But as the decade progressed, African-Americans increasingly found common cause with the federation, as well as other labor unions and liberal organizations that exerted influence over education politics.

In the late '40s, those minority, labor, and liberal groups joined forces in a failed attempt to oust the incumbent schools chief.

Out of that effort grew Save Our Schools, or SOS, an organization that brought together the teachers' federation, other labor leaders, black activists, parents, and various civic groups in efforts to increase funding, end racial discrimination, and expand community control of the schools. Between 1949 and 1961, according to Mirel, 11 of 14 candidates backed by Save Our Schools won seats on the school board.

During the 1950s, city dwellers throughout the country headed for the suburbs, and Detroiters were no exception. The exodus drained the city of many white, middle-class families who had been a fountainhead of political support for the schools.

Blacks, by contrast, continued to flock to the city that perhaps more than any other stood for high-paying jobs. The number of blacks rose by more than 60 percent during the decade, while the white population fell by nearly a quarter. By 1960, the city's overall population had dropped to 1.67 million from 1.85 million a decade earlier, but the proportion of African-Americans had jumped from 16 percent to 29 percent.

Meanwhile, the suburbs, collectively home to more than 2 million people by 1960, had overtaken the city in total population.

For the schools, one consequence of the demographic shifts was a sharp drop in property values and a resulting decline in the district's tax base. Another was a downward shift in the socioeconomic status of families using the system.

Race began to assume greater importance in the district's political dynamics. Buoyed by the U.S. Supreme Court's historic 1954 decision striking down intentional school segregation, black leaders pressed harder for integration and elimination of unequal distribution of resources. In 1955, an African-American was elected to the Detroit school board for the first time.

Besides racial issues, the big challenge facing school leaders was coping with rapid enrollment growth while the tax base was shrinking. Despite the city's overall population decline, the post-World War II baby boom pushed enrollment up from 232,230 in 1950 to 285,304 a decade later.

The growth continued until 1966, when enrollment peaked at just under 300,000. By then, the racial profile had shifted sharply, with whites making up only about 40 percent of students.

As district leaders turned to the electorate for tax increases and bond issues to keep up with rising enrollment and declining property values, voters proved harder to persuade.

In one such referendum, in April 1963, the resounding defeat of both a proposed tax increase and a school construction bond issue left the district facing the loss of nearly a third of its operating budget.

"Detroit schools were in real danger," writes Donald W. Disbrow in his 1968 book *Schools for an Urban Society.*

School officials went back to city voters the following November, seeking only to renew the existing school tax rather than raise it, and this time succeeded. But less than a year later, in September 1964, voters again turned thumbs down to a $75 million bond issue for school construction.

It was during those elections that clear signs of a color line emerged, Mirel says. Whites, who still outnumbered blacks in the voting booths though not in the schools, began rejecting spending measures at far higher rates than in the past.

Fueling the trend were race-related clashes starting in the late 1950s over school boundaries, conflicts that were to peak in the busing struggles of the 1970s. Besides alienating whites, the disputes helped turn a minority of blacks against school revenue increases.

"These elections signaled the beginning of a sea change in educational politics in the Motor City," Mirel says of the 1963 and 1964 spending votes. "In the 1930s, the business community abandoned its commitment to expanding and improving the Detroit schools. Similarly, during the racial struggles of the 1960s and early 1970s, large numbers of the white working class and a small but vocal segment of the black community would essentially do the same."

But if voters were exerting pressure on school leaders to keep spending down, an increasingly militant teaching corps was pushing in the opposite direction.

For decades, Detroit educators had divided their loyalty between the DFT, which had strong ties to organized labor, and the local affiliate of the National Education Association, which saw itself more as a professional organization than a trade union. While the two groups were active in the political arena over the years, teachers did not collectively bargain for their contracts with the district.

But beginning in 1963, encouraged by the success of New York City's AFT affiliate in gaining collective bargaining rights two years earlier, the DFT started pressing the school board to let Detroit teachers hold a similar election. After the union threatened to strike, school leaders agreed to hold an election in May of 1964.

Intense competition between the DFT and the Detroit Education Association ensued. In the end, the federation garnered about 60 percent of the vote, becoming the union designated to negotiate for all the district's teachers.

The teachers wasted no time in exercising their newfound clout. In 1965, the DFT extracted a sizable wage increase from the cash-strapped district. It did the same in 1967, after a two-week strike.

Like the teachers, African-American activists became more assertive in the middle and late '60s, as students joined community groups in protesting conditions in the schools.

By 1967, the year of race riots in the city that were among the worst in any U.S. city this century, the goal of transforming the system primarily through integration had fallen out of favor with a growing segment of the city's black residents.

Instead, some leaders advanced the view that unequal education for African-Americans could be remedied only through black control of the schools. Out of that movement came the push for community control, which culminated in a plan to decentralize the system in the early 1970s.

Looking back, some see the late 1960s as a turning point in the school system's fortunes. Before then, says John W. Porter, a former Michigan state schools chief who was the superintendent in Detroit from 1989 to 1991, the city generally benefited from concerned and supportive parents and community members, motivated students, and an effective, dedicated staff.

But after that period, he says, such conditions became harder to come by, and the quality of leadership in the district faltered.

"Governance is fragile when the socioeconomic conditions shift, and that's what happened in Detroit," Porter says.

By the end of the 1960s, Detroit's schools were in many ways unrecognizable from those of 1916. Yet the basic governance structure established that year—a seven-member school board elected at large—still endured more than half a century later.

That would change during the turbulent events of the next few years.

In April 1969, state Sen. Coleman A. Young—a former union leader who in 1974 would become the city's first black mayor—introduced legislation that called for creating regional school boards in the city, while preserving a central board with a mixture of subdistrict and at-large representatives.

Four months later, Gov. William Milliken signed the bill, which called for abolishing the seven-member board on Jan. 1, 1971.

The lame-duck school board then turned its attention to carving out the new subdistricts. Rejecting the pleas of both those who wanted to maximize black control in the regions and those who favored some largely white subdistricts, the board made racial integration its foremost concern.

On April 7, 1970, at a meeting that Mirel calls "probably the most tumultuous in the history of the school system," the school board approved a plan aimed not only at creating racially integrated regions, but also at desegregating the city's high schools.

The outcry was deafening, and weeks later, the Michigan legislature repealed the decentralization law outright, and hence the need for the controversial subdistricts.

Young promptly drew up an alternative bill to create eight regions with their own five-member boards. The central board would include the chairman of each regional board, as well as five members elected at large. The bill entrusted the delicate matter of regional boundaries to a gubernatorial commission and effectively nullified the city school board's desegregation plan. Gov. Milliken made the bill law in July 1970.

The following month, the four liberal school board members who supported the desegregation plan fell prey to a recall effort. Two weeks later, the National Association for the Advancement of Colored People sued the state and city school board to desegregate the system. The suit, *Milliken* v. *Bradley*, would make the federal courts a major player in governing the district until 1989.

After the governance change, the school board that took office in January 1971 confronted the district's worst fiscal crisis since the Depression.

Between 1968 and 1972, voters rejected six requests for tax renewals or increases. The tide finally turned in the fall of 1973, but only after the legislature had empowered the board to impose an income tax without the voters' go-ahead. Voters then approved two millage proposals in the 1973-74 school year in exchange for repeal of that unpopular income tax. But the district remained on precarious financial footing, in part because of renewed demands by teachers for higher pay.

The budget problems were exacerbated by debate over desegregation. During the 1971-72 school year, the judge in the Milliken case mandated a sweeping desegregation plan involving not only Detroit but also 52 surrounding suburban districts. That order was later scaled back to the city alone by a 1974 U.S. Supreme Court ruling. Anti-busing anger exploded, and often translated into opposition to spending measures.

Meanwhile, conflict with employee unions became a serious problem. Blaming educators for black students' academic problems, school leaders who had emerged from the community-control movement were determined to make employees more accountable. Throughout the early 1970s, the central and regional boards clashed with the DFT over efforts to do so.

"It all related to the central issue of developing the concept that teachers had some direct responsibility for student achievement, and as a result of that, teachers could be evaluated based on student outcomes," says Arthur Jefferson, the district's superintendent from 1975 to 1989.

The tension boiled over in the fall of 1973, when the teachers staged a 43-day strike, largely over accountability issues. The teachers prevailed, winning a large wage increase and effectively relegating accountability to the back burner.

But the strike was quickly followed by a racially charged dispute over an employee residency requirement the central board adopted in March 1974. The DFT and the Organization of School Administrators and Supervisors came out on top after challenging the policy in court, but not before the fight had further poisoned the relationship between district leaders and employees.

For administrators, recalls Stuart C. Rankin, who was deputy superintendent when he left the district a decade ago after 36 years, the fragmented nature of governance during the decentralization era proved frightening. "The superintendent of schools had a circus," he says. "It was a very complex and rather strange time."

In the schools, meanwhile, conditions deteriorated, as violence rose and test scores dropped. Those problems contributed to political disenchantment with decentralization.

"By 1978, opposition to decentralization was widespread," Mirel notes.

Once again, the stage was set for a turn of the governance wheel.

That change came in 1981, when state lawmakers enacted legislation requiring a referendum in the city on recentralizing the system. Residents voted resoundingly to abandon the regional boards, and a new central board of 11 members soon took office, with seven members elected from subdistricts and four chosen by voters citywide.

The schools that the new board took over continued to be hobbled by poor academic performance and violence. Many of the district's schools—showpieces in the 'teens and '20s—were falling apart. Enrollment had been shrinking for years, and was about 85,000 students lower than its 1966 peak.

Against the backdrop of a severe recession that hit the auto industry with a vengeance, the city's new school leaders confronted fiscal pressures as acute as those of a decade before. Although the political climate for tax increases had improved, the property-tax base continued to shrink.

"Detroit was no different than Chicago, and New York, and Philadelphia in that there were constant financial issues, and we tried to deal with them as best we could," Jefferson recalls.

The budget shortfalls that started in the late '70s had mounted to a cumulative debt of $160 million a decade later. The sizable salary increases granted to teachers, who shored up their bargaining position with strikes in 1982 and 1987, were a primary reason for the red ink. The union argued that the raises were essential to prevent teaching talent from flocking to the better-paying suburbs.

In retrospect, says Jefferson, "in some of those contract negotiations, we probably went too far in terms of what we could afford because we were trying so hard to be equitable and fair to our teachers."

Given the chronic fiscal problems, voters were receptive in 1988 when a slate of four candidates pledging to balance the books and devolve power to individual schools sought seats on the school board.

Much of their campaign focused on an attention-grabbing issue that attracted criticism from state officials as well: the practice of some board members of traveling first class at public expense and of being chauffeured by school employees in district-owned cars.

The reform-minded candidates, known as the HOPE team, trounced their four incumbent opponents.

Under the leadership of the new board and interim Superintendent Porter, the district got its fiscal house in order after voters approved a tax increase and bond issue in the fall of 1989. Then, in 1991, with the hiring of a new superintendent, the board sought to implement changes, including school-based management and more specialized schools.

But the effort fell apart after the DFT, which had initially supported the 1988 reform candidates, switched gears in 1992.

"They started to do things that we just couldn't live with," John M. Elliott, the president of the DFT since 1981, says of those board members.

Three of the four original HOPE candidates lost their seats, and the reconstituted board turned away from its predecessor's agenda for change.

In the ensuing years, Detroit school leaders came under growing attack for the district's management practices and lagging educational performance. Citing low student test scores and high dropout rates, Michigan Gov. John Engler put forward a proposal in 1997 that would have opened the way for the state to take over the district.

The idea made little headway in the legislature. But in early 1999, the Republican governor resurrected the idea in a revised form, pushing a plan to shift control of the 174,000-student Detroit schools to Mayor Dennis W. Archer, a Democrat.

After heated debate, lawmakers approved a measure restoring a seven-member board, with six seats appointed by the mayor and the seventh filled by the state superintendent.

The "reform board," chaired by Deputy Mayor Hendrix, took office in late March of 1999.

The board's chief responsibilities were to name a chief executive officer—to be entrusted with nearly all the powers usually vested in a school board—and to approve a strategic plan. During the search for a permanent schools chief, an interim CEO, a former president of Wayne State University, David Adamany, was tapped to run the district under a one-year contract. Detroit voters will decide in five years whether to keep the new governance scheme.

The new arrangement was loosely modeled on the 1995 governance change in Chicago that gave a small, mayorally appointed school board and a CEO extraordinary new powers to run the schools. The two cities are among a handful in which mayors have assumed control of their schools in recent years.

As in other cities, Detroit's new governance plan has drawn fire from those who say it disenfranchises city voters by stripping the elected school board of power. Hendrix acknowledges that the

AP/Wide World

complaint has resonance in a city where the vast majority of voters and more than 90 percent of public school students are black. Still, he and other supporters of the change say citizens can now hold the mayor accountable at election time.

"We have extraordinary problems here," Hendrix says, "and we need to give someone the authority to do what needs to be done."

Whether the latest arrangement succeeds will depend on many factors, including the relationship the city's new school leaders forge with educators and parents. At century's close, it's an open question whether lasting improvements are in store for a system whose status as a beacon of excellence has long since slipped into history.

"The number-one problem we face," says Porter, "is not whether you produce some reforms, but whether you can sustain those reforms." ■

Agnes Aleobua, a senior at Cass Technical High School, calls for the resignation of the mayorally appointed school board at a meeting in April 1999.

Democracy in Education— Who Needs It?

 A perspective by

good question!   ⇒

I f you fly over the prairies that stretch across the middle of the United States, you see below the farms and municipalities neatl laid out in townships composed of 3(sections, each a mile square. More tl two centuries ago, the U.S. Congress apart Section 16 in each township to support public schools. Out of the public domain thus surveyed grew new territories and, then, state after state. In the process, the United States became a massive republic composed of smaller republics. As pioneers moved into the wilderness, they could settle land where the federal government had already marked out municipal boundaries and put aside resources to create and maintain public schools.

It all sounds very neat and preplanned, and indeed some histories portray the story of public education as the inevitable product of democracy and farsighted leaders. But it was by no means

inevitable that Americans would create the most extensive array of public schools in the world. Why should citizens who were deeply distrustful of government, sometimes afraid of it, create government schools as essential to their model republic?

Puzzles abound in the story of democracy in education. Who was in charge? Not the federal government, which was a minor player until recently.

that's ridiculous   ⇒

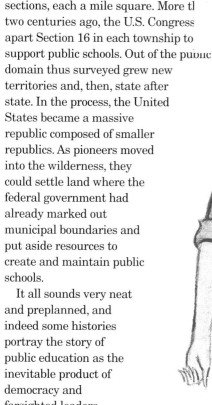

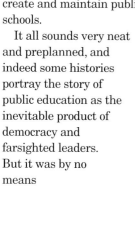

did not even mention education. A federal office of

education didn't even appear until 1867, and then was puny in size and functions. From time to time, reformers have proposed an activist role for the federal government, but not until 1954 did the U.S. Supreme Court begin its momentous impact on schooling through its landmark decisions on civil rights and civil liberties. Liberals had to wait until the 1960s to break the logjam preventing large-scale federal aid to public schools. Today, although candidates vie to become the "education president," federal programs account for only about 7 percent of public school revenues (and conservatives in Congress think even that is too much money and control).

State governments have long been legally responsible for public education within their boundaries, but their influence has been muted. Even the most famous early state superintendents, leaders like Horace Mann and Henry Barnard, had little power beyond persuasion and faced periodic threats to abolish their offices. As late as 1890, the average state department of education had only two employees, including the superintendent, and very little power to enforce laws or regulations. In the 19th century, Americans kept rewriting their state constitutions to prevent elected and appointed state officials from doing mischief. Not until the 20th century did state governments gain modest powers to legislate and monitor bureaucratic standards, usually of the sort that professional educators lobbied to install.

If both federal and state governments were minor players in controlling and financing schools until relatively recent times, who did that work? Mostly it was officials in local districts, and this generally was what citizens wanted. Both in the past and in the present (as Gallup polls show) Americans have trusted local school boards to make educational decisions far more than they trusted federal or state officials. Everyday citizens tended to agree that the best politics of education was local politics.

Although most citizens have approved of local control, in the 20th century most elite reformers have not. These professional leaders wanted to dampen, not increase, lay participation in democratic decisionmaking. They believed that professional experts kn___ what was best for children. For that reason, they wanted to centralize an_ buffer educational decisionmaking r_ than leave it to local citizens. From ti__ to time, innovators have even called for the abolition of school districts and their elected trustees. Who needs democracy of that sort? they asked. They did not abandon the rhetoric of democracy, but they redefined what it meant.

Before analyzing these re-visions of democratic governance, I'd like to revisit the origins and consequences of local control in the 19th century.

Choosing Democratic Governance.
Without a system of local control by elected trustees in the 19th century, this country might not have created the most comprehensive and popular system of public education in the world. It

was hardly inevitable that government schools would trump private ones in the 19th century. A competitive, entrepreneurial spirit among educators had created a healthy private education sector by 1850, much of this fueled by repeated religious revivals. We might

← that sounds like a better system to me!

Instead, the public school triumphed. The U.S. Census defined a public school as an institution managed by public authorities, with instruction by publicly selected teachers, taking place in a public schoolhouse. By 1890, about nine in 10 students were enrolled in such an institution. At that time, there were still differences of opinion and practice about what constituted a "public" or "private"

This system seems so much better ⇒ than today's.

Why did this happen? One set of reasons has to do with demography and geography: The population was highly scattered; one-room schools dotted the land. A single common school serving each rural neighborhood made economic sense in an era when roads were poor and transportation rudimentary, and when the local citizens paid for local schooling mostly out of their own pockets, through taxes. Because of the separation

of church and state, most Protestant denominations were willing to support a common school and to suspend their sectarian quarrels at the schoolhouse door. Americans disestablished the church, but partially established the public school in its place.

But who was to run these schools? In __st places, the answer was neighbors __ted to do the job. Under American __l control, school trustees constituted __ most numerous class of public __cials in the world; in some states, there were as many as 45,000 local school trustees, often outnumbering teachers. Decentralized governance addressed public distrust of government by putting the school and its trustees everywhere under the eye and thumb of the citizens. This provided democracy in education, meaning self-rule by elected representatives of the people. Communities were able to retain collective decisions about schooling—who would teach, how much schools would cost, and what kind of instruction to offer. If district voters disagreed with school trustees, they could elect others.

The one-room school was not only a place for children to learn the three R's. The process of making collective decisions face to face reflected the belief that governance should be close to hand and transparent. When citizens decided issues this way, they could show youth how self-rule operated in education and thus contribute to the civic education of the next generation. Education in democracy was partly a matter of book learning; a similar pedagogy of republicanism and political ideology permeated textbooks in American history, for example. But education in democracy also took place in the public life that swirled about the common school and taught the young how self-rule worked (or did not).

In state constitutions, in Fourth of July speeches, and in the rhetoric of political conventions, Americans reiterated a conviction that

representative government required educated citizens. It was part of a national ideology, but in education governance, the action took place mostly at the local level. School ~~~

[handwritten: OK now I see the problems in the old system...] ⇒

~~by state legislatures~~ (say, about Bible reading or the use of foreign languages). There was little chance that state statutes would be enforced if local citizens disagreed. "Laws on education particularly require neighborly harmony for effectiveness," wrote an observer in 1897. "The coerced minority today is liable to become the tyrannic majority tomorrow."

Questioning Lay Control.
Local control by elected school committees set a democratic stamp on public education, but policy elites at the turn of the 20th century complained that the rural school trustees gave local citizens just what they wanted: schooling that was cheap, that reflected local notions of morality and useful learning, and that gave employment to local teachers who fit in well with the community. Leaders like Stanford University professor Ellwood P. Cubberley denounced local control by district trustees as "democracy gone to seed." How could penny-pinching and provincial rural trustees prepare youth for modern society? he asked.

The easiest way to curb the influence of school trustees in these rural communities was to abolish as many districts as possible—or, euphemistically, to consolidate them. This idea was very popular among educational leaders, who wanted more professional autonomy and desired to give children an education that fit their "scientific" modern standards. But consolidation was very unpopular in communities about to lose their one-room schools and local control. In the 20th century, about nine in 10 one-room schools were eliminated along with their district boards.

Elite reformers also believed that in urban districts too many of the wrong people ran things, pointing especially to

corrupt machine politicians and immigrants who wanted the schools to respect their cultures and to hire their daughters. How could urban schools become efficient and professional with all these foxes in the chicken coops? Besides, the central urban school committees were far too large and delegated decisions to subcommittees of trustees rather than to the experts. Worse, many cities still retained ward boards that ~~~~~~~~~~~~~ th~~~

[handwritten: Good idea in theory, but who decides what expertise is best? ⇒]

[handwritten: ⇐ interesting thought...]

[handwritten: such beautiful ideals! ↗ → ↘]

radically reducing the size of city school boards. The administrative reformers were remarkably successful in eliminating ward school boards in large cities and in cutting the size of school boards in large cities. The average number of school board members dropped from 21 to seven in the three decades from 1890 to 1920. These political moves, accomplished largely by statutes and charters obtained from state legislatures, concentrated power in the

hands of the professional elite and their business and professional allies in school reform.

The solution to both rural and urban educational ills was to take the schools out of "politics," that is, to free them from the vagaries of elective office and the political representation of different social groups. Thus reformers like Cubberley wanted to abolish local trustees where ~~~~~~~~ ~~~~~~~ eliminate elected county ~~~~~~~~~ndents, appoint rather than ~~~~~~~ superintendents, and ~~~~~~ everywhere to base decisionmaking on expertise rather than on political processes. Public participation in decisionmaking was quite unnecessary in such a sanitized system, other than the school board's approving the actions of the superintendent.

Many members of the policy elite in education believed that "democracy" should mean equality of opportunity as defined by the professional educator. The school, in Cubberley's view, was an "instrument of democracy" run by apolitical experts, with authority "in the hands of those who will really represent the interests of the children." Such leaders would be able to educate all children according to their abilities and destiny in life. The people owned the schools, but experts ran them, just as a corporate chief executive managed his firm. That was the new version of democracy in governance: a socially and economically efficient system that adapted schooling to different kinds of students, thereby guaranteeing equality of opportunity.

In the first half of the 20th century, who wanted or needed democracy in education? It depended on whom you asked. Rural citizens, whose children still constituted two-thirds of students in public schools in 1915, thought democracy should mean self-rule, and they fought consolidation. Administrative reformers like Cubberley had another view of the future: The public school was essential to the health of democracy, but expert administration should, over time, replace the messiness of school politics and render it a memory of the bad old days.

No amount of wishful thinking can transform the politics of education into objective administration, for schooling is and always has been intrinsically political. The question is not *whether* politics, but *whose* politics. Nonetheless, the administrative reformers in education at the beginning of this century were so successful in carrying out their blueprint for reform of governance that political scientists in the 1950s described public education as a "closed system" in which familiar actors like city and state superintendents and their lay boards worked within a zone of political consent that made decisionmaking predictable and consensual. Ellwood Cubberley would have felt at home.

Indeed, the policy preferences of the administrative reformers of 1910 became the conventional wisdom of educators for a half-century. Big districts and big schools, they said, were better than small ones. A centralized and specialized administrative structure was more efficient and accountable than a decentralized and simple one. Differentiation of the curriculum into several tracks and hundreds of electives generated greater equality of opportunity for the students of varied ability and for the different races and genders.

Today, reformers challenge all of these conventional beliefs. They argue that small schools are better, that big districts should be decentralized, that all students should be helped to meet the same high academic standards, that academic segregation of students into tracks limits their learning, and that schools can benefit from strong involvement of parents in educational reform.

The administrative reformers of 1910 believed that if schools did a good job and tended to their public relations, citizens would be satisfied and would not need to politicize issues. For a time, that strategy seemed to work, at least so long as the voices of outsiders were not heard. But in the last half-century, the history of school governance is in large part the story of efforts to breach the buffers erected around schools during the first half of the 20th century. Groups that were excluded or unfairly treated—for example, African-Americans, Latinos, the handicapped, women—have organized in social movements and have sought access and influence in public education. Besides employing traditional democratic beliefs and political strategies, these new voices have also expanded notions of democracy; they speak, for example, of cultural democracy, of equal respect and equal rights for all cultural groups.

The politics of education has never been more fluid and complicated than in recent years. As in earlier periods of contentiousness, some activists have sought escape from democracy (roughly equated with politics). This time, however, they do not seek to replace politics with expert administration. Indeed, they think public education already too bureaucratic, too constrained by regulations inflicted by special-interest groups. The solution, they say, is to replace politics with markets. Treating schooling as a consumer good and giving parents vouchers for the education of their children solves the problem of decisionmaking: Parents choose the schools that will be best for their children. The collective choices produced by democratic institutions produced bureaucracy and gridlock. The invisible hand of the market will lead the individual to the best personal choice. The market in education will satisfy and liberate families through competition.

But wait. Is education primarily a consumer good or a common good? If Thomas Jefferson, Horace Mann, or John Dewey were now to enter policy discussions on public education, he might well ask if Americans have lost their way. Democracy is about making wise collective choices. Democracy in education and education in democracy are not quaint legacies from a distant and happier time. They have never been more essential to wise self-rule than they are today. ■

David B. Tyack is the Vida Jacks professor of education and history in the school of education at Stanford University in Stanford, Calif. His books include The One Best System: A History of American Urban Education *and, with Larry Cuban,* Tinkering Toward Utopia: A Century of Public School Reform.

> If Thomas Jefferson, Horace Mann, or John Dewey were now to enter policy discussions on public education, he might well ask if Americans have lost their way.

⇐ children should choose as well!

Index